SELF-HELP ESSENTIAL BOXED SET

LEARN HOW TO CULTIVATE HEALTHY RELATIONSHIPS, IMPROVE YOUR
HEALTH, FINANCES & MASTER YOUR OWN PSYCHOLOGY

SIMEON LINDSTROM

Contents

COPYRIGHT

INTRODUCTION

Self-help books on the market today will tell you one of two things...

   ... either that you are perfect already as you are and needn't worry, or that with just a little (well, a lot) of effort, you can reach those goals. Be the best, smartest, most successful, thinnest and relentlessly happiest version of yourself possible. *No excuses!*

   Here, you will *not* find any quick tips and tricks on how to live a fabulous life free of suffering or fear or confusion. The approach I outline in these books actually goes *against* most of the popular ways to tackle depression, anxiety or general malaise. But it is an approach that allowed *me* to dig deep into my own authenticity, be honest with myself and start to make real, lasting changes in my life.

   I was petrified to really put myself out there, to look at myself as I was, without any bullshit. But then I realized that the pain of living inauthentically was greater than the pain of taking a risk and being myself.

   The exercises and case studies I've included in this collection are borne of my own insights and experience, but they are certainly not authoritative. If you're reading this, there's a good chance that your instinct for meaning and value is alive and well within you – *trust that instinct*.

   My hope with these books is that they'll give you a starting point to begin to reconsider your relationship to yourself and, by extension, the world you live in. My hope is that you'll find something that inspires you to think differently and make different choices, ones that will leave you feeling more in control and more fulfilled than ever before.

   We each only have one life - here's to spending it wisely!

"I'M OK!"

– AND ALL THE OTHER BULLSH*T WE KEEP TELLING OURSELVES AND OTHERS: AN UNCENSORED APPROACH ON HOW TO STOP HIDING OUR UNHAPPINESS AND DEAL WITH LIFE AND OURSELVES IN A SELF-LOVING WAY

INTRODUCTION

Here, you will *not* find any quick tips and tricks on how to live a fabulous life free of suffering or fear or confusion.

The approach I outline in this book goes *against* most of the popular ways to tackle depression, anxiety or general malaise. But it is an approach that allowed me to dig deep into my own authenticity, be honest with myself and start to make real, lasting changes in my life.

I was petrified to really put myself out there, to look at myself as I was, without any bullshit. But then I realized that the pain of living inauthentically was greater than the pain of taking a risk and being myself.

Let me show you what I mean...

"How are you?"

"I'm good, you?"

"Yeah, fine."

Ladies and gentlemen, allow me to introduce everything that's wrong with the world.

I'm sure you've imagined what would happen if you told someone how you *really* felt one day when they asked you this non-question. I think every human being has fantasized that they could say something like, "well, my knees hurt and I thought about killing myself this morning, and by the way, I'd totally hit on you if we weren't at work right now" or "I'm absolutely, definitely *not* fine, and I want to talk about it badly, but I'm certain you'll judge me for it so I'll just shut up and pretend you never asked."

Hey, let me ask *you* right now, how are you? *Really*?

Just stop reading for a second and have a little look into your heart and soul, body and mind and tell me right now, are you OK? What's going on with you, right now in this moment?

Something made you choose *this* book out of many options available to you – this book with a bright cover and an expletive in the title. Why? Well, I have a little theory about this, but I'll get into it later. For now, I want to tell you what this book is about: *authenticity.*

It's also about depression, anxiety and unhappiness, and in these pages, I'm going to show you how to be depressed, anxious and unhappy with more authenticity than you ever have before. I'm not joking. In the chapters that follow, I want to show you that your depression, misery and meh-ness about life is *fantastic,* and I can't wait to show you why.

This is a self-help book like all the others, but at the same time, it's kind of an *anti-self-help* book. In it we'll begin with one basic premise: that you aren't wrong. When you wake up, feel like crap and wish you could just go back to sleep instead of even looking at your life, well, I want to tell you that this isn't necessarily a problem or a mistake.

It isn't something to deny, negate or throw Prozac at. In fact, honestly acknowledging how you really, actually feel is the first step of any real self-help. That's why before we begin, I'm going to ask nothing of you except that you keep an open mind and be 100%, completely, utterly *honest*. If you aren't, the chapters that follow will seem like abrasive nonsense. If you are, I can promise I'll make it worth your while.

Honesty is important, so I'll go first: I have suffered from depression my entire life. I was a sad child, a stroppy teenager and an angsty young adult. These days, I've moved on to being crotchety and belligerent. I have tried medication and meditation. I have sat around in support groups and cried about my father, and I've journaled, and I've exercised and taken Omega 3s, and I've paid exorbitant amounts of money to well-meaning psychologists who made precisely zero difference to my life.

For the most part, all of these things were bullshit. If I'm honest, there has just been one, and I really mean just *one* thing that has made my life better. This thing isn't a commonly accepted psychotherapy treatment, and you won't find it in any feel-good books about living every day like it's your last. In fact, this thing is a little scary, a little dangerous, a little ugly to dwell on. It's what this book is about: authenticity.

CHAPTER 1: THE BULLSHIT WE TELL OURSELVES

Here's a weird thing I've noticed...

You know how you see these rows and rows of beautifully designed self-improvement books in the books stores, filed under "psychology" or "self-help" or even "spiritual"? Those books take up so much room because people buy them. People love them. Books about how to find your tribe or speak your truth or catch a husband or lose weight by praying.

These books are hugely popular, and they must be good because their authors are laughing all the way to the bank.

But if self-help books are so popular, then why are people embarrassed to be seen reading them?

All these millions of copies of pop psychology guides have to be going somewhere ...but it's not prominently on the bookshelf in the living room. These books are not shared in book clubs and seldom recommended by friends.

Why?

I think the reason that people are drawn to but simultaneously ashamed about this kind of material is because we're ashamed of what it means: when you buy a self-help book, you're admitting that you're having difficulty with life. You wouldn't buy a how-to guide if you already knew how to, right?

Sadly, there's a weird stigma about needing guidance about the most difficult thing any of us will ever do: live. We are all seemingly OK with Googling for help on how to do our taxes or make the cat take its medicine, but it when it comes to knowing how to *live life well*, the topic suddenly seems a bit embarrassing. Hell, people may even be less bashful about sex books than they are about books that tell them how to practice social skills, or overcome childhood trauma.

"I'm OK."

The bullshit I told everyone all through my life was this: I am OK. I'm fine. I'm not having any trouble.

Do you tell people this same bullshit?

There are many flavors of this same bullshit, although it's all the same at its core:

- Everyone is having an easier time of living than I am. I'm the only one struggling with anything.

- Being an adult means not having difficulty with your life. Just sort it out. Deal with it. Suck it up, buttercup.

- If you really must have issues, take it to the appropriate outlet. Hire a professional or take a pill. Or drink, it doesn't matter, just so long as you don't make people around you too uncomfortable!

- You are insignificant, your suffering doesn't matter in the grand scheme of things.

- Being sad is a mistake, a "chemical imbalance", a character flaw, a disease. You're not, like, *right* in your appraisal of the world. If you're unhappy, it's your own fault and you'd better find a way to adapt and adjust.

I could go on but just writing these down bums me out. Maybe you believe some version of the above yourself. Maybe you buy and read self-help books in secret and take your down time to "fix" your unhappiness so that you can go out into the world and say "fine" when people say "how are you?"

Particularly if you're male, you may be so used to telling other people that you're OK that you scarcely even notice when it's bullshit anymore. Maybe you think that your own personal happiness and fulfillment in life is your own private business and something you should only indulge in on your own time.

"I Have to be OK."

Why the façade? Why the smiling mask?

Well, that's a complex question. In America in particular, there seems to be an almost aggressive push for happiness and fulfillment. While your grandparents were told to marry, find good work and be good enough citizens, newer generations are being raised on the idea that everything they should do should be meaningful, that everyone is a brilliant, unique individual who should never settle for anything but bliss and complete personal fulfillment.

Misery is something awkward, unwanted and inconvenient. People are afraid that unhappiness is contagious – and in a way, it totally is. If your entire workplace functions on the unspoken rule that everyone ought to pretend they want to be there when they don't, what happens when someone breaks that rule?

Depressed people are pitied, but for many, there is a hidden threat in their failing to be satisfied with life. Depressed people make others question their own happiness, make them face up to their own dissatisfactions – which can be very dangerous indeed. If you've been stoically enduring a broken marriage and unfulfilling job for decades, the person who's not afraid to speak out about it makes it awfully difficult to stay in denial. It's almost as though the haste with which we try to "treat" depressed people comes from our desperation to convince ourselves that there's nothing to be sad about, and the depressed person is seen as less than sane. Perhaps the sentiment is that if you have to shove your emotions down, why should they be indulged for not doing the same?

So we tell people who are unhappy that they have a disease called "depression", which is just something you more or less get randomly. We tell them and ourselves that their brains don't produce enough of the right neurotransmitters, or that they inherited it all from their parents. What we don't tell them is that their sadness is a legitimate and valid response to a world that is objectively misery-inducing.

Why would we? What would happen if the psychiatrist sat on the other side of the desk and said, "yes I know, life *does* suck"?

Whether we do it consciously or not, I think we all subtly police one another when it comes to the obligation to be happy. Of course, there are legitimate brain disorders and psychological conditions that can be successfully treated with medications. And feeling suicidal is in no way a normal state of affairs.

But somewhere along the line, we've gotten used to lumping in a whole range of genuine human emotions into the "depression" box and calling it a disorder ...with the implication that a healthy human being seldom feels that way.

Is that really true?

I think it's not.

I think it's bullshit.

Is feeling lackluster about a boring job really so unusual? Is wondering what the point of it all is really so unhealthy? For people who are depressed, the world looks dark and lonely and hostile. While being unable to see anything else in the world but negativity is probably not healthy, it doesn't mean that depressed people are delusional. In many ways, the world *is* dark and lonely and hostile, and medicating people who go on and on about it won't change that.

Why do you think people love "dark" humor? Think of all the popular comedians who talk frankly about really twisted topics, or confess things that has the audience laughing in shock but nodding their heads all the same. People laugh at twisted things because they are *relieved*. They are glad that they are not the only ones to think such dark things.

The comedian is speaking the truth.

The depressed person is also speaking the truth.

Both are being *authentic*.

So, given that there's such a need to be OK, to appear OK, and to never appear as if you're un-OK, what do you do?

"No, no I'm fine," someone says and wipes a tear from their eyes at work. It's just "personal issues". Just a temporary glitch and then everyone can return to their usual programming as soon as possible.

A particular situation develops. You have a world filled with people who know that their personal drama, their own little dissatisfactions or tragedies are nobody's problem but their own. So they tuck them away and put on a happy face. Everyone else puts on a happy face too.

Now, when you feel unhappy about your life, not only do you have to experience that sadness, you also have to experience it *alone*. You look out into the world at a sea of smiling faces. "Oh, it's only me, then" you think. And you would think so, since everyone you encounter is working really hard to convince you that they are OK, too. You see their masks, they see yours.

It all looks great, but what's happening underneath?

When two people encounter each other and interact through their masks, they never really get the opportunity to connect with *authenticity*. Just the masks engage, while the real people underneath might as well have never met. The one thing that could have been a genuine relief and source of joy for them – human connection – is forfeited so they can both play-act at being what they're not. So, they get the illusion of happiness and fulfillment instead of real happiness and fulfillment. They both go home, take their masks off and think, "why am I so alone? Why is it so hard to really connect with people? Why doesn't anyone understand the real me, the person I am deep inside?"

When we lie to others and tell them we're OK when we're not, we're killing the possibility for genuine interaction. We rob one another of authentic response to another authentic human. We forgo real conversations and honest exchange of information for role-play.

Once in a while we may lower our guard with those we feel safe with, but real honesty is the exception rather than the rule. The rule, crazily enough, is to go out and create the very same world that makes it so impossible to express your true self in the first place. Instead of having the courage to just be what you are, you hide yourself away and put on a mask.

The WORST Bit of Bullshit

So what am I ultimately getting at here?

If I sound like a strange, bitter person, well, then I ask you to take a deeper look at your own assumptions about what life is and should be. Is it really true that depression, anxiety, unhappiness etc. is something to avoid and fix at all costs? Is it really true that we should relentlessly strive for ease and positivity all the time?

Here is the biggest bit of bullshit that I hope to convince you to abandon by the time you're done reading this book:

Negative Feelings Need to be Fixed

You know what I mean because you and I have grown up in the same culture that has this principle written all over it. Do you feel out of shape and unattractive? Don't just sit there, get out there and loudly proclaim how much you love every inch of cellulite and roll of flab! Feeling stressed after work? Be proactive! Meditate! Set some goals already! Lying in bed late at night with some insomnia and the creeping sensation that something is wrong with you? Jesus, that's not normal, take a pill!

Let's stop yakking and move on to the meat of the thing.

In the rest of the book, we'll take *authenticity* to have greater value than ease or conformity. And the root of this authenticity will lie in a respect and acknowledgment of what is actually real, even if it's negative. This means that there is no rushing in to deny negative or uncomfortable feelings. There is nothing to fix and no problem. For now, there is just honesty.

I'll ask you again, how are you?

Maybe I can guess what you're thinking.

"That all sounds great, but what do you expect? That everyone just runs into the streets and starts whining and crying about how hard life is? That doesn't help anything."

If you've had a thought like this, then I want to ask you, well, so what? So what if people did run into the streets all at once and admitted how unhappy they truly are at times? If people asked "how are you?" and were met with your deepest darkest secrets and hopes and fears in life? Go on, imagine the worst outcome possible.

So what?

The fact is, nothing has really changed – people's feelings are what they are whether they are honest about them or not, right? Saying it out loud doesn't make it any more real than it was before, it only makes *you* more real. If you have this or a similar reaction (i.e. you think that civilization would crumble if people really opened up with how they felt) then I think that's evidence enough that something is wrong, don't you?

Maybe ask yourself why you think this level of self-deception is normal. Why the prospect of honesty seems so terribly frightening and untenable.

Here, I want to be clear: I am not suggesting people be anything other than what they are. Unless you are actually honest about the state you're in, right now, how could you ever hope to solve any problem? Will you just quietly read secret self-help books and smile and wither inside?

I am not suggesting that people whine and complain – rather, that only once you have the courage to express yourself and what's actually true for you, you open up the possibility to actually make meaningful changes. It's a bit of a paradox: when you can accept your unhappy feelings, you actually can derive a measure of happiness from doing so. The reverse is true: pretending to be happy has the strange effect of making you *less* happy!

A No Bullshit Self-love Meditation

Here's an exercise that I have found a lot of comfort and a good way to really tune into ...well, *you.*

Find somewhere quiet to sit where you know you won't be disturbed for around 30 minutes or more. Sit or lie down comfortably, but not so comfortable that you fall asleep!

Take a few moments to just breathe. Slow down a little and just fill and empty your lungs with clean air. Relax a little. You're not doing a big deal meditation here, you're just doing something simple: being.

Once you've found your breath, start focusing on the environment around you. Closing your eyes helps you zoom in on the sounds, smells and feelings occurring all around you. As your awareness passes over everything – the sound of birds, the feeling of the ground under you, the temperature and texture of the clothing on your back – try to accept it, as it is. This means you don't hear a sound and immediately make a judgment about it. You don't go, "oh there are some birds, what a lovely sound" or "oh it sounds like crows, I hate crows, they'd better not be eating my blueberries" or whatever. Just hear the birds, acknowledge them, and let the sound be whatever it is.

Notice that the birds are just what they are. Kind of birdy. And the cars outside are just kind of car-ish. Everything just is what it is. Don't favor any one particular sensation around you, and don't try to force your attention anywhere. Just be aware.

Next, gently turn your mind to your body, which is also a part of your environment. Notice all the sensations *inside* your body instead of outside. Feel a gurgle in your stomach, the sensation of your hair on your back, or tiny goosebumps on your forearms. Again, there is no judgment here, only awareness.

Think about each of your body parts. Just like birds or cars, they just are what they are. And just as reality is its own thing, your body is its own thing, too. Feel how it feels just to notice yourself without any judgment. You don't have to be or do anything that you aren't already being or doing. Those birds outside don't have to do something extra to be better birds, and you don't have to do anything special to be who you are.

Finally, turn your awareness to your thoughts and feelings. By now, you probably have a whole ocean of ideas swimming all around you. Even if you try, your mind *will* make judgments about things. You might have the thought, "I'm getting old" or "what an idiot, I didn't do that chore I was supposed to do this morning" or even "this exercise is lame and that book is getting on my nerves."

This part is the trickiest, though: don't judge these thoughts either. Not even the judgmental ones! Are you feeling bored? Great. Feel bored. Just watch that bored feeling and let it be. Feeling angry or sad? Do you have the same repetitive thought loops going round and round? Ok. Let it be.

As long as you can, sit with the external environment, your own internal environment and all the whirling thoughts and feeling in your head. Stand outside them, if you can, and try to see them for all they are. Now, find some phrase or word that signifies acceptance to you. You could literally say, "I accept" or "Ok" or just focus on the feeling that comes with acceptance. Look at everything, look at all of reality as it unfolds around you and try to feel it, even if just for a few seconds: I accept. Ok.

When you open your eyes, have a stretch and go back to the "real world", try to maintain this open, accepting frame of mind. You can go outside now and chase the crows away if you like, but never forget that they are just crows being crows, and you are just you being you. Notice how you can act to improve your life and achieve your goals without any judgment or self-hatred. And notice how you are fine just as you are now, without any changes at all necessary.

Congratulations, you've taken your first step away from bullshit and towards something far more satisfying: self-love and acceptance rooted in authenticity.

What I Mean When I Talk About Acceptance
- Looking at reality square in the face. Having a preference for the truth and being committed to rooting out denial or deception in yourself.
- Having the curiosity to discover what is and isn't under your control, and bravely working within those limitations to bring about what you value.
- Being OK with what is. Looking at both the positive and negative in yourself and knowing that they're part of the same person.
- Realizing that it's not so bad to be wrong, or to be criticized, or not to know what you're doing...

What I Don't Mean When I Talk About Acceptance
- Finding an "echo chamber" of people who also believe whatever you believe and speaking only to them to confirm whatever it is you've decided you wish were true.
- Deciding that you don't ever have to take any action, because where you are is good enough and so there's no impetus to improve or evolve.
- Self-pity, or the kind of martyr-like feeling you get when you tell yourself that your problems are the fault of others and that you are powerless (even if it's true!)
- Fatalism – or the belief that things can only ever be as they are now.

I'd like to call all of the above "Self-indulgence" rather than self-acceptance. It's the difference between these two statements:

1) "I'm perfect just as I am and to hell with anyone who doesn't agree."

2) "I'm imperfect. *Really* imperfect. But so what? I still deserve love and respect and consideration. And I'll start by giving that to myself!"

It's the difference between:

1) "I love myself, so I don't have to try"

2) "I love myself, and that's why I try"

When you are self-indulgent, you dive right in and try to drum up good feelings about yourself that might not have any basis in reality. And so you necessarily have to have a degree of denial. If you believe that you are perfect just as you are, then everything that you do is permissible, and you are beyond criticism. In fact, you *shouldn't* change because every change will be for the worse!

When you are self-indulgent, you give up. You say "accept" but what you really mean is "resign". You say, "no no, this is actually what I wanted for myself all along" and settle for something less than suitable because the other option entails too much risk and discomfort. A good way to know whether you are self-indulgent rather than self-accepting is to see the immediate results: if your attitude is one that immobilizes you, keeps you where you are and does nothing more than make you feel warm and fuzzy, there's a good chance it's self-indulgence.

If your attitude inspires action, if it makes you want to reach out there and connect with others, to solve problems, to better yourself and strive to reach goals, then you're probably in a self-acceptance frame of mind.

To improve, you have to acknowledge that there is a problem, i.e. something to improve on in the first place! If you are too afraid to admit fault, too afraid to take the risk of trying something new or admitting your flaws, then you shut down any possibility of being better. But if you have an attitude of self-acceptance, what you are accepting is the possibility for pain and uncertainty. You are accepting that life is sometimes hard and confusing.

Here is another paradox: the person who honestly acknowledges an ugly thing in the world is far better equipped to respond positively and create beneficial solutions for themselves than the person who refuses to even acknowledge that ugliness in the first place.

Remember how I told you that I suffered from depression for many years? Well, a big epiphany came for me one day when I was having a chat with a very smart, very switched on counselor. She simply said, "you're not wrong, you know."

A light went off in my head. I wasn't wrong. I felt how I felt. There was this painful reality following me around: I wasn't happy. Every therapist I went to had tried to convince me that I was *wrong* somehow, that my thoughts and feelings were warped and needed to be remedied, that I needed to think more positively.

What they were doing was the antithesis of acceptance. They were telling me with every fiber in their being that they did not accept my unhappiness, and that their whole job was to get me as far away from that unhappiness as possible. It was like saying that you loved and accepted crows, but not their blackness, or their birdiness, or the fact that they sometimes eat blueberries.

So I sat and looked at this counselor and felt nothing but relief. She accepted that I was unhappy. Not pessimistic. Not mistaken. Not using faulty cognitions. Unhappy. She listened to my reasons for being unhappy. She didn't jump in with a million solutions. She was just curious about my experience.

And *that* was what gave me the courage, ironically, to truly work on that unhappiness for the first time in my life. When I could just sit with my negative feelings, as they were, I could accept myself, as I was. Tension fell away. I was still depressed, but now I was *authentically*, genuinely depressed! It might sound funny, but this was one of the most positive moments of my life. Till then my depression had seemed almost taboo. I had been trying to solve the problem by pretending it wasn't there, by running away from it. But she wanted to understand that unhappiness. And so I became curious too.

The first thing I did right there and then was to *accept* my experience, whatever it was. If it was true and real, then what benefit would I gain from denying the fact? The next thing I decided was that I was done being inauthentic. I felt how I felt, and I was going to say so. If I had any hope of overcoming my negative feelings, it would only be once I had the courage to actually *have* those feelings in the first place.

Three Ways to Love Yourself Without Turning into a Self-obsessed Asshole

I bet you're an awesome person. I bet you really have your head screwed on right. And that's why I'm sure you're not interested in turning into a self-obsessed asshole.

I don't know when it happened, but somewhere and somehow, it became fashionable to work on your self-compassion. If you're old enough, some of this philosophy will seem uncannily like the confidence and self-esteem trend that predated it, just with a little Buddhist flair added. While the West should certainly be thankful for everything it's learnt from Eastern philosophy, it's probably also true that the meaning of "compassion" has been somewhat warped on its journey over.

Just as "acceptance" is a pretty convenient euphemism for "giving up", "self-love" can also be used and abused to some less than compassionate ends.

Here are 3 ways that you can start treating yourself with a little dignity, understanding and kindness ...without being an asshole about it. Allow me to demonstrate:

A little fear is a good thing

Imagine you're a woman who's been with her husband for 10 years. Like all marriages, there are ups and downs, but more ups than downs and things are on the whole happy and peaceful.

One day, her husband gets a massive promotion which entails more money, more prestige and more responsibility for him. They're both thrilled – it's a real achievement. Over the next few months, though, the husband begins to change. He starts working out more and gaining some muscle. He starts dressing a little nicer, eating a little better, holding his head a little higher. There's no doubt about it: he's transforming before her eyes.

Tensions mount as the wife begins to wonder at this new change. Was their old life not good enough for him? Is he having an affair? Does he think he's better than her or something? They discuss it and the husband is clear: he has a new lease on life and wants some of it to rub off on her. He's enthusiastic. She can also work out, get a better job and really start doing the things she's always wanted to – after all, he did it!

This doesn't motivate the wife. In fact, she feels more resentful than ever.

Asshole move: The wife consults her friends and family. They give her the message: love yourself. Don't feel intimidated by a husband who doesn't really accept you for who you are. They all agree that she's in an unfortunate position. Their advice? She should put her foot down. He's being superficial and selfish and if he doesn't stop criticizing her, she needs to leave him.

Non-asshole move: Through much soul-searching and chatting with her therapist, the wife comes to an uncomfortable conclusion: she's upset with her husband's success because deep down, she feels guilty for not doing the same for herself. Though it's painful for her to admit, her husband has a point: during their marriage, they both seemed to implicitly agree to let themselves go and quietly give up on their loftier ambitions. Now that her husband was actually pursuing those dreams, it shone a stark light on all of her unfulfilled dreams. It was as though he had now broken that unspoken promise to be mediocre together.

Though it was painful, she looked more closely at her fear and anger. Instead of trying to avoid it by creating a story where she was being unfairly judged, she just sat with it. What was she really afraid of? What was she really angry about?

The answer came to her after a few weeks of reflection: she was angry about all her goals and dreams she had given up on. She looked at herself in the mirror and had an *incredibly negative* reaction: she was overweight, overstressed, unkempt and uninspired. Instead of directing her anger and fear towards her husband, she decided to swallow her pride and take inspiration from him instead. In a year she had quit her own unfulfilling job and had started taking better care of herself in every way.

A little fear is a good thing. But it needs to be the right kind of fear. We all feel nervous at times, doubtful, unconfident or angry. Your standard self-love advice feels really good when you're in this state of mind. "Don't worry" it says, "you're good. Everything's OK. You're great as you are right now."

Don't get me wrong, it's a lovely sentiment, but sometimes, you're *not* good. Sometimes, everything's *not* OK. And pretending it is doesn't count as self-compassion so much as denial.

Ask yourself this question: what state of mind, attitude or set of beliefs is going to motivate you to take the best course of action? If you adopt an attitude of resignation, you don't act at all. You abstain entirely and stay exactly where you are. You're comfortable, sure, but you're not growing or evolving. If your anger and fear came from a very real problem in your life, well, that warning light goes unheeded and the problem remains in your life.

If the woman followed her friends' advice, she would leave her husband in a whirl of indignation, painting him in a bad light for not "accepting" her as she was. She would feel better temporarily, but the root of those ugly feelings would remain: she was living well beneath her potential and it was nobody's fault but her own.

But there's another way. By being courageous enough to sit with her unpleasant feelings, she was able to get to the root of the problem and actually have the integrity to evolve. When she looked in the mirror and hated what she saw, she didn't shrug and say, "eh, beauty standards are crazy, I'm actually amazing as I am and he'd better love me, because he's my husband and I deserve it no matter what." She had a negative reaction and stuck with it. By *honestly acknowledging* the negative, she found a positive outcome.

A little comparison is a good thing

Comparison, as they say, is the thief of joy. Don't look at what everyone else is doing and judge yourself harshly if you don't seem to be up to scratch. Sounds good. Surely I'm not about to suggest that this is bad advice?

Well, I kind of am.

When you compare something with something else, you open up the possibility to judge one thing as inferior. We live in a competitive world and usually, when you compare two things, it's only to see which is the biggest, the best, the most beautiful, the most expensive.

In this case the idea that comparison is an endless, useless activity is true. There always will be someone better than you, on whatever measure you choose. If you're trying to be the best, you're going to constantly be crushed when you realize that you aren't.

So, the solution is easy – don't compare yourself!

This is where I don't think that this advice holds. When you compare two things, you also open up the opportunity to gain a deeper understanding of both things. Some things only make sense relative to other things, especially other things that are least like them. Comparison can show you what is lacking, but it can also illuminate what is abundant. I believe that comparison is not the problem, but the way that people compare is.

If you see a good-looking, successful person walking down the street, and you instantly feel bad about yourself, what is really the *source* of your bad feeling?

1) That they exist?

2) That you compared yourself to them and found yourself wanting?

3) That you believed *you* were supposed to be most successful and best-looking person?

This may seem like a weird point to argue, but bear with me.

Asshole move: You see the person, and then look back at yourself, and see that you are less attractive, less successful. You absolutely hate the emotions it stirs up and *believe that you should never have to endure the feeling of being inferior to anyone* and so you get angry and upset. In fact, you very much would like to be *superior* to this person, and so you think of ways to do that.

You tell yourself that he may look handsome, but deep down he's probably a bit of an idiot anyway, and you're far more intelligent. You write off his success – he probably just inherited his wealth and didn't earn it, like you're trying to do. Now, there is no problem. You feel better, you've devalued his achievements and you've done little to advance your own.

Non-asshole move: You see the person, and then look back at yourself, and see that you are less attractive, less successful. You love and accept yourself, though, and you know that it's foolish to expect that you will always be the best. Instead of jealousy, you feel admiration. Because you are secure in all the things that you are, you don't feel threatened by his superiority – you only see it for what it is. You don't need to tell yourself a story about why he isn't actually superior, you can see that he is, and it's OK. You get on with your life, not by devaluing him, but by valuing you both. You realize that his success doesn't mean your failure, and even if you convince yourself that he has failed, it doesn't mean anything for how well you choose to live your own life.

Again, the differences between these two frames of mind may seem subtle, but there's an obvious way to test which one is ultimately all about self-love, and which one is about self-indulgence.

Ask yourself, which mindset motivates change, useful action, peace and joy? And which one encourages you to stay exactly the same, smug, self-satisfied and inactive? Negative emotions can be pushed away and ignored, or they can be engaged and used to power productive, compassionate action.

Compare away. Why not? Is there something to be gained from carefully avoiding the experience of being just as you are? Is it really the end of the world to occasionally be less beautiful, less accomplished or less intelligent than one of the other 7 billion people in the world?

A little isolation is a good thing

Depressed people, they say, need to get out more, to connect with a support network and share their burden with friends, family and maybe a mental health professional. This is true. When you're stuck in a depressive spiral, you can easily start to lose your grip on reality and isolate yourself.

At the same time, a little isolation is a good thing.

So far, this book has been big on having the courage to sit with a negative emotion – not as something nasty that needs to be "fixed" as soon as possible, but as a valuable clue about your next move, a warning flag, or a hint at something deeper working below the surface. I've tried to show that when you *engage* with negativity (like depression) you give yourself the chance to work through it, rather than just stuffing it away under a layer of bullshit.

Bullshit can sometimes come in the most surprising forms. It seems to me that a lot of bullshit rears its head in the very places that claim to be a *antidote* to bullshit. If you're having a problem, the automatic suggestion might be to seek advice. Involve as many other people as possible. Go to the doctor. Write to an advice column or poll your friends and family in a bid to crowdsource a solution. But I think this backfires more often than not!

Imagine a girl is having some trouble with her long-term boyfriend. She feels that she has always had poor self-esteem, and is constantly getting involved with men who treat her badly ...and he is no different. One day, a very bad argument escalates and he slaps her. He storms off and she is shattered. Her world comes to a standstill as she asks herself over and over again: what should I do?

Asshole move: Because she feels completely flooded with emotions, the first thing she does is call a friend, who rushes over immediately. They hash it out together. The friend has always hated him and gives her advice: leave him, he's awful. The girl isn't quite so sure; after all, she does love him and that just seems so harsh, doesn't it?

She speaks to her mother next and her mother, being a little more old fashioned, suggests she take some time off from the relationship and that the guy in question is just a little passionate, that's all. This also doesn't seem right. The girl grows more and more flustered. Should they break up? Was he wrong? Was she wrong?

She consults more friends, then asks an online forum. They all focus on different parts of her problem and give her different advice. She doesn't want to take any of the advice they give her, and hems and haws a little bit more. The problem escalates and causes her more stress. A resolution isn't reached. Now everyone is involved, though, and she can barely think straight trying to balance out all the factors and arrive at the best solution.

Non-asshole move: She feels flooded with emotions. But because she knows that she might make bad decisions when she's emotional, the first thing she does is try to calm down, go somewhere safe and try to center herself. There is one persistent, overwhelming emotion that won't leave her: fear. Not fear that he will hit her again, but fear that if she leaves him she will be alone.

Instead of asking a million people what their opinions are, she simply looks within: she *knows* what she has to do, but it seems quite scary and difficult. She has to break up with him. She also knows that if she asks for advice, she'll only be unconsciously looking for people to tell her what she wants to hear, or give her an excuse to stay (the easy thing) rather than leave (the more difficult thing). Once she has calmed down and had time to really think for herself, it doesn't matter what anybody's opinion is: she breaks up with him. Then, when she calls on her friends and family, it's to help her with her *real* problem, that of feeling on her own.

Of course, the girl in this story isn't an "asshole" but I hope the story illustrates that sometimes, people do the most damage when their intentions are good. Everyone loves to weigh in on a problem and give their advice. But when you look outward for guidance, you simultaneously avoid looking inward. You can probably think of people you know who ask for advice and never take it. Why? Because they are not really looking for advice. They are actively avoiding doing the one thing that would solve their problem: make a conscious choice.

Advice can muddy the waters. People around you can be well-meaning but in their attempts to soothe you, they may end up cementing your problem rather than helping you solve it. The best advice is often, "carefully look inside yourself, act according to your principles and take responsibility for the outcome" although when was the last time you heard someone give this advice? Instead, people have their own agendas, their own beliefs and ideas, their own blind spots. When you substitute their judgment for your own, you throw away an opportunity to learn what your negative emotions are trying to teach you.

The next time you have a problem, resist the urge to reach out and ask someone or something else to solve it for you. Ask if there's anything you're avoiding by deferring to someone else's analysis of your problem. Isolate yourself for a short while and be honest about your "gut feeling". You'd be amazed at how much clarity you can gain when you tune out the noise from other people telling you what you should and shouldn't feel.

"Isolate" can mean different things for different people, but I find that some quiet time away from the internet or social media, nosy friends and family, and even TV and movies can be a good way to just stop for a second and see what *you* feel, and what *you* want.

CHAPTER 4: THE COURAGE TO BE AUTHENTIC

The paradox is this: accepting your unhappiness can make you happier.

Start with being authentically you, even if that means being authentically depressed, anxious or confused.

- Start every morning by realigning with your authentic self. Before the day rushes in with its noise and distraction, take a moment to do a "status check" on your body, heart and mind. How are you? What emotions are you experiencing?

- When you discover a negative emotion, commit to staying with it, rather than avoiding it or trying to stuff it down. Take your fear, pain, sadness etc. out of its hiding place and really *look* at it. Examine it lovingly, as though it were a precious artefact. Don't judge yourself for not being happier or more put together. All you need to be is honest.

- Now sit with this emotion for a while. Notice if you try to wriggle away from it or tell yourself a story to make it all go away. Again, just watch yourself, without any judgment. Ask, what is the real source of this emotion? Ask a few times. You don't necessarily have to take your word for it, either, but ask anyway.

- Now, ask yourself what *beneficial actions* you can take to address this emotion. If you're exhausted, a beneficial action is to sleep. A less beneficial action (although one that might feel just as good in the moment) is to binge watch a TV series you actually don't like and procrastinate on doing work or chores. Don't automatically settle on the action that simply *feels* nicest. Sometimes, self-love is a little unpleasant, at least at first.

- Act. Enjoy being the free agent that you are and go out into the world and enjoy your ability to bring about your goals. Of course, you may fail. You may realize after a while that you're not actually exhausted, but bored, for example. Again, self-compassion means no judgment. Just stay open, listen carefully and be accepting of what you hear. Fear and laziness are usually the culprits – look closely and be honest, is there something you need to push yourself to do?

- Forgive yourself when you fail – but only when you actually fail! Taking concrete, beneficial, value-driven action is always a cause for celebration. Whether you succeed or not is not as important as making that decision to act intentionally. If you fail, whatever, you fail. It's just data. Forgive yourself although in all honesty, there is nothing to forgive. However, don't be tempted to forgive yourself for all those things you *don't* try. There is nothing to be gained from chickening out of taking action, then forgiving yourself because you're sure you would have failed anyway. Be hard on yourself when you're being lazy, but forgive easily for all those things you had the guts to actually attempt.

- Accept yourself. Warts and all. Really. It doesn't take any courage to say, "I'm brilliant! I'm a unique and wonderful human being! Hooray for me!" In fact, there's a certain fear hidden in the assumption that you are only worthy of full acceptance if you are perfect. Rather, say the more difficult thing, "I am who I am. I have good aspects and bad. I am responsible for myself. I am a flawed, but worthy human being. I accept all of it." True acceptance doesn't need any ornamentation. Be honest and accept what you are, right now.

- Have the courage to not hide in your acceptance and use it as an excuse to never change or grow. If you love yourself, do yourself a favor and accept criticism, and be uncomfortable once in a while. You won't die. In fact, it'll do you good.

- Don't keep yourself hidden away from others. Some people will like you better when you act the part that they have assigned you in their own personal life drama, but you don't have to stick around and play that role if you don't want to. Speak the truth about how you feel and what you want. You serve nobody by dumbing yourself down, giving up, hiding your dreams and outrageous goals, or stifling your anger or restlessness. Sometimes it hurts to evolve and grow. If you are honest and express your honesty, what is damaged as a result was not ultimately valuable to you anyway.

- Just as you'll be working on living authentically yourself, believe other people when they show you *their* authentic selves. As much as you can, praise and reward people when they are honest and genuine with you, and put less weight on interactions that are inauthentic. If you ask for honesty from others, give them the dignity of accepting their honest answers, even if you don't like it.

- Have a sense of humor about it! Keeping up appearances, wearing masks, comparing yourself to others and stressing about what you should and shouldn't do ...it's all very serious work, isn't it? Being able to laugh at yourself takes a certain kind of strength. When you are overly serious, you are intolerant of things that don't make sense, of confusing things or absurd things. But life doesn't have to make sense *all* the time. Feel how refreshing it is just to be lighthearted sometimes, to let go and see the humor in life. We're all going to die soon, we might as well laugh while we have the chance!

CHAPTER 5: NEGATIVE EMOTIONS: YOUR NEW BEST FRIENDS

Think of this chapter a bit like a roadmap for the less travelled parts of the psyche – all those dark and uninhabited places that all the feel-good self-help out there doesn't want to engage with too deeply.

We've seen that negative emotions, when experienced authentically, honestly and with awareness and intention, can be the ironic catalyst for positive change.

The next time you're feeling bad, have a look at this chapter and see if those bad emotions can't be appreciated for the gifts they are. What message are they giving you? What warnings? What encouragements?

I feel bored
- Do you need to challenge yourself a little?
- Have you outgrown a certain situation or dynamic?
- Is there something scary that you're procrastinating on?

I feel anxious
- Is there a way to stop and just be in the moment, rather than in the past or the future?
- What is the single most helpful *action* you can take right now?
- What is the precise story you're telling yourself that is the source of your panic?

I feel helpless
- Is there some way of looking at your problem that you really haven't considered before?
- Is it really reasonable that you should have control in this situation?
- Are you trying to change something that fundamentally can't be changed?

I feel unloved
- Can you find a way to love yourself for the moment?
- Have you been loving those around you? Is there someone out there who wishes you would be more compassionate with them?

I feel angry

- Have you *really* understood your options in this situation? Or is there some fact about it that you're not willing to acknowledge?
- What are you yourself doing right now to maintain your frustrating situation?
- Have you considered your situation from another person's perspective?

I feel frustrated
- Are there things you have failed to express gratitude for lately?
- What is the story behind your impatience? Is it really true that reality ought to be different from what it currently is?

I feel insignificant
- Can you think of yourself as a newborn? Can you imagine everything that must have been going through your parents' minds as they met you for the first time?
- What can you do, at your very next opportunity, to make someone's life slightly better than it was before?
- Have you been failing to really show the people around you who you are?

I feel confused
- Is there any particular reason you need to resolve everything right this instant? Or can your issue rest for a while and wait till you're ready to think it through more clearly?
- Are you taking on more than you can reasonably handle?
- Do you need to slow down?

I feel overwhelmed
- Can you commit to getting through just the next 5 minutes of your life as well as you can?
- If you could choose just one important thing that is happening to you right now, what would it be? Forget the rest.
- Could your boundaries use a little strengthening?

I feel dissatisfied
- Is it time to re-evaluate your goals and see whether they are what you really want?
- Are your expectations fair?

I feel resentful
- Do you feel bad about compromising on something that was important to you?
- Are you giving more agency to another person than they really deserve? What is your role in creating your resentment?

- Is there some place you have been inauthentic with yourself or others?

I feel clingy and needy
- Why do you feel that people around you can't or won't listen to your needs?
- Is there a way for you to give to yourself what you are asking others for?

I feel lonely
- Can you think of someone in your life you have been neglecting?

I feel disappointed
- What is your real potential?
- What can you do to bring about the things you wish you saw in the world around you?

I feel ashamed
- Is it really the end of the world if you occasionally mess up, or do something wrong/embarrassing/stupid?
- What does your shame tell you about who you *really* want to be?
- Is there someone else's critical voice you've taken as your own?
- What would happen if you ignored this feeling and chose to believe that you were lovable and worthy of compassion despite messing up?

I feel afraid
- Is your fear preventing you from growing and changing or is it a potential catalyst for change?
- Are there dangerous elements around you that you've been ignoring?
- Whose fear are you feeling, yours or somebody else's?
- Is it so bad to be afraid? Is it something unbearable that you should be apprehensive about doing something new or difficult?

I feel worried
- What can you do right now, in this moment, to bring about the things that are important to you?
- What is the state of mind that you value most? Can you focus on maintaining that state of mind for a few moments?
- Are you stressing about something that is outside of your control, or taking on the emotional "work" of someone else?

I feel exhausted

- If you were counseling a friend, what would you advise them to do right now?
    - Pick three things that you feel obliged to do right now, an forget about everything else.
    - Do you have a need that is regularly going unmet?

I feel invisible
    - What parts of yourself are you not acknowledging, even right now?
    - Have you made efforts to be your own genuine, authentic self with those around you?
    - Have you expressed your needs and boundaries?

I feel empty
    - What would be the most uncharacteristic thing you could possibly do right now? Do you have the guts to do that, and just break out of your comfort zone?
    - Have you been too engrossed in the drama of others? Or too engrossed in your own?

I feel bitter
    - What can you do today that will ensure that in the future, you don't feel like you do right now?
    - Do you feel that someone isn't listening to you? Is it time to express yourself differently or to someone who has the ability to hear?
    - What things in your life right now are blessings?
    - Can you think of a time when you were forgiven, or someone had compassion for you? Can you think of anyone you can give that feeling to yourself?

CONCLUSION

In the beginning of this book, I asked you a simple question: how are you? Maybe you brushed it off, or you had only a vague answer or thought, "well, it depends on who's asking…"

Right now, I'll ask you again.

How are you?

Maybe your answer has changed a little. Of course, I'm being glib, and real life forbids us to have a fat therapy session every time the lady at the checkout counter asks us how we are. But this is nevertheless a question that people seem reluctant to answer for themselves.

When you pick up a self-help book, you also pick up a story about who you are, and how you should be, and what your problem is. Whereas you might have sought help for a vague sense of uneasiness, your self-help book is quick to tell you why you're unhappy, that you shouldn't be, and that you should follow everything it says if you want to stop it immediately and be happy already.

In this book, I hope I have shown you that jumping in at the first hint of a negative feeling can ironically be the worst way to work through that negative feeling. Also ironically, it's only when we desperately try to force negativity out of our lives that we leave that same negativity unchecked, festering away somewhere, unacknowledged.

The approach I outline here goes against most of the popular ways to tackle depression, anxiety or general malaise. But it is an approach that allowed me to dig deep into my own authenticity, be honest with myself and start to make real, lasting changes in my life.

If you're in the same boat as I was, I can't tell you what your changes are meant to be. I can't say what goals you should make for yourself, or what you should value, or what you should do. But I *can* tell you that you will never truly understand those things for yourself unless you're courageous enough to sit comfortably with your own negativity. And nobody can do that but you. This is the height of self-love: to look at yourself, all of yourself, and accept it.

Your life right now, not the life that you are told you have or should have, or the life you paint on social media or tell people you have, but your *real* life, well, that necessarily entails some negativity. But this negativity isn't a mistake. It isn't a sign that you're doing things wrong and it isn't something that needs fixing.

Rather, pain, fear, anger and loneliness are all valuable parts of the human experience. These emotions don't limit or stop your happiness – they actively help you *shape* it, if you are brave enough to engage with them.

If anything in this book has resonated with you, even a little, I want to encourage you to stop with the bullshit – the bullshit you tell yourself, and the bullshit you tell others. I was petrified to really put myself out there, to look at myself as I was, without any bullshit. But then I realized that the pain of living inauthentically was greater than the pain of taking a risk and being myself.

Sometimes, being yourself also means being sad, angry or confused.

And that's OK.

Really OK.

SELF-COMPASSION - I DON'T HAVE TO FEEL BETTER THAN OTHERS TO FEEL GOOD ABOUT MYSELF: LEARN HOW TO SEE SELF ESTEEM THROUGH THE LENS OF SELF-LOVE AND MINDFULNESS AND CULTIVATE THE COURAGE TO BE YOU

INTRODUCTION

The world is a vast, complicated and sometimes downright hostile place.

Today, more than ever, human beings have had to learn new ways to be resilient, know themselves and have the courage to be who they are.

Our hyper connected world bombards us with images of phenomenally successful celebrities together with the expectation that we should want nothing but the best for ourselves at all times. But in a bustling world of 7 billion people, carving out a meaningful niche for ourselves can be daunting to say the least.

It's understandable that people feel the need to bolster their self esteem. Faced with millions of glossy images in the media about how we should live our lives, some have turned to trying even harder still to keep up. Others have merely given up.

It's no exaggeration that people in the 21ˢᵗ century live in a world of infinitely more possibilities than any generation before them. We have experts and gurus of all stripes telling us that the life we have now is nothing compared to what we could achieve – and yet, we're as depressed and lacking in confidence as ever.

Self help books on the market today will tell you one of two things: either that you are perfect already as you are and needn't worry, or that with just a little (well, *a lot*) of effort, you *can* reach those goals. Be the best, smartest, most successful, thinnest and relentlessly happiest version of yourself possible. No excuses!

This book takes a different approach to self esteem altogether. If you're feeling overwhelmed and worthless, inundated with information, struggling to juggle life, expectations, and disappointments... it may be time for a little self-compassion.

Unlike self esteem or an inflated confidence level, self-compassion is a different way of looking at yourself and others, warts and all, and a way more realistic acceptance of the way things are. With self-compassion, you become unflappable, calm and self-assured - without the risk of narcissism or becoming self-absorbed.

Through a series of exercises, this book will suggest a new, gentle yet extremely powerful attitude shift that can end feelings of self-hatred, doubt, shame and low self-worth forever.

CHAPTER ONE: WHAT IS SELF-COMPASSION?

You may be familiar with the idea of compassion for *others*.

When we have compassion for another person, we acknowledge that they are suffering, and feel kindness and good will towards them.

Rather than pity, self-compassion is about non-judgmentally accepting others for who they are in the here and now. Rather than judging them for their shortcomings, weaknesses or failures, compassion is about care, kindness and respect.

Self-compassion is turning this kindness to ourselves.

It's ironic that many times, people who treat others with acceptance and tenderness can't seem to summon up those same feelings for themselves. While they may be quick to forgive the transgressions of others, they berate themselves harshly for making those very same mistakes.

Self-compassion means we honor and acknowledge our humanity, our imperfection and our fragility. Self-compassion allows you to open your heart up to human condition – and no matter who we are, we all experience a shared humanity. Rather than wanting to change because we find ourselves unacceptable, we change because we *want* to, and because we can look at our shortcomings honestly and without ego.

When we are self-compassionate, we don't have to "do" anything. We can simply allow ourselves to be. Waking up to our own innate value as human beings has profound effects on the way we feel about ourselves, others and the world we live in. Self-compassion permeates all areas of our lives - the physical, emotional, psychological and spiritual. Our interactions with strangers as well as those we love will change subtly, leaving us kinder and more at peace.

Self-acceptance of our bodies

Self-compassion means observing your body with acceptance.

Our culture has an almost psychotic preoccupation with youth and beauty, but when we have compassion for our bodies, we neither love nor hate them, we only see and accept them for what they are. At any one time, people may feel that sure, they'll love themselves, just as soon as they lose a little weight or fix their hair or get rid of that zit.

Instead, try to become curious about your body. Get to know it like you would an interesting new friend. What does it like? What can it do? In what ways is it completely unlike every other body? In what ways is it completely unremarkable?

Self-acceptance of our emotions

In our self-help culture, we preach self-love from the mountaintops – except of course, if your self happens to be depressed, belligerent, strange or anxious.

In fact, the entire human experience is chopped into halves: positive emotions and negative emotions – the latter being an eternal source of consternation. Negative emotions are only tolerated as incomplete stages on the path to perfection, an assumed future where you will not struggle, will not be unsure and will not, under any circumstances, be unhappy.

But what happens to your unhappiness when you are happy to have it?

Let go of a one-sided view of what it's like to be human. Fully embrace your emotions – the pleasant as well as the not so pleasant. Be OK with the fact that sometimes, you will be unhappy. Those feelings will pass. In fact, *all* feeling will pass.

Self-acceptance of our thoughts

Closely tied to our emotions, our thoughts are also part of us. You can choose to completely identify with a thought, you can choose to deny it, or you can take a step back and merely observe it. Self-compassion means becoming comfortable with your internal landscape for what it is.

When we have self-compassion, we develop a deep, internal resilience that is unshakeable. Whether it's a hurtful comment from someone else or failing at something important to us, self-compassion allows us to look at the events of our lives with kindness. When we do so, we don't beat ourselves up when we fail to reach our goals, nor do we need to boast and brag to feel better about our achievements. The self-compassionate person doesn't look to others for validation.

Instead, they seem to generate their own self-worth, enjoying being who they are, filled with the courage to face life without needing to be perfect.

The Science of Self-compassion

Self-compassion is not just something that *sounds* good – more and more, research is being done to show that practicing compassion has real, measurable effects on our health, our work, our relationships and our lives in general.

Research has shown that when we blame others for our mistakes, we tend to feel less compassionate towards them; that when we have compassion for others our own happiness increases; that compassion makes us better parents; that it lowers stress hormones in the body and boosts the immune system; makes us better friends and can even reduce the risk of heart disease. Self-compassion floods the body with feel-good neurotransmitters, improves our sleep and reduces stress levels.

For anyone who knows how closely the mind and body are connected, this should come as no surprise.

CHAPTER TWO: SELF-COMPASSION AND SELF ESTEEM

For anyone raised in the modern Western world, "self-compassion" might sound suspiciously like regular old garden variety "self esteem". It's the reason your kindergarten teacher put "Great Job!" stickers on your crayon drawings and why group meeting leaders are told to encourage everyone to add something positive to their criticisms.

It's curious that just a few generations after the bootstrap idealism of the American Dream is over, we are left with the fuzzy democracy of the idea that everyone deserves to be special. Or rather, that everyone deserves to try and be as special as they can.

Self-compassion and self esteem are two vastly different concepts, and proponents of the confidence-for-everyone-all-the-time model have begun to see that there are limits to what at first seemed like an obviously good idea. What could be so bad about feeling good about yourself?

Well, one of the main problems with self esteem is that it's fragile. Built on external evaluation, self esteem can be instantly undermined by someone who simply does better than you. A mother who constantly gives her child affection when they perform well at school is not giving that child the message that they are intrinsically valuable as a human being. Rather, the message is that affection, achievement, recognition and feelings of self-worth are all tied to measurable external phenomenon. This means they can be taken away. That child may be said to have a high self esteem, but what will happen when they encounter a peer who does better than them at school?

Self-compassion, on the other hand, is not about measurable quantities, and there are no conditions attached to it. We should have compassion for ourselves and others because life is hard, and we are all doing the best we can. We don't have to do anything to earn self-compassion, we can enjoy it merely by virtue of being human, of living the best way we know how, of being the only thing we can be: what we are.

Creating high self esteem seems like a reasonable goal on its face, but it has a built in trap that is designed to leave us unhappier, less accomplished, less kind. What's worse, when we are constantly incentivized by praise and recognition for doing well, we eventually stop trying to do well *for its own sake*. Tying up our self-concept with external measures damages us – but it also saps the joy from doing something well, from the enjoyment of genuine achievement. It makes us believe, perhaps unwittingly, that things that others don't acknowledge as valuable actually aren't, and that good actions that aren't recognized as such don't really count.

The idealism of a high self esteem also means that being average is nowhere good enough. The irony is that we all strive to be exceptional, to be better than everyone else, but, merely by looking at the statistical reality, most of us will not be.

Let that sink in for a moment.

How does it feel, to be in the middle? To be good enough, to be fine, to be regular and average? If you've ingested any self-help material from the better portion of this century, this thought alone is probably enough to have you kicking and screaming internally. In fact, when you hear the word "average" you probably just round down to "failure". This is the reason why psychometrists who test young children are trained not to say "your child has an average score on the IQ test" but rather, "your child is scoring in the same range as his peers". For a parent, you see, being "average" is more or less the same thing as having a problem. It's far more comforting to hear the result framed as at least keeping up with everybody else.

What is on the other side of the desperate desire to be unique? What seems aspirational quickly dissolves into self-absorption, shallowness, insecurity, and vanity.

Psychologists and mental health professionals have long understood that the root of narcissism is shame. To the outsider, the narcissist simply looks like he has far too much self esteem and could probably stand to be taken down a notch. But look deeper into the mind of a narcissist and you will see that an over inflated ego very often forms in response to damage done to that ego. In other words, low self esteem and high self esteem are two sides of the same coin. Perhaps you know somebody like this. After being rejected by a particular group, they claim they never cared for the group anyway – in other words, that it is *them* who is doing the rejecting.

Self-compassion is not binary in the same way that self esteem is. To put it very simply, you needn't be better than someone else to be good. Self esteem is relativistic, competitive and zero sum. There can only be one winner, and you increase your chances of that being you by putting down anyone who threatens to take that place. It's you or them. Dog eat dog. This competition is built into our very language. Good, better, best. There is a continuum and we belong somewhere on it. When we say "better", it is implied that we mean "better than X". When our self-concept is this easy to damage, it makes sense that we are serious about defending it.

Self-compassion, on the other hand, is not about beating opponents, or even beating yourself. There is no comparison - you are kind and good to yourself simply because. Rather than look at your life, your body, your skills and your accomplishments and see only what could be improved, what is not as good as everyone else's, what is better than everyone else's, you look and see simply what is. You accept what is because... well, it is.

When we are self-compassionate we understand that realistically, most of the time we will land somewhere in the big, meaty middle of the bell curve. We understand that we can make plans, but sometimes we will fail. Sometimes we will fall short of perfection (in fact, we basically always fall short of perfection). So, instead of looking at our lives with a built in scorecard, we simply see what we see.

The joy of high self esteem tied to an external event feels great, but there's always hidden inside it a little seed of anxiety, of paranoia that recognizes that it is not permanent. Self-compassion, on the other hand, is nothing more or less than the full acknowledgement and acceptance of whatever it is that you are. It cannot be threatened.

Sure, you think, but isn't it a little dangerous to just accept everything? Isn't that the same as being passive, as completely giving up? What goals could you have if you don't strive for anything?

Sadly, most of us can't even imagine what it would look like to be motivated by anything other than shame and fear. Since we were children, we've been taught that there are only two opposite things: achievement, and failure. We are trained in school to move away from the embarrassment and disappointment of a "failure" and towards the glory and satisfaction of winning and achievement. The good guys beat the bad guys in all the movies.

But again, this is very simple, dualistic thinking. In fact, when we really accept and look at who we are - not what we wish we were or what we think we should be - we see ourselves more clearly than ever. Without either shame or excessive pride, we can see our faults clearly for what they are. Many people fail to grasp the meaning of "acceptance" simply because they have never actually experienced it themselves. It does not mean you condone what you look at. It also doesn't mean you condemn it. Instead, acceptance is neutral, obvious. What would happen if you looked at yourself the same way as you look at a blue sky? If you accepted all the things you were the same way you accepted the fact that the sky is blue?

The project of self esteem is not to realize who you are and feel good about it. The rule of self esteem is that you can only feel good about yourself as soon as you meet some goal or standard. When you have a goal, everything that doesn't affirm or lead to that goal is dismissed or ignored. This leads to denial or trivializing of the parts of your being that could actually use improvement. If looking honestly at your flaws is a painful and embarrassing process, one that only makes you feel more worthless, you're less inclined to ever really look at those flaws. And less inclined to fix them.

With self-compassion, you can look at yourself objectively and make realistic moves to learn more skills and improve on your weaknesses. Self-compassion doesn't mean shrugging our shoulders at our flaws, but rather taking a good, honest look at them and seeing them for what they are. Without judgment. When we let go of the constant need to fix ourselves up, to be better, the paradox is that we open our eyes to becoming better anyway.

Contrasting Self-Esteem and Self-Compassion:
   - Relative – you feel good *compared* to someone else feeling bad.
   - Absolute – you feel good, end of story.
   - All about competition. Feeling valuable only when ranked against others (or even an older version of yourself).
   - All about common humanity. Your value is neither undermined or enhanced by the value of others.
   - Conditional.
   - Unconditional.
   - Based on striving, which is moving away from the present reality and towards a goal.
   - Based on acceptance, which moves towards the present moment.
   - Quantifiable.
   - Non-quantifiable.
   - Reduces our empathy for others – compassion is "zero sum".
   - Enhances our empathy and compassion for others.
   - Is elite and exclusive, only exceptionalism and uniqueness is valuable.

- Is inclusive, all humans deserve to feel self-compassion.
- Too much can lead to narcissism, vanity and self-absorption.
- The concept of "too much self-compassion" is meaningless.
- Self-improvement comes from external sources, from fear and shame.
- Self-improvement is internal, proactive and aspirational.
- Flaws are not part of the picture, so are ignored or denied.
- Flaws are part of reality and accepted.
- Idealistic
- Realistic.

CHAPTER THREE: SELF-COMPASSION EXERCISES

What follows are some tools you may find useful in opening yourself up to more self-compassion in your life.

These are only suggestions though, and you should feel free to be inspired to change these exercises to suit your own unique situation. If something resonates with you, see if you can use those ideas in the way you think of yourself day to day. If not, shelve the exercise and go back instead to the ones that really speak to you.

The goal is shifting your mindset away from thinking rooted in relativistic, competitive self esteem and into a truly accepting and compassionate frame of mind – exactly how you do this is unimportant.

Exercise One: "There I Go"

There is a lot of wisdom in the truism, "the world is your mirror". The way we feel about others, about life in general, is often a reflection of how we feel about ourselves. The most important relationship you can have is with yourself, so it's no surprise that the quality of that relationship would be echoed in all of your interactions with others. It's for this reason that the following exercise can be so effective.

This exercise is a self-compassion exercise that focuses on others. We'll start with this paradoxical exercise for two reasons. Firstly, empathy and understanding for others, and empathy and understanding for ourselves, are closely linked. Strengthening our capacity for one inevitably strengthens the ability for the other. The second reason, though, is that it is often easier to have compassion for others than it is for ourselves. For a host of reasons, people seem to find it easier to look clearly at the lives of others than their own – starting with compassion for others is a good way of obliquely beginning to develop compassion for yourself.

The exercise:

Choose any day or moment to begin. You don't need to wait for an appropriate moment to start, just start now. The moment is right. As you move around your day, turn your attention outwards to the people you encounter. This includes the people you work with and family members, but also people you pass in the street for a few seconds, waiters and waitresses, people on the TV... anyone really.

As you pass them, instead of letting your self say things like "there goes that guy, look at him, walking with his dog, wearing those pants..." change the pronouns and substitute yourself, saying "there *I* go, look at *me*, walking *my* dog, wearing *my* pants". And so on.

This might feel bizarre at first. Keep it up though. Simply change your original thoughts and perceptions about other people to be about yourself.

"Look at me, screaming and having a temper tantrum in the supermarket."

"There I go, looking pretty hot to be honest."

"There I am, probably 80 years old. I feel so tired. I need a cane to walk."

Have fun with it and try it out on different people. People you like and dislike, people you are indifferent towards. People who are very, very different from you and also those you identify with. Turn all your thoughts about them, good and bad, towards yourself.

After a while of doing this, you might start to notice something strange happening. The kid screaming in the supermarket, the one who would usually elicit pure irritation from you, suddenly becomes something more familiar, especially when you invite your brain to remember, *you were once a child, too.* You probably once had a tantrum in a supermarket yourself. Maybe, you even did something more irritating as a child. Suggest this to your mind, and you open yourself to the thought that, in a way you *are* that child in the supermarket. You sometimes lose your temper, you're sometimes insufferable and sulky when you don't get what you want, aren't you? When you think about it, you have a lot in common with that child.

Human beings love to separate themselves into groups, "me" and "not me", but when you play around with these barriers, you might begin to feel that they are a lot more flexible than they at first seem. No matter who it is, you can inevitably find a way to identify with them, with their experience.

And it goes even deeper. Once you start looking at people not as separate, alien, unknowable beings far outside of you, but as people who share in the human experience, the same experience that you do, you may feel a deeper, almost inexplicable sense of connection and fellowship with them. As all of us move about our lives, we all experience difficulties and joys, we all feel the highs and lows of the human drama, we all worry about death, we all celebrate love, we all die, we all love.

This exercise can remind you that in the bigger picture, there is no competition. We are all human. If you can cultivate an amazed curiosity about others, an appreciation for everything they are, every little variation on the rich tapestry of existence, it will be that much easier to turn that lens on yourself. You are not a failure, you are not too fat or too old or too stupid. You are something much more than that: you are part of the immense human condition, and your struggles are not small, private failings – they're nothing less than part of what it means to be alive.

Exercise Two: Authentically You

Think of a famous person you know or admire (well, you don't even need to admire them, any celebrity will do). Think of all the things that make up who they are. How do people instantly recognize who this celebrity is? It could be a prominent feature, a distinct style of talking or dress, an outlandish world-view or a history of doing very particular things. Now, imagine them *without* this trait. Make Larry King sit up straight and look 10 years younger, make Marilyn Monroe a brunette or give Mick Jagger a beer belly and a conservative dress sense.

Instantly, they lose their authenticity. You could "improve" on any celebrity in this way. Make them skinnier, better looking or smarter. And they *would be* skinnier, better looking and smarter. But they wouldn't be themselves anymore, either. The thing that makes them stand out, the thing that people know and love about them, would be gone.

We have a very simplistic way of thinking of self-worth, of the value of human beings. When we position people on a continuum where one end is bad and the other end is good, we wash out all the subtle variations and idiosyncrasies that make people who they are. We are all blessed with a unique and interesting blend of characteristics, one that is truly ours and nobody else's, and yet we behave as if our being is merely a performance, one that can be quantified, measured and evaluated. Albert Einstein was famously bad at High School Maths (I don't know if this is really true, but it doesn't matter). This fact doesn't detract from his position as one of mankind's most influential thinkers, it *adds* to it.

But there is no box on your standard High School report card that the teacher can tick if she wants to express that young Albert is a restless, brilliant, and dangerously out-of-the-box thinker. She can only give him a percentage value, a letter-grade, and rank him according to his peers on how he performed on a pen and pencil test. What was the essence of Albert Einstein – the lateral thinker, the budding genius who rewrote long-held scientific tenets, the icon with the crazy hair – all of that disappears instantly.

The Exercise:
Assume you are famous. Assume, also, that you are famous exactly as you are now, sitting right here and reading this in this very moment. What are *your* prominent, memorable features? What are the things that make you who you are, "good" or "bad"? How would people instantly recognize you?

Have you got something unusual or noteworthy about your appearance? What do people usually notice about you first? What is the one way you differ from your family and group of friends? Perhaps you have a unique history, a strange way of talking, a wild personal philosophy, an unusual collection of skills, a mole shaped like a dog's head on your left butt cheek, a temper you believe you inherited from your mother, a big, ugly nose, an extra chromosome, a secret, a cat who's like your child, a job you're passionate about, the ability to eat very hot things... whatever.

Don't be tempted to only think of the odd, the unusual or the brag-worthy, though. That is just the old mechanism of "self esteem" coming through. Also think of all the ways you, to put it bluntly, suck. Maybe you never learnt to ride a bike despite trying millions of times. Maybe you have a difficult mental illness, a history with bad relationships or shocking dress sense. Think of the things you've failed at, your personal shortcomings, your mistakes, and the things that make you intensely, utterly annoying to certain people. Remember, many celebrities are famous for these "bad" things as much as anything else.

Now, sit with these things. The good and the bad. The underwhelming. Look at these things and be grateful for them as the things that make you who you are. Resist the urge to rush in and fix up. Resist the urge to deny or cover up or make things sound better than they really are. Resist the urge to judge and quantify.

If you can manage, pick one thing on the list and even *amplify* it. Just to see what happens. Really enjoy this single characteristic that is yours and only yours. Explore it to the fullest. Don't force yourself to be bubbly when you've always been quiet and a bit brooding. If you have crazy, uncontrollable hair, grow it even longer and draw attention to it, letting it be as crazy as it wants. Dress to emphasize your "figure flaws", confess to your boss that you don't know what they're talking about and if someone asks you how you spent your weekend, tell them in all honesty that you sat around in your pajamas, and loved it.

Authentic people, those who are not only comfortable and at home in their own personal reality, but who *thrive* there, these are people who are immune to the precariousness of a "high self esteem" and indifferent to other people's opinions of them. When the only yardstick you have is yourself, you are suddenly not competing with anyone else. Practice *not* ranking yourself. Merely feel what it feels like to be who you are, in all your wonderful, imperfect glory.

Exercise Three: Gratitude Journal

Perhaps "self-compassion" sounds a little soft – as if we should only have "compassion" (i.e. pity) for all the ways we fall far from the ideal. But self-compassion is not a consolation prize for not being more amazing. It's not a resignation to our flaws or merely tolerating them. Instead, self-compassion is very much about taking joy in who we are – *all* of who we are.

One of the best paths to joy is gratitude. You may have discovered this for yourself: that those who are happiest seldom have that much more than you, or know anything special that you don't yet know. Rather, they are able to access and really appreciate the sources of joy they already have in their lives.

This exercise takes you out of the standard "self-help" narrative and asks you not to build up your self esteem, not to increase competition, pursuit and achievement in your life, but to come awake to what is already perfect in your life, right now.

The Exercise:

Your Journal needn't be an actual book, but this is a good way to start. You can choose the details. The idea is to have a safe place to store your memories and feelings of joy, delight, bliss. We all have moments of transcendence in our lives, whether we find it in the eyes of our children, in a beautiful landscape, in our bodies, in the pleasure of dancing, being in nature or having a good belly laugh at the ridiculousness of life.

A gratitude journal is not about making goals or fixing yourself up, it's about being grateful for all the miracles in your life you may already be numb to, right now. When we are receptive to the beauty and wonder in life, we may start to notice that we find more of it. In strange places, even.

Things you could include in your journal:

- Memories of the happiest moments you can remember in your life – really enjoy getting into the details of who, when, why. Use all your senses when bringing them back to life.

- Pictures that capture certain emotions of bliss or joy for you – these can be artful pictures of natural beauty or silly photos of cats, it doesn't matter. It only matters that you choose images that stir something positive in you.

- Just like your mother may have asked you to do, make a list of all the things you are grateful to have in your life. Read over this list when life starts to feel a little barren or hostile. You may have forgotten how lucky you are in many, many ways.

- Put in mementos or trinkets from happy events – movie ticket stubs, photos of your loved ones, an heirloom recipe from your grandmother that whisks you back to your childhood, pressed flowers, quotes or poems that moved you, articles, jokes, even compliments you have received in the past that made you glow at the time.

Our modern fix-up culture treats the intricacies of each person's unique life as something that constantly needs a little lifestyle DIY, constantly requiring reworking and streamlining. We are told to value lists of "hacks" that help you shave off seconds of your routine so you can be just that little bit more productive, how to cram more vitamins and "super-foods" into your diet (not like, you know, the regular boring food that losers eat!), how to exercise at your desk to save time, how to always be better, better, better.

It's exhausting. And it rests on one fundamental premise: you are not good enough as you are. Life is not good enough as it is. Your daily routine? Terrible. Your diet? Shocking and shameful. Do you have a life purpose? A tribe? Do you even meditate?!

Cut this kind of thing off at the root: tune in to all the ways your life isn't, in fact, a complete and utter failure. Refuse to be mobilized and energized by shame and dissatisfaction. When you continually look at your life – your wonderful, unique, miraculous life – and wish it was something else, you are ironically cutting yourself off from the one source of joy that actually is available to you.

Exercise Four: Peace and Letting Go of Being Reactive

As long as you base your behavior on what happens around you, your behavior is not truly your own. In a reactive frame of mind, we are like a balloon getting blown around in the wind, going along with whatever breeze is strongest, liable to pop by accident, without direction or intention.

People who live reactive lives are forever caught up in the turmoil of this and that, people's opinions, fashions, habit – millions of little breezes forever pushing them in different directions. When a reactive person is pushed, they respond accordingly. They don't respond because responding is a good thing in that moment or because they want to respond. They just do it, without thinking.

When a reactive person is complimented, their mental balloon goes along with that breeze: they are happy, suddenly their self-worth is higher. But, by the same token, when someone insults them, their mental balloon bobs back in the other direction. Now, they are worthless. You could spend your whole life in this back and forth.

"Letting go" sounds like becoming loose and unconcerned, like the balloon, but the paradox is that when we can really let go of external sources of judgment and appraisal, we tap into our own personal gravity, we become more solid, less likely to be blown every which way by the breezes around us. A person who is not reactive but *active* is aware of and acknowledges both compliments and insults, but doesn't change their beliefs about their self-worth in response to either.

The Exercise:

Work on your non-reactivity. If you have done any of the previous exercises, you may have started to develop a sense of your own self-worth – *a self-worth that does not depend in the slightest on others' opinion of you.* You'll know self-compassion when you feel it. It's unshakeable. As a worthwhile human being, a being living as only you know how, there is a dignity and unflappability to everything you do. This is *your* life. What could someone possible say to undermine the value in that? Similarly, what is the value, really, in being awesome if that awesomeness rests only on whether someone else thinks so at one particular moment?

Nurture the core inside of you, that core that is beyond relative value, beyond public opinion. Let nothing disturb it. Many self esteem books on the market today want as their end goal for you to believe that you're absolutely beautiful, wonderful and uniquely amazing. A creature of unparalleled genius, rarity and excellence. You may be, of course, but chances are, you aren't. Watch out for this message – hidden in what looks like "positive thinking" is in fact the assumption that your goal should always be perfection, should always be high self esteem. That is, you need to be a winner.

Instead, nurture something better than that. Choose to be resilient enough to not need a constantly inflated sense of ego to function properly in the world. Believe, deeply, that you are neither super-fabulous nor completely worthless, but something more than both: a human being, with a life that has value, whatever the circumstances. Whatever happens, that core remains. Become a heroin addict and land up in jail? That core remains the same. Become a multi-billionaire developing a cancer cure and find the love of your life while on a humanitarian mission in the Third World? The core is the same.

Let other people's comments of you wash right off. Their opinions belong to them, not you. Don't bring it into your self-concept.

The other side of this exercise is to treat others the same way. Notice when you assign value to other people, to their actions, to their experience. Is it your right to evaluate them? Watch out for judgmental attitudes seeping into your dealings with others, even the "benign" kind of judgment:

- "I hate going to that club, the music is crap and it's full of posers" (Are you sure? What gives you specifically the ability to say what music is good or bad, or assign value to the way people dress or behave?)

- "He's just had his 50th birthday, and he *still* manages to complete a marathon every year. Age is just a number!" (If it were, it wouldn't seem so incredible to mention it. Are you maybe assuming that being older is intrinsically less valuable, and if someone appears to be doing something valuable while old, this is something that deserves a remark?)

- "You're so brave! I could never be that fearless." (From another perspective, bravery is foolhardiness. Depending on the context, caution may be more valuable. When you compare yourself to others, even favorably, even to give them a compliment, you are doing you both a disservice)

Make an effort to let value judgments pass over you instead of taking them as gospel. In ordinary life, throw-away comments like the above barely register and if you were to start dissecting them you'd likely end up with nothing to say about anything. But meaningless comments have a way of seeping deeper down into our consciousness, making themselves a part of how we actually think of ourselves. In other words, say it often enough and it becomes true. Don't accept people's judgment of you and refrain from judging others.

CHAPTER FOUR: THE ROLLER COASTER OF SELF ESTEEM

Here are some signs that you seek external validation, in other words, that your self-concept is like the balloon in the wind. See if any of these sound like they describe you, and think carefully of anything that isn't on this list, too.

- You often feel like your entire mood can be spoiled with just one mean comment.
  - You have several people in your life that you enjoy feeling superior to.
  - You sometimes tally up your achievements in a list to determine how you compare against others in life.
  - You have occasionally done something only because you knew it would get a good response.
  - You frequently pass judgment on the choices, appearance or value of people around you.
  - You bear grudges against others.
  - Alternatively, you feel deeply damaged or broken somehow, maybe even completely unlovable.
  - You feel very much worse or better than other people.
  - You think that other people get to decide whether someone is good or not.
  - You're a perfectionist.
  - You sometimes have difficulties making decisions, or accepting the one you do finally make.
  - You absolutely *hate* to receive negative feedback or criticism.
  - You worry a lot about how you come across to other people.
  - You exaggerate about how awful or how wonderful you are, even resorting to lying outright.
  - You tend to blame other people for the bad things that happen in your life.
  - You make excuses, i.e. there always seems to be something getting in your way.
  - You depend a lot on others to take care of you.
  - You sometimes feel like cutting everyone out of your life.
  - You take things in life very seriously and have trouble laughing things off.
  - You self deprecate in public or else put other people down.
  - You don't like the idea of change.
  - You feel like a lot of your identity is in the things you own.
  - You're very concerned with what others think of you, and you spend a lot of time trying to guess what exactly other people are thinking about you.

Now, you may have noticed that the above list contains "symptoms" of both high and low self esteem. This may seem strange if you've been led to believe that these things are opposites of each other.

Actually, both high and low self esteem are states of mind that result from basing our sense of self-worth on external events. When those events tell us we are worthwhile, we are said to have high self esteem, and when they tell us we're bad, we have low self esteem. But the underlying mechanism is largely the same: we are adjusting our moods, our actions and our beliefs in our worth as human beings on things that are outside ourselves.

All goes well so long as what's outside us affirms and praises who we are – nobody is immune to feeling special simply because someone has complimented them.

But we can really get a sense of how tenuous this good feeling is when that same person insults us or withdraws their praise. It's for this reason that the goal should not be increasing one's self esteem, but rather dismantling the belief that our sense of self-worth is something that other people give us or something we take or earn by doing good.

Healthier than a high self esteem is a realistic, compassionate view of ourselves – and others. Generating our sense of self-worth from within means we have a more stable self-concept – one that can endure criticism while still learning from it. One that can honestly appraise who we are as human beings – and love and respect ourselves anyway.

Wabi-Sabi – an Aesthetic of Imperfection

There is an ancient Japanese art called Kintsugi, where the chips and cracks in crockery are repaired with fine gold. Rather than throwing something that is damaged away, or even trying to invisibly repair it so that it seems like it never broke at all, a cup or vase treated with Kintsugi is honored for the broken and imperfect thing it is.

The philosophy behind this is very touching. What is damaged is merely part of the reality for the life of the item, even enhancing its value. Highlighting the seams and imperfections, we accept that breakage, wear and tear are all part of life – and that they can even be beautiful.

The Japanese have a term for this kind of aesthetic – Wabi Sabi. At the root of the philosophy behind Wabi Sabi are three principles: nothing lasts, nothing is perfect and nothing is finished. Items that show this flawed beauty, that highlight the limitations of life, are embraced and not labeled deficient. In pottery, deliberate chips or asymmetries in artifacts are seen as a reminder of the impermanence in life. The wistfulness and yearning we experience on perceiving these imperfections is understood to be an important precursor to enlightenment.

Here's the paradox: when we strive for permanence, when we tolerate only perfection and when we assume that one day our work doing both of these things will be finished and we can finally relax, we are setting ourselves up for disappointment. However, embracing the fact that everything in life, our life included, is a little wonky, a work in process and something that occasionally breaks, will lead us to a more profound sense of permanence, perfection and completeness.

Perhaps we could all learn something from the Japanese in this regard. Rather than struggling to cover up our flaws, to hide our damage or deny our imperfections, we can simply accept and even embrace them. That we can be loved, valuable and worthwhile not in spite of our flaws, but even *because* of them is something we are not often taught to do as children, or encouraged to do as adults.

Nothing lasts:

What happens when you accept and embrace the impermanence around you? Our best qualities will one day disappear with the passing of time, as will our worst. The struggles we are having now are not forever, nor are the pleasures. What remains?

Nothing is perfect:

Can you accept that there is, at least not on this earth, nothing completely faultless? Instead of mourning the impossibility of something perfect, can you love what is?

Nothing is finished:

As we attain one goal, the next goal immediately becomes apparent. Can you let go of the need to have closure, and just let life unfold as it will?

CHAPTER FIVE: PUTTING SELF-COMPASSION INTO ACTION

Daily Self-compassion: It's the Little Things

What follows are some statements and thoughts, each of them framed differently. The first two demonstrate thinking from a more traditional, self esteem framework. One shows an absence of self esteem and the other the presence of it, but both of them still place the locus of control externally instead of internally, and so both are more or less variations of one another. The third sentence shows an alternative stemming from a position of self-compassion.

First scenario:
1. "I have to lose weight to look sexy."
2. "Real men love curves. My husband adores mine."

Self-compassion: "I think that model is so beautiful. But I don't want her body – mine's fine as it is."

While the first gives power to men in general, the second gives power to just one specific man. Although the second person might be perceived as having higher self esteem, there is no real difference in the quality of the self-concept in both. The third statement doesn't argue or compete, merely asserts that the person has self-worth anyway – and that the only person who matters in this issue is themselves. Also note that the person in the third statement doesn't need to put down a beautiful model in order for them to love their own body.

Second scenario:
1. "Life is meaningless. I want to just crawl into a hole and die."
2. "Don't say that! That's such a negative way of thinking!"

Self-compassion: "Man, I'm in a bad mood today. I'm just going to veg out in front of the TV till it passes."

The first statement expresses dissatisfaction that life is a particular way, but the second sentence is no better in that it expresses dissatisfaction with particular ways of thinking. In banishing ourselves from experiencing negativity, we only, paradoxically, make the fact that we do that much worse. The third is what it is – and accepts it.

Third scenario:
1. "You did such a good job out there, I'm proud of you."
2. "It's OK, you'll do better next time, I know it."

Self-compassion: "Hm, that didn't go so well."

The first statement reaffirms that being proud of someone is connected to doing well. Implied is the reverse: that if you don't do a good job, you'll lose that pride. The second statement looks on its surface to be kind, but the subtext is: things will be better… when you get this right. The third statement is just an honest appraisal of the reality of the situation. No rushing in to make excuses or deny what is. No judgment. No implication that your failure is only acceptable if it forms part of a success later on. Just an acknowledgement.

To practice self-compassion in our daily lives, it might emerge that it's the little things that really count. The words you speak, the thoughts you think: these are what make up the texture and tone of your life. As a way to start incorporating more self-compassion into your life, start with the little things first. Beware of judging yourself for doing self-compassion "wrong". If it doesn't feel good to feel good about who you are just yet, that's OK. Choose to feel good about where you are anyway.

Daily Self-compassion: Parenting
For a while, it was popular, in the Western world at least, to help your kids develop a high confidence in themselves.

Parents were encouraged never to criticize their children or make them feel second best. As a reaction to perceived pressures in the education system and the increasing competitiveness of colleges, parents understandably wanted to let their children know that they were, in no uncertain terms, valuable. This meant telling them they were perfect and brilliant, and should never settle for anything less.

But the message has become warped over time. Somehow, making sure that your kids didn't suffer a low self esteem it became a project to make sure that their self esteem was *high*. Kids needed to feel special, to have indomitable confidence in themselves and their abilities, no matter what. The irony is that kids raised in this generation are no more secure and happy in themselves as the generations that came before them.

Psychologists are now discovering that over praising children can have the opposite effect. Telling children they're doing better than they are causes them to doubt themselves, even wonder if others are lying to them. A child who thinks they are already high achievers are less likely to take beneficial risks or get a thick enough skin to improve on their competencies. You are in effect setting them up for disappointment in the real world. What's worse, over praising achievements sends out the message: love is conditional.

How to raise children who are self-compassionate:
- Give your child the feeling that your love in them is secure by consistently being there to support – *no matter what*.
- Give your children realistic goals to aim for. Age appropriate tasks that help build competence slowly and steadily teach your child a valuable lesson in hard work.
- Whatever you do, don't compare your child to others, especially not their siblings. Speak about their worth in absolute terms, and not how they compare to their classmates.
- Don't encourage all-or-nothing perfectionism. When your child fails, don't make a big deal of it. Encourage them to keep going.
- Have compassion for yourself – children need good role models to learn how to value themselves.

But, now that we've got the children out the way, we can address the other side of the coin. For many parents, how good a job they're doing raising their children can be a constant source of worry and lack of confidence. Here are some things to help you relax and let go of the pressure to be perfect.

- Remind yourself that everyone will make a mistake here and there, and that it doesn't mean you're doing your children a disservice.
- Resist comparing yourself to other parents. You're different and you're children are different. Comparisons will only make you feel insecure.
- Try to remember that mistakes in life – yours or your child's – can always be teaching moments. Give your child a good understanding of how to be compassionate with *you*.

Daily Self-compassion: Weathering Rejection
Ginny had a really good first date with someone she found she liked a lot. She hadn't found time lately to meet and go out with people, but this guy in particular really stood out for her. But then, after they had made arrangements to meet again later the next week, her date called to cancel. When she tried to organize another meeting a few days

later, her messages were met with stone cold silence. It dawned on her slowly and then all at once: she had been rejected.

Here is an imaginary script of Ginny's "inner talk" as she stewed over the incident for a few weeks.

"I still don't get what happened. We got on SO well. We were laughing, agreeing with one another. There was such a lot of chemistry. He even said himself he couldn't wait to meet again. So what gives? Is there something I don't know? Am I just an idiot who thinks they get on well with people when I really don't? Oh God, maybe he hated every second of the date and was just humoring me all along. Maybe he saw something I didn't. Maybe everyone sees me like that. Maybe I'm really a big loser and haven't figured it out yet. Was it my dress? I knew I shouldn't have worn that. I knew it. Maybe I shouldn't have gone on and on about my holiday to Germany. He was smiling at the time but I bet he was bored to tears. I don't know why I even bother any more. I feel so humiliated. Maybe I'm just not cut out for this dating nonsense, maybe..."

And so on and so on.

Ginny's self talk may seem a bit overblown to you, but anyone who's nursed a wound of this kind will know that the negative self talk can get out of hand very quickly. Rejection of this kind can feel like an almost literal slap in the face – someone not only judged you, but they judged you and found you wanting. Here is the kind of inner talk Ginny might have had if she had a more stable self-concept and a little self-compassion after the same incident:

"I still don't get what happened. I thought we got on so well. When I think about it, I didn't say anything hurtful and I definitely wasn't rude... it must be more to do with him. Who knows? I'm feeling pretty fragile about the whole thing but since I can't find anything obviously wrong I'm just going to assume that there's a reason he didn't get in touch. Maybe he's met someone else, or maybe he likes me but realized he isn't really ready to commit to a partner right now. I get that. I mean, I've been there myself. I hate to admit it, but maybe our connection wasn't as strong as I remember. Oh well, it's a pity, but I'm not going to take it personally. I'm going to stop stressing about this now and get on with things. I don't have to be everyone's cup of tea... after all, not everybody is mine..."

A lot of dating experts will deal with Ginny's hurt at being rejected by trying to swing her self esteem the other way: not only does she *not* deserve rejection, but she's better than the date that rejected her. She's fabulous, and if he couldn't see it, then that's his problem etc. The problem with this approach is that these feelings of self-worth are not stable and lasting – when (and not if!) Ginny is rejected again, it will all fall to pieces.

Rejection can be so difficult to deal with because it strikes a blow to our ego, the very thing keeping our sense of pride and self-worth held together. Romantic rejection can be particularly painful, and being found unattractive by the very people we are attracted to can make us feel completely unworthy.

But because the stress of rejection is so heavily tied in with the ego, we can learn to moderate and manage rejection by managing our egos, too. Your ego may be telling you that if you are rejected, it must be because of who you are and what you did, and is proof that you are fundamentally wrong somehow. But think for a minute about the people *you* have rejected in your life – and yes, you have been the rejecter, at times!

You may have turned them down romantically because you just didn't "click" with them, because you were busy (really), a little unsure of yourself or simply not that interested. Maybe, in a rare instance, you felt yourself thinking, "this person is fundamentally wrong somehow", but more than likely, your reasons for the rejection were your own. Understand that people will reject you for a host of reasons, but very seldom because you are unlovable at your core.

Even at it's worst, someone will reject you because, well, they don't like you. On the other hand it's unhealthy to think that everyone will. Part of what makes being human so amazing is how different we all are. Sometimes we connect well with each other, sometimes not. There is no need to dwell on this fact, simply move on to find the people that *do* like you.

Your ego may feel bruised enough that it tries a different approach: that if someone doesn't see and agree with the beauty and perfection that you offer, then it's really their loss, and you're better off without them. As a matter of fact, they did you a favor by removing themselves from your life, and it is you who judges and rejects them. Sound familiar? This is a knee-jerk response to the pain of rejection and completely understandable, however in the long term it only reinforces the same old mechanisms that keep you trapped in a cycle of narcissism and shame, cycling between feeling wonderful and feeling awful.

The trouble with developing such a "thick skin" and sassy attitude is that it could numb you to valuable lessons. Sometimes, although we would rather die than hear it, people's criticisms of us have a kernel of truth, and were we to engage them we'd find that they are not some heartless monsters out to get us. Probably right this minute you can think of at least one person that you feel this way about: no matter what feedback they get from the world, they can't seem to "see" what you do.

In order to grow and become better, we have to admit to ourselves what isn't working. Be brutally honest with yourself – do you have any blind spots? Are there ways you could improve? But once you've realistically appraised this, the self-compassion can kick in. It's *OK* that you have blind spots and weakness. When we act from a mindful position of self-compassion, we can experience, deeply, the full range of pain at being rejected. We can see, in full clarity, our deficiencies as human beings, and we can mourn it completely. But, we can also know that even *this* pain does not negate our worth as human beings There is no need to hate ourselves or the people who reject us.

The story of the "empty boats":

There is an old Buddhist parable about "empty boats".

Imagine you are floating along a river in a boat. All of a sudden, an empty boat comes floating along and bumps into yours. What do you think of this? Probably, you're not angry about it. It's just a boat; it's just something that happened. Now, imagine instead that the boat that knocks into yours is not empty but driven by a person. In this case, you may feel irritated or even angry. Why don't they look where they're going?

The thing is, in both cases, the boats are in a sense empty. The second boat has a person inside, but that person is distracted or thinking of something else. In other words, his bumping into you is not different from an empty boat bumping into you – both have no deliberate consciousness guiding the action.

There is no point getting upset with people who wrong us by being mindless. Getting angry with such a person is like getting angry that an empty boat drifted against yours – it's just a thing that happened. Our modern world is filled with people who are quick to see fault, quick to blame and quick to seek revenge. We devolve into mindless hatred when left alone and anonymous on the Internet, and we are happy to immediately see the worst in other people's actions, to condemn them, to feel indignant.

Save your energy and don't bother reacting to empty boats. In the vast majority of cases, when you feel slighted it's not because someone was deliberately malicious towards you. Rather, we all have moments when our own lives distract us and keep us from considering others as fully as we should. This is unfortunate, but there is no point in getting angry about it.

When you feel offended, stop to ask yourself whether you might be taking it too personally. Be compassionate with people who hurt you by accident and without thinking. After all, you have almost certainly done the same to others.

CHAPTER SIX: FORGIVENESS, BOUNDARIES AND ASSERTIVENESS

How did the previous story make you feel?

For many people, forgiveness of others' transgressions is a near impossibility. They may feel angry and insulted even reading about it. What kind of a pushover would they be if they simply let everyone's boat bash into theirs all the time?

Assertiveness that stems from the ego

When a child is bullied at school and their parents tell them that the correct response is to fight back, they are sending the message that the way to reinforce personal boundaries is with violence.

Even if our parents were more conciliatory, many adults grow up with the idea that to put up a boundary and have people respect it is a process filled with conflict. When someone oversteps the mark, we are encouraged to act from our anger and retaliate. Sadly, our actions to defend ourselves start to look very much like the actions we hate experiencing ourselves.

Assertiveness from compassion

While nobody would argue that it's vital to have a healthy sense of your own boundaries, it's not necessarily healthy to act out from anger. It isn't helpful to get angry and annihilate the boat that drifted into yours. Smashing the boat to bits in a fit of indignation is not necessary, nor do you have to get the boat to admit its fault and apologize. It's just something that happened. Move the boat out of the way and get on with it.

For those unused to it, compassion may seem incompatible with assertiveness. Having kindness for others seems like an achievable goal, but what about when people abuse that kindness? What about those people that actually deliberately hurt us?

When we have compassion, we realize that every person has feelings, and if they've done something to hurt another person, chances are strong that they feel remorseful. When we are consumed with resentment and bitterness towards somebody, it can difficult to see that they are also struggling in life, trying in the way they know how to be the best they can – just like you.

We can never go back into the past and make it different from what it is. Simply by being alive, we're signed up for a degree of hurt and disappointment in life. It's just part of being human. Remember back to a time when you hurt someone. If you've been lucky enough to have experienced forgiveness yourself, remember how important it was to you at the time.

If you cannot summon up forgiveness for people who have wronged you right now, then try to do it for yourself. Have you ever looked back at your past and wished you had more grudges, more anger towards others? Let it go. We're all doing the best we can, and sometimes, it falls horribly short and we hurt one another. Forgive anyway and move on.

And you needn't be a pushover. Do not tolerate continued mistreatment from others because you have compassion for yourself, but do not mistreat them in turn because you have compassion for *them*. Learning how to set up and defend a boundary with love and kindness in your heart can be a revelation for those who have suffered abuse, resentment or bitterness in their past.

What would happen now, if you just let it go forever?

Healing grudges, forgiving and moving forward

Look deeply into the pain and anger you feel at someone else. Experience it. Don't push it away and don't chastise yourself for the feelings you have, however ugly.

Next, ask what they can teach you.

Have you allowed behavior that you shouldn't have? What do you know about yourself now that this pain has taught you? Transform your anger and hostility into defending your boundaries. Anger can mobilize and strengthen you.

But after that, let the anger go. Anger is a potent reminder of the importance of assertive boundaries, but over and above that, it only hurts the one who holds onto it.

Read through any agony and advice column and you'll see that the bulk of problems people have could be solved by saying, "I love you but I won't tolerate that". And meaning it.

CONCLUSION

To enjoy the benefits of mindful self-compassion, we merely need to change our focus.

Loving ourselves and being gentle and accepting of the reality of who we are doesn't require any special equipment, knowledge or training. It merely requires that you open your heart and mind, to yourself and to others.

At times, it can feel so easy to succumb to the hatred, impatience and judgment around us. By learning self-compassion, however, we realize the source of this negativity, and become less affected by it. When we embrace the imperfection of being human, we can be resilient enough to face criticism and rejection with grace. By developing and drawing on a deeper well of self-worth, we become immune to self-doubt, low self-confidence, blame, resentment and judgment.

In the West, the concepts of Buddhism are gradually being incorporated into all areas of our lives and appreciated for the peace and tranquility they can bring. In meditating, we learn to let thoughts come and go, and to withhold our judgment of them. Extending this, we can take our practice to include other people. People are not good or bad, and neither are we.

In fact, we are all so much more than that – we are all human beings, and truly embracing that can be the start of something profound.

INTENTIONAL LIVING - HOW TO NOT DIE WITH REGRETS BY LIVING A LIFE THAT MATTERS A 3-STEP BLUEPRINT

INTRODUCTION

"The tragedy of life is not death, but what we let die inside of us while we are still living"
- Norman Cousins

Some time ago, I stumbled across this quote – and felt as though it had slapped me across the face.

Like any thirty-something, questions of my own mortality had gradually changed from being an interesting hypothetical to something very real, and very scary.

While the first part of my life had seem filled with new beginnings and first times, the second half looked a bit more dire: I was beginning to realize that there would be *last times* for everything, too.

And like the typical thirty-something, I had a mild existential crisis about it: had I really lived my life well up until that moment? Had I wasted my youth, and was I possibly wasting my life right this minute?

When I saw this quote, it dawned on me: I wasn't actually afraid of death itself. How could I be? After all, I wouldn't be around when it happened. Rather, what I was afraid of was the crushing awareness that I wasn't living while I actually had the chance.

I looked back on my twenties and sadly realized that they were finished. I would never be in my twenties again. Life moved only forward, and the choices I had made during those years were already made, and could never be changed. In a way, it was the death of that part of my life. Was I happy with it, looking back? Did I have regrets?

I didn't know what my future looked like, but I knew that I didn't want to have that same feeling when I'd be very old and looking back on the whole of my life. I didn't want that sinking sense that I could have done more, and that there was still some life in me left unlived, some doors I had left unopened, some questions I had left unanswered. Something seemed deeply horrifying about the idea of leaving this world, thinking, "No, wait! I'm not done yet!"

And so I got to thinking about how to *not* do that, and my questions led me to writing this book. In these pages, I want to share the three key strategies that I have used to cultivate a life that, at the end of the day, actually matters.

I've learnt a lot on my journey to clearing away the rubbish and honing in on what's important. I've learnt that disappointment and self-doubt is at the root of so many people's fear of really *living*. I've learnt that sometimes the only thing holding you back from a life that is fulfilling and deeply meaningful is that you keep telling yourself stories in which you never do. Finally, I've learnt that when it comes to living a life without regrets, it's all about finding, cherishing and creating *value*, in everything you do.

The exercises I've suggested here are borne of my own insights and experience, but they are certainly not authoritative. If you've picked up this book, there's a good chance that your instinct for meaning and value is alive and well within you – trust that instinct.

Of course, before making any decisions, I ask that you keep an open mind as you read on.

Ready?

CHAPTER 1 - THE BIG DISAPPOINTMENT

When you were little, your parents probably told you that you were a very special, very clever little boy or girl who could do whatever they wanted, and achieve whatever they set their hearts to. And even if they didn't, it's a rare child who isn't completely convinced that the world is an accommodating place which will only support their dreams of becoming a president or an astronaut or a unicorn trainer.

But when was the last time you met an adult who believed something like this?

In fact, the implicit understanding is that adulthood is all about moderating your dreams. Reigning your passions in. You come to terms with your limitations, take a few hard knocks and maybe even come to believe that your life is, in the end, insignificant.

Have you ever noticed how "grow up!" is used as an insult? It's as though the adult world is intolerant of hopes and dreams that seem too fanciful, or too hopeful.

"The big disappointment" is really a series of tiny, accumulated disappointments. You realize that there is always someone better than you, even at the interests you hold most dear. You become keenly aware that life is not fair, and that others who are no more deserving than you enjoy more resources, more luck, more wealth. With your growing awareness of the complexity of the world around you, your own sphere of influence seems so small and negligible.

How could *you* ever make a difference? How could *your* life ever be meaningful when there are literally billions of other people on this earth?

Like many other people, you may have chosen to forfeit some of your most cherished dreams. You may have sternly told yourself to grow up and pushed away your loftiest and most exciting visions for yourself and your place in the world. You may have grudgingly put your head down and set your mind to more achievable, more "normal" goals, like getting on with a job. Or saving and getting a mortgage. Perhaps you quietly internalized the idea that it's foolish to try to do anything different, and that life is too expensive and unpredictable and scary to risk pursuing something that would be more meaningful to you.

If any of that resonates with you, you'll already know the problem with this approach: it doesn't work. After all, you're here right now, reading this book. No matter how thoroughly we try to forget it, our yearning for a significant, meaningful and valuable life can't just disappear.

That yearning comes out in our dreams, or late at night when we're done with work for the day and we're "free" to imagine a world where things are different. We say "one day" or daydream about having the guts to run away and start over again.

If we've been denying this instinct in ourselves for a long time, it may be second nature to never admit these dreams to anyone else. We think it's normal to work on a novel for months and then hide it in the bottom drawer. We look at successful, fulfilled people and tell ourselves, "well, of course it's easy for them, since they have so much money, influence or luck".

But our "childish" hopes and dreams for something more never really leave us. In fact, *getting older* can be an ironic catalyst for bringing some of those neglected longings out of the woodwork. Have we really done as well as we could have? Will we be able to rest on our deathbed without regrets?

As we begin this book, I want to ask you to take a look at the instinct that drove you to purchase and read it. Try to be as honest as possible: why bother at all?

Your answer to this question will provide some clues about the limitations you may have been putting on yourself thus far – and the key to removing those limitations.

- *"Nothing really made me seek this book out. It's no big deal. I read all sorts of things so reading this means nothing. I know that most self-help books are nonsense so I don't have any great expectations."*

- *"My life is a bit of a mess. Clearly solving the problems of life are too big and difficult for me, so I need guidance."*

- *"I don't know. I haven't really thought about it!"*

- *"I like reading this kind of material – it keeps me aware and engaged with my life goals."*

- *"If I'm honest, I don't know why I'm reading this – previous self-help books haven't worked, why should this one?"*

There's no need to over-analyze your motivations for starting this guide at this point, but just become aware of your attitude going in. Try to be honest and admit if you're embarking from the get-go with an attitude that fully expects to fail. Just notice if you're unconsciously limiting yourself.

Will it really cost you anything, to hope that wonderful things lie in store for you?

CHAPTER 2 - THE 3-STEP PLAN

For a positive book that is supposed to be all about intentional living, the picture I've painted so far is a pretty grim one!

If this were an infomercial, this would be the point where I jump in and tell you all about my amazing product, and how it's precisely what you need to solve all your problems.

But this *isn't* an infomercial, and there are no quick and easy fixes when it comes to the greatest task you'll ever undertake: the art of living well.

The remainder of this book will be structured around three key steps to cultivating and developing a style of life that is intentional and geared towards deep, personal fulfillment. Too many people reach the end of their time on this planet and think "I should have done this or that".

This guide is intended to pre-empt this.

What could you do right here, right now, so that you won't have to say those dreaded words on your deathbed? What could you do right now that will make your future 90-year-old self proud? How can you be and feel and act right now that will not only spare your future self these regrets, but have that version of yourself smiling and thinking, "that was a pretty good life, I'm ready to go now without any fear or sadness"?

Pretty heavy thing to think about, I know, but finding out the answers to these questions is the purpose of the chapters that follow.

The three keys are:
   1) Develop deeper intention and self-awareness
   2) Take charge of your "stories"
   3) Add value for a more valuable life

Each of these steps builds on the other two. We'll consider each of them in turn, but before we do, I want to note a few important things: firstly, the information written here is just that. Information. It's just words on a page, or pixels on a screen. And unless you actively choose to do something with what you read here, they will never be more than that.

I can't stress this enough.

Many people read inspirational material or self-help books and feel like they "don't work". Reading a book about healthy lifestyle and weight loss won't do a thing for you if you keep up with the same bad habits you always had, and reading a book about making changes to your life won't "work" if you don't actively engage with the information once you've closed the book.

Of course, there isn't anything magical in the words written here. And reading about change is not the same as changing. Change, if it happens, will happen *after* you've read and decided to put the ideas in practice. This is why each of the following keys to purposeful living not only has a section of new information, but also a practical way to *apply* that information out in the real world, right now. I've tried to include examples of real people where relevant.

Secondly, although I have given three "steps", the process outlined here is not so much three distinct steps and then you're done and finished forever. Rather, it's a never-ending cycle, one where you constantly learn to improve in increments.

As you read and try some of the suggestions in the book, my hope is you'll start feeling more aware, more in control and more joyful in your life. But that doesn't mean that on the way there you won't experience some bad days, too.

Part of change means breaking down old ways of thinking – and that process of breaking things down can be painful. Part of change is also feeling stuck occasionally, or uninspired ...or even taking a few steps back.

Before we begin, I want to encourage you to be compassionate with yourself. Change takes time. Go slowly, be kind and keep returning to the things that challenge you!

CHAPTER 3 - BEGINNING WITH INTENTION

Life isn't about finding yourself. It's about creating yourself.
   - George Bernard Shaw

Let's start with the first key to a life free of regrets: intentional living. What do we even mean when we call something *intentional*?

A clue to the whole point of living intentionally is to consider that another way of saying it is to do something "on purpose". When you act with intention, *you* come to the fore and act as the full human agent that you are. You plan ahead, you commit, and then you act in accordance with that plan to bring about goals that are meaningful to you. You are awake. You are responsible. You are deliberate.

There are immense advantages to this state of mind: a person who acts and chooses consciously is fully present for everything that unfolds in their lives. Because they are proactively choosing their actions and their responses, they have a degree of maturity and control over their fate. When adversity strikes, they can quickly recover and return to thriving.

On the other hand, when you live intentionally, you also sign up for more responsibility. The darker side of taking more control is that you can no longer blame anything or anyone but yourself. In a court of law, people will argue over whether something was accidental or pre-meditated because intention is the root of whether an action is meaningful or not. When you live "on purpose", in other words, you can be judged. You are culpable.

Living intentionally can be frightening, but it is the foundation of a regret-less, meaningful life. This cannot be emphasized enough: *there is no meaning without intention.*

If you walk down the road and find some money, well, nobody intended to leave it there for you to find. It's just luck, and there's no "meaning" to it because it's accidental and purely random. The same can be said for catching a rare disease by chance or winning the lottery. But because there is no *intention* in any of these events, there can be no meaning. Many people live their entire lives this way. What happens just happens. They experience every event as though it were as random and lacking in meaning as finding money on the street by accident.

But what if you are not satisfied to live a life that feels random and meaningless?

Well, then you can act to bring about the things you value, and in so doing, *create* meaning. This requires *intention*. You can actively decide that you will make money rather than hope to find it in the street, and work hard and educate yourself so that you can be financially successful. You can actively choose to live a healthy life to minimize your chances of getting ill.

With a firm intention in place, all your actions can be measured against this yardstick: did you live up to your goals? Instantly, your actions go from being random to being purposeful. You go from being reactive to the events others create, to being proactive, and someone that originates their own events.

But ironically, many self-help books begin with the hidden premise that you are actually *not* in control of your life. They present the equivalent of tips and tricks to finding more money on the street, or tell you to "accept" the things that make you unhappy because a lot of it's just down to luck anyway, right?

They tell you that happiness is something that you need to buy or be part of a special group to enjoy. They tell you that your problems are somebody else's fault and that you should just seek a bit of happiness in the fact that you can't do anything about it. We saw in a previous section that people are urged to succumb to the "grow up" message, which deep down is the message: "give up".

In this book we'll take a different approach: you are in control of your life. Your life *does* have meaning and you can live in a principled, focused, deliberate way that makes your time on this earth significant. You are responsible. You are in charge.

But the very first thing you must do is *decide* for all that to be the case.

Intention Exercise One: Don't Take Anyone's Word for it; Think Critically

I have a friend whose mother told her all the time that she was unintelligent and would never succeed in life. Because she was just a child when she first heard this, she believed it wholeheartedly. She kept on believing it while she sailed through school with high grades, and earned a difficult degree in record time. She believed it as people looked up to her and she became an expert in her field. She even believed it well after her mother passed away and she was surrounded by nothing but praise for her success and intelligence.

Why couldn't my friend see herself as we saw her? As a child, you trust and believe your parents. My friend, as smart as she was, never took the leap to *question* what her mother told her over and over. She took her word for it. She never sat down and asked herself what *she* thought, what *she* wanted. She took her mother's judgment and substituted it for her own.

While she suffered with low self-esteem for years and years, she never had the insight or the intention to create her own identity. Her mother had labeled her, and this was powerful enough to remain even after her mother was long gone.

In this exercise, you're going to try and question your own assumptions – about yourself, others or life in general. Don't even take your *own* word for it! How many people have wasted their lives doing things other people said would make them happy? How much happiness have you talked yourself out of because you believed your own negative self-talk?

To do this exercise, first ask yourself what you *want*.

Not what others tell you you want, not what you wish you wanted. But your deepest, truest and most lasting desires.

Imagine you're in a colossal, magical restaurant and are sitting down, ready to order a new life for yourself. What do you order? Go wild. For now, don't worry about what's practical or correct or fashionable or expected of you. Just go with it.

Do you imagine a colorful, creative existence filled with interesting people and places? A life of service and learning? An adoring family? Dig deep with this, and don't just go with whatever first pops into your head. Ask, would you *really* be happy with a lot of money? Are you too afraid to admit your real desires? Do you feel too ambitious or not ambitious enough? Just go with it.

A psychologist friend tells me that many people come to her complaining that they have achieved everything they were supposed to achieve to make them happy: impressive careers, spouses, children. But they felt deeply unfulfilled anyway. Too late they discover that those were just the things they *thought* they wanted. They had lived so long in borrowed desires that they had forgotten the joy they got from a humble vegetable patch, or that childhood hobby they dropped years ago.

What do you *want*? Not just crave in the moment, but want in a deeper sense?

Now, pick a day and go out into the world to *express* this wish, even if it's in a very small way. In your magical café visualization, maybe you imagined a more social life, where you felt more deeply connected to others. In this case, remember this desire the next time you talk to someone, and talk to them as though you already live in that fantasy life you created. If you pictured a more spiritual life, express this in the way you carry yourself for that day, even if it's just to go to the supermarket or fill your gas tank.

What happens when you begin to put your desires out there? What happens when you say, "This is what I want"?

For just this one day, listen carefully to every bit of information that comes your way and ask, "Is this what I want?" Think critically about what others tell you. Is it true? Is it really true? You can take this exercise as far as you like.

Let's imagine a woman who feels burnt out and uninspired by her life. She works all day and feels like she gets nowhere, she's not appreciated at home and her marriage has lost all its spark. So she chooses a day to ask what she really wants, and to look critically at what passes into her awareness.

She comes home after work and looks at the pile of dishes in the sink. She definitely doesn't want that. She spends an hour preparing a meal that her family seem uninterested in. But she has to feed them, right? She has no choice.

Or does she? When she thinks critically about this, she realizes it isn't necessarily true. While she has been laboring under the idea that everyone in the family wants elaborate daily meals, her included, she's missed something: that her teenaged children and busy husband don't care either way. And neither does she. What she really wants instead is just to sit down, relax and enjoy the evenings with her family rather than slave away at the things social media tells her she wants.

Such a woman doesn't need advice on how to "do it all" or how to prepare gourmet meals in even less time. She just needs to realize that doing so isn't even something she wants in the first place...

Intention Exercise Two: Making the Decision, Setting Your Intention

If you've gone a long time on autopilot, asking these questions can be a bit overwhelming at first. It's easier to default to what's expected instead of taking the time to develop your own intention. Have you ever heard someone talk about marrying their partners just because enough time has passed and it just feels like the thing they *should* do next? But by going along with external expectations for what you should want and value, you avoid asking yourself what *you* want, and why.

You forfeit your chance to make meaning for yourself, and you open the door for regrets.

The next opportunity you have, practice making decisions and flexing those intention muscles. Pick any period of time – an hour, day, or week – and then take a moment to focus in on your intention for that period. A good daily habit is to "set" your intention early every morning, but you could also do it before bed or even with each passing hour.

Find a quiet place to sit, go still inside yourself and focus on your breathing. Take a few moments to become aware of your body and your mind and just notice where you are, without any judgment.

Next, zoom in on the frame of mind you want to carry with you throughout the rest of the hour, day or week. You are not thinking of specific goals here, but rather your ideal attitude. Think of it like tuning an instrument before playing, narrowing the beam of a laser or twiddling the knob on a radio to find just the right channel.

Picture the day ahead, including all its challenges and unexpected events. Now picture yourself facing those challenges, but anchored in the intention that you have already set for yourself. Have fun with visualization, if you like.

You might, for example, decide that you want to be accepting and calm of whatever transpires that day, and visualize yourself being cloaked with a shield of light. Or you could set your intention to be strong and assertive, and imagine yourself made of steel and responding to any threats with courage. It's all up to you.

With your intention set, you're aware, awake and in control.

You may be wondering exactly *what* intention you should set, but try not to get too bogged down in doing this exercise "right". I have mentioned being calm or being strong as possible states of mind, but there's no reason that these should appeal to you. In fact, the details of the state of mind you choose don't matter that much; what does matter is that you are aware and *deliberately choosing* that state of mind.

A woman with anger problems may take the time every morning to set her intention for the day: to be calm. She focuses on this and meditates before her morning shower, visualizing herself swimming miles under the sea, in slow motion, perfectly at peace in the deep blue. She knows that no matter how stressful her day gets, she can always close her eyes and be back in that peaceful place again. In time, she realizes that her anger – and every situation – is completely within her control.

As you get more practice asking yourself what you actually want (the first exercise) and then deliberately setting your intention (the second exercise) you will find that awareness of your desires actually grows, and more specific goals will begin to form in your mind by themselves.

Eventually, you'll become less and less susceptible to external pressure and more anchored in something that is actually meaningful for you. For now, it's enough to just pause for a moment, and practice taking the reins.

CHAPTER 4 - THE POWER OF STORIES

Before we launch into the next chapter, let's take a moment to consider the previous one.

Did you dive in and engage fully? Or did you skim through, assume you understood what was being said and then skip actually doing the exercises? Remember, intellectually comprehending an idea is not the same as *experiencing* it!

Let's move on.

In this chapter, we'll be expanding on some of the ideas from the first. The previous two exercises were all about getting acquainted with your deeper desires and then taking the time to say yes, you *choose* those desires. On the surface, this seems like a pretty small thing, but it's the seed of an intentional life that's filled with meaning and purpose.

Sitting around and thinking about things is great, but of course, it's not the same as taking action. Taking action without deliberate intention is just meaningless – you'll just blow around in the winds of other people's intentions. But dwelling on your intentions without having a concrete way to realize them in the world is just as meaningless. Ideas are just ideas. Thoughts remain thoughts. Nothing changes.

The bridge between wanting something and actually achieving it is *action*. To cross a river from point A to Point B, you can build a bridge. But there are many ways to build that bridge, some ways better than others.

This is the topic for this chapter: how the stories we tell ourselves mediate our actions, and form that bridge between dream and reality.

Here's an example.

Let's imagine you would like to lose weight. As you set your intention each morning and keep asking yourself what you really want in life, the idea comes up over and over: you'd like to feel lighter and more at ease in your body. Great. But now what? If you're like millions of people, you might launch into a punishing "cleanse" or splurge on a gym membership you never use or binge and promise you'll start something on Monday.

But there's an element of mindlessness at work in solving problems this way. This is a bit like jumping into building a bridge before you have a blueprint, then building something that's all wrong and doesn't quite reach the other side. Perhaps you start an elaborate bridge and realize halfway that you should have been building a tunnel all along!

Instead, take a look at the *stories* that you're working with, i.e. the materials you're using to build the bridge from desire to reality. In our example, you might discover that you keep telling yourself the following story about your weight:

"Losing weight is hard (actually it's pretty much impossible) and I can only ever do it by going to extreme measures like getting surgery or developing an eating disorder. I'm just built fat and always will be out of control, and if I want to be skinny I'm going to have to suffer and hate every minute of it. At the end of the day, people have to

choose whether they'll be fat and happy, or skinny and miserable, and that's just a fact."

It might seem ridiculous when spelled out like that, but most of us are carrying around versions of the above story, give or take a few details. We might have carried them around so long that we barely even notice that they're there anymore. We assume that we're just witnessing reality as it is. A "story" is made of our self-talk and all the things we tell ourselves about who we are, what we're capable of and why things happen. If you're not convinced that you have any stories of your own, just listen carefully and you're bound to notice them eventually – because the best stories are those that seem invisible at first!

Stories can take any form, but the more negative ones might look like this:

- "Sure, XYZ applies to other people, but not to me. I'm different/worse somehow."

- "There is something wrong with me, at my core, and so I'll never succeed, not really."

- "Changing is scary and not worth it. It's better to stick with what you know."

- "My happiness is out of my control anyway, so there's no point trying to do something about it."

Stories are tricky because they're wrapped into our identities, and built into the foundation of our lives. Our stories might be handed down to us from our parents or given to us by our cultures or those close to us. No matter how reasonable a story is, though, it's always just that: a story.

Let's return to our example.

If you told yourself that weight loss was basically impossible and that trying to change automatically meant you'd have to be unhappy, what would happen? Well, maybe you'd go to gym for a week, and wake up very stiff one morning. In your story, trying to lose weight = pain. You feel uncomfortable. And according to your story, staying the same = happiness. Who wouldn't choose happiness over pain? It's obvious that if you've been telling yourself this story, the thing to do is give up on weight loss.

Except the problem is that your story was *a lie*. With this set of beliefs, even if you went to gym for a month and actually started to see some results, you'd look at those results through the lens of your story. *"All weight loss is only temporary and I had to sacrifice so much for such a little progress and anyway my genes are fat so I can never really change..."*

Remember that in this story, weight loss is impossible. A healthy lifestyle is painful and inconvenient. Fat is inevitable. So everything that doesn't fit that story is just pushed aside or ignored. Even success! According to the story, failure is a given. So even if you *don't* fail, you end up acting in a way that aligns with the story, rather than what you see out there in the world. It's easier to fail and stick to the story than change the story. You've built a bridge that will never carry you to where you want to go.

Story Exercise One: Learning to Listen Carefully

The only way to change a story that isn't working for you is to become aware it's even there in the first place. How do you become more aware of your own self-limiting beliefs? What stories are you carrying around with you, telling yourself over and over again? More importantly, are those stories helping you get closer to where you want to be or are they actually doing the opposite?

Well, there's no easy way around it: you have to listen!

Formal meditation is a great way of doing an inventory of everything that's swirling around in your mind. Instead of taking everything at face value, you can stop, become aware of what programming you're really running, and give yourself the chance to change it.

If you don't already meditate, well, it's easy to start. Simply find a quiet place to sit and pay attention to your breathing. That's all. You don't need to do anything fancy, just become aware. Focus on the sounds and sensations around you. Try to be aware of them without passing judgment. Turn that awareness inwards as well, and watch yourself in the same way.

What thoughts and emotions bubble up in you? Watch them from a distance instead of getting carried away with each passing change in your internal landscape. Notice what thoughts and feelings are most persistent – but remember, there's no judgment. Just become aware, then let it go. There is no way to do it wrong – just watch.

You don't have to wait till you're meditating to try and become aware, though. Carve out little moments during the day where you take a step back and breathe. What are you thinking? What are you feeling?

- Try wearing a bright band round your wrist. Every time you glance at it, pause and take a look at what "thought traffic" you're in the midst of.

- Take natural pauses during the day – on the hour, every time you go for a bathroom break or when it's time to eat. Notice your state of mind.

- During particularly emotional times, try to remember to stay aware. Your stories will come out in full force during stressful or upsetting moments, so pay attention if you can!

As you practice becoming more aware, note down some of the stories that come up again and again. Store them in a notebook somewhere, if you can.

Imagine a man who's having trouble dating. He is getting despondent, a never-ending stream of disappointing first dates and women who seem utterly uninterested in him. Instead of getting angry or forking over money for useless dating advice, he decides to try become more aware of the stories he's telling himself.

As he watches for a few months, he is soon shocked to discover a story he has been telling himself routinely for most of his life. Even though he never consciously realized it, this story was sabotaging his romantic life at every turn. The story goes: "I'm a complete loser, and I will never get a girl to be interested in me. Therefore, if a girl IS interested in me, there must be something wrong with her! I don't want a girl like that…"

Besides being untrue, this story had the same predictable result: when women were interested in him, they were immediately written off. After all, according to his story, only girls he didn't want wanted him, right? And in just the same way, his story told him that a girl who rejected him was actually the one he wanted. This story had him actively moving away from women who were interested in him and towards those who weren't. Exactly the opposite of what he wanted!

Story Exercise Two: Changing the Story

Digging down deep into your personal stories can be hard work – after all, stories are everything. They help us make sense of other people, the world and our place in it. The stories we tell are the very blueprints we build our lives on. Our stories tell us what is and isn't possible. That's why if you want to make lasting changes, it makes sense to start deep down on this level.

In this second exercise, let's take a look at those life blueprints. The key questions to ask is: what would life be like without the stories you tell yourself?

In our weight loss example, the story is clearly a limiting one. It's tricky because many people (advertisers included!) will go along with this story and encourage it. But is it really true that you have no choice but to suffer and be fat? How do you act and behave when you believe that meaningful change is impossible or unpleasant? Are you happy to act that way and is acting that way getting you the results you want in life?

Let's say the person in our example realizes the story they've been telling themselves is no good and only makes them apathetic. Because they've been practicing setting their intention and being more deliberate (the first principle), they actively decide to change this story to a more reasonable one:

"Losing weight is hard but more than possible, if I stay consistent. I'm always in control. I have made the decision to take care of myself and I'm willing to be a little uncomfortable while I adjust to a healthier, happier lifestyle. I give myself permission to go through the process."

In this story, weight loss and happiness are not set at odds; rather they are the same thing. Gone is the all-or-nothing, pessimistic thinking and instead this story acknowledges that changing takes time and occasional discomfort, but is completely possible.

Now, when such a person wakes up one morning feeling stiff from working out, they will look at the stiffness and say, "ah, this is all normal and part of the process. It's OK. I'll keep going." The story is in alignment with the ultimate goal. Change is welcomed and encouraged.

If you've written your stories down, take a look at them now and ask where you would be without them. Can you moderate them so that they're more in line with your goals? Look carefully and see how reading each of your stories makes you *feel*. Do you feel demotivated and demoralized? What changes could you make so that your stories energize you instead?

For example, if your story is "I've failed so much in my life, I'm a failure", how do you behave? How would your behavior change if the story was, "I have a chance to make each new day a success"? Would your eyes be open to new opportunities and would you be quicker to forgive yourself and focus on the future instead of the past?

Of course, you don't have to be ridiculous about making changes to your stories. You don't have to be unrealistic or overly optimistic. Neutral is just fine! The next time you catch yourself telling the same old story, deliberately step in and change it. You've taken a lifetime to develop those habits, so expect it to take a while to develop new ones. But in time, your story will change. And when your blueprint is different, your actions begin to change in alignment with it. Gradually, your life begins to shift and change shape.

- Look closely for absolute statements – these are clues that you're dealing with a story, i.e. "always", "never", "perfect", "nobody". You can often make a story less limiting merely by adjusting these extreme statements. Do you *always* fail? Really? Are you sure you don't just fail some of the time?

- Look for those statements that feel like they have the most emotional heft to them. This is a sign that you're deviating from objective reality and are in the realm of a story. "Everybody hates me" is not only emotionally painful, it's factually untrue. The more boring truth is that most people are indifferent! Look for emotive wording in the stories you tell yourself. Are you petrified or disgusting or a failure? Or are you busy adjusting and doing the best you can? The words you use matter.

- Change your stories to ones that inspire you to act. Take note which words, phrases, thoughts and beliefs leave you feeling calm, strong, level headed and ready to take meaningful action. That's the direction you should be headed. Get rid of those beliefs that immobilize you.

When you learn how to go in deep and change the stories that run your life, you make lasting, meaningful changes. If you sincerely believe that you are doomed to be overweight, no amount of well-meaning dieting or exercise advice is going to help. The problem is more fundamental than that.

But when you reach inside and become curious about the narrative you've spun for yourself, you open your eyes to new solutions and possibilities that were invisible to you before. Then, change becomes something real and possible for you. Your dreams and goals which seemed so far away before, come more sharply into focus. You realize that they were always there, within your grasp.

Let's recap.

So far, we've been slowly building on three key principles for a meaningful, purpose-driven life. In the first chapter, we looked at becoming more aware and gradually tuning into that inner compass of our own desires. In the chapter after that, we expanded on those ideas and tried to see how those desires can be honed via the stories we tell ourselves.

In this chapter, we'll expand even further and look at how to bring those new, aligned stories to life with valuable action.

How do you know whether an action is valuable or not? How do you know when you're finished with your day or your week (or life, for that matter!) that you did a good job? Well, something is valuable when it aligns with your desires and goals. Your intention is the yardstick that you measure all your actions against – when you are aligned, you act with purpose and deliberateness, and so the things you do have innate value.

Hopefully by this point you've started to try and change some of your stories. It's challenging at first, but gradually you can begin to replace limiting stories with more valuable ones. The first two chapters might have seemed a little vague, and that's because nobody can really tell you what your values and goals are!

In this chapter, they can begin to crystallize and take shape. When you act in accordance with your newfound desires, your actions become those that enrich your life, rather than just eat time and have you asking, "what's the point?"

Value Exercise Number One: Value Yourself

As you looked close at your self-talk, did you find any stories that sound like the following?

- *"I'm worthless."*
- *"I'm broken and can't be fixed."*
- *"I'm not rich/thin/young/happy enough to do X."*
- *"People are judging me. Nobody likes me and I'll never be loved and accepted."*
- *"I'm just an ordinary person, I can't do or be anything special."*

Part of learning to identify and create a meaningful life is learning how to value yourself. When you think poorly of yourself, there's just no point in trying, or in pushing to fulfil your potential – why even bother if you don't have any potential?

This exercise comes in two parts. It might strike you as a bit contrived, but try it anyway: first, take 15 minutes or so to piece together a letter to your younger self. Imagine you have the ability to reach back in time and send a message to the 5-year-old version of yourself. Picture you as you were: young, innocent, full of hope, vulnerable, good.

How do you feel towards this child? Do you feel like saying, "you're broken and you can't be fixed" to this child's face? Does it seem right to tell them that nobody loves them and that they will never be accepted? Or are you filled with tenderness and a yearning to protect that younger self? Do you admire how that little person survived and grew and did what they could to navigate the sometimes cruel and unusual world around them? Are you fond of their spirit and their resilience and joy?

Take your time with this letter. Be honest. Try to see in this child all those things that make you who you are, even today. While it's true that you're an adult now and you are responsible for the choices you make, are you really so very different now compared to then? If you wouldn't say such negative things to child-you, why say them to adult-you?

The second part is to imagine yourself travelling forwards, not backwards to the past. Picture an older, wiser version of yourself. This is the person you are at 90 years old, after a lifetime of experience and insight and pain and joy. Now, take a few minutes to write the letter that your older self would write to you as you are now.

Would an older and wiser person tell you that they wished you had been harder on yourself, or that they regretted you didn't hate your body more? Do you think they would tell you that it was the right decision to hang back and never take any risks? Picture yourself on your death bed, your body tired and old. What would you wish your younger self had done, while there was still time? What is important? What isn't important?

A woman writes a letter to her younger self and in doing so, realizes that she wishes she had been given more encouragement for who she was as a child instead of pressured to be like everyone else. Perhaps she lived her whole life in the closet, forcing herself to be what she wasn't.

In writing a letter that tells her younger self not to be afraid of being different, she hears this message now, as an adult. When she writes the letter from her older, wiser self, the theme comes up again: she realizes that if she doesn't find the courage to express who she really is, she'll eventually regret it terribly. This exercise gives her the courage to finally come out of the closet.

These two exercises have a way of making all the bluster and distraction of everyday life shrink away and reveal what is ultimately important: that you are a human being, and that you deserve compassion and understanding. If you like, keep these letters and come back to them when you're stressing about something or feeling a little lost in life.

Value Exercise Number Two: Value Others
The life of an individual has meaning only insofar as it aids in making the life of every living thing nobler and more beautiful. Life is sacred, that is to say, it is the supreme value, to which all other values are subordinate.
Albert Einstein

Of course, a meaningful and fulfilling life is not just one where you feel smug about how wonderful you are. You can't just endlessly forgive yourself every mistake or spend your time navel-gazing.

There are other people in the world! And when you value them, you plug yourself into something bigger. The paradox is that sometimes, forgetting about your ego and the petty details of your own life can be incredibly liberating; loving others more can be a surprising route to loving yourself more. Finding meaning in others has a sneaky way of rubbing off, and helping you find meaning in yourself.

You can think of this exercise as a bit like an elaborate game of "devil's advocate". When people are hostile with one another, the root of their disagreement is usually a feeling that they are completely, irremediably *different* from each other. But for the most part, these differences are not innate things that keep people apart, but superficial differences that we ourselves have put there.

In fear, it's easy to look at another human being and find things that make him a threat to you. He looks different, speaks different, holds a different set of beliefs and has a different set of behaviors. But is he really that different from you?

For this exercise, forgo focusing on differences and instead focus on what makes you the *same* as the people you encounter. This switches your brain into a collaborative, receptive mode rather than a hostile and fearful one. It opens you up to possibilities instead of problems. It lets you honor your fellow human beings' innate dignity, rather than feeling intolerant that they aren't more like you. It lets you acknowledge that sometimes, *others* are right and that your convictions may actually not be so great.

So, when you are talking with someone new, before you do anything, immediately look for something in common with them. Perhaps they're standing in a long supermarket queue and are tired and fed up, just like you. Maybe they're the same age group as you, have toddlers like you or have a similar educational background.

This exercise works best when you feel that there's nothing in common at all. But look and you'll find something. Do you think the person in front of you has ever gone through a traumatic breakup and had to stop themselves from crying at work the next day? Do you think this person ever had an upsetting argument with a family member or has some sexual fantasy that they would never tell anyone for fear of being judged?

Once you start looking, you'll realize that the people you deal with every day, from close friends to strangers in the street, all have far more in common with you than not.

Take this a step further. Maybe this person is being rude and unkind to you. Maybe they are wrong about something and being completely unreasonable. Well, now you know you *definitely* have something in common with them – just look back into your past and remember all the times you yourself said something stupid or were unkind to someone. Does this make it easier to deal with them? Knowing that this person is not doing anything that you haven't done at one point yourself?

Value Exercise Number Three: Add Value to Everything You Do
When you ask people what their regrets are, they almost never say something like, "I wish I stayed longer in that soul-sucking job" or "I wish I was better at keeping up with

my neighbors". Nobody looks back and wishes they toned things down a bit, or lived with a little less passion. And even if they look back and see the mistakes they made, they usually regret the things they *didn't* do rather than the things they tried but failed.

Once you start tuning into your intention, and once you become skilled at taking charge of your own story, everything you do becomes an opportunity to add value. When you are guided by a deeper purpose, all the noise and fuss of life has a way of disappearing into the background, and what's really important has a way of coming more clearly into focus.

For this exercise, start to think of how you can optimize on value, both the value you find in the world around you and in the value you *create* for yourself and others.

Throughout the day, stop to take a moment and become aware (luckily, you've been practicing this since the first chapter!). As you do an activity, ask, is this adding value to my life? As you engage with other people, ask yourself if they are guiding you closer or further away from the things you value. But don't stop there – ask if you are pulling you weight and doing everything you can to provide value to *them*.

Let go of people who are not truly present with you, who are working against what's important to you or using you for their own ends. At the same time, hold yourself to a high standard: are you giving all of yourself to the people you deal with, during every encounter? Are you being true to your word, compassionate, genuine? Or are you not even considering them at all?

When you constantly remind yourself to stay aligned to your values, and to *add* value, it's like gently nudging yourself closer and closer the path in life that will make you the most fulfilled. Instead of letting empty, mindless moments flit past you, never to return, you grab hold of them with decisiveness and fill them with things that are worth something.

These little moments might not seem like much at the time, but they add up to a life that feels full and worthwhile.

If you're like me, you may have read some of the above and thought, "sure, I know all this already!" and then just skimmed through. But as we've seen, intellectually understanding an idea and actually *experiencing* it are two different things.

How can you take the three keys outlined above and actually use them, in the real life you live, right now, right here?

Unfortunately, our culture values quick fixes and secret tips and tricks that you can easily do once and then never again. We hope the three day cleanse will absolve us of a lifetime of poor eating habits or that reading one book once will somehow erase a lifetime of accumulated attitudes and beliefs that go against it.

But now that we've outlined three components to a life that is meaningful, intentional and free of regrets, let's look at practical ways to *live* that information.

- Instead of aiming for big changes, focus on making things habit. In just the same way as you engage in negative self-talk or mindlessness now out of habit, you can train yourself to do the opposite, just by sticking with it and reminding yourself to keep going each and every day. A morning ritual is the simplest and best way to do this. It's free, easy to do, and doesn't take much effort – yet it can make all the difference in the world. Set your intention, become aware, breathe and focus on your goals for the day and you learn to hit "refresh" on your life each and every morning.

- Let go of all or nothing thinking. "Perfectionism" is really fear of failure in disguise. But when you're OK with doing things wrong occasionally, you take more risks and try more things – and succeed more often. Give yourself permission to be a beginner, to not know everything and to be a little afraid. Any regretful person knows that the feeling of missed opportunity is so much worse than the temporary discomfort of going out of your comfort zone once in a while!

- Keep your motivation and locus of control *internal.* The moment you hand over power to an external authority, you take away meaning from your life. Do things because you *choose* to, not because you have to or should or because someone told you to. Even if you make a mistake, the fact that you have taken responsibility for your life and chosen that mistake autonomously gives you more freedom and purpose than doing the "right thing" without really thinking about it.

- Slow down. Mindlessness often comes with a kind of rushing in life. Stop, smell the roses, and take a moment for yourself. The answers to a problem often emerge when you stop grasping or looking for distractions to fill empty moments. Stop, feel just how full and rich each passing moment in time is, and give yourself time to really process what's happening around you.

- When you catch yourself comparing your life to other peoples', ask if that feeling is actually masking another, deeper feeling. Are there some desires going unfulfilled in you? Are you feeling guilty for not living up to potential you know you have? Instead of focusing on the people who elicit these reactions in you, ask what it is about you that's being "hooked" this way.

- When it comes to your own truth, don't be moderate. Speak up on matters that concern things of great importance to you. Today, apathy is often praised as a progressive, intelligent attitude – but don't be afraid to speak out. Many people regret not living more honestly, not fully expressing themselves, biting their tongues ...and then feeling hurt that nobody knows the "real" them. If you have the courage to express your true self, you give people the chance to relate to you in a deeper, more meaningful way – and you give other people the courage to do the same!

- Be wary of people or institutions who try to tell you what you think and feel. When others try to narrate your life for you or interpret your actions using their own stories, you become disempowered. Everyone from romantic partners to colleagues to advertisers and even to therapists can have unconscious agendas for squeezing you into stories that are meaningful to *them*. But are they meaningful to you? This is why it's so important to have space every single day to tune out the noise of daily life and go quiet enough to listen to your *own* voice.

- As you become more aware, more in control and more focused on a life geared to meaning, expect that things will start to change around you. You may be thrilled to find what new doors open, but be aware that many will *close*, too. A little compassion goes a long way when you realize that certain relationships, ideas or habits are no longer part of your journey anymore. Bid a good journey to the people who are not on the same path as you and go your own way. It may hurt to lose things and people that used to be important to you, but try to focus on the space that opens up for things and people that are better aligned with your values.

- Keep healthy. The exercises in this book, though simple, take a lot of effort and presence of mind to do each and every day. You simply won't manage if your body is tired, poorly nourished or buckling under stress or illness. Turn your awareness inward regularly to see what your body needs, and take care of yourself with enough sleep, good food and exercise.

- When you're feeling challenged or as though you're not making progress, that's your clue to have a closer look at your stories. Look closely at the thought that's distressing you. If you're telling yourself the story, "I should be progressing faster than I am now" you will cause yourself stress every time you pause or take a step back. But is that story really true? Is it helpful? Perhaps, instead of getting caught up in how you should be going faster, you can spend your efforts reworking your story. Is it really so bad to go at the speed you're going? Does rushing accomplish anything?

CONCLUSION

In a way, I'm thankful for the regrets I've racked up so far. It's these regrets that have forced me to look more closely at my life and what I ultimately want to do with it.

These days, when I feel that familiar sense of panic or unease when I'm in bed late at night and can't sleep, I take it as a sign that I've strayed a little from my path and need to stop, become aware and take charge again. I no longer fear this sense of dread but welcome it as a reminder that my time on this earth is limited, and that if I want a life of meaning and value, the time to do it is *now*.

Whenever I've engaged with the techniques and exercises I've shared here, whenever I've been fully present, intentional, compassionate and tuned towards adding value, I've found that it's actually *impossible* to feel any regret. How could I?

In fact, when I can sustain these three key principles and find space for them in each and every day, my life overflows with meaning. The disappointments of life, the memories of painful things in the past, the losses all of us experience now and again and the senselessness of the world ...well, all of it is just so much easier to deal with.

I'm sharing these principles with you not because I think they are the be all and end all, but because they have been so useful in my own journey towards a life that really means something. If you are curious about what you're really capable of, I encourage you to push yourself. Give yourself permission to ask those dangerous questions and believe that your hopes and dreams are worth pursuing.

I don't know where your journey will take you, but I know for sure that if it's a meaningful journey, these three elements will feature in it, somewhere, somehow.

If you wander off your path, trust that you'll find your way back to it if you just stop, be aware and learn to really listen to yourself. And if you face adversity, trust that you have everything you need within you to overcome it, if you can only grab hold of your own intention and stay true to your values.

Live *on purpose*.

WHEN LIFE GIVES YOU LEMONS - THE POWER OF
SURRENDER, HUMOR AND COMPASSION WHEN THE
GOING GETS TOUGH

Ask a few people to tell you their quick life story and you may be surprised by a recurring pattern.

It's not obvious at first, but the person speaking invariably says something along these lines: "Well I was doing X, because I had planned for it for so long, and then I was going along, doing that, when Y happened, which was totally not what I wanted to happen. So I did Y for a bit and then had this idea to do Z, but after Q happened, stuff was just never the same again…"

You can substitute literally anything into that same story and have the life trajectories of most human beings. You were married and busy living your happily ever after when you met someone who changed the game completely. You studied for 5 years only to discover the field you were now qualified to work in no longer interested you. You expected a girl and got a boy. A windfall happened. You got in a car accident.

There are two things going on here: your plans, hopes, dreams, and beliefs about your life…

…and *life itself*.

Life, as they say, happens when you're busy making other plans.

We all have a narrative of ourselves that we hold dear, and when life "happens", we might feel a little slighted. How dare reality come and get in the way, just as we were busy trying to do our own thing? Nobody anticipates cancer, a surprise pregnancy, or being laid off of work. Nobody knows when they'll fall in love or when their uncle will die in a plane crash. But if you listen to the stories people tell, it's almost as though these random, unforeseen and unplanned for events were not distractions from life, but the main event.

"We never ever planned on having children, but it turned out to be exactly what we always wanted."

"I was very idealistic then. Ten years later, I don't believe any of that stuff anymore."

"I thought we would be together forever. I never even imagined that that could happen to *us*. Now I've moved on and found someone completely different."

This is a book about *change*.

No matter who you are, there's a good chance that life has stepped into your self-made narrative and ruined everything, probably more than once. We like to shrug and write off events like this as "accidents". We like to focus instead on tinkering with our plans even more, or changing the narrative. Life knocks our tower of blocks down and we start right back up again, building another one.

But is there another way to cope when life gives you lemons?

This book is also about *resilience to change*.

Other self-help books out there may have mountains of valuable advice on how to construct your block tower beyond your wildest imagination. Personal development is usually focused on the tower: how can you build a better one? Why are you building one in the first place? How does your tower compare to other towers and is it normal? Is it a good tower?

These are all excellent topics. But again, they don't say anything about what to do when someone comes and knocks your tower down. You could spend years meditating, cultivating an inner calm and telling yourself a grand narrative about non-attachment and letting go of ego. But then someone breaks into your home and robs you at gunpoint and all at once, your narrative shatters. Your blocks are scattered onto the ground and you're left with an ugly truth: your narrative of life and life itself are simply not compatible.

This book is for you if you've ever felt like life has thrown you a curveball. It's for you if you've ever experienced an incredible loss and thought, "Oh god what now?" or felt like your best laid plans came to a screeching halt. In the chapters that follow, we'll be looking at a quality that is seriously underappreciated in the self-help universe: resilience. Here, we won't bother with any specific narrative, but rather take an honest look at what happens when a hurricane blows through your life and strips you of that narrative.

We'll look at how resilient people differ from people who are "fragile" and how changing your thoughts (i.e. your narrative) can change how you respond and adapt to change. We'll take a slightly different approach in these pages: there are no accidents, no unforeseen circumstances – only life itself. Change is not something to fear or work against, but something to embrace and move with. In other words, getting lemons is the default!

A few years ago, life dealt me an incredible blow. Something I had taken for granted for years was snatched from me, and almost overnight, everything I held dear was called into question. I felt small, fragile and helpless. I blamed myself, everyone around me and life itself. And like so many other people who get back up after life pounds them down, I was one day able to look back fondly at that time. Today, I am *grateful* for how awful that time of life was.

Whatever trauma, hiccup, mistake or accident you've experienced in your life, my hope is that this book can show you how to roll with it, with resilience, humor, patience and compassion. Change can be a blessing, or a curse. But it *will* happen. Over and over again.

Whatever your path in life, this book is about devising a plan that will get you there, *realistically*.

CHAPTER 1: THE BEST LAID PLANS

Some people have unimaginably huge spaces between what their day-to-day living actually entails and all the things they wish it did. They may look out over their entire lives and see only something that's getting in the way of what's most important: all the things still to come. These people are waiting for their lives to align with the picture they have of themselves. They're waiting for life to start, unaware of all the time that's bleeding away with every second. "One day" everything will fall into place and things will look how they're supposed to. Until then, their actual life is negligible, just some meaningless thing to pass on the way there.

Of course, there's nothing at all wrong with goals and dreams. Unless someone had the audacity to dream up an idea of life that didn't exist yet, mankind would not have made any of the fantastic advances it has over the millennia.

But far more people use dreams, plans and goals in a completely different way. While I can think of people who've had their lives do a 180 on them, I've also know people who seem to have things fall into their laps; the chaos of life seems to fall in their favor, they go with it, they seem "lucky".

"The Thing"

Before we continue, I want to introduce the concept of The Thing. I've kept it vague because, well, The Thing always *is* vague. You've already encountered the thing yourself, undoubtedly. The Thing is sneaky, unpredictable, a bit of a nuisance at best, a huge disaster at worst.

The Thing is the way the random, chaotic nature of the world expresses itself on us. Sometimes it has the face of failed entrepreneurial projects, health problems that spring up from nowhere, financial setbacks or losses. Sometimes it looks like a bit of luck, or some happy windfall that comes just in time, just as you were giving up hope.

The Thing is random and follows no rules. By its nature, you never know when or if it will appear, and when it does, its form is always changing. The Thing *is* change. It's those irritating few dollars missing from your budget somehow. It's the genetic mutation that means you develop cancer and your friend doesn't. It's the spanner in the works, the uneven cobble stone, the typo and the plot twist.

There is no preparing for or anticipating The Thing, but it's certain: it's always there. If you look back on your own life, you can probably see a few times when The Thing pitched up, shuffled around everything in your life and left again, leaving chaos in its wake. Some changes are small but others are literally life changing: you lose a spouse, a limb, or worse, a vision of yourself in the future.

Planning that disregards The Thing

There are two ways to make plans in life. The first is the one that's usually encouraged by every personal power seminar, self-improvement book or motivational quote. Here, you begin with the assumption that you are in control, and that if only you are assertive, confident and goal-oriented enough, you can whip your life into shape, into the thing you believe it ought to be.

You want to improve, and you do so with a plan. You devise a workout schedule, set yourself the goal of a new job in 6 months, or buy a bunch of books that promise to teach you how to play the piano. In a larger, more abstract sense, you operate with a strong sense of who you are meant to be, and how your life is meant to turn out: in your vision you are in control, and events unfold in just the way you want them to.

Sounds good! But we all know what happens when life refuses to play along: tragedy. Where life and your vision of life meet, there's friction. You injure your foot and your workout schedule flies out the window. After a few months you start to wonder why you even want to get another job at all. And you sit down for an hour of piano practice and a minute later your mother shows up at your house.

The Thing comes. There's nothing in your plan that tells you how to deal with it – in fact, your plan scarcely acknowledges the existence of The Thing at all. Now, you're on the back foot. You're in a reactive frame of mind, scrambling to make a new plan, probably a little mad that you have to let go of your schedule and do this other, inconvenient thing instead. Because you're kind of invested in a path once you're on it, you choose to ignore warning signs. Or, because you're so convinced of this one course of action over another, you fail to notice a third, even better option. When The Thing comes, you aren't expecting it, and so its presence is unwanted, and threatening.

Planning that respects The Thing

Then there is a second type of planning. Here you not only acknowledge that The Thing might appear at any time, but you actually build that fact into your plan. Instead of being a rigid, static idea of what reality must look like, your plan has a few squishy places; parts that can bend and fold and accommodate change.

You don't hold onto to this plan too tightly either, realizing that you might need a new one at any moment so you'd better not get overly attached. When The Thing comes, you are expecting it, and so it's not some scary, unmanageable development – it's more or less just business as usual. Because you weren't chained to your plan, and the plan you had was malleable, The Thing doesn't impact you as strongly.

In other words, you are resilient.

How resilient are you?

Take a look at some of the following traits shared by people who make plans that go *with*, rather than against the changing nature of reality, i.e. The Thing. How many do you identify with?

"I very seldom lose my temper."

"I can apologize quickly if I see I've done something wrong."

"I would rather just try something out instead of wondering if it will work."

"I don't mind if people are a few minutes early or late."

"I always have a plan B ...and a Plan C and D!"

"I'm happy to be spontaneous sometimes."

"I'm OK with not understanding everything."

"I don't bother myself too much with other people's expectations."

"I can think on my feet."

"I'm always open to suggestions and like to mix things up."

"Things don't have to be perfect for me to be happy."

"I can always laugh at myself."

Gritty thinking

Luckily, resilience is not some inborn characteristic – it's a skill that anyone can learn. And luckily, you'll get plenty of opportunities for practice, since The Thing is everywhere!

Learning to be resilient starts with the thing you have the most control over: your own thoughts. The way that you interpret and internalize events around you has a direct consequence for the plans you make, the actions you take and the priorities you establish. Your thoughts make up the narrative you tell yourself, and give you a blueprint for how to understand change, loss and adversity.

Below, we'll look at how you might be unwittingly entertaining thoughts that are actually making you more fragile, as well as ways to reprogram those thoughts into more flexible, realistic and adaptable ones. Some of the thoughts below may seem more familiar to you than others. Some you might even disagree with, but I encourage you to read on – the portrait of resilience painted here is not what we typically think of when we imagine a "strong" person.

Fragile Thought One: The World is Hostile

So let's start: what does it mean to be tough?

What do we really mean when we describe a person as gritty, or resilient, or robust? And how are they different from those who are weak, fragile and unable to adapt and change when the going gets tough?

If you're like most people, you think of grit as a kind of *lowered sensitivity*. Tough things are not easily affected by external factors, and can endure a lot before breaking. To be tough, we think, we must be able to stand strong and not budge with any adversity. We must be like steel or leather or something immovable.

While this is a good description of resilience when it comes to building materials, it's just no good when applied to human beings! The trouble with this model of resilience is that it makes resilience and sensitivity two different things, and you can't have too much of one without compromising on the other.

In other words, when you reduce your sensitivity, you do indeed protect yourself and make it less likely that change, adversity or unpredictability can hurt you. But in the process you also shut out all the good things that come with sensitivity: social connection, intimacy, creativity, the love and enjoyment of beauty or the thrill of sensing the world around us.

Building a wall and hoping it will do the trick to protect you is one way of being resilient, but it's not the smartest. When you focus on all the dangerous and unpleasant things in life that you have to defend against, you unwittingly tune into the worst that life has to offer, and simultaneously shut yourself off from the best. When you're in this reactive, "strong" state of mind, you scan for threats and limitations, rather than opportunities. You set up a self-fulfilling prophesy where you seek out the negative and say, "Look! See? I told you it was there!" when you find it.

Fragile Thoughts:
- It's a dog-eat-dog world. Do unto others before they do to you!
- The only way to deal with negativity is with more negativity.
- It's not OK to be vulnerable.
- Shit happens. If something can go wrong, it will.
- If I shield myself, I can't be hurt.

The above thoughts are actually surprisingly common, and that's why I've begun with this as the first of five "fragile" ways of thinking. Maybe you're wondering, how can this mindset be considered fragile? Isn't it the opposite?

The trouble with this way of thinking is that it isn't realistic. If you had some undetermined food allergy, you could treat it by vowing never to eat food again. Sure, it'll solve your problem, but only in the most superficial way. You need food, and just shutting down anything that looks like it might prove problematic isn't solving that problem, it's more or less *avoiding* it. This is a fragile way of thinking.

Many people experience loss or tragedy and decide that they will seal up their hearts and never open them up again. While this is understandable in the short term, the loss of the ability to connect with the world, yourself and other human beings is a very, very high cost to pay for that safety.

Lemony Alternative:

Resilient people, on the other hand, are not "tough" in the usual sense of the word. Instead of forfeiting their human vulnerability, they hold onto it, but they moderate the way they think about threat and risk. When you see the world as full of hostility, you close up and get to experience nothing at all. If, however, you see the world as filled with both good and bad, you courageously take on the risk of occasional pain – but when you experience joy as well, it's all the sweeter.

What is *really* courageous, is to abandon black and white thinking and have the bravery to be optimistic, and see the good in life, even though you have been hurt in the past. Here are some alternative thoughts:

- No matter how dire a situation is, there are always options and opportunities.
- The world is filled with good as well as bad – and I am capable of handling both!
- It's OK for me to suffer sometimes. It's OK for me to feel a whole range of emotions.
- Being vulnerable takes courage.
- I don't have to numb myself or lower my expectations of the world to be considered rational, grown-up or smart.

Fragile Thought Two: Life is Elsewhere

When life comes along and messes up your best laid plans, your very first reaction might be one of surprise. While it's true that some events really are out of the blue, most of the time, things develop somewhat predictably, and if only you paid enough attention, you might have seen how that situation evolved.

You *can't* see things evolving in front of your eyes if you're not looking, though. If your mind is firmly stuck in the past or the future, you may notice nothing in the present at all, and something might land at your feet "out of nowhere." It's as though life is most inconvenient when it forcefully reminds us of where everything *really* takes place: in the present.

You might have missed some signals, lost awareness or stopped paying attention and then *boom*, something happens and you feel blindsided. It's not necessarily that life is unpredictable, only that you weren't really paying enough attention to predict it!

For lack of a better term, you might be living your life *elsewhere*. In regrets from the past or in dreams or worries of the future, you live in anything but the reality of the now. This is a fragile state of mind to be in because it means you have diminished awareness, reduced control and less agency in the minute to minute events of your life. You make poor choices or fail to choose at all. And when things change up, you're not prepared. You feel cheated, rushed or disconnected from the things that are happening in your world.

Fragile Thoughts:

- I know just exactly how to live a good life and do everything I want – but I'll get started on Monday, just as soon as I finish XYZ...

- I wish I could go back and change what happened in the past. My regrets. My unfulfilled hopes. Such a pity. I dwell on these thoughts all the time.
- What if...?
- In the future stuff will be better.
- Because of the way things were in the past, my future is set and can never be changed.

All of these thoughts might have more or less validity to them, but they all miss one crucial point of focus: what can you *do*, right *now*? It's metaphysically impossible to take any action in the past or the future, so if this is where your brain spends most of its time, what you're doing is training yourself to be inactive.

Of course, human beings tell themselves stories, and to do that you need to to think of the past and the future. But resilient people choose the present moment as their primary habitat, and don't make a habit of dwelling in frames of mind that limit their scope of action.

Lemony Alternatives:

Pay attention. To be resilient, to have the best possible response when life gives you lemons, you need to be present.
- When I'm in the moment, I can think on my feet, be alert and tuned in to everything that's going on around me.
- My life is not going to happen some other time, in some other place – it's *already happening*, right now.
- I don't have infinite time on this earth.
- The past is over. The future hasn't happened yet. The only thing that is real is what is happening right now.
- The only way to "miss out" is to not be present in each and every moment.

Fragile Thought Three: It's Got to Be Perfect

I'm sure you've heard someone say that their greatest flaw is being too much of a perfectionist. While they might have meant it as a sort of humble-brag, the truth is that perfectionist thinking really *is* a problem.

When you cling to the idea that your life should be nothing less than ideal and that you won't rest until you've achieved perfection, it can feel very reassuring. In a chaotic world, you tell yourself you're OK: other people can be incomplete or slightly messy or change their minds mid-plan. But not *you*. You hold high standards and hope they'll protect you from failure, or insulate you against the unexpected.

But the irony is that perfectionism is actually quite a fragile state of mind. It's rooted in the fear of loss of control, and it's almost a little superstitious: "if I do this *just right* then everything will be OK..."

You might set your heart on growing a rare and delicate orchid, clearly a perfect flower if ever there was one. But the fact that your orchid can only grow in a very narrow, very specific set of conditions is actually a disadvantage. Holding onto the image of a perfect life or outcome feels like it should be motivating, but when you decide you'll only be satisfied with that narrow range of outcomes, what you're actually doing is signing up for a *wider* range of possible failures. When it grows, an orchid is beautiful. But there are many, many more ways for an orchid to *not* grow than for other flowers. The irony in being a perfectionist is that you actually end up courting more imperfection.

Fragile Thoughts:
- There is a final, finished, complete outcome that I am striving towards. I don't know what happens once I reach it, but presumably I'll stop and my mission will finally be over.
- All my happiness will come at the end, once I'm done. But not before. There's no happiness along the way, and I won't rest at all till my plan comes to fruition.
- If I am to succeed, I must be hard on myself.
- I would rather not do something unless I can be assured that I can do it perfectly.
- I'm not like other people – I have higher standards, more exacting tastes and for me, the stakes are just higher.

Lemon Alternative:
As we've already seen, shit happens. While it might *feel* good to have a rigid set of conditions for reality and for yourself, they usually don't do much to dampen the chaos or unpredictability of life anyway. Basing your happiness on a very specific and limited set of conditions puts you in a reactive, fragile state. And even if you *do* achieve that state for a while, there's no guaranteeing that it'll last forever. Even the perfect orchid has to die eventually. Chaos and imperfection are *inevitable*, and when they occur, the perfectionist is the least equipped to deal with it.

Don't be perfect, be a work in progress.

When you are a perfectionist, you are intolerant to incompleteness. But the trouble is, the road to perfection is 100% made up of incomplete stages. That's basically all it is! The most sublime ballet performance is danced on the top of thousands of hours of ugly missteps, grubby dance shoes and sweat stained practice gear. This "imperfection" is not taking away from the glamor of the end result, it's *part of* the end result!

Try these lemony thoughts instead:
- Every single moment is full, complete and whole on its own.
- Life is not just lived to get to the end of it.
- If I am to succeed, I have to be OK with moving through the process of getting better and making mistakes.
- I don't have to do everything at once. I can be "on the way". Being "in process" is not a failure.

- If my standards prevent me from taking risks and doing hard work, then they are not perfect – they're restrictive and unrealistic.

Fragile Thought Four: It's Wrong to be Wrong

Let's build on the above fragile thought. Many perfectionists (and I used to call myself one, too!) are deathly afraid of failure. They don't want to be measured and found wanting. They don't want to try and make a mistake, and for others to see that mistake. They don't want second or third place. They don't want to get better by increments, but all at once and quickly, so they don't have to go through the awkward middle phase when they're still learning.

The core of this fragile thought is that it is undesirable to be anything other than all-knowing at all times.

Sounds extreme when you say it directly, but the idea is that all the struggles of learning are unacceptable, and if you try something, you ought to be good at it right away, even if you've never done it before.

Doesn't it seem silly?

Have you ever sat in a class or listened to someone explain something and thought, "damn, I'm stupider than I thought"? Have you had trouble with something new and unfamiliar, yet nodded your head when asked if you understood or pretended like something was easy just to save face?

Maybe this attitude comes from the days of teachers punishing students for not knowing the right answers. Who knows. The fact is, though, that no learning can happen without occasionally being wrong. Unless you can honestly admit what you don't know, how can you begin to know it? Unless you acknowledge something is a mistake, how can you do it better next time?

Fragile Thoughts:
- Being in error is embarrassing and something to be ashamed of.
- Looking like I don't know what I'm doing will undermine my credibility and people won't respect me.
- It's all or nothing – I don't want to try unless I can do it well.
- I'm the only one who finds doing new things difficult – and I have to conceal that fact!
- Doing something and then admitting you were wrong makes you unreliable.

These kind of thoughts are tricky because they focus on creating the *illusion* of control, all the while giving you less control. Think about it – if you're stubbornly refusing to admit mistakes, to do things imperfectly or to be a beginner in any way, you're robbing yourself of the opportunity to actually learn.

So, you end up saving face, but at what cost? Stubbornly avoiding the discomfort of learning means you stay longer with thoughts and actions that aren't working, and miss out on the better alternatives just around the corner, just hiding behind the admission of, "oops, that's not right, let me try again."

Lemony Alternatives:
- I don't have to know it all, and nobody is expecting that I do.
- I don't take myself too seriously – mistakes are kind of funny! I just laugh at myself and move on.
- There is no shame in incomplete knowledge, or having an only partially developed skill.
- Knowing something is better than *seeming* like you know it to others.
- If I want to be better at something, I have to be honest about all the ways I'm not actually there yet. I'm secure enough in myself that this doesn't bother me, though.

Fragile Thought Five: There's Only One Way

There is a saying that goes, "brittle things break before they bend."

There is a vicious cycle we can set up for ourselves when we try to deal with the innate unpredictability of the world. If we feel frightened and out of control, we may be tempted to clamp down and become more controlling – we make more and more plans, and those plans become more and more restrictive. It's as though we hope that with enough contingency planning and enough strictness, life can't ever get the chance to throw us a curve ball.

But when you try to constrain the natural unfolding of events around you, when you curtail spontaneity and try to force situations to be what they aren't, you end up with exactly the result you don't want. You realize how poorly real life fits into your vision of it, you realize how much work it is to maintain that vision. You paradoxically feel *less* in control than if you had held a little less tightly. You may respond to this by trying to exert even more control, and the cycle continues.

When you think about it, demanding that reality conform to your pre-made ideas of what it should look like is a little ...arrogant. What's so good about your plan, anyway? Nobody can argue that making plans is a valuable human skill. But it's possible to take that planning mindset too far, and into territory where it doesn't really work.

Like the perfectionist above, making strict plans really only maximizes the possible outcomes that will make you unhappy. When you make a "plan", it might be a demand in disguise, a secret intolerance and a disappointment waiting to happen. You say, "I'll get married before 30" and feel like you're a forward thinking, take-charge person who's taking actions to get what they want. That might be the case, but is when you get married *entirely* under your control? Do you really want to sign up for the three necessary years of misery if you only end up married at 33?

The trouble with plans and goals is that they can have the effect of *constraining* you. You put blinkers on and stop yourself from seeing something better that's right under your nose, just because it doesn't fit in with the plan you've already thought through. You might fail to heed warning signs because you're already convinced your course is the right course. Not to mention that when you live your life to a tight schedule, you sap the joy and spontaneity out of it.

Fragile Thoughts:
- There is only ever one correct and true way to do something.
- Unless I'm constantly vigilant, everything in life is going to go to shit.
- If you have good principles, you should never go back on them, never change your mind and never entertain other possibilities.
- If I do it right, I can help people see the error of their ways and help them to do what I think they should be doing.
- My life plans and standards only work out if they're followed exactly.

Lemon Alternative:

You're probably noticing some overlap with this fragile thought and the ones that came before. When you strip away all the intimidating strictness and go-getter vibe from this kind of thinking, you get to the root it: fear of change. Fear of loss of control, or of the unknown. If you can plan and control everything, then there's nothing to fear anymore, right?

This is wishful thinking, because so much of life is 100% out of our control. Trying to make it otherwise doesn't make you diligent and tough, it just sets you up for failure. When your plans don't work out, you're left with nothing. Nothing but your strong feeling that life should have gone otherwise – not exactly a frame of mind that's conducive to creative, joyful solutions.

Lemony Alternatives:
- I cannot change certain random events in the world. But I am always in control of the frame of mind I hold, so I focus on that instead.
- With the right frame of mind, I can respond spontaneously and quickly to any change in the environment.
- I am more interested in what works, and what works right now, rather than some lofty ideal I have of how the situation *should* go.
- I am flexible, and I don't mind abandoning a course of action if it repeatedly looks like it's not working.
- I am calm and in control – of *myself.* It's not my business to control others.

CHAPTER 3: HOW TO LET IT GO

As we move on, I'd like to focus on an "anti-skill", something that isn't usually thought of as an aptitude we need to develop in ourselves. This skill is the skill of letting go.

Letting go of what?

Well, everything.

Letting go of the past = forgiveness instead of resentment, despair and regrets

Letting go of the present = spontaneity, instead of being neurotic or controlling

Letting go of the future = trust, instead of stress or anxiety

Life, when it's doing its own thing, is remarkably ill-defined. It's loose, bursting with creativity and unpredictability. Life is transient and everything around us – including us – is temporary, and prone to being lost at any moment. Life flows and moves, never clinging to one particular form and never stagnating in one place for too long.

Trying to stand still, to stop up the flow or insulate yourself against change only guarantees that you'll be more unnerved by change when it eventually happens. To match life's pace, you need to *let go*.

Letting go of the past

Resentment and regret builds when we look back at what has already happened in life, and tell ourselves the story, "that *shouldn't* have been." The trouble is, of course, that what is done can never, ever be undone. When you do this, not only are you fighting with reality, but you're fighting with a version of reality that has long gone, and doesn't even exist anymore.

Holding onto things from the past is taking extra effort out of your life to keep alive a story that is already over. If we have experienced a trauma, our minds may be tempted to return back to the event over and over, perhaps in a bid to finally get some "closure", to understand what happened, to gain a measure of control over it.

But at the end of the day, the counter is reset and everything is shifted: what was real and present one moment is immediately past, immediately history. This flow is a natural state – the trees don't mourn the leaves they lost three winters ago. What is unnatural is to hold on. This takes more effort, because you are actively working against life's current. When you let go, you're letting go of your hold on something in the past, a thing that's likely taking you out of the present.

Forgiveness is one of the most straightforward things you can do ...but it is one of the hardest. There is no real secret to it. Closure is a myth. You never get to go back and change what someone did or said. All you do is decide, just like that, that you are not going to hold on anymore. Not because memories of the past don't hurt anymore, but in spite of the fact that they do.

Visualize ropes or cords that are binding you to a ship that is sinking. The ship will keep sinking, deeper and deeper into the past. And you will sink with it unless you have the courage to hack away at those cords and swim away. The problem is not the sinking ship – it will sink anyway. The problem is that you are tethered to it.

Letting go of the present

For the most part, it's far easier to get stuck with stressing about how things were or how they might still be. But if you're anything like me, then you find a way to distort even the *present* moment, too.

Rigidly holding onto plans for how the moment *must* unfold can be exhausting – and seldom even works. Loosely, people recognize this kind of mindset for what it is: stress.

But what exactly is stress anyway? In keeping with the theme of this book so far, I'd like to suggest that stress is often about fighting with reality. You're trying to do things that are sort of undoable. You're racing against the clock, or doing something that's just innately pointless or unpleasant, or you're out of control and badly want to be back in control again.

I won't try to suggest that every bit of stress you experience is just an illusion, but ...a lot of it is. Let go of it. If the reality is that you were meant to be in a meeting in 5 minutes, and you're 15 minutes away, well, there's no using fighting with reality. You will be late. Instead of using that extra 10 minutes to stress and be anxious, why not use it to accept the fact and do what you *can* do?

I'm convinced that so much of the stress we all experience is completely elective. You actively have to hold onto it. But what if you let go? The next time something in the present moment is stressing you out, ask yourself if your fighting against reality is really reasonable, and if there's a better way to spend your energy.

Letting go of the future

When you stress and worry about the future, what you do is construct a picture of that future first. You imagine what might happen, and then proceed to treat it as though it already has. If you're stressed about people's potential reactions to a presentation you have to give, you are telling yourself a story about what the future is.

Of course, nobody can say what will happen in the future. You can only act in the best way you know how, in the present, then wait and see. It simply isn't your business to decide ahead of time how events will unfold. You cannot predict other peoples' reactions to you, and you don't know what *their* vision of the future looks like. There are always going to be things you haven't considered, factors you don't even know about, complexity in cause and effect that defy the understanding of just one person in a web of many.

Having anxiety about what might be is unnatural – it is holding onto something that does not yet exist. Of course, you could lay out a million contingency plans, try to see what is in the present and make an educated guess about what might evolve in the future. But that's all it ever will be: a guess.

The terrible thing is that, unlike the future you're worried about, anxiety actually *is* real. The cortisol you flood your body with when you put images and stories in your head is actual a real chemical in your body; a chemical that can do real damage, right here in the present moment. When you act out of fear or the desire to control, you take unreal thoughts and convert them into real actions. You may bring about the very thing you're anxious about.

The future, whatever it is, will come when it comes. And when it does, you will respond in whatever way you respond. Whatever anxiety you wasted in anticipation does nothing to alter the speed at which the future comes, or what it is when it arrives. It only robs you of the only thing you have: the present moment.

Can you prepare reasonably? Can you find a way to act to the best of your abilities, given what you know? Sure. And once you've done that, let it go. There is no way to actually be in the future or the past – there is only being present and not being present.

So you might as well be present.

There is no Lemon: Ridding Yourself of 10 Common Cognitive Distortions

So far, in getting to the heart of what to do when life doesn't go quite the way you want it to, we've been making a pretty big assumption. When I talk about The Thing and how disruptive it can be, I'm assuming that …there is a Thing in the first place. I'm assuming that when you look at your life and say, "how am I going to solve this problem?" that there is even a problem there at all.

We've had a long look at fragile thoughts vs. more robust ones. We've seen that to start getting to grips with the shit life throws at you, you first need to change your mindset.

Gritty people don't necessarily endure any less adversity in their lives. In fact, they may experience more. But what's different is how they *interpret* the events around them. A fragile person thinks in ways that limit him and make life harder, whereas the more resilient person thinks in ways that keep opening up options and possibilities. They may never even "solve" their life problems in the way a more fragile person would consider satisfactory, but it hardly even matters.

I'd like to consider here the fact that for a more resilient person, the very definition of "adversity" is different. They have a different threshold for what counts as a problem for them. The same event that could send a more fragile person into a tailspin barely registers for them. Why is that?

Below, let's quickly look at some cognitive distortions – which is really just another name for a way to *create* a problem where there isn't even one.

Overgeneralization

You fail one course at college and so assume that this means you must fail every course at college. You get dumped once and conclude that the entire human race finds you repulsive. This is a neat way to take a small glitch and grow it into a full sized Lemon.

Try this instead: Be specific. Force yourself to be accurate when you speak "I messed up *today*, on this *one* task."

Emotional reasoning

You feel fat and ugly, so, therefore, you *are* fat and ugly. You feel offended by something someone said, so you believe this is proof that they deliberately hurt you, and that what they said was objectively offensive.

Try this instead: Feelings are just feelings. Remind yourself that feelings are always valid, but not necessarily true.

Personalization

Your company is doing really badly and downsizes – you get fired. Your problem is now one of unemployment, but you give yourself another problem: the sadness at being rejected by your superiors. You feel worthless.

Try this instead: Easier said than done, but try to remember that nothing other people do is ultimately because of you. Accept your responsibility in a situation, but be realistic: is everything that happens directly related to you somehow?

Black and white thinking

In an argument with your spouse, their criticism of you makes you hate them, when you loved them an hour before. You discover a new hobby or passion, and it suddenly becomes everything, and whatever you did before is nothing in comparison. In conflict, you see issues as right or wrong, and people as all-good or all-bad. No in between.

Try this instead: It takes strength to consider the grey, middle parts. Listen carefully for when you use "always" or "never" or other strong, absolute words like "perfect" or "hate". Life is complex. Try to hold both good feelings and bad feelings about the same idea – it is possible!

Filtering

You receive criticism for your work and suddenly feel that life has given you lemons. But you have focused on just a handful of criticisms while completely ignoring the hundreds of times you were praised. You have a filter on that basically only lets the problematic aspects of a situation get through!

Try this instead: It's a rare situation that doesn't have both good and bad elements. If you find yourself in a difficult situation, actively remember to look for the positives, too.

Catastrophizing

This is when you take something that is a small problem and turn it into a huge, massive problem – the biggest problem the world has ever seen, in fact. This also entails assuming the effects of a problem are going to be much worse than they are. Perhaps you botch a speech you are meant to give. That's a problem. But it doesn't mean that life as you know it is over, and that this is the worst thing that has ever happened to anyone ever.

Try this instead: Fast forward a year or five years in your life and ask if this problem is still going to be an issue then. More likely than not, the problem will be long forgotten and its effects, if there are any, are very minimal.

Prescriptive thinking

This is another common way to create a problem when there isn't one. When you have plenty of "should" and "have to" beliefs about life, everything that doesn't fit that cognition is automatically a problem. Rather than rethink the belief, you might be tempted to go into problem solving mode. You think, "My toddler should be talking by now" and so when they don't, you think something is wrong. You try to solve a problem that may not even be there. You think, "Men shouldn't cry" and so when they do, you now have a problem on your hands.

Try this instead: Be careful about making these kind of rules for yourself. Say instead, "It would be nice if..." and then work to make that thing happen. Look closely at your prescriptives – are they really true?

Mindreading

This is when you wrongly assume you have more information about other people's lives than you actually do. You might say, "everyone hates me" but really, you don't have some secret ability to know what they think and feel without them telling you.

Try this instead: Forget about what other people think and feel. That's their business. Look at what people do and say, and go from there. Stick to "*I* feel..." statements and make no assumptions about what others feel. If you're curious, reach out and communicate before you jump to conclusions.

Assuming omniscience

This is the bad habit of assuming that you know all the facts, can see things from all perspectives and have considered all possible causes and effects. Sometimes you can, but more often than not, individuals are only privy to more narrow understandings of complex situations. You might forget to ask yourself if there's something you're not thinking of. You might look at some complicated social interaction and jump to conclusions, forgetting that there are "two sides to the story".

Try this instead: Purposefully look for evidence that disproves the belief you have right now. Withhold making serious judgments until you know more. Abandon your own perspective for a while and try to see the situation from another perspective – you might be missing quite a lot of information!

Sunk cost thinking

This is a bit like having a problem, seeing that it's a problem, but failing to solve it because you've already had that problem for so long, so you might as well keep going. For example, it might feel easier to leave an abusive relationship that you've only been in for a year rather than one you've been in for 10 years, even though both might be very bad relationships. Likewise, you stick with a bad business plan because you spent so much money and time putting it together.

Try this instead: Remind yourself that however much time, effort or money you've put into something, it's *already gone*. Sticking with a bad plan because you're invested in it won't make it any less of a bad plan. In fact, all you're doing is making sure your problem lasts much longer than it needs to.

CHAPTER 5: THE STOIC'S RECIPE FOR GOOD LEMONADE

The ancient Roman stoics had some pretty amazing ideas about life. Their comprehensive philosophy is way more than this short chapter can do justice to, but I do want to look at one thing in particular: Marcus Aurelius' suggestions for how to solve general life problems.

I present to you here my own bastardized version. Some form of the following is probably the single most useful skill I have personally developed, and I can say that many others have found peace, clarity and a heightened sense of resilience when they think about problems in the following way.

Step One: Acknowledge that shit happens

I've been coy and called it "lemons" or "The Thing" but yes, life throws some very nasty, very unfair and very horrid things our way at times. The Stoics were ...well, stoic. They didn't see any virtue in going into denial or sulking or feeling entitled to a more comfortable life. Instead, they just started with the fact: life is hard. Adversity happens.

Step Two: Be reasonable. Leave the drama out of it

There's a place for emotions. But for the Stoics, you needed a cool, calm head when making important decisions about your life. Virtue, for them, meant a degree of control over your "passions", and a reliance instead of ethics and rationality. You might feel mad as hell that life has thrown you the curveball it has. But so what? That doesn't change the facts. That doesn't mean you can't make efforts to behave in the most rational way possible.

Step Three: Ask yourself how much control you truly have in a situation

Once your passions have cooled down, take a good gander at your problem. I like to divide every life problem into just three groups: the first is the category of things that I have absolutely zero control over. Think a freak accident, the fact that we all must die one day, or whether my crush likes me back. The second category is all those things that I have *some* control over. While I can't control having done something wrong in the past, for example, I can control whether I apologize right now and make amends. I can't control whether the other person accepts that apology, but I can control how I respond to them doing so.

Lastly, there are those things that I have complete control over. Now, there's no need to get too philosophical about any of this. Nothing is set in stone, but in my experience, one thing falls into this category again and again: your thoughts, behavior and attitudes. No matter what, you are always in control of those.

Step Four: Put your energy in the right place

Commit to only putting your energy into the second and third category of problems. Let's say my problem is that my wife has cheated on me. What category of problem is this? Well, I can't control the fact that she has. It's in the past for one thing, and for another thing, it's totally something only *she's* in control of.

Well, then what am I in control of? I have some control over whether she does it again, but that can never be 100%. Even if I forgive her and trust her to never do it again, it's still not entirely up to me. In a relationship, what happens is always the result of both parties, so this will always be the case. But my thoughts, attitudes and behaviors – these I *am* in complete control of. I can choose how to respond, what I say and what I do.

Now, because I'm mortal and don't have endless time on this earth, and because fighting against things I can't change is a waste of that time, I can choose to only focus on what I can realistically control. I stop worrying about what she will and won't do (not my business) or regretting what she has done (also, nothing I can do about it now) and instead focus on my thoughts. It doesn't really matter what I decide to do once I've rationally thought it through. It only matters that I've taken the situation and made the best of it. Of course I can feel a whole avalanche of emotions – but I don't allow these to get in the way of me making the best possible decision.

This technique sounds kind of simple, but try it the next time you encounter The Thing. It can be pretty hard to pull off when you're embroiled in some heavy emotions, feeling confused or pressed for time, believe me! But try it anyway, and see how much clearer you feel in spirit.

This little blueprint is a nifty way to rid yourself of all the "fragile thoughts" we discussed earlier, and gives you the dignity of controlling what you can ...and letting go of what you can't.

CONCLUSION

There is an African proverb that says: *"When there is no enemy within, the enemies outside can never hurt you."*

Resilience is not about being stronger than anyone else, or stronger than the adversity life throws at you. It's about being stronger than *yourself*, overcoming your own weakness and beating that "enemy within".

None of us has any control over the random and sometimes deeply unfair things that happen in life. But we have complete and absolute control over how we interpret these events, how we talk about them, how we feel about them and ultimately, what we choose to *do* about them in response.

I hope to have convinced you of a few things in this short guide:

1. Life hurts. Bad things happen. People die, relationships end and dreams are broken. This is not pessimistic or a mistake – it's just reality. The first step to being resilient is frankly acknowledging that the world isn't perfect, and life will never unfold in just the way you wish it did.

2. Once you can admit this, though, you can start to *embrace* change rather than avoid it or fear it. Change can be scary and destabilizing, or it can be an exciting opportunity to grow and evolve.

3. To be resilient, cultivate resilient thoughts. Look at your thinking and move away from those beliefs that immobilize you, leave you feeling powerless or unable to cope. Move towards thoughts and beliefs that focus on all the things you *can* do, right now, to adapt and thrive.

4. Let go of the past, and let go of anxiety for the future. Let go of unrealistic demands of the present. Lastly, let go of your own biases and distortions – all those thoughts that convince you that there is a problem to be solved when a subtle shift in focus would show you a completely different situation.

5. Develop your own, meaningful life philosophy to help you move forward with courage, humor and resilience. I've given a quick Stoic technique as an example, but go with a worldview that leaves you feeling energized and ready to flow *with* the changes of life, rather than against them.

When you change your focus and start to work deep at the level of your own thoughts and beliefs, a strange thing starts to happen: the random external world is just not that important anymore. You know who you are, you trust that you will adjust and adapt to life's challenges, and so you can take a step back.

You might even find yourself *relishing* the fact that your life doesn't always go to plan. After all, this is an opportunity to push yourself, to rise to the challenge and prove to your doubting mind that you can endure hardship, and you can flourish.

Adversity is then not something to avoid, or some unfortunate detour from real life, but life itself. Adversity can be understood not as something that cheapens life or makes it ugly, but which sweetens it and encourages the best from people. The next time the shit hits the fan, do something radical: be grateful and become immediately curious about all the amazing new things you are going to learn in trying to adapt to your new situation.

In the saying, "when life gives you lemons, make lemonade", there is no mention of what it was you were intending to make in the first place, or what you expected to be given instead of lemons.

But it doesn't matter!

Because lemonade is delicious.

HOW TO STOP WORRYING AND START LIVING - WHAT OTHER PEOPLE THINK OF ME IS NONE OF MY BUSINESS: LEARN STRESS MANAGEMENT AND HOW TO OVERCOME RELATIONSHIP JEALOUSY, SOCIAL ANXIETY AND STOP BEING INSECURE

INTRODUCTION

Stress is a lot like love – hard to define, but you know it when you feel it.

This book will explore the nature of stress and how it infiltrates every level of your life, including the physical, emotional, cognitive, relational and even spiritual.

You'll find ways to nurture resilience, rationality and relaxation in your every day life, and learn how to loosen the grip of worry and anxiety.

Through techniques that get to the heart of your unique stress response, and an exploration of how stress can affect your relationships, you'll discover how to control stress instead of letting it control you.

This book shows you how.

CHAPTER 1: WHY YOU SHOULD READ THIS BOOK

You wake up in the morning, swatting at the snooze button and cursing the start of a new day. You're utterly exhausted, already. Maybe you fight to get the kids up, get dressed, and start the daily errands. Work grinds on you, and your partner feels like he or she is drifting away from you as your connection wavers under endless niggles and arguments about money and housework. Everything you encounter irritates and exasperates you.

It seems like every day goes like this. You race from one thing to the next, wiped out at the end of it all and seemingly never done with everything you have to do. By the early afternoon, your brain is in a grey fog and you're snapping at everyone. You can't remember a time when you didn't feel cynical and bitter about life.

At night you collapse into bed, knowing that the following day, the same cycle will only start again. Maybe you lie there and worry about getting old or sick or dying, or worry that your life is slipping past you, or about your children or your marriage. Have you had your vitamins today? Paid the credit card? Fixed the leak in the sink? Fed the dog? Gone to gym? Called your mother? Sometimes, you're not even sure what you're anxious about. You only know that the world seems hostile, life seems hard and most of the time you simply feel overwhelmed.

Does this sound like you?

Stress has become so commonplace in our modern world that we are actually suspicious of people who claim not to be busy. Our lives keep filling up with more: more events, more responsibilities, more things, more people, more work. Like a bewildered rat in its wheel, we decide there's only one thing to do: *keep going.*

The consequences may not be obvious immediately, but the effects of stress, anxiety and worry are far-reaching. Wear and tear from stress can include heart disease, increased risk of cancer and even early death. Stress makes you feel awful, obviously, but it's far more serious than that. A stressed out body and mind are simply not everything they could be. Being overwhelmed cognitively means you are never really 100% available to make the best decisions for yourself. You're slower, get tired more quickly, and your memory suffers.

When you're constantly juggling feelings of stress, you're not *emotionally* available either. You're more prone to depression and pessimism, more likely to abandon projects you start and more likely to interpret things around you in a negative light. Stress also seeps into your relationships. The last thing you want to do is seek out others and be social, and this together with an irritable mood and short temper mean your closest connections become undermined.

You don't necessarily have to be a rushed-off-her-feet working mother or a CEO who's married to his high pressure job to understand how damaging stress can be to your relationships. For those of us with social anxiety, shyness or difficulties with dating, relationships with others are actually the *cause* of the stress. Low self esteem, paranoia about the judgment of others, inability to reach out to the opposite sex... Even when you manage to find someone, jealousy and insecurity sabotage your ability to relax and enjoy it. These are all just different manifestations of this strange frame of mind we call "stress".

Stress gets into your body, heart, mind and soul. Stress damages your ability to have trusting, open relationships with others. Saddest of all, stress weakens your relationship with yourself in the form of self doubt, low self confidence and bitterness. We tend to think of stress as nothing more serious than a certain tightness in the shoulders or a schedule that could be a little leaner. But stress can permeate every single area of our lives, right from the presence of stress hormones in the body's tissues to our bigger, overarching sense of who we are as human beings in this world. This book is for those of us pacing in our cages, tossing at night with heads full of doom and gloom, unable to trust those around us and the world at large. Here is a list of the ways that stress might manifest in different areas of life. If any of the following apply to you, this book was written for you.

Symptoms of Stress – The 5 Levels

Physical symptoms:
- Frequently having accidents, being clumsy and rushing
- Neck, shoulder and back tension. Muscle spasms and tension headaches
- Diarrhea or constipation, ulcers, indigestion or heartburn
- Increase or decrease in appetite; cravings for stimulants like caffeine
- Disturbed sleep, including nightmares, insomnia or oversleeping
- Changes in weight; weight gain particularly around the waist
- Low energy levels
- Acne, teeth grinding, dry skin, brittle nails, frequent infections
- Seeking out substances, addiction and self medication

Emotional symptoms:
- Feeling overwhelmed
- Feeling sad, or like you have no hope and might as well give up
- No longer being interested in what used to excite you
- Being irritable and having a short temper
- Feeling apathetic and indifferent
- Feeling guilty and worthless
- Feeling mistrustful and suspicious of others' motivations
- Tearfulness and sensitivity to criticism

Cognitive and behavioral symptoms:

- Absentmindedness
- Procrastination and avoidance
- Being unable to properly concentrate
- Distractibility
- Feeling unorganized and unfocused, not completing projects
- Constantly negative thoughts

Relational symptoms:
- Feeling like everyone wants a piece of you
- Cynicism about relationships or family
- Loss of libido
- Low self esteem
- Shallow connections with others
- Feeling antisocial; withdrawing socially

Spiritual symptoms:
- Feeling alone in the world
- Feeling unable to summon any hope or optimism
- A crisis of faith
- A sense of purposelessness
- Feeling disconnected from others
- Feeling that life has no meaning or is chaotic

The above list is by no means exhaustive. The way stress manifests in our lives is as unique as we are and, as you can see, stress can show its face in many different ways, along any of these 5 levels. When we are in environments that are not supportive to us, when we lack the skills to adapt to challenges around us, or when we've simply expected more of ourselves than is humanly possible, we experience stress.

But this book is not just another "anti-stress" book. Here, we will not be concerned with only reducing the *symptoms* of stress. Rather, we'll try to understand exactly *what* stress is and the role it plays in our lives. We'll attempt to dig deep to really understand the real sources of our anxiety and how to take ownership of them.

Using the power of habit and several techniques for smoothing out the stressful wrinkles in our day-to-day lives, we'll move towards a real-world solution to living with less stress, more confidence and a deep spiritual resilience that will insulate you from the inevitable pressures of life.

This book will be a little different from most stress-management tools on the market today. While most stress solutions offer relief for symptoms in only one or two of these areas, this book will show you how all 5 areas are important, and a successful stress solution will touch on each of them.

By adopting a trusting, open and relaxed attitude, we'll bring something more of ourselves to relationships of all kinds. This books will take a look at dating and relationships without stress and worry, as well as ways to bring tranquility and balance into your home and family life. Again, this book is not about eradicating stress from your life forever. We'll end with a consideration of the *positive* side of negative thinking, and how we can use stress and worry to our advantage.

CHAPTER 2: WHAT STRESS/WORRY REALLY IS

Stress is a complicated phenomenon. However, it's even more complicated than most people give it credit for. To put it simply, stress is primarily a physical response to the world around us. Almost every animal experiences stress of this kind. As creatures that needed to defend themselves and their families in sometimes hostile environments, human beings have also evolved to recognize danger and remove themselves from it as quickly as possible.

Stress, in this case, is a sudden and intense state of arousal that forces an action – running away, fighting or paying very close attention to an emergency situation. Stress is our bodies' natural way of telling us that something needs to change. We perceive a danger, and our bodies alert us to get out of that situation.

But, unless you have a particularly stressful work environment, dealing with lions and snakes and other deadly animals is simply no longer a part of daily life. Modern man has not had to deal with threats to his life to quite the same degree as his ancestors. For most people today, life is blissfully free of natural disasters, warring tribes, strange diseases and animal attacks.

Our innate stress response is older than our civilization, however, and is very much with us today. In the past, the human body perceived a threat and responded by producing hormones like cortisol and adrenaline. These hormones would make it easier for the human to "fight or flight". Stress was a useful mechanism that prepared the body to stand its ground and defend itself or else hightail it and get to safety.

Anyone with High School biology will know this. But in today's world, the things that stress us are subtler, more persistent, and more psychological than a bear lurking in the bushes. These days, our bodies react to other perceived threats – the loss of a job or a spouse, for example. While these things don't directly threaten our survival, we have come to *perceive* them as if they do. Even though we don't need to run away or fight with our bare hands anymore, *our physical response is still the same*: our bodies flood with stress hormones. Understanding this evolutionary predisposition to stress helps us understand how to deal with it. Biologically, stress evolved as a physical response to the world around us. But this helpful adaptation is sometimes... not so helpful. What may have served our ancient ancestors can be more of a hindrance to us today. Consider the example of Mike:

Mike is walking down a dark alleyway at night. He hears brisk footsteps behind him. The area is known for its crime. His pulse picks up, he becomes very alert, and he stops thinking of anything else. His entire mind and body become tuned into this possible threat. He turns around and sees a stranger in the shadows who appears to be holding something in his hand. He has the thought, " I may be in danger", which is putting it pretty accurately.

He's keenly aware that if he wants to make it out of this threatening situation, he'd better use whatever he can. He scans around, looking for other people, and speeds up his pace. Where's the nearest police station? He tries to think if he has anything on him that could be used as a weapon. His heart is throbbing in his ears – if he needs to run, he'll do it. *As fast as he can.*

The footsteps continue gaining on him. He's almost running when he finally gets to a busy intersection and quickly catches a cab to get out of there as fast as he can. He relaxes a little. The adrenaline slowly drains away and he stops shaking. He even cracks a smile – he's alive! He's safe now, and gradually allows other thoughts to enter his mind again. He thinks, "That was close, but it's over now" and he's right. He berates himself for being in such an alleyway this late at night in the first place. After 10 minutes, it's as if nothing happened.

Picture another scenario. Mike arrives home after his little ordeal in the alleyway. Instead of his wife meeting him at the door as she usually does, he sees her chatting and laughing on the phone with someone. When she sees him, she quickly ends the call and comes over to say hello. There's something different about her, but he can't say what. He has the thought, "I bet she's cheating on me."

It's a thought he won't admit to, a thought he's embarrassed to have, but it makes him angry nevertheless. As he sits down for a drink and watches some TV, his heart is racing, and he has trouble thinking of anything else. Just as he did earlier that evening, he has the unconscious feeling, "I am in danger". He has an imaginary argument with her in his mind, and doesn't notice his jaw clenching and his muscles tightening. He remembers all the other "evidence" he has to support his suspicion. The thought of his wife leaving him would tear his world apart – what would he do without her? How dare she? Does she think he's an idiot? How could she do that to him? Slowly, the thoughts pump him full of adrenaline and cortisol.

Both of these situations could be described as "stressful". But unlike the alley situation, when there was clearly a point at which the danger was gone, he has no clear way to know whether this threat of his wife's infidelity is gone or not. So he never breathes a sigh of relief and thinks, "That was a close call, but it's over now." While the first wave of stress was over as soon as the threat was, the situation with his wife is a little more complicated.

He goes to bed, the stress hormones still coursing through him, the thoughts still firmly lodged in his mind. In fact, he could live years of his life like this, a constant low grade sense of threat underscoring everything. In the same way that he couldn't think of much else when he was preoccupied with his survival in the dark alley way, he couldn't reasonably think properly when his mind was trying to process the perceived threat of his wife's cheating. Cognitively, he can't rest. He *looks* just fine, but biochemically, cognitively, even spiritually, he is a being who is laboring under a very real threat. He is safe and comfortable in his middle class house, yet at a molecular level, he resembles nothing more than a caveman running for his life. It's no wonder that people who carry such burdens end up driving themselves to early heart attacks.

The mechanisms we have evolved to deal with stress are a little primitive, but they work in situations of obvious, physical danger. Modern man, however, is a social creature and not nearly as beholden to natural laws as he was before. To put it simply, we have not evolved subtle enough ways to deal with the new "dangers" we encounter every day. What good is fight or flight when we deal with people spreading gossip about us? Or when we worry about our life choices as we lay in bed at night? Mike's teeth grinding and muscle tensing do nothing to help him out of his sticky situation with his wife.

It is not simply enough to let out bodies take care of our stress response. To cope with the demands of our culturally complex society, we need a more deliberate and more conscious way of dealing with stress. In fact, it is often our inbuilt biological mechanisms that betray us the most: the responses we have evolved over millennia are simply no match for the social landscape we find ourselves in.

The way we process stress may start out in the biological realm, but it quickly becomes more complex than that. Our physical stress response radiates out into the realm of the emotional and the cognitive, poisoning our ability to connect with others and, at the broadest level, even altering our spiritual being.

The difference between us and ancient man is that we possess a heightened consciousness and the ability to make choices about how we behave. We can become aware of our thoughts and habits, and in doing so, we can decide what thoughts to nurture and which to abandon. What follows is a conscious look at every level in which stress can have an effect.

We'll begin with a look at techniques to tame our fight or flight response, i.e. the *physical* symptoms of stress. Next, we'll explore how our thoughts can affect the way we experience stress, and look at ways to incorporate more healthful thoughts and habits into our daily life. Then, we'll look at how these thoughts are also interconnected with the way we interact emotionally with others, whether in dating or with our families.

Lastly, we'll consider the bigger, spiritual picture of stress and try to construct our own personalized "stress map".

CHAPTER 3: THE PHYSICAL LEVEL: RELIEF FROM THE PHYSICAL SYMPTOMS OF STRESS

To begin, you might want to know of ways that can reliably reduce your feelings of stress and worry, *right now.*

Sometimes, when insomnia feels like it's eating you alive, all you want is quick relief. Stress at this level looks like irritability, headaches and sore muscles. Here are some techniques that will help you soothe the first, physical level of stress that we all experience from time to time.

Progressive Muscle Relaxation:

People aren't entirely sure why, but it seems that muscles are able to go into a deeper state of relaxation when they try to relax after first tensing up a little. You can use this to your advantage with this simple method that relaxes each and every muscle and tissue in your body. Practiced once a day, progressive muscle relaxation can be a huge help for chronic pain, insomnia and general feelings of tension.

Find a quiet, comfortable place where you won't be disturbed for at least half an hour. You could also try this at bed time as you drift off to sleep. Lay down and let all your limbs hang loose. Close your eyes and take a few minutes to find your breath and slow it down, taking in fresh oxygen and slowly releasing it again.

Start at your feet and focus on the many muscles there. Become aware of them, and give each a good squeeze as you tense up the muscles in your toes or arch your feet. Really stretch and enjoy the intense feeling, holding for a few seconds.

Then, very, very slowly, let all of that tension go again. Feel your muscles loosening and expanding, and try to draw out the sensation of letting everything go. If you like, do the process again, or move onto the next body part. Travel up and tense/relax your legs, back muscles and arms. Take your time. Finish off with more deep breathing – if you're still awake, that is...

Guided imagery:

Start in much the same way as you did for the previous exercise, although you can also sit, if you prefer.

Close your eyes and let your mind wander. Breathe deeply and slowly. Think of a place - any place. Choose a special place that can be, from now on, your "sanctuary". You may choose an isolated desert, a beautiful woodland forest or the top of a fantasy castle. It doesn't matter, it's your sanctuary, so make sure it's a place that really resonates with you.

Now take your time to explore and flesh out this world. Engage all your senses as you imagine every tiniest detail. How does it smell? Feel? What can you hear? What can you see? Picture it all, and linger on the details. This is crucial. When you have painted a full and rich picture of this sanctuary, go further inward and summon up a calm, happy emotion. Dwell on your feelings of peace and bliss, and link these feelings with the new place you've built for yourself. Tell your unconscious mind that you can come here whenever you are stressed and overwhelmed.

The next time you are feeling frazzled and irritable, take a few moments out of your day to pay a visit to your special place. Just close your eyes and devote the next few minutes to reminding yourself of all the lovely, tranquil things you found there before. No matter how busy or anxious you feel, rest in the knowledge that this place is always there, and accessible with just a few breaths.

Other stress relief tips:

- Take up yoga, tai chi, gardening, hiking or any other gentle physical exercise that gets you out of your head.
- Consider doing something creative or non verbal, such as sketching, pottery or even cooking.
- Get a pet – there are studies supporting the fact that they help reduce stress levels.
- Learn to delegate. If you have too little time to do everything you need to in a day, seriously consider if you should hire some extra help or assign tasks to family or co-workers.
- Look into meditation. This is another area with a lot of scientific studies to back it up. You can do this either alone or with a group, and try to build moments of mindfulness into your schedule. Many people find Zen Buddhist literature or other spiritual principles very grounding in their journey out of stressful living.
- Vow to give up multitasking.
- Watch your diet: processed foods, alcohol, caffeine, too little water, excess sugar or too much refined carbohydrate in your diet can disrupt your mood and make it more difficult to relax and unwind.
- Speak to your doctor about a natural or mild anxiety medication – St. John's Wort has been shown in clinical trials to reduce feelings of anxiety.
- Exercise – another area with strong evidence behind it. The endorphins and sense of accomplishment are some of the best antidotes to stress.
- Give yourself breaks – and defend those breaks. So many people let work or obligations creep into their down time. Section off parts of your schedule where you don't work or fuss with other commitments. Don't let *anything* disturb that time.

CHAPTER 4: THE COGNITIVE AND EMOTIONAL LEVEL: WHAT YOU ARE (REALLY) STRESSED ABOUT, OR, HOW TO TAKE A "STRESS READING"

Now that you have a few techniques for managing the physical side of your stress response, you can pay attention to the other levels.

You may have found that no matter how much you relax your muscles, stressful thoughts can easily undo all your hard work and leave you tense and wound up again.

Imagine that stress is a kind of instrument that gives you readings about the way your body, mind and spirit are functioning. High stress, or a needle dangerously hovering into the red zone on your instrument, is not a problem in itself. It's only a *symptom* of a problem. Take sedatives, distract yourself or try to "relax" and you could coax the reading to go down a bit, but eventually, your little stress meter is going to start complaining again. The next step to taking control of the stress in your life is to learn to start respecting your body's stress alerts.

For a few days, devote a small journal to observing and recording your stress levels. For the first 3 or 4 days, try merely putting a number on the stress you feel. You could also just do what seems natural to you – you may choose to use a scale from one to ten, you may choose to map your change in stress with colors, or a diagram of a thermometer slowly rising. If you're feeling creative, you can also choose a symbol or picture to represent your stress levels.

Take a "stress reading" whenever you can manage, throughout the day. Do it first thing when you wake up and just before you go to bed. When you move from one activity or event to another, take a moment to note your stress levels and jot them down. After meals, after particular conversations or at specific times of day, you may notice patterns emerging. Resist the urge to make anything of these patterns for now, simply take faithful recordings and be curious about how you are experiencing stress as the day progresses.

Once you have a few days worth of data, start to add to this by taking fewer, but more detailed "readings". As much as you can, try to identify the *thought* that preceded the moment you took your reading. For example, you take a reading at 16:00 and rate your stress as 5/10. You're thinking, "There's never any time for anything." You note this down. Your kids come home at 16:35, and you take another reading, this one rating stress at 8/10. Your thought immediately preceding is "There's no way I can ever keep up with this." Your last reading for the day is after dinner, at 18:50, with stress at a full 10/10 and the thought, "I have failed, again."

For now, this is just data. Try not to judge the thoughts you put down, and try not to think about any of it too closely. What's important is that you are honest – there is no "right" way to do it. It's also important that your thought statements are as accurate as possible. To identify an accurate thought statement, choose a thought that you feel a strong emotional attachment to. "I'm stressed" is often implied, but try to be more detailed. What does stress mean, in that particular moment? Your underlying emotion may be one of anger, hopelessness or cynicism. Try to nail down this emotion in a thought, and write it down.

What's the point of doing all this?

Well, as we've seen, "stress" is a simple word used to describe a very complicated phenomenon. What is stressful for one could be exciting and motivating for another. Nobody experiences the world quite the same way as you do. And it's no use to try and tackle a problem that you don't have a clear understanding of.

By taking a few "stress readings" of our unique responses, we can get a better grasp of what thoughts are operating underneath our physical and emotional reactions. Our emotions, our bodies and our thoughts are all connected, and a change in one produces a change in the other. By identifying our thoughts, we also make the first step in changing them.

You may discover, after a few weeks of listening to what stress is telling you, that there seem to be some themes. In the above example, it may come up again and again that stress is tied to feelings of low self worth. The thoughts may go something along the lines of, "I am no good and I can't deal with all the things I have to do every day. Eventually, I'm going to mess up, and it's going to turn out bad when I do."

The underlying emotion here is one of shame and doubt. Such a person could look at all the things "causing" the stress and try to fix them: send the kids to daycare, take sedative medication, and choose to tell themselves over and over again to "just relax." But none of this will have much effect if they don't address the root of the problem: the thoughts and the emotions attached to them. Until the problem of low self worth is also addressed, stress will keep popping up like a weed.

So, you've gathered some information about yourself and how your mind and heart work. The next step to getting a handle on stress is to accept responsibility for the thoughts that are maintaining that stress. Sure, there may be forces out there in the world that you cannot control, but becoming a strong and resilient person requires you to own your part in perpetuating stress in your life. To change the thoughts you have identified takes courage and a willingness to do something different. If a particular thought has been with you for a long time, it will be hard at first to moderate it. But try anyway.

Your goal in this next exercise is not to identify things or people out in the world who are stressing you. It's to identify your unique response to those things and people. Often with people who are battling stress in their lives, the thoughts they have are not always accurate or healthful. The thought, "I am a failure and I'll never be able to cope" is simply not true. But when you accept it as true, it becomes the source of your stress.

At the end of a few weeks of recording data in this way, you should have a fair idea of the main thought statements that accompany stress in your life. You will start to see recurrent themes. Look at some of the following underlying thoughts and see if you can identify yourself in any of them. These are pretty common themes, but you may have thoughts and feelings very different from these.

- This is not the way the world ought to be (feeling indignant, rage, irritability)
- I have to do X to be loved or to be happy (fear and panic, low self worth)
- Nothing ever works out for me (sadness, hopelessness)
- If I don't do X, something bad will happen (guilt, worry, suspicion)

Your statements may differ, but thoughts of this kind can be recognized easily: they use words like "have to", "should" and "must", or other strong and absolute terms like "never" and "always". Look for statements in the form of conditionals ("If, then" statements) or ones that sound like rules. Statements that talk about "everything" or "nothing" are often thought statements that produce stress, as are statements about "everybody" and "nobody."

Once you have identified your key stress thoughts, write them down again. You may have one or two or a whole handful. We'll be using these statements in the next chapter, where we'll look at ways to start reworking them, unraveling stress from the root up.

Technique One: Challenging

The four example stress statements in the previous chapter are bound to lead to stress. When you fight with reality, the result is always stress and depression. But stressful thoughts only have power over us if we believe in them. If you told a child every day of his life that he was stupid, he'd likely believe it after a while. You are no different. You start to take the things you tell yourself often as absolute gospel. Or to quote Ralph Waldo Emerson: "We become what we think about all day long".

Instead, get into the habit of challenging yourself. Now that you have identified the thoughts that are holding the entire stress response together, have your ears pricked for when you notice those thoughts coming up. And when they do, be ready with a counter-thought. You don't even have to believe it at first, but argue with yourself anyway. For example, if your thought is "I can't do this", counter it with a more balanced, moderate thought. For example, when you catch yourself thinking this, immediately tell yourself, "This is difficult, but I will manage."

The goal is not to go into denial or tell yourself ridiculous stories. Merely moderating the statement is all you need – but make it realistic. So, instead of, "Life sucks", your thought could be, "Life is certainly a challenge!" or even "*Today*, life sucks." Change "always" statements to "sometimes". Ask, is your statement strictly true? There may be the odd time when it is true – but the point is to start getting used to double checking these thoughts that you have become accustomed to assuming are true.

This may seem facile on its surface – how could telling yourself a story change how much life sucks that day? The thing is, in time, your brain will begin to believe you. You will get into the habit of challenging yourself, refusing to accept statements that are overly negative and anxious. Remember, life is all about perception.

Technique Two: Do an Accounting

You may know the feeling: your brain keeps on returning to the same image, the same idea. You wake up with it already in your head. You try not to stress about it, but before you know it, your head is going like a hamster in a wheel again. For some, it may work to distract themselves, to think of "nothing", but an anxious person's mind needs to do *something*. Always something.

Instead, sit down with a piece of paper, and draw three columns. The first column should be labeled, "Things I can control", the second column, "Things I can control to some extent" and the third column, "Things I can't control."

Now, take whatever is in your head and dump it out onto the paper. Be honest and realistic. Pretend you are a little computer sorting through every thought and feeling in your head, one by one. What is stressing you out? You may have the thought, "I'm sick of trying to keep up with the housework." You spend time each day cleaning up yet feel your surroundings are always dirty. The more you clean, the more you need to clean. You want to scream and run away, maybe live in a hole in the ground you're so fed up.

Which column can you put "Too much housework" under? This will depend on your unique situation. If it's not your house and you're only staying there temporarily, put it in the last column. If you can afford a cleaner to help once or twice a week, put it in the first. If it's somewhere in between, put it in the middle column.

Be careful though, and watch your bias. Let's say you have an item, "My wife doesn't love me anymore". Where should it go? First of all, this item could be phrased better. You probably don't know this for sure (if you do, well, into the last column it goes). You cannot change how somebody else feels about you, although you can change what *you* feel about *them*. A better way to state it would be, "I am in a marriage where I don't feel loved." This can fit into either of the first two columns. When the problem is framed this way, you are open to realistic solutions. You could leave your marriage, you could seek counseling, you could do any number of things to improve the marriage or your perception of it.

Once you've gotten everything you can think of down on paper, have a good look at it. Take the last column: are there any items here that, if rephrased, can be put into other columns? Remember you are not bending reality, just reframing things. Be curious. "My dog died" certainly belongs in the last column. You can't do a thing about a dead dog. But, if reworded, the statement can also become, "I am grieving for my dog", which could go in the second column. There are many different ways to grieve, and you absolutely have *some* control over how you choose to do it.

Some things we really can't do much about, and that's to be expected. Cancer, losing a job, being born in a particular country, spilling that milk – leave these in the last column. Include here other people's opinions and behavior. You can change your response to them, but if someone doesn't love you, for instance, that's the end of it. If someone has behaved badly toward you, if you've suffered an accident or you're worried about what the weather will be like tomorrow, there's not much you can do about it. It goes in the third column.

Next: tear this column off the rest of the page. If you have a flair for the dramatic, burn it, throw it away or do whatever you need to tell yourself – *this can't be changed*. If it can't be changed, you only damage yourself by stressing about it. Catch yourself thinking about something from the third column? Stop – you already gave it all the thought that's ever going to be necessary.

Now turn to the other two columns. Start with the first column and choose just one item that you have control over. Make just one goal to address this problem. "There is too much housework" can have many possible goals, from hiring outside help, getting family to pull their weight, finding more efficient ways to clean the house, coming to terms with living in filth or moving to a smaller, easier to clean house. If you find yourself stressing about the third column you threw away, come back to the first two columns again and remind yourself: there are things you can change, there are you things you can't. Life is short. Save your energy only for the things you have a realistic chance of changing.

Items in the second column are trickier and can be dealt with once you've handled the more obvious ones. Things like, "People at work don't seem to like me", "I find calculus really hard" and "I'm addicted to heroin" can all be improved, but definitely have some elements that are *somewhat* out of your control. The trick is to slowly start filtering things into the first column. Break knotty items into pieces.

For example, "People at work don't seem to like me" can be separated into, "It's difficult for me to make friends" and "I don't have much in common with my colleagues", for example. The first can definitely be helped, but the second must be put into the last column and accepted – there's no point in stressing over what others have or do not have in common with you. Put your overactive mind to work on the things that have the best chance of changing. Instead of allowing things you can't help to stress you, tune your mind into what can be helped.

Technique Three: Reorient to the Positive

Challenging your thoughts is one thing. But nothing challenges negative thinking as well as cold, hard evidence. If you are fond of telling yourself, "I can't cope with this", try to remember all the times where you, contrary to your belief, actually *did* cope. An anxious mind can gloss over information that doesn't confirm its doom and gloom model of the universe. You may be tempted to say, "Nope, I can't think of anything", but try to cast your mind back to a time when you didn't stress about what you're stressing about now.

Don't get pessimistic about it – *everyone* has had a moment of bliss and peacefulness, a moment when they felt happy and safe and loved, maybe bursting with creativity, maybe immersed in their environment, deep in the flow of things. Put yourself back in that position. Remember it. Ask your mind to acknowledge: there were times when life was different.

It can be hard to envision a future that is better than the present, especially when we are struggling. It's much easier to look to the past and realize that things *do* change, that somewhere, somehow, you knew how to live without stress. Somewhere along the line, you didn't have the problem you have now. When we open our minds up to different possibilities, when we accept that we are living only one possible way out of many ways to live, we become receptive to solutions that we may not have perceived in our stressed out rut.

If you like, try making a list of all your achievements and make a habit of reading through them, to keep a healthy perspective. Take clues from how you have coped with stress in the past. For example, if you remember that physical activity has helped in the past, see how you can incorporate more physical activity in your life, now.

Technique Four: Learn to Metabolize Negative Feelings

The difference between resilient people and people who crumble under stress is not the amount of stress they experience, but the way they respond to stress when it happens. When you begin to think of stress and adversity as something that is inevitable, even something to embrace, you strengthen yourself against it. You realize quickly what problems are "third column problems" and just get over it.

Rather than forcing yourself to be relentlessly optimistic all the time, simply let your thoughts come. Accept them. Ask yourself, what's the worst that could happen? "My wife could leave me." Ok, really let that settle in. You'd lose your wife, you'd be devastated. And so? People get divorced and go on to live happy and successful lives every day. In fact, for some people, divorce is the best thing that's ever happened to them.

Is it the end of the world? It's tough, sure, but is it *that* terrible? Worriers are prone to catastrophizing and imagining the worst possible outcome. So, indulge yourself. Don't be afraid of the negative emotion your stress is covering. Follow things through to their natural, most disastrous conclusion. Maybe you're worried about messing up your oral presentation, losing your job and becoming the laughing stock of your company. Maybe, it gets as bad as it could possibly get. *So what?* You become a laughing stock, life goes on, you go on.

When we learn to dwell with negative emotions, to endure shame and doubt and rejection and anger, they lose some of their power over us. Many people – in fact some of the world's most successful people – started their success stories only after everything else completely fell to pieces. Human resilience is a real marvel. Yes, your entire life may end today, the things you are worried about may actually happen, and they may be absolutely terrifying. But again, so what?

On the other side of disaster, life goes on. A sense of humor will help more than any empty positive thinking platitude.

CHAPTER 6: THE RELATIONAL AND SPIRITUAL LEVEL: ANXIETY FREE DATING AND RELATIONSHIPS

The previous section looked at some possible ways to counter and reframe "stress thoughts", so that we can transform our nervous and anxious energy to a more realistic way of tackling our problems.

You may be tempted to skip this section if you are already in a happy relationship or aren't concerned with dating at this moment. But keep reading - "dating" may seem like a very specific area to focus our attention on, but actually, the way we interact with others is a key part of the topic of stress and learning to live with less of it.

To put it simply, our relationships with others are reflections of our relationship with ourselves and with the world in general. Nowhere is it more obvious how a change in mindset can change the entire tone of our living, than with dating and relationships. When we encounter others, we make ourselves vulnerable, we put our self esteem to the test, we take a risk and trust someone else with our hearts and minds. If you are one of those people tormented by your lack of "social skills", insecurity or jealousy, then a look at the role that stressful thinking plays in your relationships may be helpful.

Learning to Trust

When we first come into the world, we are naive and completely trusting. We are the most vulnerable, physically and psychologically, that we will ever be. Yet we willingly go into the arms of strangers, waddle into new and possibly dangerous situations and put any old thing into our mouths. Somewhere along the line, we develop more caution. We realize that not everything is to be trusted, and we narrow our range, trusting only those that earn that trust.

At the root of much anxiety and worry is a lack of trust. Anxiety is future oriented and its core premise is that in the future, someone or something may harm you. The response is to be vigilant, to try to prevent that harm from happening. Whether we lack trust in other people, in the world around us or even in ourselves, this orientation is simply exhausting.

Lack of Trust in Others

Fear of rejection, shyness and being withdrawn are the result of looking at the possibility of interaction with others, and overestimating the harm they could possibly bring to you. In other words, it's the absence of trust that people are fundamentally good and will treat you well. This feeling could stem from your family of origin, where you may have been taught that people never tell the truth or will hurt you if given half the chance.

In the dating realm, this manifests as the belief that almost everyone is out to get you, cynicism about the opposite sex and a tendency to interpret every behavior as proof that nobody could ever be trusted to give you what you really need. Sadly, stress that results from this can never be soothed – you have no control over how people treat you, and when you are withdrawn and unwilling to open up, the paradox is that people are less likely to trust *you*.

Lack of Trust in the World

This reflects a bigger picture – that in the world at large, we don't feel safe and cared for. We don't trust that the universe is basically a safe and reasonable place to inhabit. If we believe that most people are not to be trusted as sources of love and support, we can begin to think of the entire world that way. We sigh and succumb to "dog eat dog" laws, we think that if something can go wrong, it will. We become fatalistic in our interactions with others. We see the opposite sex as nothing more than extensions of this unfriendly world, ready to inflict more damage onto us. In other words, intimacy is something that needs to be defended against. Whether you've decided to shun people all together and live as a "self-sufficient" hermit, or whether you've latched onto hate for another group as the source of all your difficulties, a mistrustful attitude to the world hurts *you* the most.

Lack of Trust in Ourselves

Self confidence is trust in your own abilities. It is a feeling of being safe in your own competence as a human being. You may not know what the future holds, but a strong self esteem assures you that you act from you principles, and will probably be OK. Lacking trust in ourselves leads to insecurity. It is the doubt that we have any power over how our lives pan out. It is the disbelief in our own competence, our own goodness, and our own process. We may defer judgment to others simply because we don't believe we can be trusted to make good decisions ourselves. We may become dependent, choosing to forfeit our agency and believe that in general, we are helpless and hopeless.

We can see that with Mike, the man we met earlier, the details of his wife's possible infidelity are only one side of the story. Mike may have, on closer inspection, a problem with trust in general. He can't surrender to the idea that his wife will not harm him, he can't believe that the world is not hostile, not unfriendly, and worst of all, he doesn't trust that he himself is lovable enough to win his wife's continued affection. What removes Mike from him wife is not her infidelity, but Mike's own thoughts and beliefs.

On the surface, what looks like a fairly superficial first date, or a "lover's quarrel", for instance, can actually press deep anxiety buttons within us, can bring out our most fundamental beliefs about ourselves and the world, and get directly to the heart of the way we are oriented to the outside world. Relationships are stressful!

But if we put our guard up, we deny ourselves the opportunity to connect deeply with others. If we are unwilling to open up and accept the risk of pain, we are left with empty or hollow connections that don't truly satisfy us. We are unable and unwilling to metabolize negative feelings. If we lack a basic trust in ourselves, the situation is worse – we don't believe we can hold onto love even when we have it; we become jealous, dependent, suspicious.

On a deeper spiritual level, Mike is fixed in this position of mistrust. From this, the thought "she is probably cheating on me" goes unchallenged. The longer it is held onto, the more it is assumed to be truth. The idea that his wife would leave is unthinkable, and causes him great pain. These thoughts and emotions affect his physical body as much as if he had actually been attacked in the alley that night. The stress trickles down and affects each and every area of his being.

In reality, even if his wife were to leave, it may be the case that this is a good outcome, and one that he actually needs. But he is unwilling to accept and manage this "negative" emotion. He chooses not to listen to what his anxiety is telling him. He incorrectly assumes the source of his trouble is his wife, when in fact his thoughts about his wife are to blame. He tries to control her, but nothing she can do will ease his suspicions. He tries to dull his stress with substances. He forces himself to ignore it. At this point, whether his wife is or is not unfaithful is scarcely the point. What is problematic is that Mike lacks trust in himself, in others and in the world he lives in.

In the bigger picture, he doesn't trust the process he is in.

At its most basic, stress removes us from reality. Stress is future oriented, and forces our minds to live in places of "what if" rather than an appreciation for what is, right now, in the moment.

In some cases, stress is just the thing we need to kick us into gear and meet that deadline, stand up for ourselves or leave a situation that isn't working. Stress is a biological and psychological phenomenon, but it also entails a deeper, even spiritual dimension. For most people today, stress is a complicated interplay of body, mind and soul.

Stress is not something that can be fixed with tips, tricks and hacks. It is a problem with our perception of reality; it is a mistake in appraisal of the universe around us. Stress can be (temporarily) eased by managing the purely biological or cognitive dimension. But stress is, at the deepest level, a philosophical orientation and a way of thinking about the world.

To ease stress in our lives, we need to approach every aspect of the problem.

You may take a long, honest look at your life and begin to identify what is really going on, and what is really at the heart of this deceptively simple problem we call "stress". Here's an example of a "stress map" that may emerge as you start to incorporate some of these techniques and ideas into your life. This one is for the hypothetical Mike:

Physically:
Mike realizes his caffeine addiction is propping him up and damaging his cortisol levels. He quits coffee and takes up a daily breathing exercise to ensure that he is breathing deeply and slowly, something he usually forgets about when caught up in his thoughts. He chooses to actively notice when he's clenching his teeth or tightening his muscles and makes a point of having "time out" sessions to remember his breath and become mindful again.

Emotionally:
He notices how strongly tied his physical reactions are to his emotional states. Behind a lot of his suspicion and fearfulness is the underlying feeling of being small and ineffectual. He constantly feels under threat. In time, he understands this stems from being raised by parents who were inconsistent with their affection. He feels as though sooner or later, people are going to realize how terrible he is, and stop loving him. He tries to notice when he worries about rejection and actively chooses to let it go. He is stressed because he is constantly processing the thought: "I am inferior". To combat

this, he takes up martial arts and cultivates an attitude of competence and mastery over himself.

Cognitively:

To help him deal with these feelings he has, he realizes he has developed thoughts to explain this shame to himself. He tells himself, over and over and over again, "I need to be vigilant, I need to keep up or I will be a failure, I need to win people's love and be on the look out for any sign that they are going to withdraw it". These are repeated so often that the brain starts to perceive them as truth. Instead, he teaches himself to challenge these thoughts when they pop up. The more rational perspective is that he cannot change other people's behavior, only his own. He turns his attention away from stewing over his wife, and creates more opportunities for himself that prove that he is basically a good and lovable person.

Relationally:

He craves, almost more than anything, the love and acceptance of women, but at the same time he's keenly aware that they are just another thing on the list to be managed, another source of rejection. He distrusts most women, and when this shuts him out of meaningful connections with them, he takes this as evidence that they couldn't be trusted. And so his feelings of isolation deepen. With his wife, he cannot believe that she truly loves him – how could anyone love him? She must be lying. Here, Mike makes more of an effort to befriend women in casual settings.

Spiritually:

It feels as though it's him against the world. He's apathetic, anxious and mistrustful. Deep down, he believes the world is fundamentally hostile. He doesn't have the feeling that life can be left alone to carry on. So, he stresses about it. What's the meaning of it all? He grows cynical and has no faith that he is a part of something bigger, something that he can relax inside of. He starts keeping a journal and becomes reacquainted with his desire for a simpler, humbler life. He finds spiritual comfort in his martial arts practice, a minimalistic lifestyle, and begins to let in the thought that he has a purpose in life, and can surrender to the unknown and the mystery of his fate.

Mike will not be successful in reducing stress levels by taking medication (a physical solution) or consulting a psychologist to get to the root of his self-defeating thoughts (a cognitive solution) or arranging a romantic getaway with his wife (a relational solution). He could go to church or burn sage and meditate, but it will mean nothing if every other area is business as usual. His solution has to be comprehensive, and address each level.

What is *your* personal stress map?

On each of these axes, where are you now? A solution will acknowledge all of these areas, and the best solutions will link into one another. The person feeling overwhelmed with work could decide to exercise more, which will give her more confidence which will affect her sense of trust in herself. Exercising could combat the persistent thought "I can't cope with anything" - evidence of a completed marathon will definitely shift this belief.

A firmer sense of self esteem translates to healthier boundaries and expectations with other people: she may decide she is strong enough to let her guard down, and when she does, she is pleasantly surprised to learn: other people are not the cause of her stress.

Perhaps the world is not such a dark and hostile place as she thought?

Instead of neurotically stewing over what could possibly happen in the future, she becomes an active agent who has faith in her ability to change it.

What to do about the excess housework will flow naturally from this understanding.

CHAPTER 8: THE BLESSINGS OF NEGATIVE THINKING

Our positive thinking, self-help obsessed society treats stress as the common cold of the psychological world – something that everyone has, something that nobody wants. We are encouraged to do whatever we can to get rid of it.

This attitude, however, is seldom productive. Stress is not merely something that sits on top of our lives and merely needs to be taken off to reveal the tranquility underneath. Stress is a *part* of us, and indicates that something, somewhere is wrong.

Stress is a blessing in disguise that alerts us to exactly the areas that need our attention. Insomnia is not a disease that deserves a heavy sleeping tablet or alcohol, but rather proof that even if we don't understand it at the moment, our minds and spirits are working hard at fixing whatever is out of whack.

Successful people who live stress free may disappoint others who look closely at what their lives actually entail: they have exactly the same amount of stress and adversity as everyone else. They may do nothing special. But underneath is a radically different way of perceiving themselves and their worlds. If you have sought out this book and read this far, it means your instinct for growth and well-being is intact. Congratulations!

Now, what are you going to do about it?

CONCLUSION

Once you're equipped with a deeper appreciation of *why* you stress, you're in the best position to move forward in your task of reducing stress in your life – forever.

As we've seen, the multifaceted nature of stress means it needs a multifaceted solution. While meditation, supplements or a visit to a life-coach are all valuable, they are not always enough to combat stress on their own.

Instead, stress needs to be respected as the warning flag it is, and an approach that acknowledges your body, your mind, your heart and soul is going to be much more lasting and effective than a Band-Aid solution like sedative medication or "productivity hacks".

Fortunately/unfortunately, you are the only one who can truly make changes in the way you experience your life. So much of what is aimed at stress reduction fails, even if it's good advice, because people are afraid or unwilling to face up to the challenges that are keeping them locked in a cage of anxiety, self-doubt and stress.

Stress can leave us feeling helpless in a chaotic and unfriendly world. The antidote is learning to trust yourself again, and gradually taking the risks to make changes in your daily habits and the way you interact with other people. Anxiety is about a loss of control, a loss of faith and a rupture in the connection between us and others.

If you have found anything that resonates with you in this book, challenge yourself to make some changes – *now*. Not tomorrow or at some ill-defined point in the future. Become curious about yourself as you construct your own personalized "stress map" and begin keeping a journal of your thoughts. Be receptive to change and trust that you have it in you to become more relaxed, more confident and surer of your day-to-day life.

Such a stress-free person is able to face adversity head on, and knows in their heart of hearts that they will never be ruffled for long. A person who is in control of their lives is not damaged or frightened by stress, and even when it arises, they are able to engage with it and even be thankful for the lessons it can teach them about how to be better. In other words, they are robust and resilient because their sense of faith in themselves allows them to approach the world openly, with curiosity instead of fear.

Have faith that in time, *you* can become that person.

MINDFUL EATING - A HEALTHY, BALANCED AND COMPASSIONATE WAY TO STOP OVEREATING, HOW TO LOSE WEIGHT AND GET A REAL TASTE OF LIFE BY EATING MINDFULLY

INTRODUCTION

What are you hungry for - *really*?

You may have been drawn to the idea of mindful eating as an antidote to the empty promises of the diet industry, or you may have felt that it's time to pursue a more purposeful, more compassionate way of eating.

Whatever your reasons and whatever your current relationship to food and your body is, this book can help you reconsider your eating habits and whether they are truly serving your highest good.

Through an exploration of the real reasons we overeat, our thoughts and feelings around food, and coming into closer contact with our own *true* appetites, this book aims to help you craft an open and accepting attitude towards food.

CHAPTER 1: WHAT THIS BOOK IS ABOUT

You sit down to lunch with a friend one Friday afternoon and decide to order a big meal and coffee. The menu looks so good and you're in the mood for celebrating, so why not? As your friend natters on and on you tuck in, and before you know it, your cheeseburger and fries are gone, yet you scarcely remember eating them.

You feel a bit bad about scoffing it down so quickly, and penalize yourself mentally for having so little willpower. You decide that you'll just skip breakfast tomorrow to atone for it. But if you've already gone this far... why not just have a dessert while you're at it? You've already shattered your illusions of being controlled and disciplined. Plus, your friend is having one.

You get home that evening and feel a little down. You remind yourself that you are not allowed to eat until tomorrow. But then what else are you going to do? One hour and much guilt later, you've polished off some leftovers, two sandwiches and a bag of cookies your mom gave you. How did that even happen?

Maybe you have felt this sense of being out of control before. Perhaps you have eaten something and immediately thought, *why did I eat that? I didn't even enjoy it!* Perhaps you eat things that you know damage your body or make you gain weight. If that is the case, you may be a so-called "emotional eater".

This book is for you.

Mindful eating is an attitude towards food (and much more) that encourages awareness, deliberate action and an open acceptance of the present moment as it unfolds around us.

In this book, we'll look at how the conventional dieting mindset is actually damaging and counterproductive, and how mindful eating can be a refreshing break away from all the expectations that you have about yourself and food that are not serving you. The ultimate goal is to become exquisitely tuned in to your own appetites, desires and passions, and to tune out the noise and clutter from the outside world that muffle your innate intuition about what is good for you and what isn't.

When we understand our true hunger, when we realize the psychological, emotional, behavioral, physical and even spiritual causes behind our overeating, only then can we can start to take realistic steps to remedy it.

CHAPTER 2: MINDFUL EATING VS. MINDLESS EATING

Mindfulness is a concept gaining in popularity in recent times and talked of as a cure to every kind of problem, from stress to workplace conflict to parenting dilemmas.

At its core, though, mindfulness is a startlingly simple concept: to be mindful is to be aware of the present moment as it unfolds around you.

So much of what ails modern man can be remedied by a more focused awareness of the self and how it interacts with the environment. Being alert to more possibilities as they appear around us means we can make better choices, whether those choices are how to speak to your colleague, how to respond to a life crisis or merely what to have for lunch.

When we become aware, too, of our *internal* worlds, we understand ourselves better and become more resilient in the face of uncertainty. Slowing down to become keenly perceptive of your actions, thoughts, emotions and physical responses makes you more alive to the flow of each moment. When you act consciously, your actions are deliberate and purposeful instead of haphazard and reactive.

Unfortunately, even for self-aware and well-intentioned people, the arena of eating is often fraught with mindlessness, conflict and confusion. The simple act of taking in nourishment to power the body for life becomes a problem big enough to necessitate a global dieting industry. Pharmaceutical companies spending billions of dollars on obesity research and increasing numbers of people are battling eating disorders, diabetes or obesity.

It would be easy to assume that all this attention counts as mindfulness. Many people, after all, spend a good portion of their waking lives ruminating over their next meals, counting calories, weighing themselves, throwing their hopes and dreams into some new eating fad or just silently hating their bodies day in and day out. But this book will show later on that mindfulness is different from anxiety or neuroticism.

This book will also begin the same way that every other diet book begins: *with the premise that diets don't work.*

One would need a book a hundred times the size of this one to look at all the various ways people have tried to manage their weight, to look better, to feel better. There are low carb and low fat and low GI and low inflammation and vegetarian and Paleo and raw food diets. Diets that restrict what food you can eat, or when you can eat it, or in what quantity. It goes on and on.

One diet asks people to pray to a higher power for strength when the cravings hit, the other that they require a special tea; some staple closed their stomachs or wire closed their jaws to discourage eating, others will only have organic food, or local food, or only liquids, or foods that are gluten free.

If you open a diet book, within the first few pages you will discover some rules and regulations. The forbidden foods may be presented on the AVOID side, and you will be permitted to eat a few other things in abundance. What follows then is usually some sort of medical legitimizing, and a defense for why this *particular* way of eating is superior to all others. Typically some food is demonized – gluten, meat, full fat dairy, whatever – and you are urged to resist caving and eating these things.

You may start such a diet filled with vigor and determination. You decide you'll have the will and the moral determination to finally get rid of those disgusting extra kilos. But whether it's two days or two months later, temptation gets the best of you and you eat an "illegal" food and feel pretty awful about it. Maybe you take some corrective action to make up for it, or maybe you silently internalize the idea: *food is a kind of combat, some foods are bad and you are bad if you eat them.*

You bemoan the fact that everything delicious is bad for you. You feel tired and disillusioned. You start to feel like you deserve a treat for all your "hard work". Then one day, when you've had a particular rough week, you find yourself almost robotically binging on something you shouldn't be. Sound familiar?

Mindless eating is being unaware of ourselves in the present moment. It's about letting habit and familiarity take over our lives instead of asking ourselves routinely, am I hungry? What do I want right now? In the modern world, food is abundant, and we've all had the experience of scoffing down something and thinking afterwards, why did I just eat that?

The answer is that we were not mindful.

Eating when you have no appetite, eating when you are bored or sad or angry, eating because it's simply that time of the day (or month) when you're supposed to eat, eating because you want to reward yourself or soothe an unwanted emotion – all of these are examples of how we can get carried away and fail to appreciate the present moment.

Mindful eating, on the other hand, is about becoming aware of what is truly happening with us physically, emotionally, cognitively, even spiritually when we eat. When we turn our non-judgmental focus onto our appetites, we can really start to listen to our bodies, and start making choices that really nourish us.

Now, you may have the idea that mindful eating necessarily means eating sparingly, or extremely healthy at all times. Perhaps you have the image of a Buddha-like figure thoughtfully nibbling a humble vegetarian dish or something similar.

But mindful eating is not a diet. It is not about restriction, or about laying out rules that one have to follow. Rules and regulations only aim to replace your own innate wisdom – mindful eating is about tuning into that wisdom within. For our purposes, there are no bad foods, and no good foods. What *is* important, though, is the intention, and the awareness *behind* the act.

Take, for example, two colleagues at work who are busy doing their jobs when another comes merrily along with a slice of festive birthday cake for everyone. Colleague A is worried about succumbing to the family trend of pre-diabetes and has been obsessed with weight loss for most of his life. He's on a special "juice fast" and has had no breakfast. Without thinking, starvation wins out and the cake is gobbled up. Colleague A gets a bad sugar rush and an accompanying rush of negative emotions – how could he have so little will power?

Colleague B is feeling just fine and hasn't had cake in ages. He knows it's generally bad for him, but it looks delicious and he decides he'll have a little taste, to be a sport and join in the celebration. He takes a few bites and sure enough, they're amazing – the cake's pretty sweet though, and after a few bites he feels slightly sick and decides to leave the rest. He goes on with his day without another thought to the cake, to his choices about it or his worth as human being.

Now here's the thing. Both colleagues ate the cake. But the eating came from very different mindsets, and will likely have different effects on each. Colleague A might slip into self-loathing – if he's already "cheated", why not have another slice since nobody could love such a gorger anyway? Colleague B might find he isn't quite as hungry come dinner time and may turn down the next slice of cake he is offered: while it usually looks good he remembers that cake makes him feel bad afterwards, so he simply avoids it.

There is no secret formula or set of rules for mindful eating. In fact, relying too heavily on guidance from other people for what we should eat only removes us further from our own appetites. When we can observe ourselves without judgment, we can become aware of what really nourishes us.

Mindful eating, then, is more about being tuned into internal and external experiences so that we can notice, without judgment, what is the most nourishing for us.

CHAPTER 3: WHY DO WE OVEREAT?

Why eat at all?

It's a simple question, with a simple answer. We eat because food is fuel that we need to power our bodies. As biological organisms, we need to take in as much or more than we expend if we have hopes of staying alive.

But humans are quite a bit more than your average biological organism. While we are subject to the same laws that govern other animals, human beings also inhabit complex and immense social structures built around food. Food, for humans, is completely bound up with our psychology. The food landscape for the average human is vast and fraught with questions that go far beyond the simple equation of energy in versus energy out.

So, why do we overeat?

Food is the psychological equivalent of love.

Consider a tiny baby. When it comes into the world, one of the most important and urgent tasks is to find food. Babies who fail to learn to breastfeed properly or who miss out on nutrition at this crucial stage are extremely vulnerable. But this hunger of an infant's, psychologically speaking, is a hunger we can't appreciate as adults.

If you are hungry right now, excluding extreme poverty or an emergency, you can likely find something for yourself to eat without any undue crisis. An infant, on the other hand, depends entirely on others to feed it. It cannot simply go out and fetch what it needs. Think about this for a second: *the one thing you need most desperately in this world is solely in the control of other people.*

What this means is that if you're a baby, your only chance of being fed – i.e. survival – is to be fed and cared for by someone else. From our earliest beginnings, food is tied into love and affection. For a baby, it is no exaggeration to say that love and affection are a matter of life or death.

A baby who is not held and caressed will wither and become sick just the same as a baby who is denied vital nutrients. From the moment we come into the world, we have the understanding: food = love. And this we carry with us all throughout life.

Mothers show their concern for their children by urging them to eat. We give food as gifts to those we care about, to romantic partners, to congratulate people or to make them (or us) feel better.

And in the same way as we've been taught to reach for certain kinds of food when we have a cold, we may also reach for "comfort food" to nurture ourselves. Thus, even as adults, long after we learn to take care of ourselves, this association still remains.

If we feel unloved or unnoticed, the food-equals-love equation would seem to suggest that tucking into a plate of your mom's homemade spaghetti bolognaise will help. We may confuse sadness with hunger, and unfortunately fix neither problem in the process.

Food is a Habit

Life is complicated. We live in a world of over 7 billion people, consisting of more information than any one person could ever hope to digest.

"Shortcuts" in life are inevitable. Time is precious and you can't waste it solving the same problems over and over again. Instead of trying to think every single night about what you are going to eat, you usually end up sticking to a few favorite recipes that you have on rotation.

And it pays to make some things automatic. Instead of contemplating each new problem again when it pops up, you put into place some routine or habit that lets you stop thinking about it for a while. You may not need to have a shower every single day, but it's much easier to just plug it into your routine so you can get it over and done with and have it on autopilot.

Food also becomes habitual very quickly.

We all have to eat, everyday, and it's easy to get fatigued with all the choices out there. Better to hand over the decision to "rules" and stick to them. Eat three times a day, at specific times. Eat what everyone else is eating. Eat what you ate yesterday. These may not be the best choices in the moment, but they *are* low-energy and easy to stick to.

People's daily habits can be excruciatingly difficult to budge. The whole reason you have the habit, after all, is because you're too lazy to give it any more thought. Overeating is then nothing more than a ritual you become stuck in. You're used to it, so you keep doing it. Your body expects a sandwich and a Coke every day at 13:00, so you give it one, whether it's a good idea or not.

Food is culture

When enough people share the same habit for long enough, it becomes part of culture. As difficult as it may be to turn down a meal that everyone else in your family or office is eating, it's even more difficult when that meal also happens to be endorsed by society as a whole.

With things like special festivals or celebrations, hunger is almost beside the point – eating a particular way is an expression of your cultural and national identity. That little voice that tells you that you don't even like turkey and pumpkin pie is drowned out by the assumption that if it's Thanksgiving, that's just exactly what you should eat.

Westernized, capitalist culture is one of abundance. For many in the industrialized modern world, the culture around food is all about excess. People are encouraged and enabled to eat any kind of food, in any quantity, whenever they desire it.

Even if you are unlucky enough to be participating in some kind of diet, you may still find yourself encouraged to consume: buy special berries or herbal teas or novelty foods or supplements. The name of the game is variety, and never having to go without.

A culture of food that promotes excess means massive servings at restaurants, multiple courses, calorie-laden drinks and super-cheap fast foods that are available everywhere. And it also means overeating.

Food is physically addictive

Of course, there's more to it than just the psychological or cultural. Our more abstract thoughts and emotions around food are all based on certain biological realities, too. There is plenty of information out there about the many complicated ways that our bodies handle and process food. The body is a fine-tuned mechanism that is astounding in its complexity.

Take, for example, sugar. A simple substance, but one that has far-reaching and convoluted effects on the body. A food high in simple sugars spikes blood sugar levels. This in turn sparks insulin production as well as a whole orchestra of hormonal changes. The insulin processes the sugar, but in time, too many shocks to blood sugar levels lead to a less responsive system, i.e. insulin resistance. The body produces more insulin to counteract the imbalance, the effects of which cause inflammation in the cells.

This inflammation, together with disrupted hormone levels (such as testosterone, cortisol and adrenaline) all lead to weight gain. More fat in the body means an even poorer response to sugar the next time round. Eventually, the body is unable to process sugar properly, and rapidly sinks into an addictive spiral of inflammation, weight gain and hormonal disruptions.

Millions of people in the world acquire Type II diabetes in this exact way. At that point, a person may feel cravings for sugar that are legitimately as intense as those of an addict for heroin. And the effects on their bodies may be almost as bad.

The reasons we overeat are many. And our reasons overlap. Consider a fictional woman, Neena, and her "eating landscape".

She inherited a genetic predisposition to weight gain from her parents, who were both heavy and big boned. She is also from a large, boisterous Italian family that cultivated in young Neena an early appreciation for refined carbohydrates: pasta, bread and cakes. Neena's psychological associations with foods like this are complicated. Unconsciously, she links rich, heavy meals with maternal love since this was her parent's primary mode of expressing affection. She also associates eating plenty with vitality, being a "true Italian", even a certain healthful, sexy voluptuousness.

Part of her landscape contains deep beliefs about food: "the way to a man's heart is through his stomach" and "it's rude to turn down food that is offered to you" and "real women eat butter". At the same time she buys fashion magazines with the rest of the world and has other conflicting beliefs: to be thin is to be virtuous, to attain thinness is a matter of denial and effort.

Finally, Neena has her own unique biology, access to only particular foods in her environment, her personal history and routines, right down to the details of how individual substances affect her tissues and organs.

Why and how you overeat is as unique as you are. Healthy, mindful eating will be unique, too. What does your "food landscape" look like? The rest of this book will explore ways we can tune into our bodies to see what is really happening each time we take a bite.

CHAPTER 4: THE BENEFITS OF BECOMING A MINDFUL EATER

When we open our consciousness to accurately receive reality, without judgment, as it unfolds around us, we may notice that we are suddenly aware of... quite a lot.

With our fullest attention, each moment becomes rich and deep, almost endless. We can find something gentle and satisfying in the still moments between actions, and we give our spirits the opportunity to expand a little in the spaces where clutter and distraction used to be.

Mindfulness in our eating is an excellent way to begin to open up little windows of awareness in our lives, but mindfulness is not focused on any one activity. It is inevitable that when you begin to zoom in more intently on one aspect of your life, the other aspects will also come into focus.

Blame it on our modern education system, or our nonstop consumption of self-help literature, but a common reaction when starting out with mindfulness is to perceive it as work, or a chore. "No pain, no gain" we are told, and if you want to be happy, you'd better work for it.

This is where it's important to remember that mindfulness should ideally be *non-judgmental*.

Borrowing heavily from the Eastern philosophies, practicing total acceptance and detached perception is a feat in and of itself. This spirit of acceptance is what makes the difference between mindful attention and mere neuroticism. The person who is relentlessly self aware but also critical is not mindful, but rather consumed and distracted by their minds.

When we diet, for instance, we are told that certain impulses and actions are unacceptable, and we are encouraged to regulate and moderate ourselves. The literature will give you tips on what to do with your troublesome cravings or how to "think thin" – as if all your previous thoughts were fat ones. Simultaneously we are told that certain actions and thoughts are more desirable, hence the self-righteousness of gym goers or the praise we give to people who quit certain kinds of food.

Mindfulness, and mindful eating, *is not about effort*. It's about being awake to what is really happening, inside your body and out. Of course, in time you may become aware of something to an extent that it just seems to natural to act in a particular way. And you will. You will be like Colleague B, eating the cake without a tortured inner monologue or lashings of guilt.

Waking up

Become a mindful eater, and you will become more mindful at work and in your relationships, too.

When you begin to meditate on why exactly you decided to binge on cookies, you may start to naturally ask other questions. Are there other areas of your life that you also feel out of control in? How do these feelings of guilt tie in to the patterns in your life in general? Again, what are you really hungry for?

Because mindlessness often masks things we would actively like to avoid, you may find that becoming more aware leads to some changes in your life. You may start to see patterns in the way you behave and feel, and start to shift your sense of what is important and what isn't.

From a psychological perspective, being mindless is a form of defending against things we'd rather not know about ourselves or the world around us. When we remove mindless habit and ritual, we may be left with some difficult questions that need answering. In other words, you may actually find out what you are hungry for.

Agency and reactivity

Even single celled organisms have the sense to move towards nourishment and away from pain. But these organisms never make goals. They don't celebrate their achievements or feel pride or shame. A single celled organism never sits and thinks to itself: hmm, how can I be better today?

That's because such a creature lacks agency. It is not conscious and aware of itself. It more closely resembles a tiny machine or an equation: move towards food, away from pain. And that's the end of it.

Humans, on the other hand, are blessed with a sense the single celled organism doesn't have: consciousness. We can think about our actions, contemplate the world around us, even contemplate *ourselves*. We can engage in goal directed behavior. While the single celled organism merely reacts to stimuli in its environment, a human has the option to be active.

When we act spontaneously, when we engage our ability to choose, to commit to a course of action, to plan and follow through with those plans, we are active agents. This action rests on being aware in the first place – aware of ourselves, of our environment, of the options that are open to us.

But it's easy, and sometimes comforting, to fall into being a reactive single celled organism.

Besides the few ways such organism can respond to its world, it cannot act independently, because it is not aware. When we devour food without thinking or take in substances that are harmful to us, we are losing our agency in the same way. The first step to becoming an active agent is to become aware of the possibility.

The foundation, therefore, of all action, including actions to improve our lives, begins with awareness.

By this point, the talk of mindfulness has been rather abstract – we have laid out arguments for concepts like *awareness* and *consciousness*, which sound well and good as general concepts. But how does one actually *practice* mindfulness?

The idea of becoming aware in this way has its roots in Buddhist philosophy, but that doesn't mean you need to meditate on a cushion on the floor for you to truly understand the principle. In fact, practice right this moment an exercise in awareness. Put down the book, close your eyes if you want to, and become still.

What is your reaction so far to what has been outlined here? What is your gut reaction? Try not to judge this reaction you have, just look at it. See what it is, become acquainted with it. Do you feel a slight anxiety at the fact that yet another book is telling you that you have been living your life wrong all this time? Are you doubtful? Full of hope?

Do you notice a dry sort of cynicism? What's happening in your body? What thoughts are you having? Imagine a pious Buddhist monk sitting somewhere tranquil in an orange robe, being "mindful". How does it make you feel? Annoyed? Inspired?

Now, when you have felt out all the corners of your reaction, pick up the book again and withhold judgment. That reaction is yours and yours alone. Even if the voice is quiet, or conflicted, it is *your* voice nonetheless. What this book is pointing to is not hidden here in the words, but out there in that still moment that you and only you can access.

Practical ways to be mindful

If you really did the activity suggested in the paragraphs before, congratulations, you have just practiced mindfulness. That's it. If you didn't, that's OK too. Notice that you didn't, notice what you feel because you didn't. No judgment, just awareness.

In your day-to-day life, it may be helpful to rest temporarily on some deliberate activities you can do when eating. Here are some activities that may guide you to opening up those little windows of awareness.

Be a true expert

You know those fancy wine experts who claim to have an almost supernatural ability to pick up even the subtlest nuances in the wine they drink? Take a cue from them. Become an expert of what you eat. Pretend you were born yesterday and have never eaten before. Be slow – ridiculously slow at first – and notice every sight, sound, smell, taste and touch. Activate all your senses. And remember to withhold judgment: try not to label certain sensations or thoughts as wrong or bad.

Become an artist

A complicated Japanese tea ritual has nothing to do with tea. When you sit down to eat, try to pay attention to the aesthetic elements. Use pretty plates and cutlery and eat in a space that makes you feel happy and calm. Arrange the food pleasingly on the plate, and spend a moment admiring it before you tuck in.

Don't multitask

Multitasking is basically increasing the number of activities you can be mindless about in one moment. There is no cheating time – if you rush something or squeeze it in with something else, you haven't saved any time, you've merely rushed headlong into careless action. For a moment, see what happens when you eat without the TV, without chatting or reading and without stewing in your mind over everything you have to do tomorrow or what you failed to do today.

Slow down

For this moment, the only thing you have to do is eat your lunch, nothing more, nothing less. Focus on this and only this task. There is enough time. Even put your fork down between bites. Take the time to breathe or sip water between bites.

Nourish yourself

Don't be a little child who hates to eat his broccoli. Pay attention to how you feel after meals. Notice if you feel bloated, tired, energetic etc. Begin to pay attention to your natural instincts and they will tell you when a food is not truly nourishing to you. Craving fat? Eat it. Notice how you feel afterwards. Remember it.

Ask questions, don't criticize yourself

When we are curious, we have a better chance of really understanding ourselves. Criticizing yourself for doing something wrong is a trap and will only remove you from your experience. Likewise, also notice if you fall into the trap of worrying whether you are doing mindfulness "right". Ask questions. "Why am I such a pig?" is not as useful as "What happened before I ate that? What's happening now? Do I like this? Has this happened before?"

Mindfulness Exercises

We have discussed ritual and habit as something that detracts from mindfulness. To combat falling into these mental ruts, a deliberate ritual can paradoxically enhance your mindfulness. Slow, intentional ceremonies can be a way to align our outside actions with our inner awareness and intentions. Try one of the following rituals or practices.

The Quiet Dinner

Be alone for an evening. Prepare everything carefully. Choose a food that is symbolic and special to you, or simply one you really enjoy. Set some time aside to eat this meal mindfully.

Set no expectations for yourself. Be in the room with this meal as if it were a new person you have never met before. Get to know it. Take time to notice aromas, textures and flavors. Note, also, your emotions and what is changing in you. Be a scientist trying to understand this strange phenomena of eating. Simply watch and observe.

The next time you eat, see if any ideas or memories return from this quiet dinner. Were you surprised at how little you actually wanted to eat once you got going? Were you exasperated with your hunger? Did you feel any emotions come up after the meal was finished?

A Bathing Ritual

This ritual has little to do with actual eating, but involves becoming more aware of our bodies in general. Be alone for a moment. Buy a fresh, luxurious bar of soap if it feels right. Be slow and deliberate, and submerge yourself in water.

Become acquainted with your body. Look at each of your limbs, your skin, the way it folds and moves, scars and spots, the different textures. Then turn inward. Notice the emotions you attach to each body part. Hatred? Shame? Gratitude?

If it feels right, you may later decide to massage scented oil into your skin and notice how it feels to be loving and gentle with yourself. Do you feel guilty and vain? Sad? Reinvigorated? Meditate on what your body is and what it means to you.

Cooking Consciously

A final ritual involves the preparation of food. For most of mankind's history, people only ate what they could acquire and prepare themselves. Whether hunter-gatherer style or through farming, humans have always been close to the sources of the food they eat.

For this ritual, try to focus on the act of creating a meal for yourself. You can be imaginative, and try to focus on each ingredient, remembering where it came from and what it took to arrive on your table. Be mindful of the journey food takes, and how cooking is as vital a part of this journey as eating.

Watch to see if you are rushing, whether you are inclined to waste, the way you handle food. What does the recipe mean to you? Where did it come from? Do you feel strange handling raw meat? Do you feel a creative buzz putting together a dish and not knowing how it will turn out?

Not everyone likes cooking, me included, but taking a moment once in a while to prepare something from scratch for yourself can be an illuminating activity.

CHAPTER 6: DEEP BODY AWARENESS

Let's say you have felt convinced of the benefits and value in becoming more mindful in your daily life, specifically where eating is concerned. Lets say you practice some of the above techniques as well as some you may have thought of yourself. You become more and more familiar and comfortable with taking pause to notice what you are doing.

As mentioned previously, real choices can only be made when we are conscious and aware – aware of ourselves and the choices around us. Mindfulness is a gateway to becoming a more focused and autonomous human being.

In becoming more mindful, you may have noticed that much rests on your ability to go quiet and hear what your body, your mind and your hurt are truly experiencing. Without the clutter of other people's expectations, habits or inattention, the idea is that we can zoom in on something deeper and more fundamental.

Your appetite: a compass

Do you know what you want?

Your body has evolved careful and deliberate mechanisms to alert you to your needs. Dehydrated? Your body will let you know in the form of thirst. Hungry? Sick? Your body will tell you. There's a reason why poisonous foods often taste the worst, it is to help us better avoid them. Babies come into the world with a taste for fat and sugar – conveniently the nutrients they need to grow and be healthy.

Our appetite is the internal compass that lets us know what we should move towards. "Hunger is the best sauce" simply because the longer we go with an unmet need, the sweeter it is to finally satisfy that need. But the same thing that was delicious an hour before is now nausea-inducing when you're already full. In other words our appetite, our needs and wants, and our actions are tied together.

In an ideal world, our appetite is clean and elegant: we experience a lack, we gravitate towards those things that rectify the lack, and when the equilibrium is balanced again, our appetite for the same thing disappears. The above exercises are intended to focus your attention more clearly on this process as it works.

The sad truth is that these special inner compasses, our appetites and desires which are so perfectly capable of serving us, are drowned out by internal and external noise. For some people, the quiet voice of their own appetites has almost completely disappeared.

When your true appetite is masked

A little child, for reasons we can only guess at, decides to turn his head away from the spoon of food his mother is offering him. She doesn't trust her child to eat well without her guidance – in short, she doesn't believe that he has an internal compass and wants to override it: he *must* eat. In time, the child learns that there are other reasons to eat food besides the main reason of hunger.

Can you recognize times where you have eaten for other reasons? Do you eat when you are not hungry? Some of the following sources may play a role in what and how much you eat:

- Your parents and family
- Your cultural heritage
- The place you work and your office routines
- Your spouse or partner and their eating habits
- Food trends and popular diets

There are a lot of rules around food. For example, dessert comes *after* the main meal. You shouldn't eat pizza for breakfast. No carbs before bed. You must eat three meals a day. Don't skip breakfast. And on and on it goes.

Becoming more mindful means becoming more aware of instances where you may have deferred to outside judgment ("rules") about what you feel and what you crave. If you become more mindful, you may notice eventually that even though you have been dutifully forcing down breakfast for years, you are in fact never hungry in the mornings and do much better without it.

Allowing other people's judgments, or the momentum of habit, to replace our own perceptions and choices is a grave mistake – and can explain why some people can eat food that they are allergic to for years before realizing it. People in wealthy, first world countries have died of dehydration while being surrounded by water. The voice telling them to drink was so hidden that they could not hear it anymore.

When appetites become confused

Of course, this inner compass isn't limited to eating. To a greater or lesser degree, people have some inbuilt machinery that tells them who they are, what they should do, and how. We are, in essence, instruments that measure our own experience. Our "intuition" is a form of appetite and alerts us to emotional situations that may not be to our best interests, just as our taste buds tell us that bitter food has a chance of being poisonous.

Humans have many needs, and for each we have an appetite: we hunger for physical food, we crave connection and affection with others, we desire sex, we demand love and recognition, we yearn for sleep and rest and, in a big way, our spirits guide us with the biggest appetite of all: the hunger for truth and knowledge, to understand ourselves and our universe, and to know our place in this world.

Of all those appetites though, which is the easiest to satisfy?

When we have a need for love and affection, we rely on others to get it. Feeling empty and confused about life is a problem few of us have solved satisfactorily. But eating? Eating is an easy problem to solve. Eating is, in fact, *too* easy. It feels good, it distracts us, it soothes a primal need in us.

For many people, eating becomes a (unsuccessful) way to try and soothe *other* needs and hungers. Bearing in mind that it is often the case that food is though of as love at an unconscious level, food can be a way to temporary relief from the unfulfilled wish for more love and affection.

What are you hungry for?

You are taken with an idea: you want to have a hotdog with extra toppings and a side of French fries. You know it's unhealthy, but you're hungry and you really, really want it. But what kind of hunger is it?

Next time you feel hunger coming up, actively choose to deny it for a moment and pay attention to the emotion that arises. The emotion that you feel gives you a clue about what food may be helping you avoid.

Boredom

Food can be entertainment and stimulation. Your hunger is not for food in this case, but for something new, for something to do. Food can be something to occupy your hands, to keep your mouth busy, or to distract you from the fact that you are feeling uninspired, or whatever it may be. Is there something exciting that you'd like to do? Is there a void in your life?

Sadness

Food as self-medication for depression is so well understood it has become a standard trope in movies and books. The idea that women scoff down chocolate during their periods is a joke that actually shows us something serious about ourselves. Food can be a friend, or a soothing and pleasing sensation to dull pain and negative emotions. What can you do to love yourself in other ways?

Anxiety

Food can be a stress reliever, and people sometimes use a "treat" to reward themselves for enduring mentally trying moments. Instead of trying to de-stress yourself with food, is there not a more direct way to reduce the sources of stress themselves?

Emotional eating can also stem from unwanted feelings of anger, exhaustion, worry, emptiness, low self-esteem or loneliness. Food is an easy solution to these feelings, but it is temporary. To determine whether you are truly hungry, ask yourself the following questions:
- Has your hunger built up slowly?

- Do you experience physical sensations such as a grumbling stomach or a slight lightheadedness?
- Do you feel like you could eat a range of things and be satisfied?
- Once you eat, do you feel happy and satisfied?

Answering yes to the above means you are likely experiencing a true, organic hunger. One that is emanating from your real appetite. On the other hand, "hunger" that is actually another emotion or need disguised as hunger will be somewhat different. Ask yourself:

- Do you feel the "hunger" all of a sudden and very urgently?
- Do you crave one very specific thing and don't want to eat anything else?
- Once you eat, do you feel ashamed or guilty?
- Do you find you still feel "hungry", even though you have eaten the thing you were craving?

If you answered yes to the above, consider that the solution you are seeking out is not truly going to satisfy your deeper hunger. If you eat to smother feelings of shame, particularly about your body, eating in this way can lead to a negative downward spiral.

You are temporarily soothed, but experience shame after eating. This shame intensifies rather than fixes the original emotion, and before you know it, you rightly think of food as both your only friend in the world as well as your deadliest enemy.

Discovering your neutral point

Becoming acquainted with that compass again takes time. For some, our own true needs are buried so deep underneath physical addictions, confusion, negative feelings, outside expectations, habits and misinformation that they take some time and patience to uncover again.

The only way to break free of destructive patterns like these is to become aware of them. It all comes back to awareness. So, the next time you experience a craving for something, try to temporarily put off satisfying that craving. Be brave and ask yourself to endure the emotion that arises when you don't have food to drown it out.

In time, becoming able to bear our unbearable emotions takes away their sting and reduces their power over us. You may find that addressing underlying issues of loneliness and shame reduce and then eliminate your need to self medicate with food.

Your "neutral point", that special place where you can hear your own inner compass speaking to you loud and clear, can only be arrived at with patience and compassion.

Make a habit of doing a full "scan" at decision points or opportunities to eat. For instance, if it's lunchtime and everyone in the office is heading out for something to eat, take a few moments to reflect on how you feel.

Emotionally – are you sad, angry, bored or lonely? Has something just happened to make you feel "hungry"?

Physically – run your awareness over your entire body. Do you need food? Are you just thirsty perhaps? Focus on sensations in your stomach, and try to detect a real appetite versus just being able to eat.

Behaviorally – are you merely going to eat because your schedule tells you that it's "lunch time"? Are you behaving mindlessly?

Socially – is your desire to eat more about what is happening with the people around you? Do you feel pressured by others to eat?

Spiritually – do you feel that eating now would be the best thing, in the highest sense? How do you imagine you will feel after you eat?

Become skillful at scanning yourself throughout the day and you may realize how infrequently you actually are hungry and how often you eat for other reasons. You may actively decide to eat anyway, or you may decide to abstain and wait until your inner compass tells you to seek food again. It's your choice.

Surprisingly, some people find that mindful eating causes them both to eat less and yet to be more satisfied with it. You may find yourself choosing more deliberately, gravitating towards more quality food, cooking more, moving towards or away from a certain food group, etc.

In time, food will stop having quite the same power over you. Instead of viewing food as a source of confusion or shame, food becomes merely a tool. You (logically) start to move away from foods that ultimately harm you. In time, you also learn how to choose food that truly nourishes and sustains you, and hopefully this attitude trickles over into other areas of your life, too.

Compassion, vegetarianism and "orthorexia"

Perhaps now would be a good time for a note on compassion in eating.

It is possible, with deeper awareness of what and how we eat, to become cognizant of the harm done to animals to enable us to eat meat, dairy and eggs. It may well be the case that we eventually choose to eliminate these foods from our diets in the same way we eliminate other foods that we feel are simply not nourishing us. However, if you are a professional bodybuilder, it may prove difficult to completely eliminate meat from your diet. It all depends on what you are trying to achieve and what your intentions are.

However, there are complicated ideas and expectations around vegetarianism that may interfere with and warp a true desire to stop eating animal products. Someone drawn to this mode of eating would do well to question, as always, their deeper motivations. In other words, becoming vegetarian requires the same degree of mental awareness as any other food choice.

There is an aesthetic of purity, of restriction and of heightened morality associated with shunning meat that needs to be negotiated. If we fall into the trap of believing that meat is the "bad" food and only plant foods are virtuous and acceptable, we are no better than those trapped in diets that demonize sugar or wheat.

Vegetarianism often appeals to teenagers, as it can promise a way to self-definition and expression - away from the parents. Notice if this is a strong instinct within you. Meat and its consumption also have a strong gendered component, and many women opt for vegetarianism at least in part because animal products have come to represent masculinity for them. It may even be an unacknowledged attempt to adopt another weight-loss diet under the guise of a moral position.

Whatever the case is in your life, try to maintain detachment from beliefs about food, even when they claim to represent greater awareness. There is nothing innately more real or valuable about eating meat than not, and vice versa. Again, what truly matters is the intention and awareness behind your actions.

Similarly, the term "orthorexia" was introduced some years ago to address exactly this notion of becoming *too* invested in "healthy eating". Obsession with eating only the correct foods is no better than being obsessed with eating bad foods, being obsessed with eating nothing or being obsessed with heroin, for that matter. We should be mindful of becoming health Nazis in the same way as we avoid greed, anorexia or addiction. The object of the obsession is not important.

CHAPTER 7: EATING: THE MIDDLE PATH

Let's return to our fictional woman, Neena. What would Neena's life look like if she decided to become more mindful in her eating habits?

She may decide to graciously accept the fact that, because of her genetic makeup, her body is what it is, and she much prefers nurturing it to fighting against it. She makes a habit of scanning her body and mind when faced with food and slowly comes to notice that she often eats far past her need and far past what is actually enjoyable. She comes to understand that she relied heavily on eating as a way to avoid awkwardness, as a way to fill time, as a way to connect with her family.

She consciously tried to notice what happened when she turned down food, and in the space she opened up, she attempted to craft a different relationship with her family – one based around conversation rather than consumption.

She realized that there were ways to honor her Italian heritage without damaging her body. She lost a little weight but gained a deeper appreciation of what she wanted food to be in her life: a celebration, a joyful event to share with loved ones and something to nourish the soul. In this, she found that she was as much a "true Italian" as anyone.

Nowhere in Neena's journey did she try to restrict gluten, swallow stimulant drugs to "boost" her metabolism or surrender to phony hypnosis quackery for weight loss. Her journey was not about getting "bikini ready" for summer or learning to love her curves. It was also not about going on a yoga retreat and learning how to eat "clean". It was about clearing away the emotional and cognitive clutter that was preventing her from accessing her true appetite and passion.

What about you? What is your journey about?

CONCLUSION

Mindfulness is not some special trick or gimmick that you can learn to help you shave off pounds. It's not an ideology or an eating plan or a diet. Eating mindfully is simply being present, in the moment, as you make choices and move about your life – including the food you choose to take in.

What you discover as you become more mindful may well be interesting and enlightening. When we tune out the noise and clutter surrounding us we can become better at listening to our own inner wisdom and what it is telling us. And what it tells us can sometimes be very surprising.

Through practice and awareness, the destructive control that mindless eating has over our lives can be gently and gradually removed. Wouldn't it be amazing to think of food as something special, something to celebrate, and something that nurtures and heals your body rather than harms it?

Wouldn't it be good to love and cherish our bodies, outside of succumbing to the narrow images the outside world has of it and what it should be? Wouldn't it be freeing to learn to tune into our own pleasure, our own hungers and needs?

My wish for this book has been simply this: to encourage you to find that passion in yourself again – that appetite – and tune into it more clearly. I wish you the best of luck on your journey, and that you'll have yourself a real taste, as well as a huge slice - of life!

MINIMALISM - HOW TO DECLUTTER, DE-STRESS AND
SIMPLIFY YOUR LIFE WITH SIMPLE LIVING

INTRODUCTION

Today, a growing number of people are becoming dissatisfied with their lives and turning to simpler ways of working, living and raising their children.

This book will explore the philosophy of minimalism and how it can streamline your life, declutter your home, reduce stress and reconnect you to what's truly important.

You'll find ways to adopt a mindset that promotes simplicity and elegance in your every day life, and rethink your dependence on material possessions.

Whether in our wardrobes, kitchens, work lives or our deeper sense of personal and spiritual purpose, we could all do with focusing on things that align with our values and reducing the distraction of those things that pull us away from them.

This book shows you how.

CHAPTER 1: WHAT THIS BOOK IS ABOUT

For those born and raised in the height of our consumer society, the idea that happiness and personal fulfillment is found in *stuff* is more or less a given.

The capitalist machine we all live within requires only one thing of us: that we should constantly want, and the things we should want are to be found, usually, in malls. Malls that are filled with strategically placed advertising, with the sole purpose to entice and lure you, trying to convince you that you need, not want, their specific product.

Our economy relies heavily on a steady stream of consumption: better clothes, cars, bigger houses and things to fill those houses with, the newest appliances, Christmas decorations, pet toys, jewelry, office furniture, pot plants, gaming consoles, specialty tires, luxury soaps... the array of stuff is simply dazzling.

But if you are reading this there's a chance you find this overabundance just a little... exhausting. Paradoxically, there seems to be a sad sort of emptiness in filling up one's life with more things. What is simple and truly valuable often seems to be completely hidden under mountains of what is unnecessary. Although advertising tells us the best way to solve problems is to *buy* solutions, tranquility and a graceful life seem to elude us, no matter what we buy or how much of it.

Minimalism is an aesthetic, a philosophy and a way of life. This book takes a look at how deeply liberating a simpler life can be, and shows you ways you can adopt a calmer, more deliberate way of living and working. Minimalism is about clearing away the clutter that is distracting from what is really important. It's about rethinking our attitudes to ownership, to our lifestyles and to our innermost values.

This book will give practical advice on owning fewer clothes, de-cluttering your life, simplifying your daily routine and reducing mindless consumerism. It will also explore how practical changes to our surroundings can lead to a previously unknown inner peace and calm.

CHAPTER 2: LESS IS MORE: THE HISTORY OF MINIMALISM

One may think that it is only in our modern materialistic society that people have become more conscious of the way they accumulate possessions. But in fact the fundamental ideas of minimalism go back in time to mankind's earliest beginnings.

Ever since people learnt to farm animals and cultivate the land, they've thought of themselves in terms of what they own. And even the most ancient of civilizations have had individuals who have been counter cultural in their desire for simplicity.

Be it the ascetics of ancient India or the Zen Buddhists of Japan, there have always been those who decided that they *wouldn't* try to keep up with the Joneses. The Bible speaks about guarding against greed and covetousness, and most spiritual traditions, wherever they stem from, usually promote humility, grace and a simple lifestyle.

In the early 19th Century, artists, architects and designers felt a kind of relief in the aesthetic of minimalism. The extravagance and embellishment of earlier times fell away as people became interested in essential qualities, in the true nature of buildings, of furniture, even of music.

Today most people associate minimalism with the endeavors of these early artists, and think of the liberal use of white, of empty spaces and of sparse and elegant lines.

Minimalism is much more than an aesthetic though. Those seeking a simpler life are interested in the corresponding states of mind of clean concepts and graceful design. What these designers tried to express was a yearning many of us can identify with – the desire for balance, meaning and serenity.

CHAPTER 3: WHAT IT MEANS TO BE A MINIMALIST

Of course, there are plenty of trends today, especially in online communities that encourage people to be thrifty and save money.

This is a very pragmatic response to the frankly tattered economy – families who previously could afford to throw valuable things away and barely give a second thought to the thousands of products they consumed every month were suddenly forced to find creative ways to trim the budget.

As a goal in itself, thrifty living is certainly admirable and takes a certain skill and dedication to pull off well. However, being thrifty is not quite the same as being minimalist. Making do with less because you have no other choice is merely a practical concern. The spirit of minimalism is... a little different.

To willingly do with less is not a hardship, nor a punishment. It is not some unfortunate circumstance that you endure because you have to, and it is not intended as martyrdom or a denial of the self and its needs. While a minimalist and someone who has merely gone bankrupt may look a lot like one another, they come from very different places. Minimalism is not a kind of "diet". It is not asceticism or restriction of needs, but a questioning of what one's needs really are, and willingly choosing to do with less in favor of living a more intentional life.

In fact, it is sometimes the case that people who are thrown into poverty or compromised circumstances eventually experience an enrichment of their personal and spiritual lives. Gautama the Buddha, for instance, is said to have started his long journey to enlightenment by leaving the gorgeous palace walls he had lived in all his life.

So, while many who practice minimalism in their daily lives may cultivate what others would call poverty, the goal is not to do without or to suffer. The goal is to re-evaluate whether wealth and possessions actually add any happiness, and if they don't, then what does?

How can be we bring some of the elegance of minimalism into our own lives?

Think of a hot day and the strong desire to have a cool glass of water. The heat makes a tall, icy cold drink of water seem almost like a need, in fact. While very few people in the middle class Western world ever experience a true need and the true fulfillment of that need, sipping a cold glass of water when you're parched comes pretty close. It's hot and you need just one thing: water. You pour a full glass. You drink it, relishing each drop, your thirst completely quenched. The glass is empty. This is a truly elegant process, and beautiful in its simplicity.

Now imagine a less elegant process. You're thirsty, and you fill the glass up with water, but you don't have enough. You drink it up, but you're thirsty still, and your need remains with you.

Or, imagine the opposite. You pour some water into your glass but when you reach the top, you keep pouring. You're thirsty; water is good, so more water must be *better*, right? The water spills all over the counter, and now you have to clean it up. You've wasted some, and even given yourself extra work to do.

Minimalism is like trying to find just exactly the right amount of water to pour in your glass. There is no need for poverty or denial. There is also no need for excess. Instead, minimalism is looking for that sweet, elegant spot right in the middle.

When we have too much, we have to devote more of our time to taking care of the excess, i.e. cleaning up the overflowing water. When we don't have enough, we become preoccupied with our impoverishment – which is just another way to be obsessed with material things.

For most of us, the idea that you can never really have enough is practically gospel. What we don't realize is that having extra stuff can be a significant cause of stress and unhappiness in our lives. Trying to solve this deep sense of dissatisfaction in your life by buying more is like pouring more water into your glass to ease the stress of having to clean up spilled water. In other words: it doesn't make sense.

Clutter in The Home

Here's a philosophical question: what is a home? What is a home *for*?

It seems like a bizarre question, but try to answer it for yourself anyway. And be honest. Is a home a place for you to relax in between adventures in the outside world? A place to sleep? A place for your pets or your kids to run around in? Something you feel that successful adults need to have?

Probably, your answer was not, "a home is something to take up my time and money and cause me stress". And yet, this is what homes essentially are for many people. Traps. For women especially, the promise of domestic bliss, a clean, well-coordinated house and lots of pretty things to fill it with actually translates to being an indentured house servant. You may think it's efficient to pay someone else to clean and maintain your home, but somewhere along the line, you trade in your time and peace of mind in order to pay for that.

The home – the place that should be about rest and recuperation – becomes another life chore, something to juggle in the endless list of tasks that need your attention. And while you're busy maintaining all your things, do you have time to actually enjoy them? How many people in the world leave their houses empty every day to go and work elsewhere, so that they can afford those houses? Again, the question is, what is a home for?

Minimalism is not the same for everyone. The marathon runner needs to drink three glasses of water, the little child only a half. Our needs are all different, and what is important to each of us is different, too. Nevertheless, consider the following to try and streamline your home and the life you live in it.

Ask yourself what an item truly brings to your life.

You bought an expensive popcorn machine because you liked the idea of having access to fresh popcorn in your home. In reality, you don't actually eat popcorn all that often. The popcorn machine becomes like the spilled water on the counter – another thing to take care of. If you accumulate enough items like this, you may think to yourself one day that you need a bigger kitchen, more clever storage solutions, or even a maid to clean everything.

Of course, there's nothing inherently evil or useless about a popcorn machine. For another person, they may use it all the time, deriving a lot of joy from making cheap, delicious popcorn at home that they share with their family.

The question is not what the value of the item is, but what the value of the item is *for your life*. Buying something expensive and thinking that the dollar amount attached to it will have a corresponding value in your life is a mistake. An expensive phone with a hundred features that you never use is just water on the counter. Does the item serve you or do you serve the item?

Decide on a lifestyle, equip yourself accordingly.

If you were a single man, you wouldn't buy a deluxe baby crib with all the trimmings because you saw it on sale. It would be absurd, and very easy to just say, "Well, I don't need that."

But it's not always that easy to know when something truly belongs in our lives, and when it's just being heavily marketed to us. The same man may buy a deluxe golf club set with all the trimmings, even though, if he was honest with himself, he plays golf about as often as he cares for a child.

If you have a strong self-concept, it is difficult to convince you to buy something that you don't need. You become immune to advertising, peer pressure and nagging from your mother. You simply go out into the world and seek the tools that help you be yourself.

But if you've been told all your life that what you really want is an 8-seater dining table when you grow up, you may be confused by how little satisfaction it gives you when you actually have it. You may even wind up more confused because you're suddenly made aware of another need you never knew you had: you suddenly realize you need 8 people to sit there, 8 plates and bowls, 8 wine glasses and while you're at it, table decorations, too.

Instead, work from the need backwards. How often do you eat at home? If not that often, don't buy things to help you cook better. Don't buy things for the lifestyle you're told you *should* have, buy them for the lifestyle you actually *do* have.

Draw up a list of activities that you actually do in the course of a month. Make note of all the times you wished you had something, but didn't. If after a month you haven't used something you own, consider getting rid of it. Notice how much time you spend maintaining something and compare it with how much pleasure or utility it gives you. Is it beautiful? Is it functional? If not, why do you have it?

Streamlining Your Wardrobe
Beware all enterprises that require new clothes
    -Henry David Thoreau
Fashion can be a funny thing. While people laugh at the fashions their parents followed a few years before, they dutifully follow the fashions of their own time. Fashion can be a creative outlet, a platform to express ourselves and just downright fun.

But more often that not, fashion is merely a path to pure consumerism. Most items of clothing can be worn happily for years and years. So how do you get people to buy more of it? You forbid them to wear perfectly good clothing because it's not in fashion. Buying fashionable clothes becomes analogous to buying furniture that spontaneously combusts every new "season".

With other products, advertisers at least try to conceal that they are appealing to your sense of identity when marketing to you. But with fashion, the link is clear: *the clothes maketh the man.* When a company tells you that swiping on a coat of fire engine red lipstick is what you do when you want to feel confident, they are not interested in your mental health. They are interested in selling you more fire engine red lipstick. The trick is that you can't buy an emotion or an identity in the form of an item of clothing. So you try again.

You get people who have wardrobes that are literally bursting with clothing legitimately feel that they have nothing to wear. The need, whatever it was, is still there.

Think Practically
Women's magazines tell us that every savvy woman needs a "little black dress". But if you work at a game reserve nursing sick lions to health 7 days a week, you don't need a little black dress. Forget about lists that talk about "wardrobe staples" and fashion "must haves".

Think of the items of clothing you wear the most. The ones that fell to pieces and you were sad because you wanted to wear them more. The shirt that you always grab in the morning, the pair of pants that always make you feel happy to put on.

These clothes have proven value, so take them as your guide. The pile of dress shoes sitting at the back of the closet? The expensive sequined scarf that you think is beautiful but are too scared to even wear? These give you clues as well, clues on what you need a lot less of.

Embrace the idea of less, but better. One item of clothing that is well made and fits you and your life is worth much more than several items that are sort of OK, and will only end up in a landfill once you tire of them. Try to think of where your full point is on the glass, clothing-wise.

For many people, clothing that lets them get on with the business of their lives is best. Choose colors and styles that you like, whether they are in fashion or not. Avoid fussy things that need dry-cleaning and special care, things that will disintegrate after a year or less, or clothes that take as much time to care for as they do to wear them.

If you find something you like, keep it and take care of it. If the tailoring and quality are good, it will last you for years. Invest in the extra expense knowing that what you are buying is the freedom of thinking about clothes for the next while.

Be Ruthless

Look at the closet you have right now.

Ask yourself what you have worn in the last year or six months. If you haven't worn something, stop deluding yourself that you will eventually, when you have the right event to wear it to, when you lose weight or whatever. Give it away to someone who can use it and actually benefit from it.

Fix clothes that you avoid wearing because of small things like a tear or missing button. Using what you already have can be a real moment of insight. Some items can be repurposed or revived with a little clothing dye, a bit of tailoring or a good clean. Try to remember that at one point, this was a new, fancy item that you were excited to have.

Try not to let sentimentality stop you from getting rid of items that truly don't serve you. Things like "lucky" underpants, hand-me-downs from loved ones or pieces that have sentimental value need to be considered carefully. Is it the thing itself that is special, or the memory that you attach to it?

Zen Mealtimes

No matter what you do, you have a physical body that needs feeding every day.

Food is something that should nourish and nurture us, keeping us strong and healthy so that we can get on with living our lives. But ask any overwhelmed stay at home mother about food, and you'll likely find that it's just another drain on resources, just another chore.

The shopping, cooking and cleaning associated with eating every day can eat up hours of your life. If you feel that eating is more of a never-ending drudgery and not something to embrace and enjoy, it may be time to pare down.

Constantly ask yourself what is truly necessary.

If you waste time chopping vegetables and get no pleasure from it, focus instead on recipes and meals that use whole or ready-prepared vegetables. Better yet, can you find meals that barely require recipes at all? Sometimes the best meals are the simplest, the lack of recipe letting each ingredient really shine on its own.

Foods like salads, roasts and finger foods require less cooking and less cleaning up. Making a big batch of food and freezing some for later essentially halves the amount of time you spend cooking. A dishwasher may be an expensive purchase, but not when you offset it against the free time you gain to relax, be with your family or pursue something that is important to you.

Emotional Eating

It's probably no exaggeration that much of the time, what we eat is not eaten to directly address hunger.

Food is our most basic need, but also a very complicated social, cultural and psychological activity. We are told that heartbroken girls should eat buckets of ice cream, people who are celebrating should drink alcohol and those watching sports should eat hotdogs.

Nowhere is our understanding of our own desire more misunderstood than with physical hunger. For most, feeling as though you want to eat, as though you *could* eat, is mistake for actual hunger.

Try to be mindful as you eat. Think about your role as consumer, as you are literally consuming. Does the food in front of you help or harm you? If it harms you, why are you eating it, really? Do you *need* to eat it? Do you need to eat the amount that you are eating? Is there an emotion that you are soothing in yourself by eating?

When we are healthy and balanced, food is fuel that happens to be particularly delicious. When we are out of touch with our own needs, food becomes confused with representations of emotional states, just like products are. Food becomes a reward, a punishment, a celebration, a bad habit, a distraction, a companion, an enemy.

The goal should be to regain the simplicity in eating. Being hungry all the time or being stuffed full of food are both states that take your attention away from more important things. What can be removed? What is hindering rather than helping?

Being a Minimalist Parent

Ah, the baby shower. The parents to be are showered, almost literally, in gifts and goodies intended for the soon-to-be child. It's sadly fitting that the celebration we give to mankind's newest members is a showy initiation into consumerism. Having a baby? You need more *stuff*.

In the past, a baby shower had the very practical purpose of making sure that friends and family could help ease the burden that a new child could bring, while showing some support for the new parents. Children are, after all, expensive, and a little help is always appreciated.

But the baby shower can also be the first in a long line of occasions to buy unnecessarily. Tired parents of toddlers have houses cluttered with cheap colored plastic toys that get underfoot and are thrown out when they break or the baby loses interest.

Parents are encouraged to buy duplicate copies of everything for their little ones: baby spoons, baby brushes, baby baths, baby food, baby chairs, and baby soap. Advertisers have an easy job – no parent wants to worry that they are not doing the best for their child, and so consuming becomes a way to show love.

What's important

Think back to your own childhood. What are your happiest memories?

The moments that stand out to us even years later often have an ineffable quality to them. We were young and carefree, maybe feeling loved and safe, happy with the world and our place in it. Most likely, your memories have nothing to do with the material possessions you had or didn't have at the time. And if a special birthday present or something similar features, it's probably because of the emotions you associated with it, and not the thing itself.

Parents, especially first time parents, want to do the best for their children. But if you've spent any time at all with a two year old you'll realize that what's important to them are the little things – time spent playing with those they love, learning about something new and exciting, realizing that their parents are proud of them.

The best games don't need fancy, expensive equipment, and sometimes the game is to use your imagination to come up with something completely new out of what you already have. Even with infants, some first time mothers are surprised that their little angels didn't really need all the mountains of clothing and baby things they bought in anticipation.

Things we buy for our children can be held up to the same standard: are they useful? Are they ultimately enriching our children's lives? In most cases, the assumed benefit from an extra gadget or toy could just as easily be experienced without it.

Be aware of buying things that are actually intended to appeal to adults and not to their children. Tiny babies have absolutely no need for giant stuffed bears or freshly painted nursery walls. What they need is the warmth and attention of their parents – if buying them goodies takes you away from that, let go of the need to have it and focus on your child instead.

If you can cultivate a detached and balanced outlook on material things, you also give your children a lesson they can carry with them into adulthood: the lesson that happiness is not to be found in things.

By now, there's been enough mention of "utility", of asking ourselves the question of whether objects are truly necessary or not. But then the obvious question is, necessary *for what?*

It's strange to mention, but if you begin to live your life in a simpler way, with less clutter and distraction, you may find something peculiar happening: you're bored. You feel strangely lost. This feeling may be enough to convince you that your possessions and distractions were there for a very good reason, but stick with those feelings. They carry with them an important lesson.

The sad truth is, for many people life becomes almost completely about the management of our material possessions, the endless fussing with things that ultimately add little or no value to our lives or to the lives of others. For these people, there simply isn't anything to *do* after all the clutter has been removed. Their life is as meaningful as it ever was; only there is no stuff in the way to hide the fact.

So far, we've looked at very practical ways to remove material clutter from our lives, to stop buying things we don't need and to really enjoy the things we have. Excess clothing, toys and household junk are easy to identify and remove. But the minimalist philosophy extends into far more than this.

Human beings are symbolic creatures, and sometimes the "things" we let take over our lives are not even things at all. This is where the principles of elegance, of simplicity and of only that which is necessary can really change your life.

You may find it incredibly difficult to separate out your needs from your wants. And in the same way that we hold onto old magazines and knick-knacks from days gone by, we hold onto ideas and beliefs about ourselves that no longer serve us.

The minimalist philosophy extends to include every action, every event, every thought and every emotion. It is the practice of frequently stopping to ask ourselves, *is this valuable?*

And the answers may surprise you.

A new perspective

Unfortunately, it can take a brush with a life threatening illness or an accident for us to realize – none of what seems like it matters actually does. When you get into the habit of truly seeing what is necessary, what is good, and what makes you happy, you inevitably experience changes in your entire worldview.

You may lose motivation to do the same thankless and unfulfilling work, you may experience a whole new level of peace and contentment, you may find that you want and need to pursue something more spiritual for your life. You may stop being susceptible to manipulative marketing, you may leave old relationships and begin new ones, you may become interested in environmentalism or meditation.

Or, you may clean out your garage like you've always meant to and go on your way.

Minimalism is a bottom-line style of thinking and being that reminds us to keep aware of what's real and what's important. It's a life philosophy that recognizes that things and possessions are not goals in and of themselves, but merely tools to help us get to what's really important – tranquility, fulfillment, purpose.

The question, then, is to ask whether each activity, item or thought is directed towards your higher goals and values. If not, it is unnecessary, or worse, getting in the way of something that is necessary.

CHAPTER 6: MOVING FORWARD: A SIMPLE LIFE

Our time on this earth is finite and precious. We have our values and principles to guide us.

Look at your "to do" list and ask whether each item truly serves those higher values and principles. You may have had the feeling before: looking back and wondering, where did all the time go? Don't throw the present away on things that don't matter to you.

Be elegant and simple in your speech and actions. Gossip, idle chatter and negative conversations only waste time and energy. Your words are also tools, and should be used honestly and intentionally.

Reduce the barrage of choice in your day-to-day life. The constant noise of news, online media, friends and family demands, movies, music, technology etc. provides an endless stream of worthless and exhausting information. Cultivate what is enriching and avoid those things that tax and dull your senses.

Instead of multi-tasking, choose to do only one activity at a time, but well. Don't be afraid of empty space, of silence or of still moments. Resist caving when someone else tries to tell you what you should find important in your life. Make it a habit to go still inside yourself and listen to your own needs, passions and sense of purpose.

CONCLUSION

Having a simpler life is, well, simple.

But it does take effort and presence of mind to consistently hone into that thread of value and meaning in a universe cluttered with excess stuff.

Minimalism is a way of being that is counter to what is encouraged in us everyday, so you may find resistance in yourself and those around you when you choose to step back from mindless consumerism.

Start small and make slow, gradual changes that will stay with you. Deliberately open up blank spaces in your schedule and notice the effect. Choose to go quiet instead of rushing into speaking; choose to think about who you are and what you need to be your best possible self before rushing into a new purchase.

In time, a simpler and more elegant life will bring you peace and tranquility, and that little bit closer to the elusive questions of truth and purpose.

CREATIVE WRITING - LEARN HOW TO UNLEASH YOUR CREATIVE SELF

INTRODUCTION

When you were a tiny baby, your head was full of mostly nothing and the world was new and unknown. You barely had the skill to move yourself around the environment, and you most definitely lacked the skill to do what humans are most know for – *communication*.

As you grew and developed, though, something strange started to happen. The people around you, the things in your world - you began to understand that they could be *reached*. That in your infant isolation there was still a way to reach out and touch someone else's experience. You saw all around you evidence of this magical skill that you had yet to develop: language.

Almost every infant learns to talk, and many believe that impulse comes from this original yearning to reach out and connect, to speak and be heard, to breach the abyss between one and the other.

At the root of all creative expression is a deep, inborn and very human desire to be heard.

Since before we were old enough to understand it, we've tried to master this almost god-like ability to shape symbols and concepts, reach into the mind of someone else and affect their hearts and minds, to bring about changes in the world, to connect and understand and share with another human being.

I believe that it's at this early stage that writers are born. Children gradually learn that some words are more correct than others, that some have greater effect, that some words get you into trouble and some words bring you closer to what you want. And when you eventually developed a sense of identity, you realized that words are the special tool that allows you to speak your mind, to make your desires known.

Language is a window into the soul.

For the writers among us, the urge to communicate more clearly, more beautifully, and in new ways never really left us. With the right words, new worlds can be created, new ideas can be incubated and grown, great heights and depths can be reached. Every brilliant idea had its first home in the written or spoken word, and if you are a writer or aspire to be one, you most likely understand this power better than anything.

So, why write?

Why be creative at all?

Creativity is perhaps the most uniquely human characteristic, and it's no exaggeration that many have linked it to the divine. Creativity is the ability to look out over the vista of reality, and have the courage to wonder, "what if this was some other way?"

All change and growth begins with the creativity of imagining something different. In this book, we'll be talking about writing specifically, but creativity isn't fussy, and it's quite likely that opening the door on your innate creativity will invite all sorts of new skills and insights into your life, not just the verbal ones.

Let's start at the very beginning.

Our creativity journey will begin in infancy, and we'll go back to that wondering child who made the first momentous leap with his first word.

Today's exercise is broad and simple, but ponder it long enough and you'll start to uncover new, unexpected aspects. Ask yourself this simple question: *why write at all?*

Take a moment or two to answer this for yourself, but don't be satisfied with a superficial answer. It's great if your answer is, "to share my message," but take it further – what does that really *mean*? Why bother sharing your message? What's so special about that message anyway?

Once you've condensed down some of these sentiments, you'll have found something that will be incredibly valuable to your writing career, wherever it takes you: your purpose. Tapping into the deep roots of *why* you are compelled to write at all is a brilliant way to unlock your true motivations and your ultimate reason for that urge to take what's in your head and put it out there in the world.

How to find that "Big Why"

- What is the response to your writing you hope to receive, if any?

- How will you feel if nobody ever reads your work or understands what you're trying to get across?

- What, in essence, is your message?

- In the most general sense, do you feel heard in the world? Who do you have something to say to? Why? If you had the attention of the entire world for five whole minutes, what would you want to say to everybody?

- Picture people reading the best possible work you could hope to produce in this lifetime. Now, think carefully, what is their ideal reaction? In what ways do you want to move them? How will you know you've been successful?

Bear with me a little while I dwell on the fluffy stuff. Plenty of writing advice out there is focused on the nuts and bolts of writing – how to do it, when, how to market it and where, etc. But this is not that sort of book. If you want to learn to write more compellingly, with more skill and expertise, you can do it, easily. The really tricky bit, though, is understanding *why*.

Uncover this *why* for yourself and you get in touch with the inexhaustible engine of your creativity. The human core of why we bother to create at all. Get to know this root well and you will not need gimmicky books full of writing prompts to blast away your writer's block. You will not need "inspiration" or 31 awesome tips and tricks.

When you were a baby, *something* made you open your mouth and speak. Understand the thing that inspired you to do this, and you're more than half way to being the creative, productive and generative human being you were destined to be.

CHAPTER 1: DESIRE – THE ROOT OF CREATIVITY

If nothing momentous emerged for you with previous exercise, don't sweat it. You might have had a breakthrough and realized that deep down, your drive to create and express comes from a long buried need for affirmation that started in your childhood …or, you may merely feel that life is hard and you just like writing goofy things that make people laugh.

It doesn't matter. Even if an answer isn't forthcoming, keep asking it in the background. The answer may already be stirring somewhere inside you, waiting to come out soon. Let it be.

In this chapter, we move on to a more specific examination of how we can connect more authentically to that gorgeous, white hot, fantastic, almost genius kind of expression we all long for.

Have you had any moments like this?

Moments where you created something you were intensely proud of, almost gobsmacked by the joy and thrill of it being yours, and being *good*. We have all known creative competence before, and we've all known the satisfaction of making something exist that didn't exist before. It's almost an addictive feeling, isn't it?

We've briefly looked at the origin of creativity in the previous exercise. Wanting to be heard, in the most general sense, is at the core of many people's desire to write a play, paint a picture, go on stage or type out the first chapter of a sweeping sci-fi fantasy novel.

If you're feeling a little dry, or a little uninspired, there's one sure fire way to juice up your creative machine again: desire.

To reach out into the world takes a stirring, a yearning, a wanting.

What do you want?

This chapter's exercise is going to be a flight of fancy, and I'm giving you permission right now to run with it, as far as you like.

With a notebook, start jotting down ideas and impressions around the central title – *what do you want?* Don't think about it too deeply, don't dawdle and imagine someone else reading your work to see if you're "doing it right" …just ask the deepest stirrings in your heart and mind what they crave, and put it on the paper.

Do you have a hunger for more love and beauty in your life? Do you wish things made more sense? Are you lonely? Bored and desperate for something exciting to happen in life? Do you feel broke a lot of the time and feel a secret desire for ease and luxury? Do you wish your life were quirkier and more special? Do you wish you were popular? Do you crave a sense of purpose or prestige or the stability of a stable job? More money? Do you long for harmony and work that really fulfills you? Adventure? Do you want a little romance in your life? The thrill of some danger? More intellectual stimulation? Do you really really wish you could just buy an X Box already?

Go wild. Don't put any limits on yourself.

When you switch on this sense of desire and grasping in yourself, you reacquaint with the first little seeds of creativity. Necessity, as they say, is the mother of invention. Many beautiful things exist in this world solely because their creators were sick of living in a world where it didn't exist.

Have you ever had the feeling that you could do something better than how you see it being done around you? Explore that. Do you ever look at someone's life and feel a yearning to be more like them? Write it down. What is the flavor and tone of your big dreams – the stuff you'd do in a fantasy life? Look at all the things you hate about the world around you right now. After all, what do authors do, fundamentally, except argue with reality?

Writing and putting out your own unique message takes a few special elements, and the first is the desire that things *should be different somehow.* This starts with desire. Today, tap into that – this yearning and stirring is a powerful source of energy that will get you through many difficult nights of self doubt, or through many boring mornings when you feel like you lack the enthusiasm to get started.

Perhaps you're a technical writer who has a strong desire for clarity and elegance in life. Maybe you find the world utterly boring and colourless and get a thrill out of creating an alternate universe where enthralling characters battle out their bizarre story in crystal palaces in faraway galaxies. Maybe you're just damn opinionated and you're ready to give people a piece of your mind.

Whatever it is, take a moment to get cosy with your desire. Of course, this isn't a self help book and we all know that wanting something doesn't mean getting it, but knowing where to go to find your juiciest, most abundant source of creative energy is a powerful tool for any creative. Own it.

CHAPTER 2: HAVING THE GUTS TO SAY SOMETHING

So, we've had a brief look at our Big Why and started putting out feelers to find those delicious roots of desire that inform all our creative impulses.

Now, ladies and gentlemen, allow me to introduce you to the Closet Writer (although I believe you're already quite well acquainted with this character...)

The Closet Writer works some job or other, which he likes some amount but not overly so, and he has colleagues who would be shocked to learn that he writes in his spare time. The Closet Writer (let's call him Ned, shall we? In my story, I'm going to give him dark eyes and suspiciously smooth hands and a mole on his cheek with three hairs in it ...this is my story after all and that's the way I'm going to make it.)

Ned has scores of notebooks at home, all filled with the beginnings of novels, with grand plans and outlines of stories, with character sketches and bold ideas. He has poems he wrote in university that he was proud of but now hides in back pages of journals, letting them slowly go yellow. He occasionally shares these things with his mother and sometimes his girlfriend, and they like it, but then nothing happens and he goes back to scribbling behind closed doors, with vague notions of sharing his work "someday".

Deep down, Ned has one belief that keeps his scribblings hidden and almost shameful: that he doesn't have the right to speak. That artists are some sort of special species who are bright and brilliant and that he's not really one of them. So he calls himself an "*aspiring* writer" and blushes and changes the topic when people ask him about it at parties. He likes to think of himself as massively talented, but misunderstood. He doesn't take criticism well and one day, when he sees a less talented and completely ordinary friend succeed at writing something and publishing it, he gets bitter and writes off his success, "Well it's easy to get trash like that published, obviously. It's harder to find a market for stuff that's written properly, it's the sorry state of publishing today."

Any of this sounding familiar? Unlike other minority groups and closet-dwellers, however, life does not get better for Ned. He goes to the grave, as Thoreau said, "with his song still in him." Ned had the tiny flickers of desire and creativity and yearning in him, lacked the guts to put it out there, and that's that.

Millions of epic sagas, brilliant songs, beautiful poems and movies that might have been blockbusters have died along with these people who didn't believe they had the right to ask the world to pay attention. Being creative takes a certain amount of audacity, and the sorry truth is that most of us are just too afraid to speak up and say our bit.

We're taught from childhood that all our efforts will be judged and ranked along with the efforts of our peers. We're raised in school and work environments that discourage boasting and unique expression. We value conformity and like only those ideas that are financially profitable. We penalize difference and diversity in others, all the while stifling it in ourselves and trying to win approval rather than understanding our unique selves and having the guts to broadcast them.

So Ned says, "Oh nothing, don't worry, I have nothing to say" and the world doesn't argue with him, and he goes on scratching notes privately, and that, ladies and gentlemen, is a tragedy that rivals Shakespeare's.

Today, look at your desires and your Big Why. Try to see if you carry any shame or embarrassment about it. I'm not just talking about being sheepish about exploring your gift for writing absolutely filthy erotica or a hush-hush hobby where you write terribly nerdy fan fiction.

Ask yourself honestly if you censor your message in the belief that you don't deserve to have one. I can tell you one thing right now: famous authors, well-known speakers and all the rest – they weren't any more or less special than you. They didn't come into this world with their fame already in tact. They had something to say, and they took the leap of faith and said it. In fact, some authors were only really appreciated after they died. But they understood that keeping quiet when they had something to share was far worse than enduring the fear of just saying it.

- Are you secretly sabotaging yourself because you're "not a real writer"?
- Do you call yourself an "aspiring writer" or call your craft a hobby or a dream or speak about it in ways that undermine your seriousness? "Author" and "authority" share the same root – and for good reason. Do you have a sense of *authority*, literally?
- Are you generally unconfident in life? Do you hold your tongue or act like a martyr in your relationships? Do you sell yourself short?
- Do you care too much what other people think about you?

CHAPTER 3: FINDING YOUR OWN STYLE AND VOICE

It's easy to recognize a young writer – they sound like someone else. Find a fledgling author, look at the books they're busy reading at the moment and I can guarantee you their work will reflect that. This is not necessarily a bad thing, though.

Little children learn to speak from their parents, but eventually, they use that same language to express their *own* ideas. Writing is the same. It can be tricky to create something that is 100% unique and fresh, but again, this is not a problem. There are billions of people in the world, and only so many ways to say a thing, and frankly, all art is somewhere along the line "inspired" from other art.

Finding your own unique voice and style is not something that can be rushed. It's something that you grow into slowly, with practice. In the meantime, use other authors for inspiration and direction. Many people do this the wrong way round: they realize they don't have their own unique writing style, and so try to create one by deliberately tinkering with style elements until they can say, "there, that looks unique enough, I've never seen that before, I can claim this as my own now."

Often, though, "unique" is just shorthand for "authentic". An effective piece of writing is not merely a gimmick put together from a novel use of grammar and style. It's a complex blend of content, style and intention. It all goes back, in other words, to the Big Why.

A slower (but more solid) way to unearth your own personal style is just to remove anything that's getting in the way of your own natural expression. Tap into your real motivations for writing, get to the root of your message, and then write – your style will emerge on its own, if you let it.

In this chapter, we'll look at a constructive way to start including elements from writers you admire without simply aping them and losing your own unique voice.

First, start out by identifying two or three writers that you admire. Pick someone you've read a lot or even better, someone who has a very *distinctive* style.

Ask yourself, what is it about this writing that appeals to you? Go into as much details as possible. For example, you could say something like, "this author uses technically simple language and very tight, concise sentences but somehow manages to talk about very big, abstract topics. He leaves a lot to the reader's imagination. It's informal writing, almost stream of consciousness. It's got a bit of a nasty edge to it, like it comes from someone's hidden, unspoken mind. It looks like it's always in first person. It's usually about topics like relationships and family. Whenever I read this author, I feel very sad and wistful, and the stories often have a bit of bitterness in them somehow, which I like…"

Now that you've identified some elements in the style (notice how I've included not just grammar but also tone, mood, content etc.), ask yourself if there's anything in your writing that mirrors that. Look for similarities. For example, you may notice that both you and your favourite author like to dwell on the complexities of relationships, and that both have a bit of a sad tone to them. But you may also notice that where that author is curt and minimalist, you prefer writing longer, more descriptive sentences.

Do this with the other authors you've chosen.

The key here is to find out ways that other authors have already achieved something you're trying to do yourself. Look at things that resonate and then look at the cold mechanics of the thing – when your author succeeds at writing in a way you'd like, ask exactly how they did it. Feel free to incorporate *those* elements into your writing.

You could also do this by asking yourself about the ways you are different from a particular author, and amplifying that. Do you know any authors who have a similar message to you but a completely different way of expressing their thoughts? Do you read a blogger who shares your style of writing but about completely different subjects?

Merely imitating other artists and writers is not as smart as looking carefully at why and how other creative people are doing their work, and what you can learn from them. Sometimes, getting your own voice is merely a question of reading something and thinking, "Man, I could do this better!"

Writers write even when they're not writing.

When I was young, in fact, most of my "writing" involved walking around and looking at grass. By the time I turned up at the blank page, I already had fully formed ideas and my writing was merely the act of putting things down so I wouldn't forget them.

Writing is not just the physical act of typing on a laptop or scribbling in a notebook. Writing encompasses everything it takes to bring you to that moment where you're crafting the literal words – and that includes more or less your entire existence!

Everything you've experienced in your life, the dreams you have at night, your breakfast, the thoughts that bubble up as you commute to work – all of these things go directly or indirectly into your creation.

So, for this chapter, abandon the notion that writing is something you sit down to do for an hour or two and then forget about the rest of the time while you do the rest of your life. Writers are always switched on. Who knows when the next idea will come to fruition? Who knows what things you'll think of, or when a particularly awesome turn of phrase will spring to mind?

Give your brain something to work on and it will do it even when you sleep, or when you zone out and wash the dishes. Here are some daily exercises you can start doing to slip into your role as a 24/7, full time and always-on writer:

- Play with words, everywhere, all day, every day. Look at shop signs. When a person passes you in the street, quickly think of a metaphor that describes their eyes. Think of puns and jokes throughout the day. Use new words you pick up and listen carefully to the sounds of them in songs, or the rhythm and rhyme of particular words. Write down things that stand out for you.

- Keep a collection of quotes you like, copy out sentences that came out of articles and almost slapped you in the face they were so striking. Highlight bits in books you liked. Keep a dream journal for poignant and strange images to inspire you. Become curious about images, ideas, sounds and words around you ...and collect the ones that speak to you.

- If you're writing dialogue, listen to real life dialogue and get a feel for the natural flow of it. If you're writing a description of a place, go to places like it and immerse yourself there. If you're exploring a character, make it a blend of people you actually know.

- Carry a notebook around with you at all times, or else a voice recorder if you're feeling fancy. Your smartphone will do in a pinch. Many brilliant things have happened to authors while they're getting their pedicures or waiting in line at the post office – have a notebook to catch those little sparks of inspiration when they happen. Who knows what you can do with them later...

- Don't be like Ned and keep your writing stashed away all in secret. Buy organizers, files and folders – whatever you need to keep what comes out of your head safe and cherished.

- Open up. Inspiration is out there, floating, like some sort of radiation. Be receptive to it. This means making your sensory channels extra sensitive to all the fantastic things that are unfolding around you all day long. Really *look* at things. Listen to new music. Eat new foods. Touch things.

CHAPTER 5: PRIDE, EGO AND GROWTH

Writing is an inherently narcissistic activity.

You know those people who glibly mumble that they don't care about what anyone thinks because they only write for themselves and blah blah blah? Yeah, don't listen to them. We all write for a reason, and writing means nothing without an audience. Even if you never show your work to another living soul, well, you still wrote it *for* someone. That's the way that language works.

That someone may have only been in your head somewhere, and you may have been writing to them all along, unbeknownst to you. You might be writing to an imagined reader in the future, to a version of yourself, to your deceased mother, to a rival. But unless it's a grocery list, I can guarantee that every scrap of writing was written for a reason, and *for someone.*

This is a good thing. A crucial feature of any communication is that it starts at point A, and travels to *point B* – even if you're not entirely sure who's at point B just yet.

Now, as long as this is the case, you as an author are opening yourself up to a bit of a nasty reality: the possibility of a poor reception. The fact is, there is always the risk of miscommunication and misunderstanding. The possibility that even if you're understood, you can still be rejected. People who claim to not care about this are, I believe, in denial because the fact is so hard to digest.

Many people have never recovered from the first pain of having shared and expressed themselves only to find that their audience was unmoved, uninterested or worse, actively scornful. Putting out a creative effort is like baring your soul, and to have someone sneer at it can be a feeling almost worse than death.

It's no wonder that being creative and sharing your work with others is a project so fraught with ego. When someone rejects what you've slaved and laboured to create, it's easy to shut down and think they're wrong, that they're being hostile. It's easy to launch into believing that their opinion was worthless to you anyway, that they merely didn't understand you, that their taste in art was crappy all along, that you in turn judge them, that they're jealous, that they don't know what they're talking about, and on and on and on...

Now, while this reaction to criticism is entirely understandable, it doesn't mean it's something you should accept.

Luckily for writers, fantastic opportunities for growth and self-development exist. Unluckily, they exist in a difficult-to-access location on the other side of rejection and criticism. This growth is only available to those writers who have the guts to acknowledge that they could improve, and should. It's a kind of growth that only comes *after* the bravery of facing up to weaknesses and doing the difficult work of being better.

The tricky thing about big, fat, stupid egos is that nobody will ever really admit to having one! Read the following sentences and see if you've honestly ever felt them or expressed them. Tick all that apply:

- When someone doesn't like my work, I secretly think they just don't "get" it
- My writing is only for a small group of people anyway, and I'm not writing for those people who don't like me
- I'm only writing for myself, I don't care what anyone thinks
- I would join a writing group, but I'd prefer *professional* advice, not just the uninformed opinions of strangers
- Non-writers don't understand the struggle anyway, so their opinion means nothing to me
- I've done my best to express myself, if people don't understand, it's on them to try to interpret my work, not on me to explain it better
- If people don't like my work, I might as well just stop writing
- I believe people are generally vicious and cruel to writers, and I'm not willing to open myself up to that
- Unless I can be guaranteed a good reception, I don't want to risk sharing my work
- I would rather die than share an imperfect work in progress
- I prefer to write alone – other people's opinions are great and all, but I never really change anything according to their feedback

If any of the above hit a little close to home, it's likely that writing for you has a fair chunk of ego involved. Don't worry – that just happens to be the case with basically every writer that ever lived. The trick, however, is to really understand how your own ego and the need to defend it appears in your writing process.

It's OK to feel insulted and personally offended when someone doesn't like your work – but a skilled and competent writer has learnt to get over this quick so they can get to the important work of being better. Could they learn something from the criticism? If they didn't personally write this piece, what would they think of the assessment?

When you write, throw your heart and soul into the endeavor like your life depends on it. When you edit and evaluate a piece, though, take a big step back and become impersonal. A little cruel, even. This is the only way to stay vital and creative but also keep a good sense of perspective on how to improve.

An inconvenient truth

What I'm about to tell you now is an unpopular opinion and one you won't find in other writing guides. I've said above that if you are willing to accept criticism and move on, you get the reward of becoming a better writer. Abandoning your ego when necessary can lead to greater rewards and an enhanced competence as a writer. Fine and good.

But what if your original motivation for writing was no more complicated than, "I want people to praise me and to get glowing feedback. I want to be perceived as brilliant and smart and talented. I want to be popular." Now, I'm not saying that this Big Why is any less legitimate than any other. If this is your real reason, well, welcome to the club – like I said, writing is inherently narcissistic.

But it also means that you might choose to abandon writing altogether if it means you're signing up for more criticism and rejection than praise and glory. Many people have claimed to want to pursue writing because their friends and family have fed them encouragement. However, when they step out into slightly more hostile territory, and are asked to abandon the ego for a bit to do some hard work on their writing skills, they may suddenly find that writing isn't so fun after all, and that they are not in fact prepared to travel that route.

Again, this isn't necessarily a bad thing. Understanding and exploring your real motivations is always a smart thing to do. If you eventually learn that you'd rather write for friends and family or a small niche of people, there's nothing wrong with that. What doesn't make sense is signing yourself up for the sometimes grueling work it takes to improve as a writer if it doesn't actually tie in with your deeper motivation.

CHAPTER 6: YOUR WRITING WORKSHOP AND ESSENTIAL HARDWARE

Ok, so I promised that this book would not really be about the nuts and bolts of writing, but this chapter is an exception. In this chapter, we'll talk about creating a safe, productive and happy little writer's nest that you can work your magic in.

Your nest doesn't have to follow any rules other than those that will help you maximize your creative output. Most of the time, this will mean nothing more than removing distractions and interruptions to allow your natural creative spring to bubble up. Consider these elements as you set up a workspace that makes sense for you:

Concentration

You'll need a space that will allow you to do your thing without risk of pulling your energy away or putting any interruptions in your creative flow. For most people this means somewhere quiet and undisturbed, but some people also enjoy the quiet hum of a coffee shop or similar. Your place should allow you to follow a train of thought for as long as you want without distraction. Think about noise levels, other people coming to get you or things like Facebook or snacks distracting you.

Comfort

In a sense, discomfort is a kind of distraction that can pull your focus away from where it needs to be. Make sure that in your little nest, your physical needs are cared for and you are comfortable. Consider all your five senses and make sure you're treating each one right.

This means the room shouldn't be too hot, cold or draughty. Make sure your lighting is adequate, with a moderate source of preferably natural light coming from behind or to the side of you. Make sure there's enough airflow and fresh, clean air, and, obviously, make sure you're not wet or cold or somewhere dirty or untidy.

You can go full hippy with it and burn some special incense that gets your creative juices flowing, play whale music and light a candle, or you can head to a coffee shop you like and plug in your earphones while you type away with a cup of hot chamomile tea. Do what works.

If it's part of your process, buy a cheap printer (this is so you can print things out and do editing by hand with a series of pens and highlighters) and the literal files and folders you'll need to organize information. Some people like to have index cards stuck onto the wall to keep track of scenes/main ideas, other people use a whiteboard and coloured markers.

So, that's the hardware ...what about the software?

Most people find a word processor the best for writing, and use either Word or some notebook software on their laptop. There are some fantastic ones available that are very minimalist, to get rid of distractions and mimic that pure, white page in front of you.

Another idea is to get an app that cuts down on distractions (we'll look more at procrastination in, uh, a later chapter...) such as one that only allows you to look at blocked sites for a few minutes before cutting your connection and forcing you to get back to work.

CHAPTER 7: SETTING UP A WRITING COMMUNITY

Most beginner writers are like secretive moles working underground, writing alone at night where nobody can see them. But getting your work out there and in front of eyes other than your own is a vital, if sometimes painful, part of the process.

This is non negotiable.

If you think you can get away with not seeking the advice, support, opinions or feedback of others, think again. In fact, the more resistant you are to this idea, the more likely you are to benefit from it. It's not so bad!

Writing groups

I used to hate my writing group with a passion. Really. I would leave every week and secretly wish they'd all die of cancer. Sometimes I thought they were all ignorant, sometimes I got really angry with them, but occasionally, I felt like they had given me advice so valuable I don't know how I lived without it.

I'll say two things about writing groups: they are necessary, and just because you are occasionally uncomfortable with one, it doesn't mean that going isn't good for you. BUT another thing I'll say is that some writing groups are better than others, and that the whole process shouldn't be all pain and misery.

If you feel inspired at the end of your group meeting to hit the writing again, if you feel great but ready to try something new, you're probably with the right group of people. If you feel either elated that everyone thinks you're brilliant, or your soul is crushed and you feel like you can never write again, it's probably worth seeking out a group that will fit you better.

Writing groups where everyone is praised for whatever crap they put to paper (sorry) are not useful to anyone. If your group's mentality is, "everyone's a winner and nobody is allowed to offer any constructive criticism at all," your writing will not improve. Similarly, if your writing group is a den of snakes where a bunch of embittered writers take turns tearing each other down, your writing will also never improve.

You should find a group where each member is committed to improving, and where there is a culture of respect and mutual interest in growth. Follow your gut here and get away from groups dominated by fear, ego and narcissism. Also watch out for writing circles where the goal is not explicitly to improve but rather to share and chat. This ties in with the narcissism I mentioned earlier – again, it's not bad, but get stuck in a group like this and you'll feel grand but again, your writing will not improve.

Writing mentor

If you can find someone you admire and respect who is available to coach you on your writing directly, you have the chance to improve in leaps and bounds. But it becomes even more important here to be discerning. You should constantly ask yourself whether your involvement is leading to tangible benefits in your writing. Are you writing more? Are you improving on your weaknesses? Finishing projects and publishing them? Feeling inspired?

Online groups

The Internet thankfully gives you amazing access to other likeminded individuals and can be an excellent platform to elicit feedback and help. There are billions of forums, writing groups, blogs and mailing lists out there if you take the time to find them.

Again, you need to seek out that ideal balance between ego-stroking and critical enough to push you to be better. Anonymity can have its pros and cons. Consider carefully whether your online audience matches your final intended audience. Consider carefully whether your involvement with online groups is helping or hindering your overall output.

At the end of the day, a group is only as good as its effect on your writing. Your primary concern is not to feel good, to socialize or to promote yourself. It's to improve. As long as that's happening, how you choose to build your own writing community is up to you. But you do need a writing community!

Right now, think of your favourite book.

Even if you have a few, what's the first one that springs to mind? Now, immediately ask yourself what emotion you attach to that book. You should be able to answer this quickly – in fact, you might have summoned up that same emotion merely by remembering that book. Long after the details of a particular book are forgotten, the emotion it stirred up still remains.

All the best books have this in common – they have an emotional core to them that really gives us a kick in the guts, one that we don't soon forget. A book can be interesting or novel or clever, but if it has this emotional depth to it, it will far and away win our attention.

How do you make use of this fact and inject some emotional relevance into your own work? Well, if you've taken the time to carefully consider your own Big Why, like we did in the beginning of this book, you're halfway there. Speak from your heart, from this Big Why, and your emotion and enthusiasm will naturally flow.

There are other ways to make sure you're giving your writing that compelling human touch, though. Consider some of these techniques:

- When you write, build in *natural tensions* to drive the plot. For human beings, everything in life is an epic battle between two opposing forces. Really. Love versus isolation. Good versus bad. Death versus life. Knowledge versus ignorance. All the best characters demonstrate a struggle between two fundamental and conflicting principles. All the best stories show an interplay between two viable but different life philosophies. Design your stories and characters around these conflicts and your writing will naturally be compelling. Think of fundamental human archetypes, of challenges and conflicts you face in life, of your own narrative. If it's interesting to you, it's probably interesting to others.

- Mean it. I know this sounds obvious, but don't write about something you actually don't care about. If you think, "well, vampires seem to be popular," your writing is not going to be convincing, and it will show. If it riles you up, write about it. Write about it like you mean it. If even you aren't sold, how do you expect to bring your reader around?

- Don't make things too perfect. Whether you're writing fiction or not, and whoever your audience is, don't make things too easy or neat. Leave some things unsaid. Don't underestimate your reader's ability to work hard to solve innate conflicts in your narrative. Be a little ambivalent. Don't solve all your problems all at once. After all – this is what life is like, right? Life is messy and strange and full of deep mysteries. If you want to emulate it, don't create work that is easy and overly simple.

- Don't hold back. Some of the best writing in the world was writing that was shocking, ugly or frightening. Also don't be afraid to explore lofty and idealistic themes in your writing. Go large. Push your boundaries. Be bold. Don't be afraid of being a little offensive, or unpredictable. When you're done with a piece of writing, look at it and ask yourself if everything's really on the page, or if you've unconsciously toned things down a bit out of fear.

- "Kill your darlings," as they say. Don't be afraid to let go of something if it isn't working. Be honest and ask if something is really fitting, if it's reaching your gut, if it feels authentic and if it's resonating. If not? Scrap it. It's OK. The well is never empty. Keep writing and you'll get there.

CHAPTER 9: THE WRITING HABIT

A friend of mine says they write no matter what. If there's a scrap of paper in their vicinity, it gets scribbled on. This friend's home is littered with millions of notebooks. Ask them why they write and they don't have an answer. "I just do."

This is fantastic. But, sadly, it's not good enough on its own.

What do I mean?

A writing compulsion is not the same as a writing discipline. Enjoying writing and seeking it out naturally is the first step, but it's not sufficient on its own to ensure that you're reaching your potential.

No, to fine tune discipline takes boring things like work, dedication and commitment. If you're one of these people that believes that writing is a thing you do almost by accident, when the muses smile on you and gift you a fabulous idea one day when you least expect it ...well, abandon that idea now.

Inspiration is fantastic, and when it happens, you should thank your lucky stars and squeeze whatever you can from it. The hard truth, though, is that life is mostly made up of uninspiring and regular-looking moments, a whole bunch of them, and if you hope to create something special, it's more or less up to you to do it.

Be realistic. Nothing in life happens in this fairy tale way. While a flash of artistic inspiration can certainly spur you on and act as a wonderful catalyst, even the most perfect creative gift from heaven is nothing without hard work to bring it to its full potential.

Here's the bad news: if you want to be a better writer, you need to write EVEN WHEN YOU DON'T FEEL LIKE IT.

Yes, let that sink in for a bit. Consider it a job. Consider it a life obligation on par with caring for your children or paying taxes. If you want to have any success of taking your writing to the next level, you'll need to work, and you'll need to work *hard*.

This means that for every happy moment when things fall into place and you look at an awesome thing you've made, there are twenty moments where you're staring at a horrible thing that doesn't work. For every paragraph that sings, there are forty paragraphs that thunk and clunk along and need to be thrown to the scrap heap.

Think about it: *most of your work as a writer is creating horrible writing.* Like someone sifting for gold, most of what you see every day is just plain old mud.

When you commit to being a writer and working hard on your craft, you are not committing to the shiny gold bits – that's too easy. What you're committing to is all the mud in between. Are you willing to work away at it, sometimes for days and days only to backspace the whole business and start again from scratch? Are you willing to write the same sentence over 20 times until it's what you want it to be? Congratulations, you have the temperament to be a writer.

So, how are you going to do the boring day-in-day-out work of writing? How are you going to put in your hours, your blood and sweat and tears?

- Decide on a daily time commitment and stick to it. For that time, you sit on your butt and work, no excuses. It doesn't matter if you produce garbage or manage only a few good lines after an hour. Just keep the channels open and keep going. Think of writing time as non-negotiable. Turn up at the page no matter what.

- Be regular. Make writing a literal habit. Find a place in your schedule and devote it to writing. Everything else can be shuffled.

- Set yourself goals. This could be word count goals, writing group meetings or some other metric that shows you are improving. Pencil in your diary some specific times where you'll stop and ask – is this working? Then adjust as necessary.

- Always, always, always have a notebook and pen around you for if you start leaking ideas anywhere.

- Make a promise to yourself to stop being self-deprecating about your project. Tell people honestly what you're up to and be proud. Don't undermine yourself or be bashful. They may even help you to keep accountable.

- Don't share your work willy-nilly with whoever wants to see it. People's opinions are valuable, but can be a disaster if injected into the process too soon. Get your say out, and know when to take your work for criticism in a *controlled* way. Nosy partners or family can kill a new work in progress – so keep your boundaries.

CHAPTER 10: WRITER'S BLOCK AND WHY YOU SHOULD LOVE IT

I like to think of writing as a kind of therapy, and when you have writer's block, something interesting is usually going on. Don't freak out, don't rush in to try to figure out why you can't think of anything, just stop for a second and have a good look at where you are.

Writer's block can be a valuable tool if you're not afraid of it and know how to use it when it emerges. Feeling "stuck" can actually be a fantastic moment full of clues about how to proceed. The next time you feel dried up and unable to move on, ask yourself the following questions:

- Is there something on the horizon you're avoiding? Are you getting close to doing or writing something you're actually afraid of?

- Look at what happened immediately before you felt the writer's block. Do you always feel uninspired writing about a particular character or idea? Could this be a clue that this idea or character isn't working for you anymore?

- Think of the last time you bust out of writer's block and exactly what it was that got you going again. Can you recreate that now?

- Do you perhaps just need a break? If you've been going all out, heed the call and take a breather to rest and refresh.

- If you're bored ...you might be making your readers bored too. It's hard, but it might be time to admit that your idea has run its course and isn't so engrossing as you first thought.

- Have you unwittingly allowed premature criticism of your work to block you? What I mean by this is showing your work to another person before it's really ready, and then unconsciously holding this person's opinion in your mind as you write. This can be a kind of performance anxiety.

- Maybe, and don't get a big head here, maybe what you're holding back from is the fear of success. Nothing can be so threatening to your idea of yourself as a bad writer than writing something amazing, right?

"I'm not talented enough to be a writer"

A little child doesn't need a scrap of talent to learn to speak and write, he only has to keep trying until he learns. You're kind of the same. Having a natural interest in writing and feeling drawn to keep going when it's difficult may be the thing people talk about when they talk about "talent", and for sure this is better to have than not ...but by far the biggest determiner of your success as a writer is your intention and the quality of the effort you put in. Period.

"I'm just going to work on this piece until it's finished and perfect..."

Nothing in life is ever finished and perfect, especially that paragraph you've been working on for eons. The irritating reality is that a lot of the time you have to settle for "good enough" or you'll drive yourself crazy. I believe it's a good sign if you look back on past work and cringe with embarrassment – it shows you're growing. Don't be one of those people who sits churning the same idea over and over in your head. Let it go, as it is, and let the fresh ideas come. Trust that you have more in you, and that you *will* improve if you keep going.

"Only crappy, lowest-common-denominator, poor quality stuff becomes popular, so why bother with working my masterpiece when I'll never make money from it?"

This one's complicated. Somewhere out there, a deeply intelligent, hard working and talented individual was working on an epic fan fiction novel that would have brought tears to the eyes of every mom that read it, just at exactly the moment that E L James started to make obscene amounts of money with *Fifty Shades of Grey.*

As grammar teachers and general humans with a scrap of common sense wept quietly, James laughed all the way to the bank. Why bother with finely crafted sentences and rock-solid plot and character when this buffoon could make millions with writing that would have made High School scribblings look like Dickens?

Firstly, a big part of this is merely an excuse. Seriously. The fact is that high quality, innovative content *does* make money, and *does* become popular. Do your best, and let it go. Secondly, it comes back to ego. Most writers out there feel a quiet rage and indignity at the fact that James won success when she's clearly an inferior writer. Whether she is or isn't is not my business to say (ok, she is!) but she was successful for a reason, and a savvy writer can put their ego aside and ask why.

James found a way to tap into something so immensely attractive that she created a storm in a readership that was unfamiliar with light BDSM erotica but, as it turns out, pretty keen to pay for it. While people heaped scorn on her for writing trashy "mommy porn" the fact is there is not much stopping *you* from doing the same.

James and people like her, in fact, show us that success is not some airy-fairy magic, but a real possibility when all the right elements are in place. It's true that publishing and the way that people consume media is changing faster than we can think about it, but this means that there are *more* opportunities, not fewer.

Never write something you don't believe in, or create something low quality because you think you don't have to – or shouldn't – try harder. Underestimating your audience is a fatal mistake. Put your heart, soul and sweat into writing something of value, and then release it.

"I'm a writer. I don't know about the marketing side of things and I don't want to. If I create a good book, people will come. Eventually. Probably."

Having said what I just did, it's important to note that in today's world, even the most perfect bit of genius needs help with visibility. It needs to be promoted. It needs to be *seen*. I had some trouble with this myself initially, but my hesitance was mostly due to fear. If you hope to make a success of your book, you *will* need to promote your book. You *will* need to create and nurture a readership/fan base and you will need to keep them happy by giving them what they want.

If you don't, you risk becoming one of the millions of "authors" languishing alone in corners of Amazon that nobody looks at, and nobody ever will. It sucks, I know, but it's the truth. To stand out in a sea of billions of people making noise, you'll have to make sure you have something interesting to say, but you'll also have to do your best to catch attention.

We'll consider this all in a later chapter, but it can be a rude awakening for many to discover that getting the damn book finished was actually the smallest of their worries. Finding an adequate platform to launch their work, winning and keeping admirers and marketing a brand that actually has any hope of making money – *that's* where the real slog comes in.

"I'm not unique enough!"

This is another tricky one. There are two sides. One the one hand, many respectable authors do quite well creating products that are more or less rehashes of the same old themes – and it's great! They know what works and their readers love it. There's nothing wrong with this. But on the other hand, finding success initially can be difficult if you don't bring anything new to the table. Established authors get to rest on their laurels a little, but it is true that if you want to snag some attention, you're going to have to be something special.

As far as this goes, I have no advice for you. I truly believe that if you've effectively tapped into your Big Why, if you've thought through themes, characters and ideas that are compelling and have taken the time to *work* it, you will come out with something that is truly, 100%, absolutely your own and nobody else's.

This book is about creativity. No matter how full the world is, trust that you can still think of new things. Believe that no matter how crowded the market feels, that you *do* have a perspective that is all your own. Don't stress about how novel you appear, spend that energy instead on trying as hard as you can to tap into your own perspective and exploit that to its fullest.

On that note, I want to share a few ideas and techniques you can use to stimulate your own creativity and get your juices flowing.

It's important, as you try each of these exercises, to stay open. Don't go into things with your mind closed before you've even started, making assumptions about what results you'll receive. Be playfully curious, and let things *emerge* rather than wrangle them out.

Exercise 1 – Shit Happens

If life were simple and easy, there would be no stories. Shit happens, if you'll pardon the expression, and plot is what happens in response. Give your characters a bit of grief. If you don't know where to take a story, ask yourself, what's the worst thing that could happen right now? What would seriously get in the way of my character getting what they want? The rest of the story will be figuring a way around that. In non-fiction, you can do this in the form of counter-arguments. Logically create a structure where two sides are "arguing" – it's more interesting if it's a close match!

To exercise this skill of building in tensions, go around today and brainstorm all the ways your life could go wrong. If you're sitting in a café, ask how the rest of the day would play out if you were suddenly beset by zombies. What would you do if you went home this afternoon and mysteriously found everything in your home missing, with nothing but a note written in Russian stuck to the bathroom mirror? What if an alien came out of your coffee mug and told you everything you believed about the world since you were a child is completely wrong?

Take your time with this. As you walk around, really relish the thought that a great story starts when, well, shit happens. Go over the top. What's the thing you care most about in any particular moment? Think of something to get in the way of that. Then, think of ways you could *resolve* that. How could you save and redeem things?

Exercise 2 – People are Multitudes

The following exercise will help you create real, compelling characters that will crawl out of your pages - if you're writing fiction, that is.

Start by thinking of someone you know well and have a strong reaction to in general. This could be a person you're close to, but it doesn't matter if you love them to death or want to strangle them ...to death. Take a moment to think of all the things that characterize this person's essence. You could do this by creating a mind-map or just sketching out a few words, phrases, images or symbols that capture their personality.

Now, imagine another person you know who is as different from this person as possible. This might even be you! If your first person is stubborn, head strong and deeply practical, think of a friend you have who is a loosey-goosey, fickle and a head-in-the-clouds type.

Ok? Now, put those two people *together*. It might be these people actually do interact in real life, in which case you have a lot to work with, but if not, try to imagine them together. What kind of conversations do they have? What kind of arguments? Literally picture the things they would say to each other and the attitudes and emotions that would emerge when such different people collide.

Picture our example people having a fight over how boring and predictable the one is, and the boring and predictable one taking the moral high ground because at least they have some goals in life, as boring as they are. Picture the conversations in detail.

Finally, take this dynamic, this dialogue and this tension and build it into a single character. All the best characters are a little conflicted. Nobody is all one thing or all the other. No, the best characters are complex, they change, and sometimes they don't make the most sense. Think of yourself. You may consider yourself as X, Y and Z ...but if you look a little closer, you also have a tiny little bit of the unexpected Q in you, too. There's also a little part of you that is *exactly the opposite of the rest of you.*

A lot of the time, compelling characters are believable because they are flawed in this way. A strong man is compromised by his weakness, the ignorant person in the story shows that they are the wisest of everyone, the pretty girl is revealed to have an ugly, mean streak, and the evil villain of the tale is revealed to have a hidden core of compassion.

When you sketch out your characters, always embed within them this tension. Make them 90% one thing and 10% the opposite. It's the tension that will originate plot and interest and excitement. And it's up to you to decide how you will let them solve this problem!

Exercise 3 – Translations

The only way we can ever communicate with each other is through symbols. Whether you do that through mathematics, through the written or spoken word, through images or facial expressions, or whatever, every form of expression is a *translation*. A lot of creativity is merely being skilled at as many different expressive languages as possible. For example, a good piece of fiction uses many and varied symbols and so gets its message across really effectively.

To develop the skill of expression in yourself, you need to be comfortable with making synonyms and metaphors, in other words the ability to say something in many different ways. This is particularly helpful in fiction writing.

To do this exercise, go about your regular day as normal. Only, whenever you encounter something, "translate" it. Examples will show what I mean. Let's say a colleague at work literally says to you the words, "this situation has to either change or end; I've had enough."

First, try thinking of different words to express the same thing. It's now or never. Adapt or die. I'm at the "end of my tether". Think of symbols to express this same sentiment. A rope being pulled between two people, one fiber away from ripping in half. What music goes with this idea? Shrill violins that show something is about to go bad very soon? Do you find yourself holding your breath?

What colours, shapes and symbols go with all of this? What *texture* is the concept of "now or never"? If this idea were a person, what would they look like or do? Put all of it together into a scene if you can. Can you see a rock climber, holding onto a cliff with his fingernails, dangling above a gaping abyss below, the scene swelling with dark clouds and foreboding drum music as it dawns on him – things have to change or end – he has to fix things now or it's over forever for him?

Obviously, you shouldn't space out and daydream when your colleague is talking to you if you can avoid it, but you get the picture. When you do these mental conversions, what you're actually doing is flexing your creativity muscles. I'm sure you've heard the old writing adage, "show don't tell," and this exercise is just the thing to teach you how to do that. The more channels you have at your disposal to express your big idea, the more effective your message will be – and the more colourful!

Do this occasionally as you go about your life (remember that bit about being a writer even when you're not writing?) and allow your brain to go loose and let in new ideas you've never considered before. Different themes, images and ideas will emerge, and you'll develop a richer sense of imagination that will give your writing depth and believability.

Exercise 4 – Dali's trick

This final exercise is a bit of wild card but personally one of my favourites. I have no idea whether it's true or not, but there is a rumour that Salvador Dali used this technique to generate some of the bizarre imagery so distinctive to his paintings. It goes like this: sit in comfortable chair with your arm dangling off the armrest, lightly holding onto a spoon. Just below, on the floor, place a glass saucer or plate that would catch the spoon should you drop it. You should also prepare a notebook and pen within easy reach.

Now, you lean back in the chair and try as hard as you can to fall right asleep. If you're lucky, images will bubble up in your unconscious mind as you gear up to start dreaming. Right about this time your grip on the spoon will loosen and you'll drop it, where it'll fall clattering onto the plate and wake you up. Before you even know what's happening, you reach for the notebook and scribble down whatever was in your mind at just that moment you were slipping off into dream world.

It sounds cheesy, I know, but I have frequently found insight and arresting imagery by plumbing my dreams for content. Do this carefully. You may even deliberately ask your unconscious mind while awake to work on a problem and then wait and see what your dreams throw up. You could choose to keep a dream journal beside your bed and write in it every morning before the ideas of the night past evaporate. You may well not come up with anything – but then again you might.

Exercise 5 – As Good as a Holiday

This is not so much an exercise as a way of life, and something you might consider doing indefinitely. The heart of a creative response to life, the root of creating things in this world rests in novelty. Creativity doesn't lie in your stale old routine or in the things you already know about. It's *out there*, new, fresh, and a little scary. It's something, by definition, that you haven't done before.

To get well acquainted with it, you need to get comfortable with newness, with taking risks and doing things you never have before. The more new things you try, the more channels you open for potential creativity to flow.

Do new things. Shun routine and stop making assumptions:

- Eat food you haven't eaten before. Try new recipes or strange food combinations. All the best sci fi writers, I'm sure, have put something bizarre on toast just to see what would happen.

- Listen to music you're not familiar with, watch TV and movies you find strange and branch out with your reading material. Act out of character and try something you thought you hated.

- Go travelling without any plan of where you're going. See places with fresh eyes and act spontaneously.

- Take up a new hobby that uses a completely unfamiliar skillset. Flamenco dancing, pottery or beat poetry may all be that special ingredient your writing could use.

- Try other art forms. Take up watercolour painting or do crafts to loosen any interesting ideas you may have hidden in your brain. When I say "art forms," I'm not excluding Play Doh sculptures or drawing smiley faces on lemons.

- Exercise – the blood flow is good for your brain and the endorphins will keep you resilient and productive.

- Dress uncharacteristically and practice expressing yourself out of what's normal for you. Why can't you take a risk and wear something you're a bit too shy to? Try a new scent, wear a colour you never do or buy something whimsical to wear.

Writing is a habit that you can develop just like you can develop other habits. This chapter is all about ineffective, inelegant and inefficient ways to write, and how you could remedy them to make better use of your time, energy and creativity.

Procrastination

Ok, here it is. Here's the section on procrastination.

The best thing you can do to kill this filthy habit is to understand *why* you do it. For many writers, procrastination is protective. You've convinced yourself you're not good enough, you're scared of failure, scared of the effort, and so you put it off with fantastic excuses so that eventually, you can look back and say, "see? I can't do anything."

If this is you, you need to start small.

Give yourself lots of opportunities to prove yourself wrong. Don't make grand plans, just give yourself assignments you know you can do. Write 100 words one day. Praise yourself. Write 200 the next day. Don't catastrophize if you fail, just ask yourself why and then get back on it the next day. 300 words. And so on.

A good technique is to just start. Promise yourself that no matter what happens, you'll at least sit down for five minutes every day, come hell or high water. What usually happens is you get stuck into it and want to carry on writing after all.

If you procrastinate because you're a lazy bastard, like me, then there's no way around it: you have to stop being a lazy bastard, and that's about all.

Choose your most productive time of day (for me, it's the morning) and then schedule your writing for then. Write no matter what. Tell others if their knowing would push you to write each day. Reward yourself if it helps. Say affirmations in the mirror, track your progress with an app or say a little prayer and remember your Big Why every time you feel like you'd rather watch TV and veg out than write.

It doesn't really matter what "tips and tricks" you use – at the end of the day, you either write or you don't. You either reach your goal, or you don't. This is not a motivational book (can you tell?) and I can't say exactly what will be the most inspiring thing for you, but I can say this: you *could* watch TV instead of write. You *could* put this off till tomorrow, or next week. Or, you could be better than that. Decide what you want and do it. There are millions of hopeful, unfulfilled authors out there who will never amount to anything, but there are zero authors who are successful who got there by watching TV and vegging out. The choice is yours.

Perfectionism

Do you notice how often people claim perfectionism as one of those "good vices" – you know, a bit like caring too much or being too handsome? Fact is, perfectionism is one of the *worst* habits you can have. Perfectionists often end up producing the least, and having the hardest time with criticism. Perfectionists never finish. At root, the perfectionist is driven by fear, and as long as that fear is in place, growth will be limited.

It takes courage to be in process. What I mean is it takes a lot of guts to look at yourself, *as you are right now*, and accept it. You may think you are motivating yourself by being harsh and having impossible standards, but what you are really doing is shutting yourself off from the very process that would actually make you better.

This is because failing is an intrinsic part of succeeding. The messy business of trial and error is actually the place where you learn to be excellent. If you're unwilling to dwell in that vulnerability and uncertainty – you don't learn, plain and simple. And so "perfection" becomes stubbornness, pride and stagnation.

Routinely tell yourself it's OK to mess up. In fact, *plan* to mess up. Reframing "mess ups" as your goal. Mistakes and imperfect attempts are really just a way to learn, and if you accept them for that, they're not so scary any more. Laugh at yourself a little. Shrug off looking like a fool – you won't die. Switch your goal temporarily from quality to quantity. Just write – you can edit and "fix it" later.

Disorganization

You wander, lonely as a cloud, and tumble into a quaint coffee shop that speaks to your heart. You sit down and curl yourself round a hot chocolate, taking out your Moleskin notebook and pink pen, ready to start the day's writing. You're distracted for the next 10 minutes thinking about whether to order cake and then your friend calls and you spend the 10 minutes after that having a chat. Then you remember that you actually have to be in town in an hour and a half and so you cut your dreamy writing session short. You've only written one line, but that's OK, these things can't be rushed. You'll try again that evening.

Except that evening, you're tired, and you realize that whoops! you left your beautiful notebook at the café. Your table is covered with quilting supplies anyway so even if you had your notebook you wouldn't have anywhere to sit and write. But you went to the café this morning, so that counts, right? The next morning you write "characters" at the top of a loose piece of paper and brainstorm some random ideas. You lose that paper the following day while talking to your friend on the phone again...

This, ladies and gentlemen, is disorganization, and it's not cute.

I don't mean to crush your artist's spirit, but at some point, you're going to need files. You're going to need a dedicated place to write and a space in your schedule that's cordoned off for this and nothing else. You'll need paper, mountains of it, and a way to organize it. You'll need files on your computer and they'll need to be organized logically, where you can get at them. You'll need a small notebook to carry with you and endless, endless pens.

Maintaining focus while writing

- If you don't already, start supplementing with Omega 3 fatty acids from fish oil or similar. Make sure you're getting adequate sleep at night and make sure you're doing what you need to keep any medical issues manageable. A diet rich in fiber, low GI grains and high quality fats (coconut, olive and macadamia nut oils, for example) will keep your energy levels stable and help you keep focused while writing. Stay hydrated and avoid too much caffeine, alcohol or sugar spikes – they'll give you a temporary boost but you'll pay later.

- Write for 20 minutes or half an hour and then get up to stretch, walk around, drink some tea or gaze out the window. Think of it as a periodic refresh to stop things from getting stale.

- Mix things up a bit – write in different locations or with slightly varying stimuli around you to keep your brain active and engaged. Write outside when the weather's good or occasionally write with a friend (if they're not chatty!) I like burning incense as I work as I find it pulls me back into the moment and gives my writing sessions a sense of ceremony. Try what works for you and enjoy it.

- Take up an auxiliary meditation practice – the skill of opening up still, aware moments within your day will benefit your writing enormously.

- Make sure you're exercising often. Disengage your brain completely at times and flood it with oxygen and endorphins – you'll feel fresh and strengthened when you return to the page.

Boosting productivity

- Of course, the golden rule is quality and not quantity, but if you're starting out you will need to ramp up your output gradually until you reach a good momentum. Give yourself small, incremental goals every day – increase your writing quota every day by 100 words until you find a comfortable pace.

- Be firm with friends and family who think nothing of interrupting you or don't respect the time and space you've carved out to do your writing. If you need to, have a serious chat in which you explain just how important it is that you are left 100% alone during writing time. Get a sign for your door, work when the kids are at school or work away from home entirely – do whatever you can to minimize disruptions to your flow.

- Write when you have nothing to say. Write when you don't feel like it. Be OK with putting pen to paper in the morning when things are dry and it looks like nothing's coming out. Trust that once you've warmed up a bit, things will flow again. Some people do "morning pages" as a ritual. Start out the day with putting down some "word vomit" first thing in the morning. It doesn't matter, just start writing and don't stop. Write anything. *Anything.* Do this for 10 minutes and then stop. Think of this as stretching your writing muscles for the writing jog ahead of you.

- If you're frequently distracted by Facebook or the Internet in general, get an app that cuts your access to certain sites during certain periods, or which will block access after a specified amount of time. Some writing apps allow you to write with nothing on the desktop except a blank page that cannot be closed until your writing session is over. Explore some of these to see if one of them can work for you.

Fine tuning your time management

- You are never too busy. Don't self sabotage by scheduling your writing time when you know you'll be busy. Choose your freshest, most optimal time in the day and schedule your writing for then. Writing when everyone else is sleeping (early in the morning or late at night) is a good and time-honoured trick, but do what works for you.

- Don't rely on the goodness of your own heart to motivate you to write. Have a schedule, *and don't deviate from it.* Plan it and respect the dates as though they were as important as your wedding date or an important job interview. In other words, something pretty serious has to happen to stop you from going.

- What's that, something serious happened? That's OK, life is tricky, I know. But make a plan. Work something out. Carry your notebook around with you and scratch a few lines even if you're stuck on a bus in traffic. Do a thought exercise while driving on your way to an impromptu meeting. Remember, writers are still writers even when they're not writing. Keep going, even if conditions temporarily become difficult.

- It's more important in the beginning to be regular than to be prolific. It's better to earn yourself a daily 20-minute writing habit that lasts for 2 years than to go big with 4 hours a day that lasts for a month and then never happens again.

Dealing with a lull in motivation

- Writing can feel like a long endless slog with no light at the end of the tunnel. When you're feeling spunky and motivated, write your future tired self a letter reminding them why you're doing what you're doing, and why they should keep going. Whip this out when you're low on energy and thinking of giving up.

- Try to tap into your Big Why any time you feel your enthusiasm waning. A drop in energy can hint at a place where you need to ramp things up or inject more feeling into your writing. If you're bored, write until you're interested again. Use your boredom as a rudder or a compass and adjust continuously. What would it take to get your interest again? Write towards that.

- Reach out to others. Often, a drop in motivation happens because we feel like we're trekking alone on our journey. Connect with other writers for some support, positive feedback or even some commiserating. You won't feel so alone and you may even learn a few new strategies for getting the stamina to keep going.

- Think back to some happy writing moments – moments where you were praised or recognized, moments where you were in the "zone" and writing effortlessly. Try to recapture what exactly was special about those moments – there are more in future if you keep going.

CHAPTER 15: THE EDITING PROCESS

Here be dragons. Editing can be the cauldron in which you brew up your unfinished scratchings into perfect literary elixirs – or it can be a whole lot of bubble and trouble.

A good process is to have some sort of rough draft period where you write down what you need to without restraint. Give yourself the creative free-reign to just put pen to paper (or finger to keyboard) and get everything out. Write quickly and don't go back or pause to fix anything. The name of the game here is speed, and to get *volume.*

Once you're satisfied you've got it all out, it's up to you to decide where you'll take the editing process from there. There are a few approaches:

Write Fat, Edit Lean

The idea is to spew out a lot of words, and then go back later, picking through the rubble to find the gems. Your editing here is getting rid of the junk to reveal the good stuff hidden within. This is a good method if you like banging away a keyboard and like to build up a good momentum. Avoid this technique if you don't ever feel like you get a good rhythm going and don't get the impression you could just sit and write for 10 minutes solid.

Write Lean, then Plump It Up

The other way is to first piece together a skeleton and then go back later to fatten it up with "prettier" writing. I personally find this style less appealing, and I believe it may be more useful for non-fiction writing ...but it's really up to you.

Once you have your initial chunk and you're ready to do your editing, you also need to decide on your method. You could print things out with large font and generous spacing and then manually go through with a highlighter or red pen (this is fantastic and I love doing it this way) or you could simply do multiple "sweeps" over your text using the same word processor you wrote it in.

Some people like to print things out, then literally chop up the paragraphs and shift them around if part of their editing means changing up the order and pacing of events. Another good technique is to read it all aloud to find places where the flow is "sticky" and where you need to adjust punctuation. If it sounds good, it'll probably read nicely, too.

A good technique to do rather extensive editing is to go through the text with different coloured highlighters. Make marks on the paper depending on how you *feel* as you read. For example, use pink to make a mark the moment you start losing interest. Use green to show where you felt a little confused. Use yellow to show where you were reading faster because you were really excited about what would happen next.

This is a fun exercise to ask someone else to help you with – the kind of feedback you'll get from them will be far more useful than anything else they'll give you. Look at the response and ask yourself – why did they lose interest here? Are my sentences too long? Am I just repeating myself in this paragraph? Do this a couple of times with different people if you like.

You might like to take your editing process to your writing group, if they do that sort of thing. They will most likely only be able to give you general feedback ("I don't like the first person voice here") but it's a good start. Alternatively, hire a freelancer online to go through your work and give you feedback. It'll help if you ask them to answer specific questions for you:

- What part did you like best?
- What part did you like least?
- Can you find any grammatical errors?
- Can you find any spelling errors?
- Can you find places where the word choice or sentence structure can be changed so the meaning is clearer?
- What do you think about the length of the piece in general?
- What do you think of the tone?
- Is the "voice" correct and consistent? (i.e. first, second or third person)
- Are then tenses consistent?
- Are there any logical inconsistencies?
- Did you generally *like* the piece?
- Where the characters relatable, real and likeable?
- Was the argument, if there was one, persuasive?
- What would you change?
- Would you like to read more of the same? Why or why not?
- What do you think about the paragraph length and sentence length?
- Are there any overused words or expressions?

If you're eliciting the feedback and help from another person, be a grownup and be prepared for whatever they tell you. Make it safe for people to tell you the truth, or you're asking to be put in a bubble to protect your ego. Anonymous feedback is often the best for this reason – people have no incentive to lie to you. Thank the person for their perspective (even if it makes you feel bad) and use the information wisely. You're not compelled to change everything a person doesn't like, but try to be neutral and rational about it.

Finally, the editing process must, at some point, *stop*.

This is tricky because for the most part, you could go on forever if you wanted to. Don't expect to ever reach perfection. Don't expect a moment where you'll be so thrilled with a piece you can't imagine changing a single thing. But do try to reach a point where you know you've put in the work, where you're sure the message is there, more or less, and where you're happy to take the lessons you've learnt from it and move on.

Often, the real improvements come with the next piece, and in a sense, everything you write is a rehash of the same story you keep on telling throughout your life. The key is not to let obsession with the perfection of one piece keep you from working on other things, or sap your energy and self esteem to keep writing.

Many times, the temptation to tinker with something you've already written is just a procrastination technique to stop you from writing *something else*. Do your best. Work on it, a lot. Then know when to let go and try something else.

CHAPTER 16: WRITING BLUNDERS

And now, just for fun, let's look at a few all-too-common yet easily avoidable writing mistakes that even the seasoned pros make occasionally.

It's the age of the Internet: I have no doubt that you can source obvious writing tips from literally anywhere, but I have nevertheless compiled a handy collection of those crimes I know are easy to commit – and how to avoid them.

As you work through your editing process, skim over these to make sure you haven't inadvertently made a writing blunder.

- Don't introduce the reader to a character by having them stare at themselves in the mirror or get dressed in the morning. It's boring and overdone. Put your character in a real life situation instead, to show their character.

- Don't date your work by referring to particular celebrities, the prices of things or Internet memes. Ask yourself if a reference to a song or product will hold up in 2 years or so. If not, drop it.

- It goes without saying, but if you're writing sex scenes, be very, *very* careful about your tone. Unless it's obviously erotica, avoid rude slang and expletives and leave most of if to your readers' imagination. Trust me. A good rule of thumb is to avoid writing about sex at all in regular fiction.

- It's dead basic, I know – but make sure you're actually formatting paragraphs correctly. They should all be of roughly the same length, contain a topic sentence and have one idea per paragraph.

- Choose a spelling convention – American or British – and stick to it.

- Avoid making your characters speak in over-the-top slang/vernacular. It's tiresome to read someone spelling out an accent, and can even be offensive. Throw in a little here and there if you want, but try to show character, ethnicity and social class in other ways.

- I'll say it again: show, don't tell. Never write something like, "he was furious." Instead, use your words to tell the reader about the exact red colour that went to his face and the vein that throbbed in his temple. Exercise 3 above is great for this.

- Try to avoid second person voice. This involves writing things like, "You wake up to the smell of burning gas. You wonder what's burning…" Although it can be a great way to create an immediacy and intimacy in writing, it's not really suited to longer works and can be hard to get right. Most of the time, you can achieve the same result in more conventional ways.

- Avoid the "as you know, Bob" mistake. This is when you get your characters to explain to the reader what's going on, although to another character who would reasonably know it already. Think, "Oh, brother, ever since our mother died, you know I've been a little distant, and when we sold the farm last year it was worse…" Again, show instead of tell. Put clues here and there – your reader will figure things out for themselves.

- Don't have a crush on your characters. This might seem funny to some people, but it's actually pretty common. Don't launch into a description of a character that sounds like you're a stalker admiring every mole and freckle. It's a convention in some genres of romance to make the hero and heroine impossibly hot, but in all other writing, this is to be avoided. Regular people are more believable and relatable.

- Don't waste words and time on boring details. Begin scenes in the middle of action, rather than making the reader wade through a character arriving at a coffee shop and faffing around for 10 minutes before his friend arrives and the juicy dialogue begins. Don't bother telling about the little actions they do, unless they're applicable somehow. Your reader will fill in the gaps – focus on what's important.

- To make your dialogue authentic, read it aloud. Resist the urge to make characters grandstand and give soliloquys about your personal views. Believable dialogue is more fragmented.

- Don't be clever and try to change up the standard "dialogue tags" *he said* and *she said*. They're good enough on their own, I promise, and will be invisible to most readers anyway. Try being fancy and saying, "she explained" or "he wondered" and it only looks clunky. Instead, try to embed those meanings into the quoted words themselves, or use punctuation (! Or ?) to communicate the way someone spoke.

- In the same vein, kill adverbs. I love adverbs, and it's my greatest failing in life. Sometimes I catch myself thinking, "maybe I can just put an adverb in here…" but then I stop myself. Ask if there's not a *verb* you can use instead. Kill adverbs and reincarnate them as noble verbs. If you really can't, default to an adverb or nothing at all. For a very simple example, don't say "she put her glass down loudly on the table," say "she slammed her glass on the table." And so on.

- Keep variety in your sentence length. Keep a mix of long and short sentences. Those with the same length over and over and over again can be so boring they almost hypnotize the writer. Short sentences grab attention. Long, languid ones slow the tension down and ask the reader to wait a while…

- I know it goes without saying, but if you're bad at this, be extra extra doubly sure that you're not making common grammatical mistakes (you're vs. your for instance, or principal instead of principle) and be careful with easy-to-make errors like "I could care less" or "for all intensive purposes."

- Don't put two punctuation marks together. Ever!!

- Don't write for nothing. After reading a scene, paragraph, chapter, whatever, something must have *changed* somehow. There must be some kind of development. Before you begin writing it, ask yourself what the point of that part is – to show a change in the character? To reveal new information? If you haven't actually succeeded in doing that, scrap the paragraph entirely.

- Make sure you're not over using some words. Whip out your thesaurus. Word processors will let you search for every instance of a particular word. Don't use "giggle" or "bright" or say how a character "shot back" in dialogue every few lines. Mix it up.

- When naming characters, don't spend half a year pondering on the perfect name as you would your own child. It's incredibly awkward when a name seems like something fanciful and over-the-top, just to tickle the author. Long, unpronounceable names can be incredibly alienating – the reader will often skip over it mentally and lose that connection with them. This is bad especially if you have a lot of characters. Use an online random name generator or go through the phone book for natural sounding names, unless you're writing fantasy or something similar. Avoid "stripper names" ("Melody Lovemore", "Trixxie Jones", "Brandi Griffyn") ...unless, you know, you're writing about strippers.

CHAPTER 17: A STEP-BY-STEP PROCESS FOR HANDLING REJECTION WITH GRACE

First things first: rejection *will* happen.

You may be one of those people who think they'll just sidestep the whole nasty business by never showing their work to anyone, but I hope I have convinced you so far that that's not an option if you take your writing seriously.

But in showing your work, you open yourself to criticism, and you are made vulnerable to the awful, terrible, no-good feelings that come with being rejected. A good way to make sure you handle it well is to be prepared for it before it even happens. Here's a step by step process that I can suggest that will help you get a handle on the icky emotions and give you a way to squeeze the most out of the experience.

Rejection is an opportunity to learn and be better, and a great attitude is where you actually *want* and anticipate rejection. I'm not suggesting you become a masochist, but merely take a different perspective. Stephen King explained how he gleefully pinned all his rejection letters on the wall of his office, collecting them by the dozen and papering the walls of the very room he worked in. It wasn't some sick way to belittle himself (or maybe it was, Stephen King is a strange man) but a way to cultivate resilience.

Step One: Don't React Immediately

The first thing most people do when they are criticized is fight back. This makes sense. You perceive an attack (in this case, an attack to your self worth, to your identity and all the rest) and your instinct is to defend and protect yourself. You may get angry. Hurt. Miserable.

The problem is, criticism is not quite an attack, and so responding like it is will ensure you miss the learning opportunities hidden within it. Resist the urge to argue, even if you're only doing it quietly to yourself. I know some people who respect and admire their friends, but the second one of those friends says an unflattering word about their writing, they instantly take this as proof that the friend isn't as great as they thought they were. They instantly demote that person's opinion and taste, instantly try to neutralize the "attack" by invalidating the feedback they receive.

We all do this, and we all suck because of it. The first and best thing you can do when you are criticized is to stop and get a control of your emotions, gaining composure before you do anything else. Withhold on making a judgment. Don't jump to conclusions and say, "well, who is he to judge – have you read *his* stories?"

Watch for the temptation to snap back at another person, or to coolly write off their criticism because, well, what do they know? Simply hear the message, thank the person for their opinion and shelve it. They may be right, they may be wrong. You will only be able to appraise their criticism properly when you are feeling calm and levelheaded.

Take a moment to scream and cry into your pillow, put on a stop watch and give yourself 5 minutes to wallow and be the poor maligned misunderstood artist – but then get over it. Shake it off and move on to step two.

Step Two: Evaluate the Criticism

Once you've gotten the nasty feelings out of your system, or at the least sectioned them off to deal with in a more appropriate way some other time, it's time to look carefully at the data you've just received. I'm suggesting that you be clear headed and open to the criticism you receive, but I'm not saying you can't get feedback that is completely worthless. I'm not saying every bit of criticism you receive is worth the same and deserves the same consideration.

The next thing you have to do is ask yourself, as honestly as you possibly can, if there is any truth in the feedback. If somebody says, "your work is hard to follow and confusing at times," then your job is to go to your work and look with honest eyes to see if they're on to something. If they say something like, "I just didn't like this, it's not really my cup of tea," then you can shrug and move on with life. Not everyone has to like you or what you make.

If you look hard at your work and can admit that yes, the criticism may actually have a basis in reality ...excellent! You can thank the person *again* for uncovering this new aspect for you. Truly, they've given you something more valuable than a hundred "good job" comments. This is something you can work with. With this gift, your writing can become better.

The most likely outcome of this step is that you will look at your work and see a mix – maybe there's *some* truth in what has been said, but it's not the whole story. In this case, you suspend your judgment and wait till you have more data. If ten people tell you your work is confusing, take the hint. If only one ever does, you can be a bit more confident in writing that off as their problem. It's your call – but it's a call you can only make when you drop any ego and look at the situation rationally.

Step Three: Adjust and Repeat

Don't keep throwing your work at people who routinely say they don't care for it. Don't spend years of your life and valuable self esteem writing to people who can't and don't want to listen to what you have to say. Likewise, don't keep asking for feedback from people and never doing anything about what they tell you.

Feedback and criticism is valuable if something changes because of it. Let the process be dynamic and intelligent. You are not a performer on a stage pandering for attention or likes on social media. You're an artisan, and you need to keep working on your craft until it's the best it can be.

Take feedback to heart, make changes that you believe in and then seek feedback again to compare. Remember, you don't have to agree with the response you get. But give the process its due diligence. If you feel pressured to go one way and really want to go the other, there's only one solution: go your way and then see what happens. Even if you never get feedback from another human being, the world itself will be your critic and let you know how you did. If you enjoy writing something, have people who enjoy reading it and even make money from it, what could be better?

Things To Remember When You're Feeling Rejected

- Don't be tempted to think, "everyone is special, we're all great in our own ways, my work is just not appreciated right now for some reason..." I mean it. This kind of thinking will make you feel better in the short term but is toxic in the long term. Yes, *it is possible for you to write something crappy.* And it's OK! Write badly, it's not the end of the world. Don't be the kind of person who looks at shoddy writing and shrugs and says, "well that's just the honest expression of where I am in my artist's journey..." or whatever. No. There is good writing and there is bad writing. Strive to write well, but don't be horrified about writing poorly. Oh, you wrote something awful? So what? Look at it, admit it's *bad*, and move on.

- Everyone fails. Everyone turns out truly embarrassing, ugly, headache-inducing writing at times. In fact, I would suggest that even your favourite authors in the world have some dirty secrets you don't know about. It doesn't matter though. What matters is that they had the spirit and courage to keep going and get closer to the good stuff.

- The key to being resilient is not to give a damn. If you ever catch yourself censoring what you have to say because you are worried about what people may think, try think of it this way: imagine yourself on your death bed, at the end of your life. That's it, it's over for you. Have you got some untold stories you didn't get out while you had the chance? Have you hidden from the world the very things that made you special? Have you bitten your tongue and are now going to your grave never knowing what would have happened if you had the guts to speak up and be seen...?

- Remember that sometimes, critics really are just frustrated artists themselves. Trust your gut on this. It's so easy for someone who hasn't taken the chance to be vulnerable and expose themselves to pass judgment on someone who has. Take it for what it's worth. Sometimes, people will be mean because unconsciously, they are jealous that you're doing what they don't yet have the courage to do. Be kind to them and move on. You may inspire them to take the leap themselves one day.

- Rejection gets easier the more you do it. And you may as well get used to it, because as long as you're writing and putting stuff out there, there will someone with something to say about it. Grow a callous and accept that criticism and rejection are just part of the deal.

- If you're floundering and feeling bad about your competence, it may help to remember the praise you've received. Balance out any catastrophic thoughts you may have by remembering that although you've written something less than fabulous, there have been times when you've hit the mark perfectly. Keep going and you'll find those sweet spots again.

- Try to separate out your worth as a person from your skill as a writer. This can be tricky. Have the balls to feel great about yourself no matter how you perform.

Remember to tell yourself that you're still a writer, you're still a good person and that you still have permission to keep writing!

   - Lastly, treat positive feedback the same way: be neutral about it and evaluate it carefully. Are people just flattering you? How astute is their commentary anyway? Don't let these judgments disturb your core values and stay calm – appraise positive comments just the same as you would the negative ones.

CHAPTER 18: WHAT ABOUT A GHOSTWRITER?

You know, I understand if you have a good, hard look at your life and think to yourself that honestly, you just can't be bothered. Maybe you really don't have the time. Maybe you've tried to improve but your writing is just atrocious and that's the end of it. Maybe you hate writing or English is not your first language.

Even still, though, I believe you should write your own work.

Why?

There are ghostwriters out there who are talented, hardworking and just the kind of people who will take your grand ideas and spin them into something special, without all the effort of, you know, writing it out yourself. With enough money, in fact, you could actually just *buy* yourself a good novel, put your name on it and call it a day.

Many "authors" do this, and if you're a fan of any famous bloggers, self help writers or other sundry famous folk, there's a good chance what you read was actually written by a ghostwriter. I'm not about to tell you what I think of the ethics of this (I think it's fine) and I'm not about to tell you whether you should go for one (you can) but I am going to say one thing.

Ghostwritten work is missing a crucial ingredient. It's something that you can't actually pay for, even if you had the money. It's not something you can describe to a freelancer you've never met and tell them to whip it up for you in a few weeks. Throughout this book, we've been going round and round this idea of creativity, this beautiful, elusive quality, this *thing* that makes dead words on a page come alive. I've tried to suggest ways you can cultivate this in yourself, ways to coax out this magic in ways that make sense for you, and ways to nurture it when you find it so that your writing is vibrant, human and completely captivating.

Ghostwritten work can be good. It can *very* good. But it can never capture this magic. Not even close. I'll be blunt to make my point: in the same way as you wouldn't expect to find love and romance with a prostitute, you can't expect to find personal, high quality and unique work merely by paying a ghostwriter.

Now, if the work you are commissioning is merely a how-to book, a compilation or guide, something light and silly, or, I don't know, a recipe book – it will be less obvious. Here, I would say go ahead and save yourself the trouble by hiring a professional and carrying on with the rest of your life.

But if you have a tender, special idea you've been nurturing for a while, yearning to grow it up into a big strapping book that people will read and be moved by – then *don't* go for a ghostwriter. They can craft you a convincing replica of what you tell them, sure, but it will lack the soul and punch that a book you wrote yourself would have.

There won't be the same level of conviction present in a book written by somebody who's approaching the thing as more of a technical exercise. Your efforts may even be a bit rougher, a little less polished and a little less sophisticated than theirs – but it will be *authentic*. And readers respond to authenticity.

Once you've actually written the thing, you're going to need to find people to read it and hopefully, with a bit of luck, love it to death.

The topic of how to promote, market and sell your work is massive and beyond the scope of this book, but we'll consider here briefly the elements you'll need in place.

Ideally, you'll start marketing your book before it even exists. If you're one of the many informal, unpublished authors who want to make a name for themselves on their own steam, you'll need to have a good idea of how to self publish.

The Internet has made all aspects of publishing – from the writing to the promotion to the actual exchange of money – easier and more accessible than ever before. Truly, someone today can write a book, design the cover, format it for Kindle, promote and sell it on Amazon or other platforms and collect money from sales directly – all without the help of anyone else.

But it's daunting. The real work of self-publishing is far, far greater than merely putting the book together, but consider the following questions to help guide your consideration for how you'll actually publish your baby:

Will You Self Publish At All?

First decide if you'll pitch to agents or publishing houses or go it alone and publish your book on a platform like Amazon. The former may never work out and may take a lot of stress and rejection, but still retains something of a gold standard in terms of the prestige of having a house's name behind you; the latter is less prestigious but more realistic if you really want the work out there and money in your pocket.

How Will You Cultivate An Online Presence?

This has gone from something that authors could optionally do to something mandatory. Authors these days are expected to be masters of self-promotion, so think of how to get your name and brand out there. A blog? A website with promotions, teasers and special discounts? A Twitter feed? A podcast? You could hire someone specifically to help with the promotion of your book or you could use any of the billions of marketing resources out there to piece together a campaign of your own. But it needs to be done, and it needs to be done *continuously*.

Who Is Your Audience, and How Can You Connect With Them?

Your audience should already be built into your work, and you should already have a firm idea of your demographic before you begin writing. But also brainstorm ways you'll form actual relationships with them, rather than just market your book in their general direction. How will you get feedback and requests from them? How will you reward their loyalty? What else does your audience want and how can you give that to them?

What Is Your Brand?

I know some aspiring authors are repulsed by the idea of marketing themselves and their work like a brand, but it needs to be done. Chat to a marketing expert or consult some literature on putting together a coherent image that you can communicate to potential readers. Try to really understand the market you are entering. Work alone or with a graphic designer to put together logos and book covers that are professional and consistent. Cultivate *yourself* as the creator of all this. What image do you wish to convey? What do you offer readers that they can't get anywhere else?

How Will You Price Your Work?

Will you write millions of short, serialized pieces that sell for nothing on Amazon and hope that in bulk, they'll amount to good exposure and a tidy profit? Or are you going to write longer, more quality pieces less frequently and charge more for them? Both strategies are valid. Do research on optimal lengths and prices for things, factoring into it the effort you've put in. One book will not be enough. Will you need multiple personas? A pseudonym? Will you launch on multiple platforms or just one? Will you offer initial discounts or a free run to get people interested?

What Can You Do Consistently To Maintain Your Marketing Campaign?

You'll be working your butt off to promote a new book, but it doesn't stop there. Decide upfront what level of engagement you're comfortable with *for the long term.* Can you maintain a blog for the next three years? A Twitter account? Will you hire someone to do it for you?

Ultimately, the best way to start with publishing yourself is to just do it. Just start. It will be inelegant at first, and your first attempt may very well bomb, but it's good to just start, and begin sooner rather than later to learn the hands-on lessons.

Through trial and error you can gradually build something effective and all your own. Self-publishing is a lot like being an entrepreneur: you learn by doing. Fail early and fail small, and you'll arrive more quickly at the place you want to be eventually.

CONCLUSION

And so, we arrive at the conclusion, although a writer's life, to be dramatic for a moment, is never really concluded. There are no easy answers, no quick hacks and tips. No shortcuts. But it is my hope that with this short guide, I have spoken to something in you, or at the very least, that you have disagreed with me enough to be spurred into action.

The creative process is possibly one of the most rewarding things in life. It's also a treacherous journey – sadly, many people never fulfill their real potential as writers.

This book has tried to focus on some of the earlier, less examined aspects of the journey – the urge to create at all, and how you can harness that and use it make your writing more powerful and effective. Wherever your journey as a writer takes you, I hope that the ideas in this book have convinced you to go a little further, and a little deeper with your message.

On to new beginnings...

THE HOUSE THAT LOVE BUILT - UNEARTH THE
FOUNDATION OF LOVE AND THE FUNDAMENTAL
PRINCIPLES OF WHAT MAKES LOVE STRONG ENOUGH
TO LAST A LIFETIME

INTRODUCTION

In your mind's eye, *picture a house.*

You can make this house whatever you want it to be: grand or humble, multiple stories or made of a single room, beautiful or run down. Picture the rooms and the furniture inside those rooms. Picture the number of beds and the kinds of things you'd find in the kitchen cupboards. Is there a TV? A nursery room? A garden?

Now once you've visualized everything, ask yourself, is this house *suitable*?

Well, you might naturally ask, suitable ...for what?

In this book, we won't be talking about the best, most correct way to build "houses". Instead, we'll look at what makes something like a house suitable in the first place: *whether it suits the needs of the family living there.*

This is a book about relationships, but perhaps not in the everyday way we use the word "relationship". In the chapters that follow, we'll look at a set of three fundamental principles of real loving relationships. These are the kind of human connections that stand the test of time, and this book is about how you can start creating them right now, no matter what your "house" looks like.

This book takes an approach that's a little different from what you'll see in other books about love, relationships or family. Following relationship advice can sometimes feel like building a house for a family that doesn't exist, or one that you've never met before. It's like deciding that a house is suitable for someone's needs without knowing what those needs are.

In this book, we turn things around and look at the family first, and *then* consider the best house for that family to live in. Because no two people are the same, and no two families are the same, the "best" will never be just one thing.

Before we continue, I want to address a thought you might already be having: "wait a second, I don't have a family yet, I'm just looking for advice about how to make the relationship with my wife/husband better."

Here's another principle that we'll begin this book with: everyone is in a family.

The TV tells us about the standard "family unit". It's invariably a mom and a dad with two or three school-aged children who all live together in a house. But try to think for a second just how many people you know who actually fit this description.

While most of us immediately picture this setup when we hear "family", the reality is that we are surrounded by people who are divorced, remarried, single, childless or childfree, in gay relationships, in open or casual relationships, estranged from their parents or some colorful mix of all of the above...

So what *is* a family then, if not this standard "unit"?

In the pages that follow, we'll understand a family as any set of emotional connections. That's it. If you are unmarried and have no children, you may not consider yourself as having or being part of the classic family, but you are nevertheless surrounded by a constellation of connections and relations to other people that defines your experience and gives your life meaning and character. You *do* have a family. And it is unlike any other.

To get the best out of this web of "relations" ... that's the topic of this book.

To improve this family and help it fulfill its potential, we'll be looking at the *connections* between people, rather than the people themselves. These kinds of families are living, breathing entities and they are always changing. And this means that no matter what your situation is right now, you can take steps to help that family grow and develop into something else, something amazing.

Using three key principles that underlie all human interaction and connection, we'll look at kind, compassionate and intelligent ways to start taking control of the relationships in your life, right now. Whatever problem you're dealing with right now, the principles in this book will help you tackle them with compassion and awareness.

Whatever drew you to this book, and whatever your current life situation, this book is for you.

Maybe you've had a miscarriage, or you're thinking about proposing, or you're having difficulties with your children. Maybe you're recently divorced and in transition, or your parents are moving into your home. Maybe you're pregnant or recently a step parent. Maybe you really did have the traditional "unit" with all the trimmings ...and then your partner cheated. Because this book is not about a single solution for a single family, the ideas here are meant for every one of these situations, and more.

I started by asking you to imagine a house. Now, I'll ask you to do something a little more difficult: imagine a family, *your* family.

If you're like most people, you might have a little trouble deciding who to include and who not to include. You may be drawing a blank and feeling that nobody really fits the bill as your family member, or you might feel as though you're including many smaller families into one big, complicated mess. By the time you are done reading this book, my hope is that your answers to both of these questions will have changed a little.

But enough rambling, let's get on with the book.

We'll start where every self-help book starts.

With *you*.

CHAPTER 1: IT'S NOT ABOUT YOU

Now, don't take offense if I tell you that even though you're the one reading this book right now, you really are only a small part of whatever problems you're experiencing. I know that in the vastness of our own minds, it can feel like our perspectives and our experiences are all that there is. Of course we see problems from inside our own filters – how else could it be?

But our limited perceptions are not the full story. If you're having difficulty right now, hold the problem you're experiencing in your mind and just look at it for a second. You may only feel the pain of whatever emotions this situation causes for *you*, or you may only see yourself in it, a victim of circumstances or other people, desperately trying to live your life while other people get in your way.

But, this is where this book departs from others like it: it's not about you. Really.

The First Principle

The most fundamental idea of this guide is that there are, at the end of the day, no individuals, only connections. This is like "no man is an island" although it goes a step further, in that there isn't really a separate "man" either.

This is not as bizarre as it seems at first, it simply means that we, as humans, are constantly defining each other. Whatever we are, we are that only *in relation* to others who are. A word is mostly meaningless just floating on a page; it needs the company of other words, or a sentence, to starts meaning anything. People are the same.

Think of all the things you are, right now. In whatever way you define yourself, you'll soon see that you are never those things in an absolute sense, but a relative one. If you think of yourself as "patient", then ask, patient to whom? And with what? You are never just standing by yourself, being patient. Rather, your patience is expressed when you encounter others, when you work together with someone on something.

You cannot call yourself a mother if there is no child, or a doctor if you have no patients. Even if you define yourself as an anti-social, lone wolf, you still need the help of others to define yourself against. You still need somebody that allows you to say, "I am not like them".

Of course, we can delve into a philosophical argument about what it means to be a person and all the rest, but most people can intuitively sense the fact that human beings are all connected. And those connections can get pretty complicated!

Later in this book, we'll explore how this shift in perspective is actually the first step to a deeper understanding of yourself and others; for now, try to remember that whatever problem you're facing, you're only facing it from one perspective. Also remember that whatever you are right now, you are that in relation to those around you.

Most self-help advice positions people as free-standing individuals, whole and complete. The idea is that these individuals then go out and encounter others. When there's a problem, it's up to the individual to change himself or the other individual until the problem goes away. In this book, we'll do the opposite. Here, there are no individuals, only relationships. When there is a problem, it is not either individual who is responsible for fixing themselves, since it's not about them. Rather, it's the *connection* between both that is the problem.

Let me give an example to show the difference in mindset.

A mother brings her child to therapy: he's badly behaved, can't seem to pay attention to anything and fights with his siblings at home. Mother believes he has ADHD and needs medication. The thing is, the son is happy at school, getting good grades and doing well with his peers.

What is the real problem here, anyway?

If we assume that there are only individuals, we'll zoom in on the son and look at his "symptoms". To solve the problem, we'll think of ways to make him stop doing what he's doing. We might send him, alone, to a therapist and assume that once he changes, or takes the right medication, the problem will go away.

But was the son ever the problem at all? What if it's the mother? Well, we'll see that the mother has completely different relationships with her other children, and of course, never had this issue before her children were born in the first place. It doesn't seem like it's entirely the mother who's "to blame" here either.

If we switch our focus to connections and relationships, we might see that the problem is not the son, and not the mother, but the relation between them both. The mother is fine, the son is fine. But their connection itself is the problem, and it's this *connection* that needs to go to therapy!

If we use this perspective, we might see that the mother and son have a complex and malfunctioning set of patterns when they deal with each other. The son is playing the role of the naughty child, and the mother the role of the only one who can reign him in. The problem is the drama they play *together*. Medicating the son doesn't do a thing for the root of the problem.

Take a moment to think of the last person you connected with before reading this. Can you think of all the ways that your connection with them is 100% unique, and how neither of you share that with anyone else? Does this single relationship define everything that you are? Does it define everything that they are?

The Second Principle

Remember the "family unit"? Perhaps you thought of some family who *used to* fit the mold. But then their kids grew up! People are born, people die, and in between, people grow and age. That means that a family can never stay the same. The second principle is pretty obvious: relationships and connections are always transient.

Imagine the mother and son from the previous example. Now picture the same situation, a few decades into the future. Much time has passed, many insults are forgiven and forgotten. The son is now an adult and the mother is older too and in a completely different stage of life.

Their connection now could not be more different. They relate on friendly terms now, and they are actually very fond of each other. The relationship has changed because the individuals, the environment and life itself changed around them. The particular connection they shared was temporary, and eventually gave way to another, different connection.

In this case, the new relation is "better" than the old one, but very often, changes in the connection between two people can be for the worse. Think about the relationship problems you're experiencing right now. Chances are, the problem emerged because the nature of the connection changed somehow.

A connection dissolved or became less significant, such as with divorce, breaking up or drifting apart.

A connection intensified and became more significant, but perhaps in an uneven or disruptive way. Think of an affair, or a couple who are on different pages when it comes to having children or retiring.

A connection can change in what it fundamentally is, such as when people grow up and relate to their parents as adults rather than dependent children. The transition can spell some awkwardness, at best.

Change is the rule, rather than the exception.

But read any relationship advice column and you'll get the impression that any change is some kind of horrible mistake. A husband loses interest in his wife and is chastised and immediately given a million tips and tricks to spice up the relationship again, i.e. to *resist* that change. A woman is told to leave her indecisive boyfriend because he doesn't want to move in with her just yet, and their change in expectations of one another is to be *resisted*. A mother is encouraged to put more rules and restrictions on her budding teenagers in an attempt to stop them from growing up, *resisting* the fact that her old relationship with them is gone forever.

But using this principle, we won't resist the natural changes that come with any relationship. In fact, we'll assume that just as you can't argue with birth or death, you can't argue with inevitable changes in connections. All you can do is embrace them!

Take a moment to think of your own life. Rewind back to a decade ago, if you can, and think of all the people you knew then. Picture in detail your most important relationship at the time, but also all the less significant ones.

Are they the same as today? Are YOU the same now as you were then? If you go back even further, do you see the same people or a whole different set? Picture yourself a decade or two into the future. What is still the same? And what has changed?

The Third Principle

If the first two principles seemed a little grim, well, they kind of are. There is nothing we can do to change these two facts. We all rely on other human beings for our existence, and there is no arguing that we all exist as part of a bigger whole. And because human life itself is always changing, our connections with one another will always be in flux, too.

If you believe in the "standard unit" narrative, you might believe that any change to this ideal setup is automatically a problem. Children grow up and rebel, threatening the status quo. People change their minds, or more likely, they change their *hearts*. Financial circumstances change, people move, people fall in and out of love. The closer you look, the crazier it seems to expect any relationship to be one thing, forever. Why bother at all if nothing is permanent?

But there is one more principle that takes these two facts and makes them a source of meaning, rather than something to get depressed about. The third principle is that if relationships are always changing ...then they can change for the better, too.

Connections are not *real* in this sense, as they are nothing more than what the people involved have agreed to. In our example, the mother and son can stop their script and choose to relate in a completely new and different way. In fact, only one of them needs to change to change the relationship between both. At any time, you can make conscious, meaningful changes to the way you relate to others.

And so, we arrive at the point of this book. When you narrow down your perspective and zoom in on yourself and your own small part in the bigger picture, it's easy to feel overwhelmed. It can seem like you have no options, no choice but to carry on with the way things are.

If you blame others, you are unable to see all the ways that *you* hold power, and that you can improve your situation. On the other hand, if you assume all responsibility and fail to see the role others play, you set yourself up for disappointment when you try to change things that aren't rightly up to you to change.

But if you take the broadest possible view, you see all the connections surrounding you. You realize that change is natural, and you are able to move with those changes instead of against them. And when those relationships evolve and develop, you are aware and conscious enough to act, not as an individual, but as a part of a much bigger, much more complex relationship machine.

Thinking about your own life, try to remember when last you acted deliberately and with conscious effort in some relationship or other. Do you "go with the flow" and feel like things just happen to you, or are you proactively working to bring about changes in your life? If not, why not?

How to Use This Book

This book is for you if:

- You have ever loved or want to
- You have a mother, father, siblings or children
- You work with people or for them
- You have friends

In other words, it's for everybody!

Using the three principles we've outlined here, we're going to build a model for dealing with love, relationships and families, from the ground up. Whoever you are and whatever challenges you're experiencing, we'll look at how to apply these principles with compassion and self-awareness.

But when are you going to get to the relationship advice?

If you've read this far, you might be wondering when I get into the good stuff and start explaining *how* to have better relationships with your partner, your children etc. I should give a disclaimer here: this book contains no advice. What it does contain, however, is a comprehensive *method of creating your own advice.*

Think of the techniques and ideas in this book not as some quick fix to get you out of relationship drama, but as a method to save you from that drama in the first place. The ideas here are not just intended to resolve any relationship issues you have right now, but all those issues you will have in future, with people you haven't even met yet.

In the second part of this book, I'll suggest some concrete exercises and techniques to help you start taking control of the relationships you're a part of. You'll start making changes towards a life that not only make *you* happier, but is for the well-being of *everyone* you encounter.

I encourage you to read with an open mind. And an open heart! More importantly, I encourage you to actually try some of the exercises here. These ideas are nothing more than dead words on a page until you apply them, out there in your real life.

CHAPTER 2: FAMILY - NOT A TREE, BUT A FOREST

We've looked at the three key principles that guide this book, and we've set up a new, broader definition of "family":

Your family is your own personal constellation of human connections.

Most families are bonded together by blood or marriage. But there are very many more ways for one human being to bind to another – some ways can even be stronger than blood ties.

There are 7 billion people living on this planet, right now. In a sense, every single one of them is connected to every other. You may not know it, but there are distant, convoluted paths linking you to a stranger in China at this very moment, or to a family living in the Dutch countryside. Every time you work, buy something, or share information online, you are doing so through this web of connections. It's not a family "tree" so much as an entire family ecosystem. The more immediate links (your mother, your spouse) are the obvious ones, but you are connected, in some way or other, to every other human being, past and present.

When defining your own family, it's really just a question of where you draw the line!

In this chapter, we'll be piecing together your own family network, including those people who have the most influence on your life right now. Of course, because relationships are always transient, this may change at any time.

The following is an exercise designed to bring your own web of "family" connections into focus. This may seem deceptively simple at first. When people ask about families, it's easy to rattle off a list of your parents, your siblings, your significant other... This is *not* what we're doing here now, though.

We'll be constructing a family tree, but one where ALL the different flavors of human connection are represented, not just those from blood or marriage. Once you have a better understanding of what you're working with in your own life, all the rest of the book's exercises will make more sense.

Don't be tempted to rush this exercise. It only *seems* simple. If you really spend the time with it, you may be surprised by the insights you gain. Try this even if you're seeking insight into just one particular relationship – your understanding of it will be so much deeper, I promise. Incidentally, many mental health workers and therapists of all kinds use this technique with their clients.

Step One: Lay it Out

There are many different ways people connect with each other. The significant connections are not necessarily the longest or most official. The ones that ultimately matter are those that have changed you, those people who you've shared a deeper experience with or who you trust and depend on greatly.

Start with a blank piece of paper and a pen. Think of all the people in your life. Now draw yourself at the center of this page, in a circle. Draw your parents, friends and colleagues around this circle. Arrange them according to how significant each of them are to you. You could write important people's names larger, or put them closer to your own name. Or both. Use colors and symbols if you like.

Step Two: Kinds of Connection

Connect yourself to the names around you with a directional line. This line should symbolize the *type* of connection you share with this person. Be creative: for a difficult relationship, draw three jagged lightning bolts, from them to you, for example. If you feel that you're constantly protecting your partner, draw the line as a shield or umbrella over their name. You get the idea. Try not to overthink it at this point, just make sure that you're representing the relationship honestly. If you have practically zero relationship with someone you're supposed to love, draw only a faint line …or no line at all.

Remember, you are drawing the *connection* now, not the people who are connecting. There isn't much information in family titles, so don't just draw an arrow to represent "sister". Rather, think of the kinds of actions or emotions between you and a particular person in your web.

What kind of information travels between you both? How frequently do you interact and what is usually the outcome of those interactions? Is the connection equal or unequal? Carefree? Unstable? For example, instead of "sister" you can draw a line that represents playful competition, but make it quite light since the relationship is not particularly intense.

Here are some types of relationship that might appear in your diagram, with examples:
- Protecting or defending (like an older brother defending his younger sister)
- Undermining (a manipulative work colleague)
- Supporting (a mentor or grandparent)
- Conspiring together (siblings, friends)
- Enabling (a "doormat" mother)
- Hiding (a dependent girlfriend or boyfriend)
- Celebrating and having fun (friends, colleagues)
- Working together (parents of toddlers)
- Fighting against someone or something else ("Us versus the world" style couples)
- Encouraging (schoolmates)
- Limiting (parole officer or course coordinator)

As you're filling in the connections between the people in your web, remember also that relationships go both ways. The same sentiment might be reciprocated, or you might behave towards them in a way very different from how they behave to you. Draw two arrows (or more!) to represent the connection as accurately as possible.

Step Three: Edit

Put in everyone you can think of. Your paper may get crowded or seem lopsided – this is fine, just go with it. Add in work colleagues, old crushes, teachers or enemies. Anyone who has played or is playing a significant role in your life.

When you're done, look at your web. It'll probably be messy! If you're like most people, you may notice that your "official" family tree doesn't quite match up with your unofficial one. The people who actually play the biggest role in your life may be quite different from what you first assume. You might have put your husband close to you but on second thought, found that the lines between you and your two best friends are far, far more significant.

Look without judgment and if you need to, redraw your family tree according to who is *really* the most significant to you. Make a neater, more compact version. If you're having trouble with this, ask the following questions to really zoom in on the key players in your life right now.

- Do you notice one particular person in your web that is really prominent? Maybe they have a lot of lines going outward from their name to everyone else, or maybe a lot of lines direct *to* them. Maybe that person is you?

- Are there any spots where all the connections seem negative? Does one sub section seem dominated by a particular kind of relationship? For example, are all the relationships on one side of your family exclusively financial and obligatory in nature? Are they all particularly weak or particularly strong?

- Most people draw their support and energy from just a handful of people. Who are these people for you? Are you surprised by how many people there are?

- Are there any "black sheep", forgotten people, members who have been expelled or left the group, or is the memory of someone passed still making itself felt in your family? There's no reason why you can't include deceased people or those you haven't had contact with for years – if they have an impact in your life right now, you have a connection with them, and so they deserve to be in your diagram.

- What kind of relationship is most common in your web? Are there any kinds of relationship that are completely absent? For example, you may notice that all your friendships are really work-related, or that you have no close confidantes at all. Maybe you notice that you have plenty of "limiting" type connections with others, for example.

If you'd like to, make a note of two or three insights that you've gained from this web, or the things that seem most prominent to you. They might look like this:

- "My wife is serving the role of friend, family, therapist, work colleague …she plays every role!"

   - "My family is mostly made up of connections from the past, and all the people I know are those I grew up with. There don't seem to be any new people at all."

   - "Though my family and I are very close knit, it does seem that our interactions are mostly negative, with my aunt being the instigator for a lot of the negativity."

And so on.

   What you put down at first with this exercise might not necessarily be the truth. Sometimes in families, things are not what they seem. Just remember to look not at the individual, but at the *connections* they share with other individuals. You are curious about the lines, rather than the people that share those lines.

CHAPTER 3: LOVE VS. CHANGE

Let's move on.

Armed with your new family tree and the understanding of how you fit into the world, it's time to look at the three principles we mentioned earlier on. In the following chapters, we'll see how these general principles can be applied to specific relationship problems of any kind ...including whatever problems you're having with your loved ones right now.

The first principle was that there are no individuals, only connections. There is no "husband" or "wife", there is only the unique relationship they share *together*.

So what's the problem? Focusing in on your issue

Chances are you didn't start reading this book because everything in your life was going perfectly and you just needed something to read! Your relationship issues may be vague or very specific, long standing or recent. Whatever they are, take a moment to write them down now, clearly.

Creating your family web might have brought the problems into focus a little more clearly. See if you can condense your problem down into one or two sentences. For example:

- "My husband and I are drifting further and further apart and we're both not financially secure enough to separate."

- "My girlfriend cheated on me and we've moved on, but the trust is gone and it seems like things will never be the same again."

- "I've broken up with what I thought was the love of my life, and I'm getting depressed with how difficult it is to meet new people again."

Once you've focused in on your issues and written them down, put them somewhere safe. We'll be returning to these notes again soon.

Framing the problem: a perspective shift

So, why do relationships "fail" anyway?

Ask this question and you'll get a million answers: People change. Husbands cheat. People drift apart or have a big fallout. It's his fault. It's her fault.

Here, I'd like to suggest that most of what we think of as relationship "failure" is not failure at all, but simply relationship *change*.

Because connections are transitory, it's normal that they evolve and grow with time, just like the people that they connect. The problem comes when we try to force these natural, evolving connections into a fixed shape. When the relationship evolves (as it always does) then we notice that it doesn't conform to our expectations anymore. We call it a problem and try to fix it, which in this case means forcing it into the shape it was before.

Marriages are classic examples. A man and woman vow to one another that they will always love the other, always be true and devoted, and stay together forever and ever. This is a script. This is a performance where both people agree to play their respective roles. Some marriages do naturally follow this script. But others? I don't have to tell you how many people divorce, cheat, break up or live in dead, unhappy marriages. I don't need to tell you because it's so common that it isn't really news!

Example 1:

A man and a woman marry. They are very happy for 10 years. They love each other. Eventually, they each grow in different directions. They still love each other, but things are different now. They start to pull in different directions. Both panic when this happens. Have they fallen out of love? Are they going to be a humiliating statistic after all? They rush to counselling, take a second honeymoon. They fight. The more their relationship changes, the more they resist it. They *have to* stop fighting, the script says so! Eventually, after much bitterness and regret, the two divorce, and hurt each other greatly in the process.

Example 2:

The same man and the same woman marry. They are very happy for 10 years. They love each other. When they start growing in different directions, they don't panic. They talk about it, are honest about their changing relationship, and vow only to treat each other with kindness. Eventually, they discover that they are moving into a new era in their relationship. Their old way of relating is indeed over, but there is a *new* one developing: they still have the same affection for one another, but spend less time together, and sleep in separate rooms. There is no need to divorce. After their relationship transitions, they accept its new state, always being kind to one another. Whatever happens, they do it mindfully and with compassion towards each other. The script is not important – only the actual relationship they share, with each moment.

The way you frame a problem determines the way you engage with it.

So let's return to the question, why do relationships fail? I would like to suggest that no relationship is *ever* a failure, and what are sometimes called "problems" are merely growing pains. Here are common "relationship problems" that I'd like to suggest are not problems at all, but changes from one kind of connection to another:

- Loss of sexual chemistry, or a decrease (or increase!) in libido

- Interest in other people
- Drifting apart and feeling like there is not much in common anymore
- Needing a break from a person
- Becoming very comfortable or even bored with someone

The typical advice for any of the problems above is to *fight them*. Fell in love with someone else? Forget them and force yourself to only love your spouse! Feeling resentful? Force yourself to forgive and move on! Restless and wanting change or something new? Tough luck, you'd better find a way to be satisfied with what you have!

Have a look at the problems you wrote down earlier, but with a different perspective. Instead of trying to solve the "problem", become curious about the *changes* you are experiencing.

Imagine a couple who fight about money. With a problem mindset, they might look at the problem and try to solve it with budgets, financial advice or couple's counseling.

Instead, they could try a mindset where they gently acknowledge the change, and where it's going. See if you can do the same:

- What new relationship is developing, and in what ways is the old one not working anymore?
- Have you been treating the individual as the problem, rather than the connection?
- Are you following some "script"?
- Fear and suffering is information. If you listen, it tells you something important about your life right now. What lesson can you learn from the trouble you're experiencing?

Often times, a problem actually disappears when you realize it's only a problem because of the narrative you're trying to maintain. When you let this go, you realize the problem wasn't really a problem at all, but a growth opportunity, and sometimes even a *good* thing.

Now, instead of "My husband and I can't stop fighting about money," you have the following:

"I'm becoming more financially independent and my connection with my husband is changing. We are moving from a relationship where I depend on him financially to one where we are more equal. There are some hiccups as we make the transition."

Do you see how the above is so much less negative? There is no resisting, no forcing. Better still, in this frame of mind, all thoughts are now geared towards actual *solutions*. If you had dwelt on tinkering with budgets as your solution, you would have gotten nowhere.

But by embracing the change, you turn your mind to making the transition easier. The solutions suggest themselves easily now. You can more clearly communicate that the old way is past and that you intend to move into the new way, compassionately and with kindness.

Love flourishes and grows when it can be *what it is*. It withers inside scripts. It only blossoms between two people who are genuinely themselves. It never thrives between people who are playing out roles or wearing masks.

Love isn't lust, or dependence, or obligation, or fear. It is only that fleeting and beautiful connection that springs up between two people. The irony is that trying to hold onto it, constrain it or force it in one direction over another, only kills it.

When you see signs of trouble in a connection of any kind, *relax.*

Remember that there is no way to fail in a relationship. There is only being authentic, or nothing.

So look again at your list of relationship problems:

- Is this really a problem after all?
- How can you embrace the change with compassion rather than fight it?
- Are you honoring a "script" instead of the real, lived experience you're actually in?
- How can you make the transition easier?
- What is the truest, most authentic expression of the connection between you and this other person? In what ways are you helping that and in what ways are you hindering that?

If you can, rewrite your problems. Of course, simply changing the way you talk about a problem doesn't mean it magically goes away! But framing your issues the right way is an important first step. Reframing your issues this way will make it easier to start applying the three principles, one at a time.

Changing mindsets in this way takes a little practice, and can feel strange at first.

Making significant changes means trying out ways of thinking that may seem awkward or uncomfortable at first, so don't worry if trying these exercises feels a little phony.

By applying the first principle, you let go of blame and stop trying to force people to be what you believe they should be, and instead focus on the connection you share. By applying the second principle, you move with change, rather than fighting it. And the third principle? In the previous chapter, I asked you to look at your relationship problems in a different light. In this chapter, we'll expand this view.

Perhaps you've read all this and thought, "it's fine to just float around life and never be bothered by relationship problems, but the reality is that I have goals and wants and needs. I *do* have a script. Is that so bad?"

Perhaps you realize that you'd be happiest with a long term, monogamous partner who you can settle down with and trust to build a home together, having children and working together, as a unit. What could be wrong with this? Well, nothing at all.

You are your own 100% unique and legitimate human being, and your wants and needs are all your own. We all have our own limits, our own desires, deal breakers, goals and deadlines. And I would be a fool to suggest that you abandon those. For women who want to have children, for example, it's just a fact of life that time is limited.

So, people create "scripts" about how their lives *must* play out. But then that script extends to what *other* people must do. Herein lies the problem. The moment you allow someone else's actions to determine whether you are happy or not, you lose control.

Abandon Your Scripts

A script about how a relationship ought to be is unnecessary. So how do you ensure that your boundaries are respected, and that you get what you want? Not with a script, but with a *mindset*. Here's the difference.

A script:
- Is set in stone
- Is weak and destroyed with any change
- Tells other people what *they* should do
- Is disempowering
- Draws attention to problems (i.e. places where life doesn't fit the script)

- Can be unkind
- Is about WHAT

A mindset:
  - Is flexible and robust
  - Remains fundamentally the same, no matter what changes around it
  - Tells you what *you* should you
  - Is empowering
  - Draws attention to solutions
  - Is compassionate
  - Is about HOW

I can understand how scary it must seem to abandon your scripts. But remember, a script is not a magical spell that prevents you from pain or loss or confusion in life. A script is just the *illusion* that you have control, it's not control itself. More often than not, holding onto some fixed idea about what should be blinds you to all great things that *could* be, or all the great things that already are but which are invisible to you.

Instead of scripts, focus on cultivating the right *mindset*.

You can never force people to feel or behave exactly the way you want them to. You can never live a life without change. And yes, some changes will be for the worse. But no matter what, you can always maintain a frame of mind that is consistent with your principles.

If you know your own values, your own limits and your own desires, you can gently hold that mindset as you move through the world. You naturally move towards those people and relationships that fit your mindset, and away from those that don't. There is no need for a script because everything that you do, if it aligns with your mindset, is the correct thing to do.

If you're running a script that says you must be married by 30 no matter what, you might squash and squeeze your current situation until it fits: you marry whoever's closest at the time and badger them until they resemble the picture you have in your head. Ironically, you may even marry someone completely wrong for you. Your script ends up forcing exactly the situation you don't want!

On the other hand, if you hold a *mindset* that you value long term relationships and are seriously looking for one, you simply never get involved with people who want something else. There is no wrong person to marry by accident because your mindset has ensured that only those who align with you are in your web in the first place.

You hold your goals, but lightly. You have standards, but only for yourself. You don't waste time fighting with others because they aren't what you want; instead you spend your energy finding those people who already align with your values.

It's a subtle, but massive difference.

This chapter is about "building a home". Did you look at your web and find that you didn't like what you saw? Well, you can change it. You can start, right now, to bring the right people into your web. When you build a home, the blueprint you start with is your own mindset.

Once you've determined your own wants, needs, goals, and boundaries, you can build a web around you that makes you happy, fulfills you and connects you to the world in a meaningful way. This is your "home", and it starts within you.

Look at your web and see if you have any scripts that you hold yourself or others to. Are these scripts obscuring things? Go through each of these scripts and change them to a mindset that you can hold instead:

Script: "We *have to* do Christmas every year at my mother's, and I hate it, and it's a problem."

Change to: "Christmas is important to my mother but not to me. I love her and I know she'll appreciate if I visit for a few days over the Christmas period, but from now on I'll spend that time with friends I love, doing other things I enjoy. There is no problem."

Script: "It's wrong to be a virgin at 25, and I'm ashamed, and it *should* have happened by now, and it's a problem."

Change to: "I *am* a virgin at 25. There's no problem. I want it to happen with the right person and at the right time, so I'm going to make sure I'm attracting that kind of person and putting myself in the way of those opportunities. Until then, I won't stress about it."

Script: "It's the third date and we *have to* sleep together, but I don't want to, and it's a problem."

Change to: "It's the third date. I want to get to know this person better. There is no problem. I'm in control. I'm going to focus on nurturing the connection we have, and see what happens…"

Listen closely if you use phrases like "have to" or "must" …these are clues you might be running a script! Instead, stop and tell yourself there is no problem. Look at the facts. Then, instead of forcing anything or getting angry that others aren't doing what you want, look at yourself and *reaffirm your own mindset.*

Do you want to be calm and composed? Full of compassion? Carefree and independent? Well, focus on the thoughts and actions that help you maintain that frame of mind. Stay aligned, and the actions of others don't matter as much.

If it's important for you to maintain a level-headed attitude, you will eventually weed out all those people who create drama and arguments. If you focus on maintaining a loving and accepting frame of mind, you'll notice immediately all those people and interactions that don't fit. You'll easily be able to move on from them. And there is no problem.

By now, I'm hoping that you can see how these three principles come together. While you may not find specific answers for your specific relationship problem here, my hope is that you find a valuable *technique* for dealing with every relationship problem, now and in the future.

You could troubleshoot each little relationship problem that comes your way. Or, you could cultivate the mindset of a person who doesn't encounter those problems in the first place.

Take some time now to see how you can get rid of your own scripts, and focus on what mindset you want to create and maintain.

Cultivate the right mindset

A mindset is the "right" one when it affirms your values.

If you're not sure exactly what mindset you need to be focusing on, it's easy to find out. Simply look back on your life and ask yourself when and where you felt most alive, most yourself, most "in the zone". Everyone has these peak moments once in a while. What were yours?

Think back to those moments and try to remember your thoughts, emotions and actions at the time. Were you buzzing with creative energy? Filled with calm and a deep sense of wellbeing? Tuned into others and overflowing with empathy?

These peak experiences give you a glimpse into your most cherished values. Building your own "home" starts with you, and with these values. Once you've identified your mindset, there are many ways to nurture it:

- Meditate. Devote some time each day to deliberately find that state of mind and maintain it.

- Start each morning with a small ritual that "sets" your mindset for the day. Say an affirmation, journal or do some exercise to get your head in the right place.

- Practice being aware. During the day, as you go about all your activities and engage with people, regularly remind yourself to stop, and become aware of what you're doing and thinking and saying. Take a moment to re-align yourself.

CHAPTER 5 - TAKING CONTROL

It's time to move onto our third and final principle, and the most powerful one of all of them. This principle says: you are in control.

You can make conscious, meaningful changes – *right now.*

There is something very *vulnerable* in the process of connecting with others. We all feel the desire to love and be loved by others, and we all know the pain of rejection. Loneliness has been shown time and time again to be linked to shorter lifespans and poorer health. Those without good support networks have weaker immune systems and heal more slowly from illness. Death and bereavement can almost feel like it literally breaks the heart. More than anything, human beings *need* to connect to other human beings.

And yet each time we reach out, we risk being turned down, disappointed, hurt or ignored. How frightening it is to know that this deep need of ours is up to others to fulfil ...others who could choose to hurt us instead.

It's easy to see why anyone would feel powerless when it comes to relationships. You have no control over what someone feels for you, what they say to you, or what their actions are.

Still, you *can* make conscious, meaningful changes.

This is because there is always something you are 100% in control of: yourself! The next time you hear someone complain about a relationship problem or ask for advice about an issue with a boss or a spouse, listen closely. You'll probably hear some version of the same old complaint, "the people and situations around me are not what I want them to be, and there's nothing I can do about it, and I'm so unhappy." You might have even made this complaint yourself.

But remember the first two principles. There are only connections, and those connections are always changing. And *you* can change those connections, too. When you're deep in a relationship of any kind, it's easy to believe that you have no power over how things unfold. You might start to think that because another person holds your affection, that they also hold the key to your happiness. That it's *them* that decides.

But this is not really the case. If a connection between you and another person isn't working, it can be changed or, in some cases, dissolved completely. This might sound kind of obvious, but how many people do you know who refuse to leave a bad relationship, almost as though they were under a spell?

When you learn to take control of the connections you share with others, you do two things. Firstly, you protect yourself from relationships that don't serve you. But there's a second benefit, which is that taking responsibility also makes you a better partner to share a connection with. You have firm boundaries, you know when to apologize, and you don't get sucked into "drama".

How can you start to take control of the connections in your web, right now?

In every discussion, argument or interaction, get into the habit of asking yourself what is *yours* and what is *theirs*.

The answer might not always be clear. But it pays to remind yourself not to blame others for your emotions, or take on responsibility for emotions that aren't yours. For example, if your partner is slamming doors and ignoring you, and you ask what the problem is and get "nothing" as the reply, then you can safely say that this is their problem and not yours. Taking control of a situation sometimes means seeing exactly the ways in which you aren't in control, and letting go of things you can't change. Many abusive relationships have these blurred boundaries in common. Take control by letting go of the things that are not yours to control in the first place.

Another example:

You may be angry with a friend for something they said. If it was an accident and they apologized sincerely, then move on. If you feel particularly hurt because the comment hit your own insecurities, then that is yours, and not theirs. Instead of saying, "you *made* me feel X" you can simply say "I feel X". Instantly, you gain more control over the situation and yourself. You don't waste time trying to change the past. It already happened. But you can ask yourself about your insecurities and what *you* can do to avoid the same situation in the future.

Know your own triggers and "hooks", and learn how to de-escalate

The first step to being in control is to be aware. You can have no mastery over something you aren't even aware is happening! Of course, it's easy to be calm and collected when you're not in the middle of a heated argument. The time when you most need presence of mind is the time you're most likely to forget yourself.

Before you get into arguments with others, take some time to understand your own "hooks". A hook is anything that can disrupt your state of mind and pull you into being reactive. For example, a couple fight and argue, but the moment a particular issue is brought up, the argument gets worse and soon both are saying things they regret.

What hooks you? What situations, people or ideas have the power to "push your buttons"? We all have wounds from the past, and we all have blind spots. If you know what yours are, however, you can recognize them before they have the chance to overwhelm you. Then, even if you're in the middle of an upsetting conversation, you can stop, take a breath, and center yourself before carrying on.

Change what you can, accept what you can't

Perhaps relationships are so difficult because they can make us feel so irrational. In just the same way as you'd ask what is "yours" and what is "theirs", also remember to ask whether some issue or problem is *anyone's*. Some issues in life are really not for us to change, and trying to fight against them only causes more unhappiness.

Ask yourself:
- Are my wants and needs here really reasonable?
- What exactly can I control in this situation and what can't I control?
- What can I do to let go of the things that I can't control?
- If I didn't feel any strong emotions about this issue, how would I act?
- If I was advising someone else with my problem, what would I suggest?

A Relationship "Crisis Kit"

Something's wrong. You've had an upsetting fight with someone you care about. You're in a difficult situation that needs to be resolved soon. You're unhappy and something needs to change. These "crisis" points happen to everyone at some point or other, and it's easy to forget yourself in these high stress moments and make poor decisions.

But if you're in a crisis right now, try going through the following steps to gain some clarity.

1. Don't panic! No matter how bad things seem now, try to remember that it's temporary, and that you *will* find a solution, one way or another. Everyone struggles at times, so don't worry.

2. First things first: can you get some distance from your problem? It's hard to see clearly when you're caught up in an issue. Is it possible to take a break, step away from the person/situation for a moment or delay any big decisions? This will give you some time to process.

3. Next, make sure you are taking care of your basic needs and even though you might not feel like it, eat well, sleep well and try not to disrupt your daily life.

4. When you're calm, try to see the issue from as many different perspectives as you can. What is your part in the problem? Is there a miscommunication? What does the issue look like from "the other side"? What do both parties ultimately want? Can you zoom in on the real problem here? Note: if you still think the problem is that they're just a big idiot, you're likely missing something!

5. Remember to focus on the connection, rather than the people involved. Can you separate out people's actions from who they fundamentally are? Can you address behavior, actions, words etc. without attacking the other person?

6. Can you frame the problem in a more positive way? Look closely to see if your relationship with this person is just in transition. Are there positives that you are overlooking?

7. If you have something deliberate to communicate, prepare carefully and start a discussion with the other person. Where you go from here will depend on what you learn about the problem you share.

8. Don't worry if things aren't resolved immediately. Keep reminding yourself of your values, of what is your responsibility and what isn't, and what you can change in this situation.

9. Be aware of your own blind spots and keep asking: are you missing anything? Is there a lesson here I could learn? How can I prevent myself being "hooked" into drama?

10. Keep coming back to your own boundaries and goals. Sometimes, the best thing for any relationship is for it to end. If this is the direction you're moving, stay aware and be curious about the most compassionate way you can do this.

The Three Principles in Action

These principles are quite abstract, I know. What do they look like, out in the real world? And can they really be applied to the problems you are experiencing right now with your own relationships?

In this chapter I want to give examples to show that these three simple principles can be applied to *every* possible relationship problem. You could read a self-help book on marriage, or a separate one on how to deal with your children, or one on good communication skills at work.

If you read all of them, however, you might start to notice the same patterns emerging over and over. I believe these patterns are the principles we've just explored. If you can grasp and master them, any problem that involves another human being becomes something you can understand and work through.

Example one: Cutting the apron strings

Marie and her daughter have a very strong bond. Marie is a single parent who had her daughter Clara when she was just 16 years old, and the two have been each other's support system ever since.

As Clara gets older, though, she begins to drift further away from her mother and closer to her peers and eventually, her boyfriend. Marie is devastated. She begins policing her daughter, believing that she is protecting her from the same bad decisions she made as a young woman. Clara fights back, feeling that she's ready to be independent and that her mother needs her own life. The situation comes to a head when Clara wants to move out and in with her boyfriend.

What should Marie do?

Principle 1: *There are no individuals, just connections*

Looking at this problem, it's easy to fall back onto stereotypes: single mothers behave like this, teenager daughters behave like that. But when you look at people only as roles in a script, you fail to see them in all their complexity. For example, you fail to see that Clara is not only a daughter, but her own person. Importantly, she is someone else's girlfriend. Likewise, Marie is more than just a mother – and definitely more than just a single teen mother stereotype. If we just look at these two people as the labels they have on them, we don't see potential solutions, only more of the same problem. What other parts of their personalities could be developed here?

The problem here is not in Clara or Marie, but in their connection. Neither is to blame, neither is a victim and neither is the "good guy".

Principle 2: Every relationship changes over time

Marie is laboring under a misconception: that the way she relates to her daughter is the way she should *always* relate to her. Of course, this isn't true. Her daughter is growing and changing. And so is Marie! Eventually, Clara will stop being a dependent teenage daughter, and Marie will stop being the mother of a dependent teenage daughter.

If Marie focuses on resisting the negative aspects of the change, she never allows herself to see the positives: that there can be a new, even better relationship with her daughter. If she allows herself to accept the changes in this relationship, she may discover something else: that she is also ready to move on, to find another partner, to be more independent herself.

Principle 3: You are in control

When two people are dependent on each other, it's difficult to see who is responsible for what. Especially where parents are concerned, it can be difficult to let go and let your children make their own mistakes. In this case, this principle might show Marie that *her daughter* is also in control, and that she no longer has to treat her like a child.

Reaffirming that both Marie and Clara are in control of themselves can be just the thing to start a new relationship; one between two equal, mature adults.

Example two: A commitment puzzle

Like many of their 20-something friends, Mike and Leah had a "casual" start to their relationship. Neither of them can point to a specific date they met, and they both never really discussed their relationship. After two years Leah starts to notice that their relationship hasn't reached any of the "milestones" a relationship should: Mike hasn't said "I love you", hasn't mentioned marriage, hasn't moved in. This makes her feel awful and so after much fighting she issues him an ultimatum: commit or else. Mike, completely taken by surprise, feels like he's being manipulated and calls her bluff, breaking up with her.

Both of them are pretty unhappy. Leah regrets the decision, but at the same time, she wasn't happy without any firm commitment from Mike either.

What should Leah do?

Principle 1: There are no individuals, just connections

This is the kind of problem people like to pick sides over. Some will say Leah is pushy and entitled, others will say that Mike is an immature commitment-phobe. But there are no individuals, just connections, and this connection is evolving in a lopsided way.

Leah is not to blame and neither is Mike. They do have different ideas of their respective roles in their "family", though. If you focus on who's to blame, you don't really get anywhere. But if you focus on the real problem – that the connection is not reciprocal – then you can actually start solving it.

Principle 2: *Every relationship changes and grows over time*

What Leah and Mike are experiencing is so common it's almost the norm. As their connection grows and changes, they'll need to adapt and learn new ways of being with each other.

But Leah's script for what her relationship *should* look like has blinded her to what it actually is. Mike, too, has failed to take notice of the changes and hasn't taken responsibility for his part in the dynamic, turning a blind eye to Leah's concerns. A relationship of two years is different to one of two months. Instead of seeing the changes as something scary and problematic, both Leah and Mike could welcome the changes. What better time to learn about one another's values and goals?

Principle 3: *You are in control*

In this situation, both Leah and Mike are forfeiting their right to take control. Since the beginning, they have both avoided deciding what they want from their connection. Because they are both unaware of their wants, needs, limits and weaknesses, they are taken by surprise when they appear. Leah is unable to decide what she wants from Mike, and so resorts to ultimatums; Mike doesn't know how to respond and so resorts to an equally extreme measure: breaking up.

Standard dating advice will tell Leah to dump poor Mike and find herself a marriage-minded man, and Mike will probably not get any relationship advice at all, because stressing about marriage is a woman's thing, at least according to his script.

Using the three principles, though, the perspective can be shifted. After the breakup, Leah could spend some time alone to tune into what she really wants, without a "script". Mike could do the same. After some time, the couple could have their first frank discussion about their expectations. They could talk honestly about the changes to their connection, what they both want, and whether their mindsets are compatible.

It might turn out that they both had very different ideas about where their relationship was going. Maybe Leah moves on and in a few years, marries someone else. Or maybe the breakup marks the start of a completely new and different connection between the two, one that honors both of their values a little better.

Whatever the outcome, the path getting them there will be one of compassion and self-awareness.

Your problem

What about you?

Let's look at how you can apply the three principles to whatever relationship problem you're experiencing right now.

Principle 1: *There are no individuals, just connections*

- First, take the focus off of who's to blame or who is the cause of this or that. See if you can shift your focus onto the connection rather than you or the other person.

- Notice if you think things like "she makes me feel X" or "because of her..." and rather speak only about your own actions and feelings. What is yours and what is theirs?

- Where does this person, and this problem, fit into your web? And how do you fit into theirs?

Principle 2: *Connections always change*

- Are you experiencing a problem or just a change from one kind of connection to another?

- Are there some positives to your situation that you haven't considered?

- Are you following a script?

Principle 3: *You are in control*

- Have you been focusing on what the other person needs to do in order for you to be happy instead of taking responsibility for your own happiness?

- In the broadest sense, what do you want?

- What is the mindset you want to maintain, in this problem and in general?

In the following chapter, we'll look at a technique for having those awkward conversations that seem to accompany relationship problems. Now that you've seen the three principles, seen how they can be applied and put them to use on your own situation, it's time to reach out and try to make a change. Most likely, the first step will be to communicate with the other person.

Let's see how.

CHAPTER 6 - MINDFUL COMMUNICATION FOR THOSE AWKWARD "CHATS"

This chapter is about a conscious, compassionate way to have difficult conversations.

Whether you want to discuss a relationship problem, break up with someone, make a complaint, address a misunderstanding or apologize for messing up, your chat be much easier if you follow these steps. So many relationship issues hinge around difficult conversations just like these. Instead of avoiding the awkwardness or launching into a fight instead, you can master mindful communication.

Step One: Prepare

Have you ever sat down for a serious talk with someone only to have the whole thing take a strange turn and end up being the opposite of what you wanted? Conversations can get derailed or lose focus if there's a lack of planning.

The kind of conversation you're about to have is not like an ordinary chat. It has a very special and distinctive *purpose*. This means that it's not enough to simply start talking and hope that things will resolve themselves. You are in control, so take some time to prepare.

If you read through the previous chapters and engaged with the ideas there, you've probably already done plenty of preparation. But crystallize your ideas now, so you are not tempted to stray off your topic once you start talking.

- What do you want?
- What exactly do you want the other person to hear and understand?
- What is the most important thing about your position, right now?
- What is it you're asking the other person to actually do, i.e. what response do you want from them?
- What mindset and attitude are you maintaining through the discussion?
- What do you expect to change after you're done talking?
- What are you going to do differently?

Think through all of this very carefully. Be prepared. Next, think of a good time and place to have this discussion. Even if it's just a small thing, you don't want to be interrupted or risk getting distracted by something else. It's a good idea to let the other person know your intentions, then give them a moment to process and organize themselves. Say something like, "I wanted to talk about X when you had a free moment. I'm available tomorrow evening at 7. Think about it and let me know if that works for you." This means you're not springing anything on anyone, and won't feel rushed in the moment.

Step Two: Set the tone

As the person calling the discussion, you have an advantage: you get to set the tone. The other person will be looking to you to do this, so begin on the right foot and take control. In the beginning, more important than *what* you say is *how* you say it. Do what you need to beforehand to get into the right frame of mind. Meditate, do a visualization or breathing exercise or just carefully organize yourself.

If you start out by creating an atmosphere of accusation or resentment, you may lose the other person's cooperation immediately. Instead, focus on creating rapport first and foremost.

Don't launch into your topic immediately. Spend a little time affirming your connection first: what is great about the other person and the relationship you share? What are you happy about? What's working well so far? Let them know.

"We've been working working really well on this project and I'm pleased we're in the same team."

"I know how difficult this last weekend was and I wanted to tell you that I was impressed with the way you handled things."

"You know I've always admired X about you."

Keep open body language, be relaxed and take the lead.

Step Three: State Your Experience

Nobody responds well to being talked at or told what they should feel and why. So avoid doing this with other people. Instead of beginning with *them* (their actions, their words) focus on yourself. As clearly as possible, lay out your own personal experience, and nothing more. This is the time to use "I" statements and clearly state your observations, thoughts and feelings.

You don't even need to interpret things or identify the reason you've had the experience you do, just state it. Be clear, avoid blaming, and take ownership.

"For the last week I've been very frustrated with how we're repeatedly missing deadlines. I feel unappreciated. I've noticed that the quality of my work is suffering as well."

"To me, it seems like we've misunderstood each other. I worry you haven't heard me."

"When you said X the other day, I felt really hurt and angry."

For this last example, note that it's different from saying, "you made me feel hurt and angry" or "I'm hurt and angry because of you". This is not strictly true and will put the other person on the back foot immediately. Don't try to tell them what their experience is, just explain your own.

Step Four: Give Them a Chance to Respond

You've probably spent some time thinking about this problem, and have had the opportunity to plan ahead. But they haven't. So be considerate and stop speaking, pausing long enough so that they can process what you've said. Say something like, "what do you think?" or "what's your take on this?" to invite them to respond, and don't rush anything.

When they respond, actually listen! It's tempting to start thinking about all the ways you're going to respond or even argue, but imagine you have nothing more to say and only want to understand as deeply as possible what their position is.

To help with this, ask them questions to make sure you've received their message loud and clear. Repeat what you've heard and ask if you've understood correctly. This shows that you're paying attention and care about getting it right, rather than just waiting for your turn to barge in again.

Say things like, "So what I hear you saying is X... is that right?" or "I'm trying to understand. Do you mean X?" Then paraphrase what they've just told you. Once you feel sure you've heard them properly, move onto the next step.

Step Five: Express Your Need and/or Boundary

Note, this is a need, not a demand, not an ultimatum and certainly not a threat. Again, it's kind of neutral. You're merely stating the things you need for you to be happy in the current situation. It's up to the other person whether they choose to address that.

It's difficult sometimes but avoid blaming or accusing. It's not important what has happened in the past – just focus on your need now, in the present. If you feel offended or hurt, you might need to assert your boundary and stand up for yourself. It's perfectly fine for you to feel angry, fearful or even as though you want revenge, but try to hold those emotions instead of forcing them on the other person.

You are not asking permission here, or begging, or admonishing. Just stating what is true for you. Luckily, you've spent some time honing in on what you want, and the mindset you want to hold. It's not your job to force the other person, only to communicate clearly and compassionately.

"For me to feel happy and safe in this relationship, I need to trust that my partner will never lie to me."

"I draw a line at family members showing up unannounced at my home. I'm busy so I always need a day or two's notice before guests show up."

"I'm quite an introvert and need some down-time after I hang out with friends."

Note that none of these is making any claim or demand on anyone else – simply stating a need.

Here, beware of getting "hooked". If you're a pushover, simply state your needs and then stop. You never need to justify yourself. You're allowed to have whatever needs and boundaries you have! Be careful here of getting drawn into other issues. Separate problems can wait for their own chat – just deal with one issue at a time.

Step Six: Give Them an Opportunity to Respond, Again

Depending on what you've said, you might be met with a range of reactions. Anger, understanding, bewilderment. The thing is, you can't really predict. Remember, you are in control, but of yourself only, not others.

They may respond once and that might spell the end of the discussion, or you could go back and forth many times. Keep talking only as long as you know you are maintaining your mindset, and you're not getting distracted or "hooked". If you feel yourself getting emotional or losing track, simply ask that you pause and continue the conversation later. Nothing good will come of talking in the wrong frame of mind. You might need to step back and clear your mind a little before reaching out again.

What you are interested in is whether the other person is receptive and respectful of the needs you just stated. Have they really heard you? If they present some new information, listen closely and try to see their point of view.

Step Seven: Ask for What You Want, Then Close

The goal is not to chat forever. Finish in the same way you started, and reaffirm any positive feelings. The idea is that even though there is an issue now, neither of you are "wrong" and that the reason you are speaking at all is to preserve the connection and all the good things it entails.

Remember that you don't have to resolve everything all at once. If you're dealing with a big, difficult problem, this may be only the first of many conversations. That's OK. Thank the other person for their time and consideration, and keep reminding yourself to maintain your frame of mind.

Before you finish off, leave the other person with a concrete, specific action that you'd like them to take, as well as an idea of what actions you'll be taking.

"I want to ask you to turn up to work on time from now on."

"I'm asking you to stop sending texts to your ex."

"I want you to stop making hurtful comments about my lifestyle choices."

Then, follow up with what you'll do. Again, this isn't a threat, but rather a clear explanation of what your boundaries and needs are, and what they can expect from you. A boundary means nothing if it cannot be asserted, and you're stating your needs in the hope they'll be fulfilled. Lay out the stakes and your own expectations. Adjust your assertiveness to the situation at hand. If your boundaries have been violated, you may need to be very firm. If the situation is not so serious, merely let the other person know what they can expect from you.

"If you're late in future our policy does mean I'll have to write you up for a warning."

"As I've explained, when you message your ex, I feel really doubtful about us. When I see that you don't stop despite me asking you to, those doubts are confirmed. Eventually, I'm going to assume you don't care about my limits and I'll need to reconsider our relationship."

"I won't be engaging in any further discussion on this topic."

Follow up

For relatively simple situations, communicating clearly and early on is usually enough to avert problems or solve little ones as they come up. Keep reminding yourself to maintain your frame of mind and trust that if you follow your values, you will naturally gravitate to the people and situations you need.

Stay curious about *change* and how it can be an opportunity rather than a threat. Lastly, don't forget that the person you're speaking to is a human being who deserves your respect and compassion. No matter how badly damaged the connection between you, stay mindful and be kind.

You might end with an invitation to talk again in the future, maybe to re-evaluate whether anything has changed. Follow through on what you've promised, and take note about their behavior, too.

CHAPTER 7 - MINDFULLY MOVING ON

If you read the previous steps and cynically thought, "yeah right!", don't worry, I understand. In an ideal world, everyone would communicate clearly and rationally, staying compassionate throughout. In the real world ...communication of this kind will always be a little hit and miss.

You can talk yourself in circles, use "I" statements, assert your boundaries and be mindful till you're blue in the face – sometimes a connection with someone is just *bad*. In this chapter, we'll take a look at what to do when a connection needs to be cut, once and for all.

We live in a consumerist world where people are quick to throw things away or abandon projects when they're too difficult. It's true that modern man has a lower tolerance for discomfort and higher expectations for the relationships around us. Nevertheless, not every relationship serves us, and not every connection is worth keeping.

The first step is making the decision that a connection does, in fact, need to be severed. I personally know a few people who've spent *years* stuck in this stage, unsure of whether they'd be making a huge mistake to split.

Ask yourself the following questions to determine whether a particular connection has well and truly run its course:

- Does this relationship align well with your values? This means that the connection actively supports the mindset you want to maintain. Take note – the person themselves doesn't have to share your mindset, but the *connection* should. At the very least, are they not hindering you in your values and principles?

- Look at it from the other side: are you aligning well with the other person's values? It's easy to see relationships in terms of what benefits we get from them, but are you actively serving the other person? Are they better for knowing you, and do you support them, even if it doesn't necessarily benefit you?

- Every human being is imperfect, and so every relationship will be, too. But is your relationship with this person more good than bad? Friction, disagreements and misunderstandings can be a great way to deepen a connection ...but is that *all* you do with this person?

- Is your connection here preventing you from forming better connections elsewhere?

- Have you done your "due diligence"? This means taking the time to communicate, accept your responsibility in any problem and try something new. Have you really done your best to honor this connection or are you taking the easy way out by cutting it?

- Are the problems you're experiencing only temporary? Have you given the connection enough time to change and adjust if you're in transition?

- Is it possible to let this connection fade naturally? Sometimes, relationships run their natural course and peter out of their own accord. Perhaps you don't need to do anything besides maintaining your own mindset.

- Every serious relationship experiences trouble and discord eventually. The question is what happens with this discord. Do you feel that disagreements ultimately push you to become a better person, to be more empathetic and to communicate better? Or do these disagreements "hook" you, bringing out your worst characteristics?

- Is the only reason you haven't cut this connection yet because of fear? Perhaps obligation, financial worries, guilt, duty or even momentum are stopping you from ending the relationship. Is this really enough of a reason to stay with someone who makes you unhappy?

Deciding that you want to end a relationship takes courage. It speaks to the third principle – that you are always in control. At any time, you can decide whether you want to remain in a relationship or not. Even if you've known the person your whole life. Even if they're family. Even if you work for them!

And if you've read through the questions above and still can't come to a decision, remember: you don't actually need a reason at all. You can want to leave a relationship simply ...because you want to.

Remember also that if you *don't* leave, you are actively choosing to stay in that relationship. People like to blame others for the bad situations they are stuck in, but the fact never changes: you can always remove yourself. It might be incredibly painful, or inconvenient, or embarrassing, or stressful, or disruptive. And let's be honest, if the relationship is a marriage, money and children may pose massive difficulties if the connection dissolves.

But still, you are in control.

Mindfully severing a connection

How you break a connection will depend on what that connection is, and they're all unique. But in keeping with the spirit of this book, do it mindfully and with compassion.

- Ending a relationship doesn't mean it's a failure. So don't speak about it that way. Rather, frame it as moving on to other things. Emphasize your appreciation for the relationship that was had, even though it's ending now. Stay positive and affirming, and share what you believe are the benefits of cutting ties.

- Don't make accusations, place blame or narrate the other person's experience for them. All of that is irrelevant and, if you've done your due diligence, should have been addressed by now anyway. Instead, look to the future. What have you learnt from the relationship? What's next?

- Be clear. It's unkind to string people along, or keep them in limbo. Be straightforward about exactly the *ways* your connection is ending. Will you be moving out? Will you be transferring to another team? Do you expect to never speak to them again or are you still going to be friendly when you see them around?

Try not to worry about getting "closure". This is usually a script in disguise: they *should* say or do this or that, and you can only move on once they do this or that. Take control and end the relationship because you want to, and not because you hope to elicit any particular response from them. Give the other person time to respond but remember, you actually don't need any one's permission to end anything. If you've considered everything carefully and the cut aligns with your values, then it doesn't really matter, does it?

Unless someone has seriously violated your boundaries or the connection is really dangerous to your wellbeing, don't burn those bridges. Principles two says that your web is continually evolving. You never know what new shoots will grow on an old tree stump!

If you're compassionate and mindful, old relationships can fade away and make room for new, better ones.

If a house has been built on poor foundations, you'll never fix anything by going in and changing the paint on the walls, or putting a nice throw on the sofa.

Likewise, if you've constructed your "house" of relationships on a foundation of fear, mindlessness and "scripts", you'll never change anything by winning a single petty argument with a single person. In both cases, you need to start from the ground up.

The foundation of all good relationships is mindful compassion – or love, as it's also known!

There's no point in resolving relationship tensions if the discord is *within you*. Fix your own mindset and then your relationship issues resolve themselves. When you've cultivated a spirit of love, every person you meet becomes a wonderful opportunity to express yourself, affirm your values and learn something new.

It's not feasible (or necessary!) to tear down your whole life and start fresh. Like many homes, you'll have to make alterations as you go. But after a while, all the old parts are replaced and you effectively have a new home.

In the beginning of this book, I asked you to imagine a home. A home for who? Well, for you!

Can you start constructing a web of connections that will make the best and most suitable home for your values and goals? A family with four children needs a house with with enough rooms. In the same way, your web of connections needs to be just the right shape and size to accommodate who you are, with all your unique values, hopes and dreams.

We'll finish this book with a few simple but powerful exercises. These are simple to read through, but difficult to *do*. You can do all of them or just the ones that really speak to you, but keep an open mind and have faith that if done sincerely, they have the power to work for you.

Exercise One

Look at the diagram of your "family". What kind of relationships are missing? Try to think of one kind of connection that you wish you had but don't. Maybe you wish that you had more encouragement at work or that someone would pay you some romantic attention. Just for one day, do whatever you can to bring about that relationship *yourself*. Find someone in your web to encourage. Find someone who looks like they might be receptive to some romantic attention. See what's missing in your life but instead of wishing someone else would make it so, take control and create it yourself.

Exercise Two

You already know what all your connections to others look like. But what about your relationship with yourself? If you drew yourself as a separate person in your web, what kind of connection would you have there? Do you support or enable or criticize or limit? Is this really the relationship you want to have with yourself? If not, dedicate the day to treating yourself in the same way as a long lost family member, one who you're trying to build up a friendship with.

Exercise Three

Look closely at your web again and try to identify places that need "trimming". Are there connections that drain your energy, compromise your values or just plain old serve no purpose at all? Gently let them go. If you're feeling guilty about ending relationships, just remember that if you aren't happy with a connection, there's a good chance the other person isn't, either. Do both of you a favor and clear some new space for better, more authentic connections. For today, make an active move *away* from all those connections that no longer work for you. It doesn't matter if it's just a small move for now!

Exercise Four

The most influential people in our lives are sometimes the most invisible. Even though a long lost parent hasn't spoken to you in years, you may still hear their critical words in your head every day. Are you carrying around any extra weight in the form of old resentments? Are their "ghosts" in your family web or people you hold grudges against? Let them go, too. There really is no easy way to forgive someone, you just have to decide that you are done carrying that weight. Then let it go. Forgive all those that have hurt you. While you're at it, forgive all the past versions of yourself that you still hold onto. When you let all of that go, you release that energy and can spend it on the present, instead.

Exercise Five

Think of someone you know who you have a faint connection with right now, but that you wish was a little stronger. The most fantastic things can happen when you draw on these distant connections! The great thing about nurturing existing relationships like this is that you get the chance to start anew. Have you been neglecting someone? Is there someone out there who would appreciate you reaching out? Today, take that faint connection and take action to make it something better. Do them a favor, pay them a compliment, or suggest an activity. You could even ask them for help or advice.

One of these exercises can be done each day, but there's no reason you have to stop there. Using the three principles and with your own values and mindset firmly in place, every day is a chance to build on your own "house", and improve the web of human connections around you. With awareness and compassion, you can slowly weed out those relationships that harm you and cultivate those that help you instead.

CHAPTER 9 - LOVE IS A HABIT

Love is authentic, and never hides behind labels, rules or scripts.

There is no "should" only "is".

Love is never forceful or controlling.

Love isn't mindless and automatic – it takes regular, deliberate effort to cultivate and develop. It is a muscle to train, a skill and an art. It needs to be practiced in every moment of every day.

Love isn't possessive. Love is happy to share, because when you give it, there's more of it!

Love has nothing to do with fear. Love stays because it wants to, not because it has to.

There is no competition when it comes to love, no race, no prize, no goal. Love is its own reward.

Love is not a "what" but a "how".

Love isn't something to own, but to give away.

To love another is to honor them, and everything that they are.

What is love to *you*?

CONCLUSION

I've made a big deal in this book about the three principles that I believe are most important for an authentic, compassionate and self-aware life. I've tried to show that the right mindset is the first and most important step in building a network of relationships that will leave you satisfied and fulfilled.

To be honest though, there is nothing particularly special about my three principles. At the end of the day, I hope they form a useful framework, but they are just one way of many to speak about something deeper, something very important. At the root of all three of these principles is just a single one: love.

The house that love built will always be changing and growing. It's a happy house; one that's filled with honesty, joy and peace. You may find many more ways to bring love into your home than I've mentioned here, and that's because love takes on as many forms as there are people to share it.

I encourage you to take what you like from this book, and add to it your own wisdom. Every one of us knows, deep down, what love is and how to do it. When we tap into this inborn sense, we are able to start turning outward in love, shaping the world around us to match the world within.

When I'm tired, or ill or fed up with life in general, I boil it all down to one thing: *am I acting in love, in this moment?*

Simply asking this question as often as possible has done more than you can imagine. It's a call to stop, be aware and realign. It has the most amazing ability to make life's unimportant noise just float away...

Start building a home for yourself now.

The blueprint is *within*.

WHERE DID OUR LOVE GO, AND WHERE DO I GO FROM HERE? - LEARN HOW TO REDISCOVER, REKINDLE AND BRING BACK THE PASSION TO YOUR RELATIONSHIP

INTRODUCTION

This book is for everyone who feels that the passion and fire of their relationship have gone, and they aren't happy about it.

"Where did our love go?" is a simple question, but it can have some very complicated answers. In the chapters that follow, we'll look at ways to arrive at an answer that will respect your unique relationship, with all its strengths and flaws.

As the years tick on in a marriage, most people know to expect a slow fading of intense lust and the gradual development of a deeper, but more stable connection. But the transition from one to the other can be challenging!

"Passion" in a relationship is a strange thing. The moment you try to put your finger on it, it wriggles away. If you're like many couples, you may have already tried some of the usual suggestions, like sexy lingerie or going on a holiday together. But these things, while certainly in the right direction, are seldom enough.

If you find yourself in this position, then read on. This book is all about getting to the *root* of the problem of waning passion. By looking at the deeper workings of your marriage, you don't just "fix" the lack of passion, you rebuild your whole relationship over again, this time placing love and passion at the center. By carefully understanding your personal ideas of commitment, action and passion, we'll be able to slowly rework them, and create a long term relationship that is healthy, fulfilling and *real*.

Before we continue, I'd like to clarify that the ideas and exercises that follow are not just for those who are married. No two people are the same, and so no relationship is ever like any other. Because of that, your idea of a "committed, long term relationship" might look very different to someone else's.

There are people who are committed who aren't married ...and people who are married who aren't committed! There are those who have been together for five years and are still in their "honeymoon period" and those who have a mortgage, two kids and a simmering resentment for one another at the two-year mark. This is why I'll be using "marriage" or "relationship" interchangeably. And it's also why I'll leave it you to decide on how long a "long term" relationship is, married or not.

The first half of this book will be about dissecting and truly understanding the baggage we all bring to relationships, in the stories we tell ourselves about what love, commitment and passion actually mean to us. We'll look at *why* relationships fade, and what our role is in letting that happen. We all have baggage – think of the first half of this book as checking in your baggage at the airport before you fly.

The remainder of the book is about putting those ideas into practice. Using a series of exercises designed to be used by both people in a relationship, we begin the process of building a more genuine, more passionate connection. If you're asking where your love went, these exercises can have you saying, "Oh! *There* it is..."

If you're ready to step out of your comfort zone, courageous enough to confront your demons and curious enough to be a little playful about this crazy thing we call "love", then let's dive right in...

CHAPTER 1: TOO GOOD TO LEAVE, TOO BAD TO STAY

I want to describe a story that friends, clients and colleagues have often described to me in one form or other: marriage limbo.

Perhaps they began to experience problems in their marriages and seek out advice. Now the first question is, what's the problem? Does your husband beat you? Does your wife cheat? Do you want another child and they don't?

If you've asked someone for marriage advice before, they might have assumed that your problem is one of these classic marriage issues. Infidelity, money problems, one of you drinks and won't stop, the sex has fizzled out, you suspect the other one is emotionally abusive...

Don't have any of those problems? Well, lucky you!

Somewhere along the line, we all collectively agreed that so long as everyone is more or less faithful and nobody's getting abused, it's not a bad marriage. But the problem is ...it's not a *good* marriage, either.

And so, you land up in marriage limbo. A place where things are ...fine. But that's all they are.

You will find no shortage of books out there about dealing with messy divorces. There's plenty of help and support for abuse victims, for those managing infidelity or deception in their marriages, or those whose life partners slowly became their worst enemies.

But this book isn't for those people. Instead, it was written for those long term relationships that are just fine. These are the kind of relationships that people remain in for decades, convinced it's the best they can do. They're grey, tired, empty relationships. A bit like an old woolen sweater that's ugly and doesn't even keep you warm anymore, but which you keep because you've had it so long and you feel bad throwing it out.

Try to look for a problem in these relationships and you won't find one. Because there aren't any! The marriage limbo is all about what *isn't* there: passion. This may sound strange, but all those couples that get into hideous fights? Those husbands and wives whose marriages are like soap operas and who split and make up a hundred times each weekend? They have problems *because* they have passion.

In marriage limbo, however, there's no enthusiasm for anything, good or bad. Without passion, there are no heated arguments and fiery make up sex. No divorce threats and ultimatums and tearful confessions ...but there's not much else either.

Do You Have a "Too Good to Leave, Too Bad to Stay" Limbo Relationship?

Have a look at the following statements and see if they apply to you and the marriage you share with your partner. How many do you agree with?

1. You think of leaving often, but you're sure you wouldn't find someone else, and don't want to risk dating all over again.
2. Both of you deal with problems in the relationship by just withdrawing: you'll ignore each other for a few days, or do your own thing till things blow over or you each forget.
3. The best thing you can say about your relationship is how long it's lasted! You can't speak to how good it's been, but at least you've stuck it out all these years!
4. When you think of leaving, you're put off by all the bureaucracy involved. Divorce is expensive, and time consuming, and just extra admin...
5. You and your spouse have both gained weight, or "let yourselves go" in some way since you married.
6. In a way, you've kind of given up on the notion of love. You're a little disillusioned, sure, but that's just what happens when you grow up, right? You're just happy that things aren't worse.
7. You don't hate your spouse or anything, but you wonder often what life would have been like without them.
8. When you think of your marriage, the emotions that you feel are all *low energy*: pessimism, tiredness, disappointment.
9. You guys have been through so much, you're basically family. In fact, you're so much like family, you treat each other like brother and sister.
10. You feel a yearning, but you're not sure for what. You feel trapped and unsure. Leaving seems extreme, but you're bored to death of the way things are.
11. Your relationship kind of "just happened". It seemed like one day you were independent and carefree and the next day you were saddled with kids and debt and a spouse.
12. You're not sure what *you* want anymore.
13. Your partner and you don't share any new information with each other, and you don't do any new activities together. Instead, you engage in the same, narrow set of actions and conversations, again and again and again.
14. You can't remember the last time your partner surprised you or did something unexpected.
15. You've said, or thought, "I love them, but I'm not *in* love with them anymore."

But isn't all of this normal?
Limbo relationships are all around us, and way more common than you think. In fact, this kind of low-grade dissatisfaction and apathy is so typical, many people think that commitment *is the same thing as* boredom, and that in a long term relationship, it's normal and expected that both parties are numb, a little irritable with each other, dispassionate.

Maybe you've seen your own parents model this kind of attitude to each other, or maybe you've watched any of the hundreds of movies and TV shows that show long term couples bickering like children. Have you ever heard a man playfully call his wife his "ball and chain"? It's cute, in a way ...but is it really the *best* that relationships can be? Is it really true that people can't be expected to sustain loving, respectful and passionate relationships for decades?

If you take a moment to think of all the people you know who have been together long term, how many of them still laugh and joke together, or show spontaneous affection?

WHY the Spark Dies

Now, I think I might be able to guess your response to the previous section. You might think, *of course* people gradually lose the passion and heat from the beginning of a relationship. That's normal. The spark dies down and gives way to a more mature, less lust-fueled, more somber relationship. Everyone knows that.

The standard narrative tells us that after the "honeymoon period", a couple calms down and gets on with regular business of marriage. No more dates, spontaneous holidays or silly stuff in bed. They're not kids anymore, and they're a little bored with each other, but they're *committed*, so it's all good.

When someone cheats in a relationship, we get angry with them not because they had the impulse in the first place, but because they didn't have the discipline to resist it. Just think about that assumption for a second and what it tells you about how we think of commitment in the long term.

So, let's go with the narrative and assume that yes, every long term relationship eventually does fizzle out in the passion department. You've seen them naked a bazillion times, you know all their nasty flaws and weaknesses and you've been putting up with their stupid habits and quirks for years. In the place of true love and whimsy, you now have only a flesh and blood, mostly imperfect, human being. Now what?

Follow the common wisdom and they'll tell you: tone down your expectations. Romance is for the first year, after that the drudgery kicks in. Deal with it. Forget about how you used to tear their clothes off at every opportunity and just take out the trash already. Pick up your kids from school. Squeeze your aging body into novelty lingerie every Valentine's day and get it over with till next year.

As you can guess, I take a grim view of this "solution". While it's a little true that the spark dies eventually in a relationship, I've always been curious: *why* does it? How could a couple who were so madly in love eventually find themselves farting on the couch together on a Friday evening, arguing about who's turn it is to take the dog out?

In other words, where did the love go?

In this book, we'll begin with a radical and unpopular fundamental belief: that even though loss of love in a long term relationship is common, *it's not normal.*

Yes, I'm here to tell you that boredom, disillusionment and a vague sense of comfortable resentment – all of it is completely unnecessary.

I also want to say that a deeply fulfilling, loving, affectionate relationship is not only "possible" for you, but it's actually the normal state of loving long term relationships (do you sneer internally just reading that?)

In the previous chapter, how many of the statements did you agree to? Just a handful? The whole list?

Now let me ask you, did any single item on there have anything to do with *hate*? Not a single one.

The opposite of love is not hate. It's APATHY.

Limbo marriages are all about the absence of love. Call it "settling down" or "growing up" but it all comes down to the same thing: the love disappears, leaving a big, grey, bald patch where your affection used to be. But it doesn't have to be that way.

Models of romantic love: a history lesson

Now, I know you're probably not interested in too much "theory" here, but it's illuminating to consider that mankind hasn't always organized his relationships exactly the same way through history as he does now.

For a long time, marriage was merely a practical institution. If you were part of the upper class, your marriage had political or social significance, if you weren't, it was still a way to cement your role in the community and make sure you were managing children and assets in the approved ways.

Marriage has always been a tool to disseminate religious doctrine, a way to strengthen the tribe, keep women and men in the places society outlined for them, and give structure to the project of raising offspring.

What it *didn't* have much to do with was love. In fact, most of the wedding traditions we all know and assume are "traditional" are recent and had their beginning in the 40s and 50s. The notion that a man and woman can come together in nothing but romantic love to build a life together and bond forever is ...surprisingly modern!

If you examine all cultures, through all eras, you'll see only one common theme: marriage and long term relationships are many things, but *they are never just one thing.*

So what? What does this mean for you and your relationship now, whether it's in limbo or not?

Well, if the concept of marriage is arbitrary, then it means something very exciting: that it can be anything you want it to be.

What do I mean by that? Well, if people have been changing and re-changing the definition of marriage throughout history, there's nothing to stop *you* from doing the same thing, right now. In other words, there's nothing to stop you from saying, "being mildly dissatisfied with my long term partner is not normal, and I don't accept it as normal anymore."

There's nothing to stop you from taking actions to bring about the kind of marriage you *do* want. With conscious, compassionate action, you can CHOOSE to have the relationship you want, this very instant.

Apathy is the opposite of love. It's the opposite of deliberately choosing, of conscious action, of control, of commitment. Apathy is forfeiting the gift of defining your life as you want it, and letting something or someone else define it for you.

You may have noticed something while reading through my list of signs that you may be in a limbo relationship. All the statements are decidedly *passive*. They're about lack. They're what happens when you let go of your right to take control of your life, and the dull, helpless feeling you experience as a result.

"I want to leave, but I just *can't*..."

"I've wanted a divorce for years, but she's so dependent on me..."

"Even if I left, I'm so old now, who would want me?"

When reading these sentences, do you feel how utterly *exhausting* they are? This is because in each one, there is no conscious control, no choosing, no action. Only the sad resignation of submitting to something or someone that's out of your control. And it's tiring to be at the mercy of something out of your control!

By the time people realize their relationships are not what they want them to be, they usually find out it's too late: they already have kids and a mortgage and the thought of dividing up the kitchen appliances seems horrific. So they blame external circumstances, or their spouse, and *fail to take action*.

They're apathetic, in other words.

CHAPTER 3: THE 3 MYTHS THAT ARE EATING AWAY AT YOUR MARRIAGE

Marriages get this way not because it's the natural order of things, but because we *choose* for them to be that way. In this chapter, we'll look at the ways you are actively (even if unconsciously!) choosing to kill the passion that your relationship began with.

Myth 1: They have to stay with me, they promised!

Marriage, in many ways, is nothing more than a promise that you'll never leave. In fact, most wedding vows are just a list of all the things that a married couple promises to endure, rather than succumbing to and leaving. In sickness and in health. For richer and poorer. For better or worse. The message is clear: *no matter how bad things get*, you have to stay.

The sentiment is great, in many ways. But it's also unrealistic. In almost every area of life, there are consequences for "better" and consequences for "worse". We don't expect our bosses to keep paying us no matter what our performance in the office. We don't expect to maintain friendships if we treat our friends badly for years. We don't expect our cars to run well without proper fuel and maintenance. And yet, with marriage, many people assume that their spouses *owe* them, no matter what.

The intention of this "myth" is easy to see. People do sometimes struggle, people lose their jobs and they fall ill. A good partner isn't scared off at the first sign of trouble and will help their spouse through both their trials and their celebrations.

But the dark side of this is obvious, too. When you take your partner's commitment for granted, no matter what, the pressure's off. If they're supposed to love you as much in the "better" as in the "worse", you don't have an incentive to cultivate the "better", do you?

It's not the most PC thing to say, but both men and women fear this very thing in long term relationships. The vows are made and the woman gains weight and stops doing her nails, the man stops buying her little gifts and remembering her birthday. They're little things, they don't *really* matter. Don't be so shallow, we're told, that kind of thing is sexist anyway, true love should go deeper than all that. Right?

Wrong.

There's a very simple name for behaving any old way you like because you know your actions won't have serious consequences: it's called taking advantage.

Ask yourself, do you regularly assume your partner has to put up with poor behavior from you, because they're your partner, and they owe it to you? Do you accept behavior from your spouse that you wouldn't dream of putting up with from a friend or family member or colleague? Or even a younger version of your partner?

If you're reading this book, the question in the back of your mind might be, *what has this relationship ever done for me? What good is my partner to me anyway?*

Turn the question around and ask what *you* have actively done for your partner and your relationship. Ask yourself what you have done to deserve the treatment you feel entitled to.

Myth 2: Married couples are supposed to be a little unhappy

Again, we come to the idea that a little boredom and irritation in long term relationships is just the way things are.

This myth does more than any other to keep people trapped in situations their gut tells them is wrong, but which society tells them is perfectly reasonable. Instead of taking that gut feeling and doing something useful with it, you might be tempted shrug your shoulders and carry on.

We've all heard that after the honeymoon period is over, it's not fair to expect romance and white-hot passion anymore. And this is true! But there is a second part to this story that people forget about. While the old white-hot passion burns off, in healthy relationships, it's meant to give way to *a different type of love.*

It's not normal for love to disappear completely. Quite the opposite. The initial lust and thrill of getting to know someone new is fantastic, but it's short-lived for a reason. The chemical cocktail buzzing around in your brain gives new relationships an intense quality. You don't have to do anything special, this pheromone storm just happens on its own, and you enjoy it.

But then trust, familiarity and companionship develop. The hormonal side of things calms down and you begin to see your partner clearly – warts and all. If a couple survives this transition back to reality, they can enjoy moving on with a love that is solid, deeper, and more substantial.

Nowhere in that story though, is there any need for contempt, bitterness, resignation or disappointment in your partner. Transitioning from the intensity of early love to the deeper, subtler love of a long term relationship is just that: a transition. Not a loss.

Happy couples may have a few hiccups along the way, but they eventually settle into a love that's less all-consuming and more stable. The quality of their love matures and deepen, but it doesn't disappear.

Ask yourself whether you're being mature and adult in your relationship expectations ...or whether you've actually lowered your standards too much. Ask if you're hiding your relationship's lack of love inside the narrative that tells us that love is meant to mellow a little. It's in the nature of love to change with time and with the people who experience it. But if love is *gone*, that's a problem.

Myth 3: You only work on a marriage when you're having problems

This is a two-part myth. Let me give you an example. If I told you, "This is Adam, he's been working really hard on his marriage this last year", what would you think about Adam and his relationship?

If you're like most people, your response might be: "Oh poor Adam, what's the problem? I guess there must have been some issues with his wife. I hope he fixes everything!"

In this response hides a persistent but damaging belief: that you aren't supposed to "work" in a marriage. That falling in love is effortless, and so staying in love must be effortless too. It's the old "love is enough" myth, and it tells us subtly or not so subtly that real love doesn't require effort, it just happens.

The other face of this myth is the implication that comes with it: that if you are working hard on your marriage, something must be wrong, and if you're doing nothing at all, things must be fine.

Because you're reading a self-help book on marriage, I'm going to assume you're less susceptible to this particular myth than most. But could you be buying into this idea all the same?

"Chemistry" happens on its own. Falling in love is easy. Once the spark has happened though, and the fire is lit, well, it won't last forever. A fire, no matter how big and powerful, requires a constant supply of fuel to keep going. Cut off the fuel supply and the fire will consume what it has *and then die.*

So not only is this myth not true, it's actually the opposite of the way things really are: good marriages require constant effort.

Too many people assume that they needn't actively work on their relationships, and even if they do, it's usually only once things have gotten so bad and it's already too late. It's a little ironic: we think there is something shameful about couples counseling and the like, as though it was an admission that your relationship was failing. Yet making the effort in this way could well be the thing that makes sure your relationship *isn't* a failure!

Go a little deeper and this myth rests on the assumption that relationships are never supposed to be difficult or effortful, and that working on them is proof that something is wrong. Ask people who've known each other for two years and they'll tell you that the most important thing is shared interests, respect, communication, passion ...ask those same couples two decades later and they'll tell you the most important thing in a marriage is to *keep working on it.*

Keep adding fuel to the fire. Allowing the flames to die down and then being sad that your fire is gone is not proof that love never lasts – it's only proof that you didn't cultivate your love while it did last.

In this chapter, I want to turn the 3 big myths from the previous chapter on their head.

I believe that holding on to these ideas about how relationships *should* be limits your own growth and prevents your relationships from being everything they *can* be. But as we've seen, you can change, and you can make the decision to do something new and different with your life, right this instant.

Let's take each myth and invert it. Instead of being passive and accepting whatever stories we've been told about what relationships can and can't be, let's start by assuming that these rules *aren't* true.

New story 1: You aren't entitled to anything but the present moment

What I want to suggest is a bit radical, and at its core contradicts what most people think of when they think of marriage. It's this: you don't owe anyone anything, and they don't owe you anything.

Everyone you encounter, in any capacity, *chooses* to interact with you. And you choose to interact with them! At any point, one or both of you can consciously choose to step away and change the dynamic. In other words, there is no "script", there is no rule, there is only a pair of people, in the moment, making choices.

In a marriage, the exact opposite can sometimes feel like it's true, but you are always *free*. Free to leave, free to stay. With love, there are no obligations. So your partner is free to leave, and free to stay, as well.

Think of all the vows you've said to your spouse, on your wedding day. Now, imagine that you say those vows, and really express them with all your being, every single second of the day. Rather than committing less, staying in the moment is about committing *more*. It's because you take your commitments so seriously, that you renew them each and every passing moment.

By the same token, you can re-evaluate those commitments with each moment. You can stop at any time and say, "is this commitment still true for me? Is my heart still in this? Am I living my vows and not just going through the motions?"

The vows of marriage are paradoxical. If love were so important, wouldn't you want its expression to be spontaneous and elective, rather than enforced? If you felt your love so deeply that you wanted to make a vow, wouldn't the vow be unnecessary, given how solid your love was?

I'd like to suggest a different way to look at commitment.

Most commitments are future based. They tell the other party what they can expect from you in the future. "Till death do us part" a man may say to his wife, not really sure that he'll feel the same way about her in a few years, let alone at the very end of his life.

Most commitments are feelings based. The promise is for ever-lasting love and devotion, rather than concrete actions. "To have and to hold" is kind of *static*. What does such a promise actually look like, day in and day out?

Most commitments promise things that are not actually under your control. How many people made commitments (and meant them!) and then met someone who was a complete game-changer for them? The fact is, they made their commitment with imperfect information. They promised that they would always behave in the same way, forever. But since none of us know what's in store for us in the future, how on earth can we promise that? How can we know what our beliefs or priorities will be in 10 or 20 years? We can't, and so when we promise that we will, we are guaranteeing something that is actually not up to us.

Of course, commitment is a valuable thing for a reason. The sentiment behind commitment is so valuable, that marriage is the single biggest decision some people will ever make in life. Earning another person's trust is priceless, and if you can be devoted and stay the course to your goals, you are a valuable partner.

But there are two kinds of commitment. One is TV-movie commitment; glossy, done all at once in a wedding ceremony using fancy words, but lacking a certain depth. This kind of commitment is given before truly understanding what is being promised. The commitment is offered because the *idea* of it seems nice. But it's untested, unsubstantial.

The second kind of commitment is different. It's not future based, it's *present based*.

It's a sustained, alert presence of mind, not just in some abstract, Valentine's card way, but in a real, every-day-and-right-now way. It's not feeling based, but actions based. It's effort and real-world work. It's the dedication not to the pretty "After" picture of a relationship, but to the process, and all the middle bits and difficult conversations and compromises that come with constant improvement.

This second kind of commitment doesn't make any claims on what the future has in store for anyone. Life is uncertain. But it promises to stay conscious, to take charge and to be kind in the moment – something that you can maintain always, no matter what.

It's romantic to say, "I will be your husband and I want you to be my wife" but what does it actually mean? It's a vague, almost-empty *sentiment*, nothing more. It is worth more to commit to the ups and downs of a human relationship, not as husband and wife, but as two unique individuals, individuals who have problems. It's the difference between saying, "my love is eternal" and "in every passing moment, my focus is to prioritize loving you in real, active ways."

The paradox is that it's *easy* to promise away your whole life, but difficult to devote this moment, right now, completely and fully to the person you are sharing your life with. Someone can be glib and easy with grand promises – but can they stay with you, in the fullness of this moment right now, and be committed to you, as you are?

All any of us have is the present moment. Can you commit *right now*?

New story 2: True love changes, but never disappears

As we saw in a previous section, it's normal for love to evolve and change with time. People are only the vessels of love, and since people themselves are always changing and growing, so too will the way that they express and experience that love. What works in early life might not work later on.

But it's cause for concern if love "disappears" completely.

I always find it terribly sad that people just assume that married couples are always a little miserable. We laugh when men make jokes about being shackled to their wives, or when wives make jokes about having three kids: two plus the one they married. The advice on how to have good marriages can be a little grim: forgive easily. Pick your battles. Get over it.

Here is the next "inversion": there is absolutely no reason that love should "fade" with time.

Love is not something you buy and maintain, hoping it doesn't fall to bits before its time. It isn't a game that becomes boring the more you play it, or a delicate treasure that loses its color if you leave it out in the rain.

Lust, on the other hand, is very much like this. So is infatuation, or a temporary crush. Novelty, the momentary excitement of someone new ...these are all things that can fizzle and disappear with time. It's just the nature of the beast.

But love is not like this.

Can you imagine gradually falling out of love with your children? Just think of it now: imagine them at twelve years old, and thinking to yourself, "you know what, they're OK, I guess, but you just can't expect to have that some intense love for your children as you did when they were five, you know? We get on OK now, but man, it's nothing like those early days..."

It sounds ridiculous! And it is. While the novelty of having a child may soon wear off, the fact is that this novelty wasn't the *reason* you loved them. You just loved them. This love was vast, immeasurable and total. They could grow up, they could change, they could teeth and graduate and leave home and get married and more ...and your relationship would change with every step of their (and your!) development.

But that love would never go anywhere.

True love changes, but it never disappears. Just like a drop of water can be cloud, or ocean, or river at any one point in time, but still be what it essentially is: water. Love can change forms too. It can go from high energy, lustful, exciting early-love and change into slow-burning, warm, comfortable love ...and back again.

An old friend of the family once told me about how differently you think of love once you're been married for decades. He told me that while a younger couple might have a few days where they fight, or a "rough patch", for an older couple, this rough patch could last *years*. The scale of a relationship can get very large. He recounted to me moments in his marriage where he hated his wife, loved her again, hated her again. He told me about years where they seemed to be in the first few months of their relationship all over again, and felt infatuated with each other as though they had just met. He remembered the crazy years raising toddlers, the quiet years after they moved out, the busy working years, the houses, the pets that came and went, the money, the lack of money. Everything. When he spoke about his relationship, he understood that throughout everything, his love would change. He came from an era when people didn't divorce as easily, which might have something to do with it, but his story stuck with me.

Relationships have their ups and downs. But apathy is neither, and it's not normal. You don't have to shrug and think, well, that's just what happens. It isn't. Give your partner – and yourself – more credit.

New Story 3: True love is something you work for

If what I've said so far has me seeming like a bit of a romantic, well, let me get rid of that idea right now! The common idea is that genuine love is so special that it doesn't need anything to help it along. It's a bit like magic, or luck – and there's nothing you can do to make it more or less likely.

This is the final myth I want to invert. I believe the opposite is true. Genuine love is so special ...that it needs all the help it can get!

The old man in the last section, he wasn't just sitting on his butt, waiting to see what his marriage would turn out to be. At every step of the way, he was *working* at it. Nobody earns a degree in a subject just because they're really interested in it. Nobody builds a house just by really liking the blueprints.

A good, happy relationship is not a feeling. It's not a sentiment or an idea or a wish. Though relationships have their foundation in our emotions, that's just where they begin. Where they come to life though, where they are expressed and where they live or die, is in action.

You can have the most profound and beautiful love for someone, but it is nothing more than a private bit of indulgence if you never *express* that love in real, concrete action. Two people are forever strangers to one another unless they can find meaningful ways to reach out and connect over the distance.

In the previous chapter, we saw that there is a reluctance to do relationship maintenance ...why fix it if it's not broken, right? But think of it this way, those parts of your relationship that are not expressly actions you've taken, what are they? Chance. Luck. Randomness. I'm sure you have a few of these relationships in your life, actually. Certain circumstances make them happen and then when the circumstances don't exist anymore ...the relationship dissolves as well.

True love is effortful. It's the kind of love that compels you to pick up a violin and push yourself to play, day in and day out, because you want more than anything to create beautiful music. You could walk up to the violin, try it out, find that you're not naturally talented and then forget the whole thing, of course. And many people do!

But ask anyone who's had a long, deeply satisfactory and meaningful relationship and I bet you not a single one of them will shrug and say, "well, it just kind of happened by accident." Love is not that different from most other valuable things in life: the bigger the effort, the bigger the payoff. The more you risk by being vulnerable, the greater the reward.

It's all about sustained focus and effort. Working on a relationship means you care.

CHAPTER 5: SPACES IN YOUR TOGETHERNESS

We've had a look at length at all the subtle but powerful beliefs that could be quietly wearing away at the fabric of your marriage.

And I've suggested ways to turn those beliefs on their head. While my inverted beliefs may not be the stuff of romance novels, my hope is that just entertaining the alternative can start to open up new thoughts in your mind, or new behaviors in your daily life. Perhaps my suggestions might seem a little lackluster, but you'd be amazed at how far gratitude, hard work and flexibility can take you.

If you've read the previous chapters and make an honest effort to try and change the way you think of your relationship, I congratulate you. But at the same time, the too-good-to-leave-too-bad-to-stay relationship may subscribe to none of these beliefs and still lack that special something. That's the difficulty with this kind of marriage: it ticks all the boxes.

Sort of.

The following three chapters are about taking charge and *actively* working on the kind of marriage that you want. It's great to take an honest look and ask yourself if you've become complacent, if you're taking your partner for granted or if you've succumbed to damaging myths about how couples are supposed to feel about each other in the long term.

But the next step is to take action.

What kind of relationship do you want to create?

Some counterintuitive advice for women

Before we move on, though, I want to address a tricky topic that I feel doesn't get enough attention. It's this: when it comes to relationships, marriages, keeping peace in the home, or general social maintenance, there is a hidden assumption that it's all *women's work*. In fact, I have myself assumed that many of you reading this book right now are women.

What should we do with this fact? Culturally, we train little girls to think of others before themselves, to be polite and accommodating and to care for others, like they see their mothers doing. Perhaps we all unconsciously assume that women are natural nurturers, and that if a relationship is in trouble somehow, it falls on them to fix it.

And so you see marriage advice mostly in women's magazine and not men's, and you see women becoming marriage counselors – or insisting that their partners go to see one with them.

Women devour books explaining how to be better mothers, wives and girlfriends, and the expectation is that men *don't*. If you're here reading this right now, I want to ask, what is your partner (assuming he is male) doing about the problems you believe exist in your relationship?

Think honestly about it. My guess is: nothing.

While it may or may not be true that women are better communicators, more empathetic, or just more interested in these topics, I think it pays to ask how this bias plays out in your own relationship.

The counterintuitive advice I want to give, particularly for women, is this: instead of focusing more and more intently on crafting a good relationship, *turn outward from your relationship.*

If you're a super-nurturer, occasional doormat or like to think of yourself as in charge of relationship duties, this suggestion will probably seem preposterous. If you thought, "well then who will give a damn about our relationship? How will it ever get better?" then I want you to look carefully at what those thoughts and fears are telling you.

I'm going to explain soon what I mean when I say "turn outward" but first, I want to ask that if you're a woman, and you've been in Relationship Problem Solver Mode for many years, that the hardest and most beneficial thing you can do might be to step back, rather than ramping up your efforts.

A surprising problem: you are too close!

Kahlil Gibran is famous for his writings on love in The Prophet:

"Let there be spaces in your togetherness, And let the winds of the heavens dance between you. Love one another but make not a bond of love: Let it rather be a moving sea between the shores of your souls. Fill each other's cup but drink not from one cup. Give one another of your bread but eat not from the same loaf. Sing and dance together and be joyous, but let each one of you be alone, Even as the strings of a lute are alone though they quiver with the same music. Give your hearts, but not into each other's keeping. For only the hand of Life can contain your hearts. And stand together, yet not too near together: For the pillars of the temple stand apart, And the oak tree and the cypress grow not in each other's shadow."

Like a chain, a relationship can never be stronger than the two individual people it's made from. If a marriage consists of two people who have a deep and abiding self-hatred, how good can the love they have for each other really be?

Have you ever seen a really old couple out together, maybe at a restaurant, and they just sit in silence? They share their meal and go about everything with scarcely a glance at each other. There's nothing to say because they've already heard one another's same old stories, a million times over. There's no new funny anecdote to share because they spent the whole day together (not to mention every day for the last forty years) and were likely both there when it happened. Neither of them have changed in a decade so there really is nothing extra to share or even argue about.

What's happened is that these two people have forgotten their individuality. They have blended into an "us" and forgot about their own separate interests, separate ideas or goals. The "us" is a safe, comfortable bubble, but there's largely no new information coming in or going out. When they were dating, they could each excitedly tell the other about everything that happened since they last were together. Their differentness was like a breath of fresh air into the bubble.

There were, as Gibran says, *spaces* in their togetherness. And in these spaces, fresh, exciting new energy flowed. Things didn't grow stale and predictable. There was even a little excitement and a feeling of risk. As you get to know someone better, it's natural to want to close up all those spaces, and chalk it up as intimacy. And it is. But squeeze out those spaces and you kill the attraction that comes with being two different, separate people.

What advice would you give that old couple in the restaurant? What effect do you think it would have if they both trotted off to couple's counseling together, and forced each other to stick to a sex schedule and daily, grueling "chats" about the state of their relationship?

If any of this is hitting a nerve, the solution to the loss of passion in your relationship may be the opposite of what you may think at first: *turn outward from your relationship.*

If you're a woman, you may feel an irresistible urge to reach out, to talk, to get your partner to "open up" ...and unwittingly squeeze close even what tiny spaces remain open between you. Instead, why not try injecting a little fresh air into your relationship?

A good marriage is made of two people. Working on your relationship is great, but in what ways can you become a better person, not just a better partner?

In what ways can you make sure you have something interesting to say the next time you share a meal with your partner at a restaurant?

When was the last time you truly taught them something, or surprised them, or shared something about yourself that was exciting? Have you neglected parts of yourself because now you're not a "me" anymore but a "we"? What parts of you are your own, separate from your partner entirely, private or even secret?

CHAPTER 6: THE ALL OR NOTHING MARRIAGE: IT'S ABOUT PASSION

Relationship limbo is, in a way, worse than an outright broken marriage.

At least when a relationship is broken, there is the promise of fixing it! But when passion fizzles, the people involved might not even have the motivation to *care* that it has. You have people who couldn't keep their hands off each other and then 5 years later, can't stand to look at one another day after day.

So far, I've asked you to be honest in appraising your own marriage. Since no two are the same, you might have agreed wholeheartedly with some things here and not others. Nevertheless, you may have come to a few sad or discouraging conclusions.

Maybe you've read the previous chapters and thought, well, what's the point in saving such a marriage? Perhaps an apathetic, static marriage is actually not so bad, and when you start digging, you realize that your boredom and dissatisfaction is actually covering over a much more serious unhappiness. Now what?

There are two ways to get out of marriage limbo. The first way is to take a leap of faith, find the love and passion you used to share for your partner and reignite it, then move onto a new relationship, one where the terms of engagement are different. The other way is to break up. There's more on this second outcome, later in the book.

When I talk about "passion" here, I'm talking about boldly and firmly taking a stand. Of choosing. Instead of lingering around in low-key limbo, you *decide*. You deliberately act according to your values and principles – and take on the responsibility for the consequences. In other words, adding some passion to your life might have the unexpected result of forcing your hand on decisions that you've long left unmade. If you decide that what you want is more authenticity, more connection, more vulnerability …then you also open yourself up the chance that the most authentic path for your relationship to take would be to end.

And so we come to the "all or nothing" marriage.

The all or nothing marriage is not about giving ultimatums or being a perfectionist. It's about deciding that the actions you take are going to be a reflection of your principles, or they aren't. It's the sentiment that says that when it comes to your most important values, to who you are deep down and what you ultimately want from your life, there are no half measures. No almosts or nearlies.

Let me give you an example to show you what I mean. Let's say a woman does some soul-searching and comes to understand that what she really values and wants out of a romantic relationship is *honesty*. Not just the absence of deceit, but the presence of a spirit that values being direct, forthright and genuine.

Now after she comes to this understanding, she looks at her marriage. She tells herself that her husband's reluctance to willingly share anything with her is a problem. He doesn't *lie*, it's true. In fact, she could stay forever in a marriage with a man who technically didn't lie or cheat. While she could go along with this, telling herself that no marriage is perfect, that her husband isn't really a bad guy etc. etc., the truth is, she'd be putting herself on a path to a stale, limbo relationship. Her "it's fine" would slowly turn into "I don't love you anymore". She'd "put up" with her husband, quietly racking up resentment for him for something that he's not actually obliged to change.

But she's not only holding her husband accountable. She realizes that it's also her responsibility to act towards the things that matter to her. She has *passion*. She values honesty so she commits to being honest with him: she tells him she isn't happy, and she requires XYZ in order to be happy. He can now choose to take responsibility himself, respond actively and communicate with her ...or he can choose not to. It doesn't matter from here which way the relationship goes, however, because it's fundamentally different from a limbo one: it's *real*. It's alive and fresh. It has passion in it now.

Look at your relationships now and ask yourself, do you bring your whole, genuine self to your relationships, whatever your whole, genuine self looks like? Are you *present* in your relationships? Do you know your values and do you consciously act to bring them about in your words and deeds?

I want to suggest that unless you're choosing to live the "all" every single day, then what you are actually doing is living the "nothing".

I had a long chat with a marriage counselor once and I asked her if she ever felt bad that so many of the couples who came to see her ultimately ended up separating. She said she didn't. In fact, she didn't see herself as causing the break ups at all. Simply deciding to take an action in your marriage, to act decisively, can be enough to unravel a marriage built on years of momentum, assumptions and "going through the motions" ...a limbo marriage, in other words. She said to me, "most of the time, their relationships had ended years ago, it's just that coming to see me made them both admit that for the first time."

A marriage that is not in limbo, but instead buzzing with passion and vibrancy:

- Can end any time. Both partners treat the fact that they are together as a happy, lucky bonus they've achieved in life, and appreciate it all the more, renewing their commitment to each other every single day.

- Is filled with intimacy of all kinds – sex, meaningful conversation in which both parties feel heard, joint efforts on the children or household, shared activities, physical affection...

- May have conflict. There might even be a lot of conflict. But you're always fighting *for* something. You fight because of the things that are important to you both.

- Is fun and carefree and doesn't take itself too seriously. After all, if relationships are not enjoyable, what's the point?

- Means you know your partner better than anyone. But there are just some parts of each other's lives that are private. And you both give each other that privacy, happily.

- Means you are not afraid to engage with strong emotions, to hash things out, to talk or to change things up. You don't move away from heavy emotions, but into them.

Make the Commitment

The trouble with a word like "commitment" is how terribly vague it is. When you hear that word, I'm sure you instantly have some sense of what it means ...but do you? Try for a second to think of a simple, one-line definition for "commitment". How would you explain this word to an alien?

I believe that people fail to live up to one another's relationship expectations not because committing in itself is hard to do, but because most people share wildly different ideas of what commitment is in the first place! If a woman tells her friends, "Oh, he has a real problem with commitment" they may all nod and agree, but have they really understood her? Has the woman herself really understood what's going on in her relationship?

In this chapter, I want to talk about commitment. In the previous chapter, we looked at the power of taking deliberate, decisive action when it comes to your relationships. What comes after that?

Commitment.

Understanding The Promise

When you tried to think of a definition for commitment, did you just imagine a handful of synonyms like "dedication" or "promise". But think of this: can you imagine someone coming to you, a deadly serious look on their face, as they take your hand in theirs and tell you earnestly, "I promise."

You might think they've lost their mind. Promise *what* exactly? To simply say "I promise" is completely meaningless. Unless you promise *something specific*, then it's an empty statement.

And yet, how often do people do exactly that with their partners, when the word is "commitment"?

We have a set of assumptions we hold about everything it means when someone is "committed" in a relationship and we hope that the people we encounter share a similar definition. We say, "he's committed to his wife" or "she made a commitment to him" and then leave it at that.

But what are you committing to? What does commitment actually mean? *Who* is doing the committing? And why?

The word commitment is like relationship "shorthand". It's just a single, simple word but it actually points to a very complex subject. While this is inevitably the way that language works, the problem is when you forget the complexity you're trying to grapple with and get distracted by the words, the symbols or the images associated with that complexity.

I'll give you an example. A woman has a whole cluster of ideas, feelings and thoughts stored under the word "commitment" in her mind. For her, she values a partner who is tuned into her needs and more than willing to hold them as a priority. What's more, she thinks this will naturally lead to things like elaborate proposals and expensive engagement rings. The problem comes when her boyfriend not only fails to make an elaborate proposal with an expensive ring, but actually suggests they go shopping together for a ring.

The woman is upset because this is proof that her boyfriend isn't "committed" enough. She may fail to see that actually, he cares so much about getting the right ring that he wouldn't dream of picking it himself and getting the wrong one. His actions are directly in line with everything she wants in a partner, i.e. for them to be considerate and put her needs as a priority. But they end up fighting – not because they are not committed, but because they don't share the same definition of commitment.

The previous chapter was all about choosing. Commitment is all about the follow through. But it's not enough to simply say, "sure, I commit." You have to engage with the complexity behind that word.

What are you committing TO?

Have you ever noticed how some people say, "I'm ready to be married now" and marry whoever's hanging around and seems up to the task?

This person is very committed ...to an *idea*.

Many relationships are held together not by dedication flowing towards the individuals involved, but by dedication towards the idea of that relationship. Perhaps you've felt this yourself, after a breakup. You might have liked the feeling of being in relationship, even if not specifically with that person!

When you say, "I commit" are you only committing to the rosy picture of what you hope and expect your relationship should be? Or are you committing to the hard times too, not just the hard times you can imagine right now, but even the hard times that you can't even picture right now? If your commitment only extends to a healthy, functioning relationship, then it will dissolve the moment you believe that the relationship isn't what you agreed to.

Of course, though people like to think it's not the case, commitment does come with conditions. How far does your commitment extend? What are your (unspoken) conditions?

When you commit, are you committing to a *feeling* or a concrete set of *actions*? We all like to promise undying love but the nasty truth is that your ethereal emotions can be some of the hardest things to predict and control. People seldom make promises about something that is far more under their control: the actions they take. When you tell yourself or others that you are committed, are you imagining that this is merely a state of mind, an attitude or a feeling? Or can you see the concrete actions that are required of you, and the work and effort that you'll do to maintain what's important?

What does your commitment mean?

It's bad news to understand the limits to your own or your partner's commitment when it's already too late. For many people, commitments mean next to nothing. They may say the *words*, but the words boil down to something like, "I promise to keep doing this thing that I like doing as long as I keep on liking to do it". The moment the feelings waver, or circumstances change, such a flimsy commitment will disappear instantly.

When you commit, what are you actually saying? Strip away all the romantic language and borrowed clichés and look at what you are actually promising to your partner. Take a look at the following:

- I will always consider your needs on par with my own, and think of you in everything I do, and every decision I make.

- I will always give you the benefit of the doubt, and trust you, and be forgiving and understanding of all your weaknesses.

- I will pretend not to be interested in anyone else so long as you agree to do the same.

- I will put our family and the home we put together first, always. Our standing in the community, our children, those things are important. I commit to building that together with you, no matter what the state of our relationship.

- I will never leave you, no matter how badly you treat me.

- I will stop thinking of myself as "available", and actively discourage involvement with anyone who would make you feel jealous.

- I will love and support you to become the person you want to be in this life, no matter what. Even if we split up, I'm your ally for life and will do all I can for you.

All of these are "commitments". And they're all very different! Maybe some seem romantic to you. Maybe some of them seem kind of sad or creepy or unhealthy. Thinking of your own relationship now, what is the commitment between you both? Do the commitments match up? Have you both been making assumptions about the other? Do you have an "official" commitment and a not-so-nice, unspoken one?

Commitment: Prescriptive versus Descriptive

I want to say one more thing about commitment before we move onto the more practical section of this book. It's the difference between *prescriptive* and *descriptive* commitment. It might sound needlessly complicated, but it's basically the difference between saying what *is*, and saying what *ought* to be.

Here is the root of confusion when it comes to the way different people think of commitment. As we've seen, some people say "I do" and, consciously or unconsciously, mean "I do right now". Right in that moment, they feel happy and passionate and in love with their partners, so it's easy to say sure, they're committed. They'd travel to the ends of the earth for them, why not. This kind of commitment is purely descriptive. It just tells you what the current situation is like. How many people have you heard say things like, "I married him, and I loved him, and when I said my wedding vows, I really meant it. At the time"? Those wedding vows were descriptive.

The other kind is less common, and less talked about. This is prescriptive commitment, and tells us what we want to be the case, rather than what is. In other words, it's more like saying "I will" than "I do." It's the kind of commitment that kicks in not when you're filled with warm fuzzies and happy to promise your life away, but the feeling you get when you're angry, sad and unhappy with your relationship. It's the impetus to work on your relationship even though committing at that moment is very hard.

To put it directly: descriptive commitment is the promise you make because it's easy to do so in the moment. Prescriptive commitment is the promise you make, *in spite of it* not being easy. The former kicks in because of hormones and convenience. The latter kicks in when hormones and convenience run out!

When you're wondering where the love in your relationship went, it might be a good idea to take a fresh look at the kind of commitment you share with your partner. It may not be that something is wrong or missing, but rather that it was never quite there in the first place. Perhaps now is the time to start thinking about what you really want, and truly *committing* to it.

Commitment to Yourself

This is the only exercise in this book that can be done on your own. It's all about making commitment to yourself, before you enter into agreements with others. The idea is that if you know and understand yourself, you're in a better position to make promises to others; similarly, you have a better grasp on what *you* want from your partner.

You don't have to have your commitments laid out like an actual set of vows, like I've done below, but I think it's nice to have something written down, just for a bit of ceremony. Read this every day, in the morning or evening, and do a little ritual to help cement the ideas in your life and in your mind. Here's an example of a possible commitment you could go with.

I commit to the work it takes to maintain calm self-awareness in everything that I do. I commit to treating myself and others with kindness and compassion, even when things don't go my way, or I have limited understanding in the moment. I commit to being honest and genuine in everything I do, expressing my own needs and having the presence of mind to hear others' needs. I commit to keeping anchored in love and acceptance, no matter what.

Mine sounds a little fruity, I know, so don't worry if you'd like to go with something less new-agey. "I commit to staying aware of myself and taking responsibility for my actions" is just as powerful.

Write your commitment down, if it's long, and make sure to return to it often. Don't let it be just words on a page though. Ask yourself what it looks like out in the world as a living, breathing value that guides your *action*, not just an empty idea. Think about the following when putting your commitment together:

- What is ultimately the most important thing in the world to you? Learning? Family? Success? Self-expression?

- What aspects of you have stayed the same, no matter what relationships come and go? What are the best things about you?

- Look back on past conflicts and try to remember times when you dealt with things in a way that made you proud. What actions and what state of mind did you have then, and how can you recreate that now?

CHAPTER 7: REDISCOVERING ONE ANOTHER: A TOOLKIT

It's time to move onto concrete exercises to try and put some of these ideas into practice. How you use these exercises is up to you. And up to your partner, too! Do one a week, one a day or just choose one or two that look the most relevant.

Exercise One: Memories

If you go to therapy, some counselors might ask you, can you remember a time when you *didn't* have this problem? The idea is to get you thinking about solutions, and to find out what, if anything, is different now compared to then.

If you've lost some spark and passion in your relationship, ask yourself this question: can you remember a time when you had loads of spark and passion? For this exercise, spend some time thinking back to that fabled "honeymoon period". Really try to remember exactly what it was that was so different.

Now, together with your partner or on your own, write down three separate things that you've stopped doing since then. Keep focused on concrete actions. You might discover that you've stopped going on "dates", or you've stopped putting on makeup on the weekends, or you've stopped bringing home flowers every Thursday.

I know what you're thinking – you only stopped doing those things because the passion disappeared, and not the other way round. But for this exercise, take a leap of faith and just see what happens when you try to do those actions again. Schedule these activities back into your life and commit to doing them again. Try to capture exactly what made those actions or activities so special, if you can. Was it the sense of having your partner all to yourself on Sunday morning brunch dates? The feeling that you were remembered during a busy workday whenever you got a cute text at lunch?

Many couples find that even *talking* about what originally attracted them to one another is a wakeup call: they discover that they're actively taking each other for granted in the present.

Exercise Two: The Daily Marriage

We've spoken at length about the kinds of commitment, and how love and passion can fizzle in a relationship when the commitment is not what it should be.

For this exercise, you're going to do something a little strange: forget about all your long term commitments to your partner. Really. Whether you're married or not, forget about your vows and all the assumptions that go with them. You can of course come right back to them when you're finished with this exercise, but try as much as possible to clear the slate, and approach your partner from scratch, with no expectations, no assumptions and no demands.

The exercise goes like this: each and every day, set aside a fixed time where you will "marry" your partner. The details of how you do this are up to you, but the idea is to set a fresh, living commitment *for the day and nothing more*. What this does is removes your focus from big, abstract, ultimately empty concepts ...and puts it firmly back in the present moment. Can you love your partner, right now? Can you look deep inside them and appreciate everything that they are, as they are, in this moment? Not tomorrow or when the kids have grown up or once you get your promotion – but *now*?

Deliberately refreshing your commitment like this also keeps reminding you of what's important: taking concrete, beneficial actions each and every day. How many people do you know who treat each other horribly, but since they never technically break up, they gloat about having a successful relationship simply because they've been together so long?

You'll be doing the opposite. Instead of promising eternal devotion and love and then failing to have the presence of mind to pick up your socks or ask your partner how their day went, you'll go the other way. You'll forget about grand gestures and 70th wedding anniversaries and focus on what really matters: the person in front of you right now, in the life you have, today.

You can just sit quietly and meditate together, or do a little ritual like saying mini "vows", kissing or shaking hands. But keep it anchored in real life. Focus on the meat-and-bones of your commitments, and say things like, "I'm going to do my best today to think of you and ways to make you happy, and I'm committing to not offloading my work complaints on you when I walk in the front door."

This may sound flippant, but take it very seriously. Nothing that happens that day can sway the vows you've made. It's just one day anyway! Whatever transpires, keep your vow. Stay mindful, keep compassionate and be present.

If you can't? Don't make the commitment. Don't get married that day. You're under no obligation, for this exercise. Be honest and if you are too resentful or too sad to stick to your commitments, say so and try again tomorrow. But ask if there's something you do want to commit to. Even if it's just a small thing. Can you commit to not making a fight worse today? Can you commit to giving yourself a day to cool down, if you're angry? Can you commit to keeping an open mind and seeing how you feel later on?

Commitment, ultimately, is not about the content or the size of the promise, but the *intention* to keep it. Try this exercise for a week and then see what results you have. Watch out for, "this feels weird, I have nothing to vow and no promise to make, it's just both of us doing our everyday lives..." Become curious about why it's not easy for you, and whether you are still hiding out in relationship limbo.

Exercise Three: Something to Share

If you've become that old couple with nothing left to say to each other, this exercise is for you. Date nights are great. Chatting to a knowledgeable counselor and learning to communicate better is also great. But this paradoxical exercise is designed to bring you closer together by opening up exciting spaces *in between*.

The task is this: agree on a day and time where both of you go out on a date ...not with each other, but with yourselves. Think of it as going into the big wide world to gather something fresh and new and shiny to then bring back into your relationship; something that will bring fresh air into things and even better, the very exciting idea: your partner is an *individual*.

They are similar to you, but ultimately different. Rather than a source of friction or disappointment, this difference can be interesting and exciting ...and even a little sexy. A close friend described to me the moment she saw her boyfriend of 10 years raucously socializing with old school friends she had never met. She was surprised by how *attractive* he seemed at that moment. Even after 10 years, there were still parts of his life that were new and mysterious to her. He had unexpected talents and anecdotes and ways of speaking and being. And so did she!

A little tension, a little distance and a little mystery can inject massive amounts of new energy into an old relationship. In this exercise, you'll take the energy you develop by living your own awesome life and bring it back to your partner. When you've settled on a day and time, each go out and do your own thing. Then come back and "report" to your partner. Make sure you pick something that you find really interesting or exciting, and then explain to them why. Show them a new skill you've learnt at a class, tell them a fascinating anecdote or share with them some pictures you've taken or a curio you've picked up.

The point is, sharing is exciting, but you can't enjoy the thrill of exchange if you're both always doing, thinking, saying, eating the same things. Give yourself something *to* share. Remember how fascinating your partner seemed to you in the beginning? How you could both listen to each other talk for hours and you couldn't wait to learn more about them? Do this exercise and you're giving yourself the chance to experience all that again.

Exercise Four: The Element of Surprise

This exercise is primarily about sex. We've avoided mentioning sex explicitly so far, but of course this arena of the long term relationship can be where many of our big themes are played out.

Sex, like all forms of passion and attraction, dies under obligation. Knowing that you *have to* have sex X number of times every week or month can be the single biggest thing stopping you from doing just that. Not feeling the lust organically but pushing yourself to go through the motions anyway is something some sex therapists recommend, but I won't be recommending it here.

The trouble with "scheduling sex" is that it positions it as a chore; just one more thing you have to do. Then instead of thinking of intimate time with your partner as a fun and relaxing escape, it becomes a stressful thing you need to escape *from*. Instead, take the pressure off. In a long term relationship, yes, the sex is a "sure thing". Yes, you don't technically have to win your partner's continued interest ...but act as though you do!

Decide with your partner on a fixed period of time, let's say a week. At the beginning of that week, choose some small tokens to use to keep "score". Whether it's coins, pencils, stones or spoons, make sure you have four (possibly six) of them. Decide also on exactly what these tokens represent. You can keep things open ended, and say that each spoon represents someone "initiating" sexual contact of any kind. Or you can be more specific and say that one token counts as cuddling or oral sex, two as full sex. Decide on something you both like the sound of.

Now, the "rules" go like this: when a partner uses one of their tokens (say, by laying it down on the bedside table), the other partner has 24 hours to respond. They have 24 hours to meet their partner's loving request for sex. Because there are only 2 tokens each, each partner can only initiate twice before they run out. If you have no tokens, you have to wait till your partner plays theirs, which you can keep and spend later. At the end of the chosen period, however, the tokens are reset. This means that nobody gets to stockpile tokens while the other anxiously waits for them to be played.

This may seem silly, but the idea is to keep up the effort and "work" in your sex life, without introducing any passion-killing sense of obligation and stress. It becomes a game, but one that favors neither partner. The frequency of sex is determined by both, and nobody's libido is allowed to dominate. This is also great for people who feel pressured in the moment to succumb to their partner's initiations, since there's a 24-hour period to be "spontaneous". It's the best of both – they can acknowledge their partner's needs, but in a more natural way.

Provided both partners respect the rules, this game can be a great way to learn new skills in asking for, and giving, pleasure. After a week, change up the rules to suit your relationship, if you like. You can have a lot of fun with it: if one partner has a kink the other doesn't quite share, make it so that only half the tokens can be used for the kink. Adjust the number of tokens or the response time to suit your own needs. Remember, it's about finding a clever balance between expected, predictable and safe on one side and unexpected, exciting and sexy on the other.

Exercise Five: Play dates

In keeping with the theme of low-obligation exercises, here's a final one that focuses on dates ...but perhaps not the kind of dates you might be imagining.

These are dates you'll organize with your partner, but they'll be centered around one thing: fun. Think of traditional romantic dinner dates, for example. You get dressed up, you go somewhere to spend a lot of money and eat something nice, and then you both proceed to do all the little dating "rituals", almost like a human mating dance. You're supposed to flirt on such a date, so you flirt. You're supposed to have sex afterwards, so everyone quietly expects that. There's a script that everyone must follow. It might be romantic, it might not be, but one thing's for sure, it isn't fun or spontaneous!

If you've been together for years and years, these kind of dates are especially lacking in the fun department. So, forget about the scripts for a second. Do something truly, actually fun, for both of you. Choose one activity at a time and agree to it, then make only one rule: you only do it so long as you're both enjoying yourselves.

Play games.

Literally, go out to a field and play catch and argue over the rules about how many kisses the winner gets. Play practical jokes on one another, cook a bizarre and complicated dish together, or follow your noses in a new city and see where you land up. Think pillow fights or blanket forts. Do crafts together or sing karaoke in the living room. Go out on dinner dates but pretend to be different people and see how long you can keep the game up.

Your imagination is the limit!

CHAPTER 8: WITH COMMITMENT AND COMPASSION, THERE ARE NO ENDS, ONLY BEGINNINGS

If you've given the previous exercises an honest go and have thought carefully about your needs, your wants and what you can commit to in your relationship, I can guarantee that moving forward, your connection will be more genuine.

But the disclaimer is this: "more genuine" can mean "genuinely broken up."

Sometimes, the most honest and authentic form a relationship can take is for it to end. Sometimes, people linger in relationship limbo because both are unconsciously avoiding the fact that the relationship is already over.

The answer to the question, "where did our love go?" may be, "it morphed into respectful and compassionate distance".

It may be that your relationship was built on conditions that no longer exist, and that's OK. Perhaps you've both taught one another a great deal, but are being pulled in different directions. It may be that you tried these exercises and can honestly say: there is no passion left here anymore.

It can be a heavy thought. It's not something people like to think of, no matter what stage their relationship is in. The thought that a relationship can be well and truly over, empty of affection and having run its course is ...hard. It feels like failure. But it isn't!

If you've done the work of understanding your own needs, values and weaknesses, congratulations are in order, even if your relationship ends.

It can be hard to tell yourself that a break up or divorce is not the end of the world, but in this final chapter, we'll be looking at why it isn't. In fact, a break up is just as good as any life event to practice compassion, self-awareness and acceptance.

Staying committed through a separation

It might sound strange, but you can break up with dignity, respect ...and commitment! Breaking up is obviously the biggest transition your relationship will ever undergo. But instead of thinking that this means your commitment to that person is over, think of how the commitment is there, but adjusted to fit the new situation.

Ask yourself, even in breaking up, what are you committed *to*? Can you dedicate yourself to being kind and taking responsibility for any hurt you've caused? Can you commit to the *person*, even if you're no longer committed to the old relationship you shared with them? Can you commit to maintaining your own mindset, and behaving in ways that fit your values, even if your ex is no longer playing along with those values?

Commitment doesn't go out the window just because you're breaking up!

"Breaking up" is not the only solution

Life is not like a hospital intake form that you have to fill out, and you can only check one of four "relationship status" boxes. In fact, you can define your relationship any old way you feel like! I believe that many people are quick to "throw away" people because they don't fit into their fixed ideas of what their relationship with them *should* look like. If your husband no longer acts like what you believe a husband should act like, the solution seems to remove the label "husband" and divorce.

But breaking up is not the only option. There are many, many more labels …and you don't even have to use a label, ultimately!

Just because a marriage no longer looks much like a marriage, it doesn't mean that your connection to that person is dead and gone. It simply means that it has changed, and you might need a different label now.

Where did our love go?

Maybe it turned into friendship! Maybe it turned into "fond memories". Maybe the woman who was your muse and lover for twenty years grows up to become your mentor and lifelong ally. All the brilliant and subtle ways that people can love one another will never be adequately contained by the little boxes on the intake form.

If both of you have done the work to understand your values, and your definition of commitment, you can relax and let life unfold as it will, and let love blossom into the forms it wants to take.

People may discover that they want to revisit the idea of monogamy, or decide that the thing to save their marriage is to never go on a holiday together again. Some may renew their vows, some may decide that old vows need to be bid farewell and respectful buried. Maybe you need new promises. Maybe you just need to dust off the old ones you already have and give them a bit of TLC.

This is where I want to return to the "Commitment to Myself" exercise from earlier in the book. While this may seem like a bit of indulgence in a book that's about relationships, it comes in very handy at transition moments like this. Whatever happens, if you maintain a compassionate and self-aware frame of mind, then it almost doesn't matter what label you give your relationships.

With compassion, there are no endings, only endless beginnings. With commitment to our values, there is nothing to lose, and nothing to fear. There is only *change* and the privilege of accompanying someone on the path that winds through this change.

CONCLUSION

On the surface, being slightly bored and uninspired in your relationships seems like a small problem to have. But it's a kind of "iceberg problem" in that the closer you look, the more you realize is hidden under the surface than would first seem.

The symptoms of a "limbo relationship" are not so bad. They're so mild, in fact, that you can scarcely notice them creeping up on you, and even when you do, a lackluster relationship isn't the end of the world, is it?

Well, pull on that thread and you might discover that "mild' dissatisfaction with your relationship can lead you down a path of getting to know your desires, values, wants and needs intimately ... perhaps for the first time!

The first step is to believe that dull dissatisfaction is not "normal". If you choose to do nothing about the love slowly dying and sputtering out in your relationship, you are still making an active choice, even though it feels like you're putting things on hold, or avoiding making any scary decisions.

But this is the road to apathy and eventually, loss of love. Passion takes awareness, action and commitment. And yes, in the process of making proactive decisions about your life and the lives of others you're sharing, you may discover that your futures lie in different directions.

When you ask "where did the love go?" you are in a reactive, passive state of mind. Instead, get into the habit of asking yourself, "What do I want? What am I committed to doing to bring that state about, right now?"

Nevermind where the love went. Become curious, instead, about *now*.

Where is the love in your life, right now, and what form is it taking? And if it doesn't look like you want it to, what actions can you take to make it so?

CODEPENDENCY - "LOVES ME, LOVES ME NOT": LEARN HOW TO CULTIVATE HEALTHY RELATIONSHIPS, OVERCOME RELATIONSHIP JEALOUSY, STOP CONTROLLING OTHERS AND BE CODEPENDENT NO MORE

INTRODUCTION

Codependent partners are not necessarily together because they want to be, they are because they *have* to be...

If you've had difficulty with starting or maintaining relationships, issues with feeling jealous and possessive or find that your connections with others are more a source of distress than anything else, this book is for you.

We'll begin with a look at the phenomenon of codependency, what it has traditionally meant in the psychological realm and how these traits and patterns can be traced back to issues of self-worth, compassion and more deliberate action.

We'll examine how mindfulness can be the magic ingredient to getting a hold of the codependency cycle, and some of the characteristics of happy, mindful relationships.

Finally, we'll explore a model for mindful communication and ways that you can begin to implement immediately in order to make a commitment to stronger, more compassionate relationships with others.

CHAPTER 1: WHAT IS CODEPENDENCY?

"Codependency" is one of those words that sound more harmless than it is.

On the face of it, it sounds normal and healthy to be mutually "dependent" with other people, doesn't it? This might explain why people frequently use this term incorrectly, putting the label on any relationship that looks enmeshed, unbalanced or unhappy.

But what does codependency really mean?

This concept comes from the field of addictions counseling. Very early on, psychologists and social workers realized that it was not enough to merely treat a substance problem by treating the person who happened to end up in rehab. Rather, when you look closely, you begin to understand that addiction is a problem that affects all the relationships in an addict's life. Even though the addict's friends or family or romantic interests don't themselves have a problem with the substance, their behavior is nevertheless warped and changed by the presence of addiction anyway. In other words, the addict is dependent, and the people in the addict's life are "codependent". While an individual is under the control of a substance, the people closest to him are in turn controlled and manipulated by the addict.

Imagine a man with a gambling addiction. He is a little "rough around the edges", and has always attracted supremely feminine, kind and long-suffering women into his life. His wife is his counterfoil. Although she hates gambling, she is as much a part of the problem as he is. Because she enjoys playing savior, and secretly relishes moments where people wonder aloud how such a lovely woman could end up with such a troubled man, she keeps re-enacting moments when she has to "save" him or play the martyr. Because she enjoys feeling needed by her husband, she unconsciously avoids anything that would end his addiction. The husband in turn is caught in a never-ending cycle of crime and forgiveness, unwilling to break his addiction since in all honesty, it forms the basis of his connection with his wife. If they never argued about gambling, what would they even talk about?

The term "codependent" has come to loosely describe any relationship that forms around a dysfunction, where one partner is unhealthily preoccupied with the needs of the other instead of their own. A codependent relationship is one where the boundaries between individuals are blurred, constantly violated or non-existent. Such people may be trapped in cycles and patterns of destructive behavior that both can't seem to break out of. Connections are tumultuous, conflict frequent. These are the couples that everyone quietly wonders, why are they even together?

In codependent relationships, manipulation, guilt and resentment take the place of healthy, balanced affection. Codependent partners are not necessarily together because they want to be, they are because they *have to* be, because they don't know how to live otherwise. One partner may bring a history of abuse, a "personality disorder" or mental illness into a relationship; the ways the other partner responds to this may be healthy or not, but if they bring their *own* issues to the table too, they may find that the bond of their love is more accurately described as a shared and complementary dysfunction.

CHAPTER 2: COULD YOU BE CODEPENDENT?

Because we are human, we all occasionally show traits and behaviors that leave something to be desired. However, codependency is about a *pattern* of behaviors, and is something that is stable over time. Read over the following traits, behaviors and themes that are common with those with more codependent tendencies and see if any feel as though they describe you.

- You feel as though you absolutely need to be in a relationship, and if you aren't, you frantically search for one.
- You often feel responsible for the mistakes that others make.
- You sometimes find it hard to know exactly what you, personally, think about something without comparing notes with others first.
- You feel, at times, entitled to be loved and cared for by others.
- You feel that in many circumstances, you can't really be held accountable for your actions.
- You like the idea of saving people.
- You feel as though you sometimes confuse pity with love.
- You often behave like the parent in relationships or friendships.
- You find yourself attracted to and attracting the same kind of people over and over again.
- You often feel like a "doormat" - you put your foot down but people don't seem to respect you.
- You have the same fights over and over again with the people closest to you.
- You feel intensely jealous of people who could threaten your relationships.
- You find it difficult to trust others.
- You believe, deep down, that a bad relationship is better than no relationship at all.
- You have a long history of broken and drama-filled relationships.
- People have sometimes accused you of being passive aggressive.
- You tend to idealize your partners.
- Even though a relationship is bad, you tend to delay ending it, or just pretend it isn't that bad.
- You enjoy the image of being saintly, a "mother hen" or completely selfless.
- You have very romantic notions of relationships: you hope that love will redeem everything.
- You have a self esteem that seems to fluctuate wildly - and criticism from those that matter to you can be absolutely devastating.
- You feel possessive over your partner, and hold them accountable for jealousy you feel.
- You often look back at an ended relationship and wonder at how you ever behaved like that.
- You feel that self-sacrifice is just a part of all relationships, i.e. "love hurts".

- You find yourself "punishing" others by withdrawing, sulking or holding grudges.
- You think of your relationship as a kind of "project".
- You tend to think of yourself as a victim. You feel constantly persecuted, and outraged about it.
- You often feel out of control.
- You've had issues with phobias, shyness and depression.
- When someone criticizes your partner, you feel personally insulted.

Now, you won't find a description of codependency in the Diagnostic and Statistical Manual, the handbook that helps mental health practitioners diagnose psychological disorders.

In fact, most of the time, this kind of complicated, intricate dysfunction is hard for most psychologists and counselors to even see at first. The reason for this is because for many marriages, families and even friendships, it's not "codependency", it's just business as usual.

Whatever you call it, you may have witnessed these patterns in yourself or others. Being caught up in a codependent dynamic means each person's boundaries become muddled, the sense of responsibility is murky, and self-identity becomes fused within the relationship.

But no matter how painful and confusing the relationship is, it never seems to come to an end. For many, codependency is the natural complement to narcissistic or borderline personality disorder or substance addiction.

Codependency is like the complement to these disorders, the flip side, or a "passive" disorder.

CHAPTER 3: THE CHARACTERISTICS OF MINDFUL RELATIONSHIPS

An antidote to mindless, reactive relationships is to become more aware - not only of other people and their needs, but of ourselves and *our* needs.

When we are mindful, we can slow our interactions down, take a step back and make sure we are not responding out of habit, anger or fear. We can become more aware of what we are feeling, and so we're less likely to feel emotional without understanding why.

When we can take an objective, neutral look at the emotions and thoughts that fill us, we can begin to make better decisions for ourselves, suddenly aware of choices we never knew we had before. Here are some ways mindfulness can manifest in healthy relationships.

Mindful Relationships are not Attachment Based

What do you think of those couples who say to one another, "you're my everything" or "I don't know what I'd do without you"? Crazy romantic or just crazy?

When we are little children, we come into the world completely hopeless and dependent on others. It's normal that we look to other people to satisfy our needs - and everyone on this earth at one time relied on the charity and love of someone else to get where they are today. But the other part of development for human beings is to eventually break away from that. Even when we are toddlers, we step out, try to explore the world, find ourselves. It's good to know that Mom is always there, should things get tricky, but as a child grows, she eventually dismantles those bonds of dependency.

Later, sometimes very much later, it's easier for a grown adult to take a mature and honest look at their parents and love them deeply, even though they no longer depend for their very survival on them.

Dependency is not the same as love. When we are dependent on others, our affection and attention is coming from a place of fear and need. As something temporary, as with little children who are still growing, dependence can be understandable, but as a relationship model for mature adults, it's far from healthy. Later in this book, we'll look at ways to begin communicating from the mature, adult parts of ourselves rather than the insecure and dependent child part.

Mindful Relationships are Compassionate

It may feel sometimes that an intense and serious connection with someone is proof of the depth of the feeling you have for one another. But be careful, obsession is not the same as love.

In the codependent relationship, the partners never really *connect* with each other. They do endless, complicated dances around one another's problems, but what they never do is make an honest human connection. What does connect is the *problem*. When we have unresolved issues or dysfunctional ways of being, these patterns are there, on the top of our consciousness, being projected to the whole world.

You may feel like the worst parts of you are hidden, but when you encounter someone with a complementary or resonant issue, you "click". This may feel like a strong bond, an instant connection, even love at first sight, but what it really is is the things that are broken in you recognizing the things that are broken in another person. Is a connection of this kind powerful and hypnotic and attractive? Absolutely. But it is not love, and it is not compassion.

For Buddhists, the greeting of "Namaste" expresses something close to "the divine in me recognizes the divine in you". It is a noble and touching sentiment. We all have higher selves, and when we deliberately make a point of letting only the best of ourselves interface with the best in others, love and compassion is inevitable.

Think of obsession, possessiveness and dependence as being a "Reverse-Namaste" - the worst in you recognizes the worst in someone else. It may serve your ego to be with someone, to behave in a certain way. It may make you feel good. But is it for your highest good? Is it for theirs?

Mindful Relationships are Free From Perfection and Striving

When we are mindful in our lives, we may come to a place where we accept ourselves for who and what we are. We accept, not with resignation but with joy, the fact that life is often wonky, unfathomable and a bit of a mess. But each present moment is a gift, is breathtaking in its beauty and simplicity.

Mindfulness in relationships means viewing the ones we love through this same lens. The idea of "The One" in popular culture is framed as a deeply romantic notion but is actually a sad and almost violent concept that is the exact opposite of romantic. What it means is that we begin to look at human beings like "love capitalists" - we compare the miraculous person in front of us with our mental checklist of what the love of our life is "supposed to be". We score and rate people according to how well they fulfill some arbitrary needs of our egos, and we ask all the time, "Yes, but what's in it for *me*?"

Because we are human, because life is never perfect or finished, a mindful relationship means letting go of striving and accepting relationships for what they are, as they emerge. Young women in the modern world are trained to force conclusions from relationships. What do they call their connection? How does it rank? What category does it fall into? When confronted with a unique and completely spontaneous connection with another human being, they cannot enjoy it fully because they want to know, what's the bottom line here?

In mindful relationships, everything is 100%, gloriously and exuberantly what it is. Nothing more, nothing less. There is no need to push it this way or that way. When two partners come together from a place of health and compassion, they can separate in the same way if it doesn't work. There is nothing to hold onto, no effort, no "game".

Mindful Relationships are not Possessive

For some bizarre reason, jealousy in relationships is seen as something of a compliment, even a little bit cute in the right context. If someone is jealous of your relationship, and you feel a little glad about it, what it really means is that you are pleased that someone else is, in some way, dependent on you. Rather than proof of their love, it's proof of your ego being stroked.

In a mindful relationship, the partners are together because they want to be. The single thing that determines the quality of that relationship is the two of them - their compatibility, theirs plans. If they are secure in that connection, everything else is irrelevant. Nobody can "steal" anybody away, nobody need worry about wandering attentions.

Jealousy can be one of the most difficult things for couples to wrap their heads around. It seems almost like an inborn reaction, something out of our control. But it is in your control. Here are some ways to think about jealousy if you've had trouble with it in the past.

Try to distinguish between feeling some way, and having someone else *make* you feel that way. For example, one partner may feel distrustful and suspicious of the other. They may demand proof of their exclusivity, wanting to be soothed and put at ease. The problem is, the source of the jealous feelings is not in the other partner, but in the one having them. In other words, j*ust because you feel jealous, it doesn't mean someone is making you feel jealous. Just because you feel unloved, it doesn't mean someone is making you feel unloved.*

This can feel like a revelation when put into practice. What it means is that your focus should not be on your partner and finding ways that they are responsible for what happens inside your own head. This is a recipe for disaster. You ask for proof, they give it. It's not enough, so you demand more. The problem is, it will never be enough because your partner was not the source of the negativity, *you* were.

Start with your own needs. What (reasonable) needs do you have as an equal member of your partnership? Next, are those needs being fulfilled? Very often, at the root of jealous feelings is not the fear of what your partner may be doing with someone else. That is just a mask for feelings that really, your partner is not doing those things with *you*. You can notice this with couples that have a healthy attitude to jealousy: a woman whose husband occasionally ogles beautiful women in the street doesn't feel the slightest jealousy because her needs are met. In her relationship, she is told so regularly how utterly gorgeous her partner finds her, so what does it matter? She is so confident in these feelings he has for her, what feelings he has for others are kind of beside the point.

Jealousy is like projecting our fears for our relationships onto others. When we are not secure in our sense of safety in a relationship, it's easy to see external things as threats. But healthy, balanced relationships build on trust and compassion and are therefore not threatened by others. The quality of their connection, remember, rests with them and only them.

Naturally, our feelings can also be a good source of information - sometimes we grow jealous because we have reason to believe that our feelings are warranted. In this case, there is no point in demanding certain behaviors from our partners. If you do not trust someone, they are not likely to be for your best interests. Let them go. Assert your boundary to not be lied to or deceived, and then move on.

Mindful Relationships are Well Marked

Between healthy, mindful partners in a relationship, there are clear boundaries, a firm understanding of the respective responsibility of each and the expectation that as unique individuals, they will do their own work. Doesn't sound very romantic, does it? What about "two becoming one"? What about the bliss of melding your hearts together?

Romantic, maybe, but not practical. A codependent bond forms when partners are over involved with one another, when they agree to take on responsibilities that are not theirs, to do "emotional work" that rightfully belongs to the other partner or when they violate one another's boundaries.

The paradox with healthy relationships is that the "two becoming one" idea is only really possible with two distinct, well-developed individuals. You are not doing anyone any favors by pitching up to a relationship with holes in your heart and a mind that need filling. All this means is you'll attract someone with complementary lumps on their heart and a mind that fit with yours, and together you'll make a sort of misshapen jigsaw puzzle. Now *that's* not very romantic.

Good fences, as they say, make good neighbors.

An individual with a mature, well-developed sense of themselves has the most to offer someone else. They have their own lives, their own sense of self-worth, their own strength. "But then you don't *need* the other person!" you might say. Why even bother with relationships if you want to be so completely independent?

The reason is, when you remove need, and fear, and obsession and desperation, you open up the way for love and affection *just for its own sake.* Love is many things, but it's cheapened when held hostage by the ego. Connections formed around ego and fear may be strong and lasting, but what keeps them going is mutual need. What could be more romantic than, "I don't need to be with you. You don't complete me at all. I am happy and stable and fulfilled without you. But I still want to be with you, because you're awesome"?

A note on "Emotional Work"

Quick, picture this: one partner decides they've had enough in the marriage and pushes to see a couple's counselor. The other partner goes along reluctantly. The counselor says to them both, I want us to work together on better communication, etc. Hold this image in your mind. Really imagine the couple and the couple's counselor.

Now, in your mental picture, was it the wife that pushed to see the counselor? Did you imagine that it was the husband who came dragging his feet? Lastly, what gender was the couple's counselor? I'd bet anything that you imagined her as female.

If you did, what are we to make of this? For whatever reason, most cultures in the world seem to think that the maintenance of relationships is "women's work", like housekeeping and childcare. We think that men are morons in the EQ department and can't be expected to do things like talk about their emotions, and that if it happens in a relationship, it's up to the woman to sort it out.

This is a mild, institutionalized form of dependency. We let men get off the hook for responsible adult behavior, and we expect women to step up and do a little bit more than their share when it comes to managing the health of the relationship. We suspect nothing is wrong if the woman is reading magazine articles on how to increase intimacy and the man shrugs his shoulders and wants nothing to do with it.

Mindful Relationships Have a Balance Between Intimacy and Non-Attachment

In that small space between caring too much and caring too little, in that narrow margin in the middle of throwing yourself into the life of someone else and being aloof and distant, there rests a balanced relationship.

The paradox is, it's only when we are vulnerable and open ourselves up to hurt that we allow ourselves to make deep connections with others, but at the same time, it is only when we have a firm sense of distance and independence that we can form healthy relationships at all.

Mindful relationships have to constantly renegotiate this barrier. Sometimes, we show our strength by reaching out to others and asking them, in our weakness, to help us out. Sometimes, we demonstrate a cynicism and fragility in shutting ourselves off from others and never allowing them to get close.

So, what constitutes balance? Who knows. This might be something that each couple needs to figure out for themselves. Ask yourself, is this behavior bringing me closer to my partner or further from them? Does this behavior come from fear or does it come from a place of good will and compassion?

It would be silly to claim that there is a way to engage in relationships with other people without getting hurt. Getting hurt is more or less the price of admission when we connect with others, in much the same way as dying at the end is the price of admission for life.

But it's a decision people make over and over again, probably because, in sum, it's worth it.

That may be all very well and good, but how can you be one of those people, the kind who attracts only partners who have integrity, so that they can have successful, mature and fulfilling relationships?

If the sheer ocean of dating advice out there is anything to go by, this is basically the opposite of most people's experience.

The problem with dating advice is that it's dating advice: if you were truly committed to having the best relationships with people, you would focus on *yourself* first. You could do more to improve your "datability" and the chance that your connections will be more fulfilling and satisfying by taking a class, losing some weight or going to therapy. Trying to fix yourself through trying to fix your relationships is a backwards way of looking at things.

On the ground, in the nitty gritty of life, we can reduce a massive thing like "Relationships" down to smaller, more manageable units. Everything from the deepest and most profound romantic and spiritual union to sharing a joke with the cashier at the supermarket rests on one thing: communication. Whether it's through words or not, we are constantly communicating, and the accumulation of these little units creates this big thing we call a relationship.

So, we'll start there, with communication. What follows is a method of communication that you can use to become aware of the messages that you are sending out as well as the messages others are sending you. By becoming mindful of the "place" we come from when we communicate, we understand ourselves a little better and what's more, we can start to control and manage the kind of dynamics we enter into with other people.

Parent, Child or Adult?

The model we'll use here is very old and was popularized in the 60s by Dr. Eric Berne under the name "Transactional Analysis". Though there's a mountain of material out there to explore if you are interested, the fundamental principles of this theory are really quite simple, and make intuitive sense to almost everyone.

To begin with, there are three "ego states", or states of mind and heart that we can be in at any one time. We can change these states or have a preference for only one. We may be in one particular state exclusively with one person and a completely different state with another.

The states are as follows.

The "parent" state is what it sounds like. The positive expression of this state of mind is all the good things we associate with a loving parental role: support, encouragement, unconditional love and wisdom and care offered in the form of advice. The negative manifestation, we are also familiar with: being judgmental, critical, forbidding and harsh. A negative "parent" state means we withhold love, undermine through our bossy criticism, mistrust others and put arbitrary limits on them because we don't trust their ability to do it for themselves. We have all experienced both the positive and negative sides from our own parents, and so these traits might be very obvious to you. Even if we are not parents ourselves, though, we retain a memory of this way of being and communicating.

"Parent" State:

Here are some things that "parents" may say:

"Most new businesses fail, you know, you'd better be careful is all I'm saying" (negative parent).

"You'll figure it out, I'm sure" (positive parent).

"You behave like such a hooligan when you're drunk" (negative parent).

"Haha! I remember being your age, what a blast" (positive parent).

"Child" State:

What about "child" state? Again, you can imagine it. The positive manifestation of the child ego state is the kind of joyfulness, spontaneity and wonder that we have all seen in little children. They are loving, vulnerable, and curious about the world and full of energy and creativity. The negative manifestation? Brattiness, a failure to take responsibility, rebellion against authority, lying, impulsiveness, sulking and over-reliance on others to sort things out for them. Again, each of us has it in ourselves to show, at times, both of these traits.

Here's the child expressing itself:

"Who's my little love noodle? My little fluffalump? You are! Yes you!" (positive child).

"I don't care what you say, I'm entitled to my opinion" (negative child).

"Wow! Check this out! I've never seen something so cool before!" (positive child).

"This is SO unfair" (negative child).

Now, as you can imagine, "parents" and "children" are naturally complementary, even if the chronological child is actually in the parental mindset and the chronological parent is in the child mindset. Below are some conversations; see if you can identify who is the "parent" and who is the "child" in each of these interactions.

Example 1:

"Only losers spend that much time on computer games. I'm putting a hiatus on this relationship until you can figure out what's *actually* important to you."

"Fine. While you're at it you can put a little leash on me and keep me in the garage."

Example 2:
   "What do you think of this one?"
   "Wow. It looks great".
   "Really? You think I look OK? Do you like it?"
   "It's beautiful. You're beautiful".
   "Are you sure? Is my hair OK...?"

Example 3:
   "Look! It's an ant farm!"
   "Oh my god, you are so immature".

In the first, exchange, a negative, judgmental Parent is passing judgment on a sulky, petulant child. There is no neutral discussion of the facts. Both come from a negative frame of mind, and the first is the definite parent in the relationship.

In the second, a loving, supportive parent is interacting with an insecure, clinging child. The child in the second person keeps demanding affirmation and praise from the supportive parent.

In the last conversation, a happy, silly child is being playful with a negative, judgmental adult. In this dynamic, the joyfulness and spontaneity of the child in the first person is seen as a nuisance to the long-suffering adult of the second person.

Of course, we have all at times been in both negative and positive forms of both parent and adult. We are all petulant and stubborn at times, we have all felt the joy in falling in love, we all have a responsible, supportive side to us and likewise we also have judgmental, boring sides to us, too. Importantly, age has nothing to do with it.

"Adult" State:
What about the third mindset, the adult?

Well, the adult is the neutral, rational midpoint between the two. The adult is good at solving problems, getting things done and managing the impulses from both the stodgy parent and the sometimes-out-of-control child. Being in Adult state is being calm, in control and conscious. In the adult state, you can indulge in the joy and chaos of being a child without getting out of hand, and you can draw on the good sense of conservatism of the parent to get things done. The adult is the only one who acts with conscious awareness. While the child and the parent are reactive and unaware, the adult appraises reality neutrally, and makes the best choices to achieve his goals.

To be effective people, the theory goes, we need to be mostly in adult state, but be able to consciously draw on the other two states when appropriate. Spending a fun date at a funfair with a new partner means the child can come out and play. Likewise, when we need to discipline an employee at work, the parent needs to come out.

The trouble comes in when we get stuck in patterns of connecting with others and are unaware of the circle we're going around in. Here's the thing: with a "complementary" state, the communication goes on and on forever, until someone steps into the adult state. The negative parent says, "Clean your room!" and the negative child says, "Leave me alone!" and nothing ever changes. These kinds of interactions are "stable" in the sense that there is no impetus to change. Both may be very unhappy with the situation, but, they push each other's buttons, the jigsaw fits, so the miscommunication continues. The only way to break out of this sort of thing is by one or both entering into the adult state. Here are the same conversations, with the person responding from an Adult state:

"Only losers spend that much time on video games. I'm putting a hiatus on this relationship until you can figure out what's *actually* important to you."

"Well, you can do that. But I would prefer to address the issue at hand. Let me know when you'd like to talk together about a way out of this."

Here, there is no sulky retaliation or sarcasm in response. There is also not a negative parent response in return (you can imagine it: "Honey, good luck finding someone who doesn't" is just like a condescending adult who knows how the world works and assumes the other person doesn't). Rather, the response is focused on the reality of the situation and is geared towards finding solutions. If the second person responds in this way, it makes it a little more difficult for the second to respond as the negative parent. This is the awesome thing about the adult: it encourages other people to be adult, too. Here's the second:

"What do you think of this one?"

"Wow. It looks great".

"Really? You think I look OK? Do you like it?"

"Yup. I'll just go and start the car in the mean time".

Here, the adult has their eye on what's important: getting them both to wherever they're going. Recognizing that the cycle of validation could go on indefinitely, the adult just removes themselves from the situation. They could have responded in child themselves ("You always do this!" - Can you hear the pouting?) or from a negative parent ("You know, you should see a professional about this nonsense") but they don't engage and instead focus on the realities at hand.

Here's the last:

"Look! It's an ant farm!"

"That's amazing! I've never seen one like that before. Have you managed to find what we're looking for?"

Here, the playful silliness of the child is responded to with some playfulness in return, but then the adult kicks in and drives the conversation back towards the practical.

As you've probably noticed, there's nothing really "bad" about any of these states, only that trouble comes up when we cannot adjust and change what state we are in, or if our state is inappropriate. We cannot be negative children at work, and literal children cannot be expected to be parents to their own literal parents. Think about yourself: what state do you most commonly address other people from? Are you sometimes a child to get out of your obligations? Are you the boring parent type who spoils everyone's fun?

Jealousy, possessiveness, mistrust, dependency and all the rest stem from either the parent or child state. They dissolve when the adult in us is activated. You could read a lot about effective communication strategies, but as long as you are in the adult state and speak to people from a place of neutral respect, you'll likely say the right thing. People who are caught up in manipulative or dysfunctional behavior (i.e. those in the other two states) can't get much of a foothold if you never enter into playing parent/child "games" with them.

If one person is in the adult state, things never escalate past a certain point. The kind of endless on-again-off-again relationships of the codependent type are not possible, because the adult will end that conversation or change it. The adult realizes when something in someone else is triggering something in them and makes the deliberate decision to be non-reactive. The *compassionate* adult respects that people are all in different places in their lives, but that that doesn't mean they have to engage with them in pointless or harmful behavior.

How to use this model in your daily communication

The next time you encounter someone, anyone and in any capacity, try to identify what state they are approaching you in. Try to notice what state you are in as a response. Notice, also, if they are trying to "position" you in any way. In order to carry on the conversation, do you feel like you need to "play along" in the state that fits with theirs? Also, ask yourself: what is most appropriate in this particular moment? Is there a way to bring in aspects from your child or parent? What are your shared goals and how can you move both of you towards those goals?

Lastly, if you are unsure of how to proceed with another person, ask yourself, are you being compassionate?

CHAPTER 5: WHAT YOU NEED TO KNOW ABOUT NARCISSISM, PERSONALITY DISORDERS AND ABUSE

Somewhere in the last decade or so, it became fashionable to call everyone who had slighted you a narcissist. Though it is arguably a real "personality disorder", something about the empathy-less "psychopath" captured the imaginations of people who suddenly combed through their histories to determine if the people who had dumped them were in fact mentally ill in doing so.

Perhaps this is a bit too glib. The question of whether a person can be completely heartless and without feelings of guilt and the question of what to do about that is beyond the scope of this book. However, the codependent personality often attracts its complementary, and that person very often resembles a narcissist. Where the codependent is unsure of themselves, weak, latching onto others, the narcissist is overly confident, pushy and ready to boss others around. While the codependent person is constantly on the look out for someone to save and to latch on to, the narcissist gathers them up like disciples and proceeds to treat them exactly as badly as you'd imagine.

There has been plenty written recently about how to spot psychopaths, what it means to be one, whether *you* could be one etc. But I sincerely believe that when it comes to "toxic people", predatory personality types or any person who is hurt and wants to hurt others, the single best thing you can do is go quiet within yourself and be mindful. A person who knows and believes their own self-worth, who is compassionate and has respect will likely not fall prey to such a person, and if they do, they will not stick around for long. Someone seeking open, honest and compassionate connections with others is simply not on the same wavelength as a "psychopath" and, well, whatever it is they are looking for.

What other people do, their own weaknesses or failings, these are not really your concern. When you project calmness, dignity and compassion, you'll likely attract similar people into your world. If you meet someone who is abusive, irrational or whatever the case may be, have compassion. You can acknowledge the goodness in them, but have enough self-compassion to move on.

CHAPTER 6: TRAUMA, HEALING AND FORGIVENESS

Here is an exercise/meditation that is a simple yet powerful way of regularly opening your heart, letting go of past hurts and resentments and becoming receptive to those "higher parts" of yourself and others. It's called a Loving-Kindness meditation, and can have profound effects on your ability to empathize and be compassionate.

You need no previous experience or familiarity with meditation. Find a quiet place where you can be sure you won't be disturbed, and get comfortable - but not so comfortable you want to sleep. Clear your mind, and take a few deep breaths to focus on your body in the present moment. Find little places of tension in your body and breathe into them to release them. Become aware of sounds and smells around you, and take a moment to notice your surroundings as well as the thoughts flitting around our mind.

Next, conjure up the image of a person who you love dearly in this world. A parent, partner, child or friend. Take your time picturing their face, their voice, what you love about them. Imagine a glowing sphere at your center, golden bright and warm, and imagine that this is pure love, pure acceptance and the most unimaginable joy. Visualize yourself "beaming" this out to them. Think of all their good qualities, think of how you love and accept them - every part of them. Without conditions, without judgment or fear. Just enjoy how good it feels to love.

Next, turn your attention to someone you respect and admire, although not necessarily "love". Do the same with them. Notice that no matter how much love you found for the previous person, you have still more to give this one. Imagine the glowing light, and enjoy, again, the feeling of warmth and peace in your heart.

Next, move onto someone you usually feel neutral towards. This could be a very distant family relative, a coworker, a celebrity or someone you walked past on the street. Go with whoever pops into your mind. Again, cultivate the glowing love, kindness, acceptance and good will and direct it to them. This may be a bit trickier - but don't move on until you have felt a real, genuine experience of compassion for them.

Lastly, bring into your mind a person you actively dislike. Think of your enemies, those who have hurt you or those you simply can't stand. Summon up your feelings of open acceptance and love for them and try to direct it towards this person who it is much, much easier to hate. You don't need to "love" their actions, or their beliefs. Your goal is to see their humanity, and to accept and love that with compassion. This might be insanely difficult and you may encounter all sorts of resistance. Try anyway.

If it helps, picture the people in their life who love them dearly - as much, in fact, as you love your most dear ones. Picture them as children, new and fresh in the world, just like you were. Remind yourself that they have hopes and dreams too; that they have fears and have also been hurt and confused. Try to put aside hostility towards them and connect with a deeper sense of shared humanity. No matter how horrible you feel this person is, they have also experienced weakness and joy, pain and pleasure.

Before you end your meditation, turn to yourself and try to consolidate your feelings of love and acceptance for your own path. For some, unfortunately, this may be even more difficult to do than for their worst enemy. Forgive yourself for finding it hard to forgive others. Acknowledge your imperfections. See all the ways that you are terrible, and all the ways you are amazing, and love yourself anyway simply because you are a human being.

When you are ready, open your eyes and carry on with your day, trying to hold on to that warm glow and your feelings of compassion. Like many things in life, your compassion is a skill that can be exercised.

Reactivity and Hooks:

If you are on this earth long enough, eventually, someone will hurt you. Like a physical wound, the area may heal eventually but if it's bad enough it will leave a scar, or a permanent limp. Rather than view this as an unacceptable and awful part of life, be mindful and grateful of your wounds, of the trauma and unfinished business you carry around with you. Why? What could be so good about *damage*?

There is a bittersweetness in being fragile. It's only when we are open and vulnerable to another that we can experience love, but sometimes being open leaves us vulnerable to injury, and in being injured, it is more difficult to trust and open up again.

We all have our "hooks" - the tender spots inside us where we have been hurt, the memories of injury, prejudice from long ago, grudges against those who have harmed us, small disappointments...

Sometimes we encounter others with wounds that are similar to ours. They "hook" us. We feel like they are kindred spirits, that they understand us. Sometimes, we are "hooked" when we encounter someone who reminds us of the person who originally hurt us. In both cases, we are not responding genuinely in the moment. It is our pain that is responding. In other words, we are being reactive.

For many people, their worst fear in the world has actually already happened. And even though they keep waking up to fresh new days with fresh new people in them, they relive this fear over and over again. Men who hate women and women who hate men have allowed the pain they feel to shut themselves off from the very thing that could have soothed them of that pain: compassion for "the other side".

If you are ready to let go of old injuries and move into the present, you'll need to identify your hooks. You'll need to become aware of the moments where you are being triggered. Only then can you deliberately learn to respond not from your pain, but from your compassion, joy and acceptance. And no matter how bitter or cynical we may feel, no matter how hurt or mistrustful or full of hate we are right now, we all have compassion and joy within us.

Case Studies

Zara:

Zara was always the shy and retiring type - coming from a large and boisterous family, her best defense was to shrink into the background and hope nobody noticed her. Considered the "ugly sister", Zara's self esteem was so much in tatters that the very first boy who showed her attention was clung to for dear life. Zara didn't disagree when her new boyfriend eventually told her she was worthless, and she only felt grateful that he would even stick around with her in the first place.

It took many years for her to realize that her self-worth stemmed from inside her, and not from whoever deemed her worthy enough for proper treatment. She made a vow to herself never let another person define who she was but herself. For most of her 20s she remained single as a result, but eventually she developed a sense of self that was solid enough that she could open up and share it with someone else.

Ted:

For Ted, women were always around. Women cleaned for him, cooked for him, sorted out his files at work, served him at restaurants. For him, his "shopping" for the perfect wife was just a natural extension of his belief that a good woman was just, well, a natural extension of *him*. He considered himself a dominant, "alpha" type who was successful enough not to have to "settle" for anything less than perfection. The trouble was, no relationship of this kind ever lasted longer than a few weeks. Just as people would get close to him, he'd cut things off and make up a reason why they weren't good enough for him.

As his 50th birthday approached, though, he had to admit that something had to change if he was going to avoid dying alone. In therapy, he realized that he had been completely unwilling to be even the slightest bit vulnerable in a relationship, seeing intimacy as a loss of control and dominance. If he admitted desire and love for someone, it had meant that they had "won", and that they had some power over him - something he couldn't bear. So, with the help of his therapist, Ted decided to cool off on the dating and work instead on learning to open up to people.

Ellie:

After she divorced her husband of 23 years, Ellie was ready for something new and different. Just two seconds on the dating scene, however, and she had the sinking suspicion that she wasn't brave enough for some of the callousness she discovered on her first few dates with others. Her friends gave her dating books, encouraged her to play it cool, to never call first, to be mean even.

This never felt right. Ellie followed her heart and pursued someone she was interested in. Rather than the world imploding because she had broken this dating "rule", she instead stumbled upon someone who was open, confident and straightforward - like her.

Here's a list of daily habits that I'd like to encourage you to implement in your relationship:

- ***Mindful couples are really present with one another.*** Living together makes it easy to assume you are always "with" one another - but unless your mind is actively engaged in the moment and your partner, you may as well be in different countries. Happy couples don't multitask or answer emails or messages during conversations. They listen. They are there, open and receptive, enjoying just being in the moment with their partner.

- ***Mindful couples are deliberate.*** They don't expect the strength of their feeling for one another to be the magic element that makes everything work - they know that if things work, it's because they *make* the work. By being constantly aware of the subtle changes in themselves, their partners and their environments, a mindful person is able to perceive more options, and make better choices. They take charge of their own emotions and actions, and never say things like "I just don't know what got into me".

- ***A mindful person doesn't need to manipulate others and also will not tolerate being controlled by someone else.*** The need to control and dominate often stems from fear, and the mindful person bases their interactions with others on love and acceptance instead.

- ***A mindful person accepts who they are and gives that same respect to the people that share in his/her life.*** Making comparisons cheapens what is unique about a person. Being mindful means refusing to compare your life path with others, and also never expecting your partner to be someone who they are not.

- ***Mindful couples are not afraid of disagreement.*** Expecting that the ones we love always agree with us perfectly and on every topic is unrealistic, and striving to force ourselves into that perfection means we miss the beauty in the moment, the paradox, the humor, the bittersweetness. A mindful couple can share love, acceptance and compassion for one another, even when they completely disagree with one another.

- ***Mindful couples are not afraid of impermanence.*** In matters of the heart, many people are encouraged to think of endless, infinite love as the only standard to measure our connection, and anything less is not "true love". We celebrate 50-year wedding anniversaries and feel sorry for those who've never had a relationship past 3 months. However, a mindful couple is OK with any length of relationship, if it means that the connection was compassionate and honest. An amazing meal wasn't any less delicious because you got to the end of it.

- ***Mindful couples don't need their partners to complete them.*** Making another person responsible for your happiness means that you are using them as a means to an end, and not simply because you enjoy being with them. A mindful partner will have the courage to face up to his/her own "psychological work" and not expect to hash it out with someone else. Likewise, they'll have enough self-compassion to resist being put into the position of completing somebody *else.*

   - ***Mindful couples are constantly grateful.*** It's easy, once we have "won" someone over, to stop wooing them, to stop feeling thrilled that our attentions are reciprocated. A mindful couple never gets tired of those magical little things they fell in love with in the first place. They keep their minds, hearts and spirits fresh and thankful, knowing how much of a blessing it is to be intimate with someone, and they express their gratitude constantly. Little compliments, favors, saying thank you - these are all things that a mindful partner will keep up with, whether it's been 6 months or 60 years.

   - ***Mindful partners can take a step back.*** When you meditate or learn to be mindful in your daily life, you learn that just because a thought drifts into your awareness, doesn't mean you have to cling onto it or identify with it. Mindful couples are able to take a step back in emotional moments, still their minds and come back to their partners with clear, open hearts. This way, nothing is said in anger.

   - ***A mindful couple acts as a team.*** In very real ways, we are *all* connected. A successful, happy couple work as one. Though they have their own separate lives as individuals, they come together as a couple and work on shared goals. There is no competition, only encouragement.

   - ***Lastly, mindful partners are compassionate, with themselves and one another.*** Perhaps nowhere else is it as evident than in a long-term relationship that people occasionally mess up and hurt one another. A mindful partner values openness and tranquility above holding onto grudges. They forgive not because they like the higher ground, but because they know that they, too, have also made mistakes. A mindful couple works through feelings of hurt, guilt, resentment and all the rest as quickly as possible, so they can get back to their connection.

CHAPTER 8: A MINDFUL RELATIONSHIP INVENTORY

What follows are some questions that you can turn to periodically to hone in on your current feelings about others and yourself.

These questions can be asked at the end of the day to focus on areas you'd like to become more present and compassionate in, or just once or twice to become familiar with your "hooks", your strengths and your goals when it comes to mindful relationships.

- When do you notice yourself getting very emotional, defensive or angry? Can you see a pattern in what "sets you off"? What "hooks" you and why is it that this particular spot is so tender?

- Have you been careless with your words? Are you taking care to think before you speak? Do you tend to speak to people from a position of child, parent or adult?

- Take a moment to remind yourself of your boundaries. Remember that you are an individual. What lines can never be crossed? Have you respected those lines in others?

- In your relationships, do you regularly strive to bring the best out of everyone? In what ways could you help those around you be more true to themselves?

- Likewise, do the people around you encourage you to be your best self - not who they want you to be, but who *you* want to be?

- The activities and conversations that you engage with others in - are these designed to bring you closer to each other, or merely give the illusion of that? Do you have "frenemies" or people you spend time with just because you always have, but don't connect with them in any beneficial way?

- Do you ever give people love, compassion and acceptance that you are denying yourself?

- Those that you hate and reject, in what way does your hatred of them harm you? Is there anything you can learn from them?

- Have you been mindful in your communication, in your actions and in your body?

- If in doubt, ask yourself, does this come from the best part of me? If not, have compassion for yourself that with patience and awareness, you can make this your default.

An Exercise: "Writing Your Vows"

At a marriage ceremony, the soon-to-be-wed couple goes through the ritual of making their promises to one another explicit. They stand honestly before the other and vow to do their best and to love their spouse till the end. It's such a lovely sentiment, that you wonder why people don't make vows more often. Marriage is a big deal, sure, but isn't every interaction with another human being a chance for something special? Why should only the marriage relationships be treated as sacred and honored?

This last exercise asks you to outline your own vows, not to your future husband or wife, but to *everyone* you encounter in life, whatever you end up doing with them. It is a promise we hold ourselves accountable to. We prepare ourselves beforehand so that when we encounter someone, we do it according to our highest principles, and not just mindlessly.

The relationships we are in can never be better than the relationships we have with ourselves. Two unhappy people together never make a happy couple together. We cannot treat other people in ways we have never taken the time to consider before, and we cannot communicate properly if we are not even sure what it is we need to communicate in the first place.

Wedding vows might emphasize fidelity, loyalty, trust or forgiveness of the small things. What will you emphasize? It's only by being deliberate and aware that we can decide to be compassionate. If you are single or coupled or something in between, take the time now to write your "vows".

Here is an example of vows written by the hypothetical Zara from the case study above:

"I vow to be the best person I can be first. I vow to seek out only those who nourish who I am, and to pass by those who would undermine me. I vow that I will never place the responsibility of my own happiness in the hands of anyone else. I vow that when I find love, I won't cling to it because I know that I am strong enough without it, and that there is always enough love in the world."

Serious stuff, for sure, but you could also make your vow simple and to the point:

"I vow to treat everyone I meet as though they were and old friend."

Or even simpler still:

"I promise I will not be a jerk, and will try as hard as I can to forgive those who are."

CONCLUSION

Even for the most well-balanced among us, successful relationships can be tricky to navigate.

Much of the relationship advice out there focuses on what your *partner* does and doesn't do, but it's only by becoming more mindful of ourselves that we can be fully present with another human being.

I hope something in these pages has resonated, and that the next time you meet someone new or have an argument with someone you know already, you'll remember to invite your calmest, most rational and most compassionate adult self into the moment.

When we have respect for ourselves and others, we gravitate towards connections that encourage that. By coming to terms with our own weaknesses, past hurts and "hooks", we take the first step to letting them go and meeting people anew in the present moment.

By staying in an "adult" mindset, we remind ourselves to focus and pay attention only to what is happening around us, as well as encouraging others to do the same.

UNLOCKING ONE ANOTHER - 30 DAYS TO IMPROVING
YOUR RELATIONSHIP COMMUNICATION

INTRODUCTION

Have you ever noticed how often people say they wish they could "find" love?

As if love were something beautiful to just stumble upon on the side of the road. Yet when you speak to happily married couples, especially those that have been married for decades, they never ascribe their success and happiness to luck. Instead, they'll probably tell you that a good relationship takes work - lots of it - and the continued effort and maintenance from both sides.

Love is a *verb*.

It is not something only some people are fortunate enough to catch and then merely set aside. It's not a prize you win or a box to tick on your life's checklist. Instead, love has to be kindled and rebuilt *every day*; it has to be invited in, nurtured, cultivated. Love is not something passive that you simply have or don't have - it's an active process and the continual expression of what's in your heart, mind and soul.

In this book, love is not a noun. It isn't some mysterious gift from the gods that falls into our laps, but something that we can work on and build with intention. So, in that spirit, this book will not be a dispassionate list of relationship advice, or theories about the way people work together, or tips to heat up your sex life.

Instead, this book will ask you to become *actively* involved, to not just read but to constantly apply what has been read to your own life. And since we are on the topic of heart-to-heart communication, you're naturally going to need to rope in your partner, too. The exercises are experiential, meaning, simply, that you have to actually *do* them in order to benefit from them.

You'll be asked to be honest with yourself, get out there into the world and even make yourself vulnerable. Some of these exercises will be fun, others will scare and challenge you - but they are all designed to open your heart to more effective communication with others, so that the relationships you build are strong, heart centered and compassionate.

This book is written for anyone who feels that they are not living (and loving!) to their full potential. Whether you crave deeper connections with others or want to reignite relationships you are already in, this book was written to help you master the art of good communication.

In fact, it would be ideal for you to think of this book itself as one of the first of many new and interesting conversations you're going to have. Although I don't know you and cannot be sure of your response to what's written in these pages, I want for to engage with and respond to everything here as though I was sitting right there in the room with you.

You don't have to agree with everything, or like the principles outlined here. The important thing, though, is that in opening up the dialogue, you are already taking those first few steps to becoming more conscious, compassionate lovers and partners.

When we risk nothing, we gain nothing. When we don't open ourselves to love, we don't love deeply. My wish is that this book leaves you feeling open and receptive to love - your own ability to give it as well as the privilege of receiving it. And I hope that you have high expectations for yourself in reading it, too.

When two people come together, in any capacity, there is the chance for something special to happen. Every great romance began with a meeting of two hearts, with the first word of the first conversation.

Let's begin this book with the first word. I am pleased to meet you, dear reader, and hope that in moving through this book together, we can jointly create a little more love, a little more tenderness and a little more understanding in the world than there was to begin with.

CHAPTER 1: MAP OF A DYSFUNCTIONAL RELATIONSHIP

Well, it may be a strange place to start, but let's begin our conversation with all those ways relationships *don't* work.

If you're reading this book, chances are you've had difficulty with relationships in the past, or are currently unhappy in your situation. You can find plenty of information out there on codependent relationships, on partners who abuse, on relationships built around jealousy and guilt, and much more.

But perhaps all "bad" relationships, whatever their particular challenges, have some common elements. Here are ten characteristics of a style of relating with others that may be destructive, counterproductive or even dangerous. You'll notice that what makes a bad relationship is not the behavior or the individuals that make it, but *the pattern of relating* between them.

As you prepare to start your 30 days, use these beginning chapters to try and map out your challenging areas - just be receptive: if you notice any strong feelings for a particular topic, make a note. After each characteristic, answer the questions and see if some of these themes resonate with you.

In dysfunctional relationships, affection is a zero sum game

Everyone has 24 hours in their day, a finite amount of money in their bank accounts and only so many seats in their car. For most things in life, an increase on one side means taking away from the other side. In other words, it's "zero sum".

But love isn't like this. There is no need for a scarcity mentality when it comes to love and affection for others, because love is not a quantity that you can count or run out of. Think about it now: after spending quality time with those you love, after caring for them and lashing plenty of affection and attention on them, do you feel like you've "spent" all your love and now it's finished?

Of course not. If anything, the more love you give, the more love there is to give.

An unhealthy relationship treats warmth, affection and kindness as if they were measurable substances that can be given, earned or even bartered with. What else is jealousy but the fear that should somebody else receive love, there will somehow be less of it available for you?

Jealousy is damaging in relationships because it puts us in a fearful instead of thankful mindset. When we are jealous, we turn our attention to being defensive against perceived dangers, instead of enjoying what we do have.

Of course, jealousy doesn't only manifest in the form of fear of other people. Everyone knows that jealous partner who can't seem to let their boyfriend or girlfriend enjoy their lives without them being involved. Whether it's a hobby, family commitments or work, a jealous partner will be threatened if the object of their affection experiences happiness that doesn't come directly from them.

The problem with this way of thinking is that it shuts off the ability to see how much love and affection there is around us at all times. Intense and possessive partners can become so wrapped up in their beloved that they forget that there is a whole world out there, and that it doesn't really make sense to fearfully hold onto one "source" of love as if it was the only one.

Do you have any of the following beliefs about love? Be honest and tick all that apply.

- I feel like love is something I have to earn by working hard to get it
- I don't want to *ever* hear about my partner's exes - I hate that they've been with other people.
- A bad relationship is better than none at all.
- I feel that if my partner were to be attracted to someone else, it would immediately invalidate their attraction to me.
- I believe in soul mates.

In dysfunctional relationships, vulnerability is used as a weapon

In every relationship, people need to lower their defensive veils and take the risk of truly connecting with another person. And when we make that love connection, we're even more vulnerable: a person we love can hurt us so much more than anyone else.

But the risk is worth it - and of course it is, considering how many people take the plunge over and over again. Opening up to someone else can be so beautiful precisely *because* we are vulnerable - and loved anyway.

In an unhealthy relationship, people use one another's vulnerability to their own advantage. Gentleness, affection and the willingness to share deep and intimate parts of yourself are merely seen as tools to hurt the other if it comes down to it.

You've heard this story before: a woman, repeatedly beaten and mistreated by her husband, claims she could never leave him. Why? Because she loves him. Her love for her husband is not seen as a precious thing to be protected and nurtured, but as a means to have power over her, a tool of manipulation.

For many people, openly admitting feelings, confessing desires and sharing their deepest selves is more or less the same thing as weakness - a weakness to be exploited. Relationships where vulnerability is not cherished are easy to spot: communication is based on warped power dynamics, abuse of "authority" and manipulation take the place of compassion.

Abusive relationships of all kinds fall into this category, but so do partners who seemingly keep each other at arm's length for years. Denying your partner sexual intimacy as a punishment, threatening to leave unless you get your way, using guilt to get them to do what you want - all of these are ways of taking what should be a tender and safe space and turning it into a battleground.

Do you have some of these beliefs?

- If you don't ever trust people, then you can never get hurt.
- If someone loves me, then it's their responsibility to keep me happy and give me what I need.
- I often feel humiliated and used after a breakup.
- It's better to find someone who loves you more than you love them.
- In fights, I know exactly what to say and do to push my partner's buttons.

In dysfunctional relationships, people compete rather than cooperate

As teenagers, our main challenge in life is to sort ourselves out - find our identities, refine what we believe in and work on our own life code and worldview. Adulthood is different, however. Assuming our sense of self is more or less settled, we're expected to start caring more about others the older we get.

By becoming parents, we forever give up ourselves as the main focus of our attention and learn to take into account someone else's well being - the child's. Even if you're never a parent, though, there comes a time as an adult when you need to build collaborative relationships with others.

In partnered relationships, there is necessarily a degree of compromise. By working as a team on shared goals, a couple can achieve and experience so much more than otherwise.

Unhealthy relationships, however, lack this sense of cooperation. When both partners merely see the other as an extension of their own individual life plan, as a means to an end or even someone to directly compete with, the partnership can never be a collaboration.

People who aren't interested in or supportive of their partner's success and failure, those who don't actively try to be a part of their partner's dreams and goals, those that insist on maintaining the lifestyle they had when they were single and simply expect the other to adapt - these partners are not working together with their partner but *against* them.

Do you have any of these beliefs?

- It's not my problem if my partner fails at something.
- I get uncomfortable if my partner always performs better than me.
- When we fight, it's always about getting each other to comply with the other one's idea of what's right.
- Major life decisions are mine to make and have nothing to do with my partner.
- I sometimes feel very smothered by my partner.

In dysfunctional relationships, there is no deep recognition of each other's being

Happy, long term couples look at one another, warts and all, and embrace the full package. It sort of goes without saying but a healthy relationship is one where two people... actually like one another.

Dysfunctional relationships are characterized by a complete and utter disregard for the very things that make your partner who they are. A person's personality, heart, mind and soul are not dishes at a buffet that you can pick and choose from. Loving one part and hating another does a great disservice to your partner.

Of course, loving partners know when to call the other on their bad behavior, and they don't tolerate it. But *acceptance* of what your partner's weaknesses are communicates that your love is not half-baked, but applies to *all* of them.

Maybe you know a couple who are like this. Their irritation with one another goes deeper than niggles over bad habits - it seems to go to the very core of the person's being. When you don't respect and accept what makes your partner who they are, there simply just isn't room for a healthy relationship to develop.

This may seem obvious to some people, but less obvious perhaps is the fact that many nurture relationships in which there is no active appreciation of one another, even though there is the absence of actual hostility. Does your partner think you're awesome? Do you really *like* them, as people?

In some relationships, the practical or physical benefits of a union can become so much a point of focus that everyone forgets that they were meant to really, truly and on a deep level, approve of their partners.

Relationships where there is a lack of affirmation of one another will leave both feeling drained and uninvested. Such a relationship always feels like an uphill battle - the kind of ordeal that has you asking, what's the point?

Do you have any of the following beliefs?

- My partner doesn't really "get" me as a person.
- There are some values my partner has or choices he or she has made that I simply don't respect.
- I think there are definite ways my partner could improve themselves that would make them easier to love.
- We spend a lot of time negotiating and criticizing each other.
- I'm often disappointed with my partner for not meeting my expectations.
- I feel like I could probably do better.

Dysfunctional relationships are fear based

"Why don't you leave her?"
"I don't know what I'd do without her."

In an unhealthy relationship, the driving force behind the connection is *negative*. The union may not be that great, for example, but it's better than nothing. Rather than cherished for what it is, this kind of relationship's best feature is what it *isn't*. Compare the above with:

"Why don't you leave her?"
"I love spending time with her. She makes everything so much lighter and happier."

There are plenty of things that keep people locked into relationships that are objectively not so great. It could be the fact that you are afraid of the financial ramifications of divorcing, or you're afraid of what your friends and family will think of you if you're single at your particular age, or you're afraid that your partner will be a miserable failure without you.

Maybe you're afraid you'll never find anyone else, or you're afraid that your partner will seek revenge or worse, harm you physically, or you're just afraid of having to start dating again if you had to break up. Whatever the reason, all of these are rooted in fear and not in the benefits you actually get from staying together. It could be the worst relationship in the world, but as long as it's better than the alternative, it's tolerated.

Do you have any of these beliefs?

- I can't imagine anyone else ever finding me attractive.
- My relationship benefits those around me more than it benefits me.
- I'm with my partner because I depend on them completely.
- I've thought a lot about ending my relationship but never do.
- Sometimes, you just have to settle.

Of course, you may be able to identify many more themes common to dysfunctional relationships - perhaps even some that apply to you directly. Take a moment to reflect on what you think are your most prominent relationship challenges.

At the end of the day, in unhealthy connections, people bring out the worst, and not the best in one another.

CHAPTER 2: WHAT IS A HEART-CENTERED RELATIONSHIP?

In the book *Anna Karenina*, Tolstoy says that all happy families are all alike, but unhappy families are unhappy in their own completely unique ways.

I think relationships are similar.

No matter the details, happy, heart centered and compassionate couples work from a basis of love, respect and honesty in the way they relate to one another. Here are some characteristics of such relationships.

Respect

Never calling your partner names, belittling them or undermining the value of what they believe and do. Taking their projects seriously and valuing their insight and input during conversations. A respected partner is not even necessarily one that you always agree with, only that you respect their ability to hold different opinions.

Honesty

Without trust, there can be no real depth of connection. Honest partners go above and beyond simply refraining from lying, they actively try to be transparent with their partners, communicating their experience and not hiding things that their partner would prefer to know. Honest partners don't support each other's denial, either, and expect that for any meaningful communication to happen, everyone needs to be on the same page.

You may say, sure, I'm honest, I've never tried to deceive my partner, but sometimes this isn't enough. Have you wrangled the truth a little to serve your own needs, even if not directly lying? Is there something that would be better if said instead of just assumed?

Trust

On the flip side, relationships with heart do not operate with mistrust and suspicion. In a healthy partnership, someone is innocent until proven guilty. Trust is given freely and not as some sort of reward or bonus. Partners assume the best of each other and have no need to snoop on them or demand they prove their loyalty.

Encouragement

The right partner will love to see you happy and successful. They'll push you to be the best version of yourself, because they believe in you. This kind of love is selfless - such a partner cares about what you're doing with your life for no reason other than that they want you to live well. Partners who are each other's cheerleaders will never be alone when it comes to weathering life's difficulties.

Variety and spontaneity
It's easy to be endlessly fascinated with your partner in the early days. Later on, when they are less of a mystery to you, you'll both need to take deliberate action to maintain the proverbial spice of life. Routine is death for a relationship. In a strong, healthy relationship, both partners constantly strive to try to new things, go places, learn things and rediscover their partner over and over again. It may sound like a bit of a paradox, but spontaneity is something that can be planned and controlled!

Boundaries
Though we've seen how important it is to work as a team, a relationship needs well-defined boundaries on both sides. You need to know exactly where you draw the line and know how to calmly and reasonably assert that boundary if it gets crossed. Maintaining a strong personal identity means there's more to bring to your partner when you do connect. Happy partners know when they begin and where their partner ends - and they take responsibility for the their actions.

The list could go on an on; love, passion, romance, good communication skills, plenty of fun activities, a life away from your partner, shared goals etc. etc.

Ultimately, a heart centered relationship is one that acknowledges and affirms both partners at their very core, with compassion and acceptance. A relationship is strong when it draws on the fact that both partners sincerely want the best for the other - they don't want their partner to be who they aren't, or to be whatever would benefit *them* the most, but to be a congruent, fulfilled and happy individual.

Heartfelt compassion doesn't cling or demand, it isn't panicky and insecure, needing to be propped up by outside affection. This kind of love is big and expansive, growing and changing as each partner develops, built on solid communication, honesty and genuine desire for the happiness of the other.

A mature, heart-centered relationship is a thing of beauty - light, warm and a source of energy and inspiration. Sounds good, doesn't it?

Take some time now to reflect on some of your most deeply held beliefs about what love is and isn't. Here are some questions to guide your exploration of your own personal mythology, your own store of memories, dreams, hopes and fears when it comes to love.

- What do you most want from you partner - and when was the last time you gave that to someone else?
- What would you say to an alien from outer space who landed on earth and asked you what 'love' was?

- What is missing from where your life is now to where you want it to be?
- At the end of the day, what is your passion in life?

CHAPTER 3: THE ART OF COMMUNICATION

What is a relationship other than a long string of small conversations?

Every time you reach out to your partner or shut them off, when you choose to use certain words and not others, when you smile or turn your body away from them, even when you are completely silent - you are communicating.

Communication is that strange interface, that curious place in between two people where they must find a way to bridge the gap. Of course communication is not just verbal. When we reach out in any way, when we try to make ourselves understood or when we try to understand others, we are attempting to communicate.

We can make our intentions known through the way we use our bodies, our words, our facial expressions, and our actions. When we communicate with someone else, we are temporarily inviting them to become a part of our experience. We're saying, *listen to me! What I have to say is important.*

When we communicate properly, a healthy and happy relationship naturally follows. And why not? When both partners know what the other is experiencing, when everyone understand the mutual goals and expectations, when fights are sorted out before they even begin, a relationship cannot help but be a successful one.

But, this is easier said than done. "Conscious" communication is choosing to become aware of the messages we are sending to our partner, to ourselves and out into the world in general. Becoming more perceptive means we can also tune into the messages of those around us, hearing what is actually said rather than what we wish was said.

How can you become a more conscious communicator?

The answer is simple: pay attention. Pay attention to what is happening inside your own heart and mind. Notice the rise and fall of emotions, thoughts that you have, notice unquestioning beliefs, fears and expectations.

Turn your antennae, too, towards the outside and really listen to what your partner is communicating. Even those who are not the most skilled of communicators know that when people say "I'm fine" with just the right tone of voice and body language, they actually mean exactly the opposite.

Learning to become more responsive, more aware and more in tune with yourself and others means you'll communicate your own needs better as well as understand others. You'll reduce the chance of misunderstandings or harmful assumptions.

Here are some smart ways to start being more deliberate in the way you communicate. Once you begin your 30 days, you may need to refer back to some of these skills and techniques to help reach your partner and express yourself. As you read, consider whether each particular skill is a strength or a challenge for you.

Acknowledge emotional content first

Here is a tip that many marriage counselors, divorce mediators and even hostage negotiators know how to use wisely: acknowledge the emotional content of what is said. People use words, sometimes a lot of words, but when people have conversations, there is always a more subtle undercurrent of emotional communication.

When you communicate to those close to you, make a point of hearing this emotional undercurrent as well as the words spoken. When you respond to this, you cut away the clutter and small talk - in a deeper way, you "hear" the person more fully.

A classic example is the woman who complains at the end of a long day to her partner. She tells him how irritating everyone was, how rude her clients, how naughty the children, how bad the traffic. Instead of hearing the exasperation and defeat in her voice (i.e. the emotional content) her partner only hears a string of complaints and problems. So, he sets to helping her solve them.

Had he responded to the emotional content first, he would have seen that the emotional message was, *I'm having a hard time, please sympathize with me*. When he instead responds, "Well, maybe you should take another route home from work if traffic is such a big deal" he is communicating to her that he hasn't "heard" properly at all. This misunderstanding likely just gets added to her list of the irritations of the day.

Instead, if he simply says something like, "Wow, you've had a lot to deal with today. Sit down, I'll make us some tea", the communication is instantly more conscious and compassionate.

Become familiar with different styles of communication

If you have not already, it's a great idea to read the book *The Five Love Languages* by Gary Chapman. Even when we believe we are expressing ourselves loud and clear, sometimes we are just on different "wavelengths" than our partners.

The five love languages, according to this book, are physical touch, acts of service, quality time, gifts and words of affirmation (food is also a suggested language). But you may have your own special blend of languages or require that people express their affection in particular ways.

While it's good to know your own preference, the trick is to make sure that you are communicating in the language that your *partner* prefers when you interact with them. You may choose to express affection through a hug or sex, or your partner may hear you clearest when you praise them and build up their self esteem with compliments and affirmations.

Your partner might notice your love the most when you help out around the house, do little chores for him to make his life easier or stand up for him in difficult moments. If their language of love is gifts, you would show your partner your love by regularly observing occasions with carefully planned gifts, taking them to dinner and surprising them with little trinkets or hidden notes.

In understanding what your own language is, you can learn to make reasonable and clear requests of your partner. Don't feel strange saying something like, "I love it when you X, it really makes me feel appreciated". Pay close attention to your partner's language, too, and you'll ensure that when you speak to them, the right channel is open.

Start smart conversations and survive "we need to talk"

As we've seen, a good relationship is a single, constant, flowing conversation, but once in a while you'll need to deliberately start a conversation with your partner, possibly a difficult one.

Step One: Sort out your intention

There's nothing worse than instigating a difficult conversation without clearly understanding exactly why you're doing it. Your partner will get that you are unhappy somehow, but without any focus and forethought, you may end up aggravating matters without coming to any conclusion.

Before you approach anyone to talk, figure out what you want. The first, and most important step, is to ask yourself what the purpose of the talk is, and exactly what you see as the end point. But be honest. Many people would say, "I want to express my feelings about such and so", which seems pretty innocuous, but on closer inspection, what they really want to do is blame someone, or even punish them. Be honest about ulterior motives.

Sometimes, when you examine your intention, you may discover that it's best not to say anything. Does your talk improve on the silence? Are there better ways to express yourself? Sometimes, as they say, actions speak louder than words. If you've identified a reasonable, heart centered goal that will be improved by speaking to your partner, go ahead to the next step.

Step Two: Identify the position of the other person

This is vital. To communicate, you always have to know whom you are communicating *to*. Here are some questions you can ask to zero in on the other person's perspective. Compare the answers to those you'd give for yourself.

- Are you making any assumptions about their position that are not strictly supported?
- What emotions have they communicated to you so far?
- Is there any chance you will be misinterpreted?
- How do you think you will be perceived and how can you make sure it's accurately conveyed?
- How do your goals compare with your partner's? How can you find out?
- What have you done to contribute to the problem you are bringing up?

- Can you anticipate the issues your partner will bring to the conversation?

Step Three: Begin like Socrates
In Socratic dialogue, you start any enquiry assuming you know absolutely nothing and are trying to learn. Clear your mind of assumptions and past experiences. Try to really listen. Imagine you are approaching the problem for the first time. Open a conversation by letting your partner speak first. Let them say everything they need to. Listen without thinking of what you'll say when they're done. Repeat what you heard back to them to confirm you have understood. Take it slow and give them ample room to express their side of things. Try to truly consider their perspective. Open with statements like:
- "There's something I wanted to talk about with you and I'm hoping it will help us communicate better."
- "I've really wanted to talk about X with you. First, I'd like to get your opinion on it."
- "It seems like we have different ideas about X, and I'd like to really understand why you think Y."
- "I would really appreciate if you could help me understand something I've been having trouble with…"
- "I really would like to share my perspective with you about X. Maybe you can tell me your feelings first?"

Remember to be respectful. Your first task is not to win someone over or convince them to accept your way. Initially, you are just trying to get a very thorough understanding of one another. A good technique is to be actively reflective as you talk: if you notice that the other person seems defensive, comment on it. Say something like, "I noticed that you seemed to get defensive just there. Am I right? I'm curious about what made you feel that way."

A good way to start with this sort of discussion is to constantly acknowledge and affirm the information coming from the other side. Say things like, "It seems to me that I feel X and you feel Y. Do you agree?" or "I can see that X means a lot to you. Let me explain why I don't agree…"

Step Four: Focus the discussion on solutions
The beginning of the discussion is the time to air and acknowledge everyone's feelings. However long this takes, each person should feel that they've had sufficient time to express themselves and that they have been heard. Don't feel awkward about saying things like, "Okay, it seems like you're saying X. Have I heard you correctly?" or, "I'd like to explain again, because I don't feel as though you've understood just yet…"

At a certain point, though, an issue is only resolved with realistic, action oriented discussion. The second half of the discussion should focus on rational solutions to the issues raised. A good thing to think of throughout the discussion is: in what ways do we want the same thing? Identify and build on this, for example, "I see we have different ideas, but fundamentally we both seem to want X. Maybe we can think together of ways to get X for both of us."

If conflict arises again, start back at step one. If you seem to be going in circles, it may be prudent to stop and assess whether the discussion may be better had later on when emotions have cooled. Here are some useful phrases that are heart centered and focused on finding workable solutions for everyone.

- "I understand what you're saying. I have often felt like that, too. However..."
- "I'm feeling very unhappy about this. I really want to resolve it because I am used to being honest and open with you and I don't want anything to disrupt that."
- "What can I do to make this easier for you?"
- "You make me very happy. I'd like to ask that you do X."

Life is complicated and confrontations like this, as much as we try, can often be awkward, gut wrenching and sometimes end quite badly. Remember, the price of affection we pay is the risk of rejection and hurt. Try to accept things gracefully and calmly. Take some time afterwards to process your emotions. If you're at a loss, a good compass to follow is: is this for your highest good? For the highest good of your partner?

Take responsibility and enforce your own boundaries

Responsibility and boundaries go hand in hand. In partnerships, it is our responsibility to erect meaningful emotional boundaries, and our partner's responsibility to respect them. It is our responsibility to enforce those boundaries when they are violated.

In romantic relationships, it can be hard to draw the line between what is ours, what is our partner's and what is shared in the relationship. Make a habit of sorting issues out into these categories. Here's an example.

Lets say a "we need to talk" conversation arises. John tells Beth that he has become increasingly bothered by her weight gain. Over the years, stress and lack of good diet and exercise have left her in poor shape, and he attempts to start a dialogue about it.

Beth, who has a history of disordered eating and is currently under a lot of stress at work, feels her self esteem is at rock bottom and is understandably hurt and humiliated at what John has to say.

Now, in this scenario, who is to "blame"? Where, exactly, is the source of the problem? In other words, what is Beth's, what is John's and what is both of theirs? Lets examine the boundaries and responsibilities of each.

John:
John has a right to find whatever he finds desirable, and the right to express that. His boundary takes the form of asserting that he cannot be attracted to what he isn't attracted to, and if Beth gains a significant amount of weight, he is put in an awkward position. He has a right to express that.

What he doesn't have a right to, however, is what Beth does with her body. He can merely express his own standard and preference - but his right stops at Beth's right to be however she wants to be. For John to assert a healthy boundary without violating the boundaries of Beth, he has to acknowledge this.

Beth:

Beth has a right to be stressed, to process her stress and to have difficulty in life. She has the right to struggle occasionally and the right to ask for sympathy and understanding while she does so. She can assert that boundary by demanding nothing but thoughtful respect from John.

What she doesn't have the right to, however, is John's unconditional attraction. She doesn't have any claim on what his experience is, or how he perceives her. While she is free to gain or lose weight or any other thing, John's reaction to this is entirely his own.

How can they both resolve the issue?

In any ensuing discussion, it is Beth's responsibility to own what's hers. She cannot accuse John of making her feel bad if she experiences low self esteem. That is hers and hers alone. Similarly, John can express himself freely when it comes to his feelings and expectations, but he can never demand that it's Beth's responsibility to give him that. He might prefer a skinny wife, but it is not Beth's responsibility to give it to him.

What is in both Beth and John's best interest? What addresses their highest good?

As they hash the situation out, they may discover that it's beneficial for both if Beth can have some sympathy and understanding while John encourages her to start living a healthier lifestyle. There is no blame, no expectation and entitlement, only a loving, realistic and compassionate working together on the problem.

Watch out for statements such as:

"You make me feel..."

Nobody *makes* you feel anything. You and only you decide how to feel about something. You are in charge of your own emotional response, and nobody can interfere with that - unless you give them permission to. Don't blame your choices - whether they are obvious actions or less obvious emotions - on someone else. Say instead, "I feel..."

"You should be more..."

You can have a preference for something. You can really wish something were the case. You can want with all your heart that the word be a certain way. But it doesn't entitle you to getting it. And it doesn't entitle you to demand it of your partner. Instead of saying, "You should be thoughtful!", say something like, "When you say things like that, I feel attacked."

It is your decision to feel attacked, and your partner's decision about whether to alter their behavior to accommodate you. Someone who doesn't respect your boundaries deserves no place in your life, but they should respect those boundaries because they want to, not because you tell them to.

"I'm sorry, I just..."

Whatever you feel, you feel. Don't make apologies for it or try to soften what you think and feel. Put it out there, and own it. Of course, your feelings don't entitle you to any particular claim on the world, but they are *yours*. Be proud of them. Assert your experience. Apologizing for the way you feel is like apologizing for digesting or breathing. You don't have to be sorry for what happens naturally. How you deal with those feelings, however, is completely under your conscious and deliberate control.

CHAPTER 4: NURTURING THE FLAME

We've had a look at the various characteristics of a healthy and a not-so-healthy relationship. But what if, like so many people in long-term relationships - everything is, well, just *fine*? You know what "fine" means: not bad enough to leave. Comfortable. OK. Tolerable.

You could communicate like champions, never fight and have a genuinely respectful and low-drama relationship - but then again, you may be more or less the same as two roommates who get on well.

Maybe human beings will never find a comfortable and permanent way to negotiate monogamy. Maybe love, no matter how good it starts out, eventually fades. For whatever reason, sometimes the zing just... disappears. It's not a matter of communication or being compassionate.

First things first: a relationship that doesn't last is not necessarily a failed one.

You can enjoy a meal, a ballet performance or a good novel even though there comes a time when it's finished. Just because it had a finite duration, doesn't mean it was worth any less. Having said that, our culture does put a premium on connections that last - and for sure relationships that go on for years have the chance to develop and mellow in ways shorter connections can't.

In many ways, finding love is not the most difficult - *keeping* love is. Flirting and catching the right kind of people is like the miracle of getting a seed to germinate - but a long-term commitment is like growing that seed into a massive tree, season after season, through winter and spring.

Here are some things to consider if your situation is, well - if it's fine. Just fine.

- Think of the way you dressed, spoke and behaved when you first met your partner. Do you do that still? Why not?
- In the last week, have you shared something new, interesting or entertaining with your partner? If you're always together, of course, you can never have exciting conversations about the developments in each other's lives.
- Make a commitment right now to stop gross "roommate behavior": close the bathroom door, refrain from belching or picking your teeth in front of them, throw away disgusting socks you routinely wear around the house and maintain good hygiene. There is a natural and comfortable set point that a couple reaches - but don't let it slide.
- Go on holiday. Leave behind chores and obligations and carve out a space where you can just enjoy each other for a while.
- Sometimes the best way to reinvigorate a stale relationship is to stop focusing on it at all. Have a break from each other, from talking about the relationship, from shared anything. Go out with friends, pursue hobbies. Then, bring that freshness back to your partner.
- Forget about it. Forget about all the things they've done, all the ways they're wrong. You don't need to forgive them, to hash it out, to punish them. Just forget it - really.

Couples who have been through a few seasons know that sometimes, you just make the decision that you're going to get along, and that's the end of it.

- Dampened libidos and routine sex can be awful - why even have sex if it's going to be exactly what it was the previous 678 times? No matter how long you've known your partner, they are guaranteed to have some erotic terrain that you have not explored. Be playful and start a conversation about kinks or fantasies. Be naughty about it. Do something you've never done before.

- If it's something big, share it with your partner - don't let issues fester and poison the relationship. If they do something small to irritate you, do one of two things: call them out on it there and then, or forget it ever happened. Holding onto every little slight and crime is a recipe for resentment. Actively address it or let it go. The time to bring up your hurt feelings over something is not four months later during a fight about something else.

Long-term relationships have special challenges - see if you can identify your own particular issues before embarking on the 30 days. Before we start, lets take a quick look at one more issue that plagues many couples of all kinds.

CHAPTER 5: LOVE IN THE TIME OF SOCIAL NETWORKS

Back in the day, you only knew the people who lived in your neighborhood and your immediate friends and family. Even further back in the day, you would likely only have ever encountered a small band of around 150 people at most who lived in your immediate tribe. The point is, for much of the history of the world, human beings never had the massive connectedness to one another that we do now.

The Internet and communication technology have meant that we have access to more people that we don't know than ever before. Think about this for a second. In the past, your average caveman would have *only* seen people he knew day in and day out. Today, walking on the streets, going about our lives, we encounter hundreds of people that we don't and won't ever know.

We may know more celebrities than we do actual people in our social circles. We have the strange new relationship category of "Facebook friend". At any time, we can reach out to people, strangers or otherwise, all over the world.

It's no surprise then, that the way we relate to one another and how we connect in relationships has also changed. Here are some ways to negotiate intimacy in an era of extreme connectedness, especially when it comes to social networks.

Don't assume - make boundaries clear

In the past, "thou shalt not covet or commit adultery" etc. was pretty much the sum total of the rules and regulations of most relationships. Today, the world is more complex. The only way to negotiate the new social landscape is to be explicit in your expectations and boundaries. Talk about it. What, exactly, do you consider infidelity? What counts as flirting?

Don't snoop

In the same way, respect your partner's boundaries. Don't poke around on their Facebook pages looking for "clues", don't guess their passwords, don't read over their shoulders and don't go through their browser history. Either you trust them, or you don't. Do be tempted to be one of those people who "accidentally stumbled" upon something upsetting. If you have suspicions or doubts, the person to speak to you is your partner.

Be congruent

It's easy to lead a double-life online. Make a point to conduct yourself online as you would offline. Don't leave room for misunderstandings or grey areas. If you are in a committed relationship, is that communicated in all the relevant places?

Maintain privacy

If it concerns your partner, think twice about sharing information online. You may have different ideas of what is appropriate to share in a public space. The whole point of a relationship is that at some point, there is something that belongs to the two of you and only to you two. Try not to over share when it comes to your relationship.

CHAPTER 6: RELATIONSHIP CARDIO: 30 DAYS TO A STRONGER HEART

Now that we've spent some time getting to grips with some fundamental communication strategies, it's time to put it all into practice.

Most likely, you're reading this book because something, somehow in your relationship is not quite what you feel it could be. Perhaps you're onto the last straw of a long and difficult partnership and feel pretty close to giving up, or perhaps you've noticed the shine coming off what seemed to be a loving and close relationship.

Either way, the following exercises are designed to open up and initiate the kind of conversations that move you - and your partner - forward. Some of them will focus on your side of the dynamic exclusively - after all, this is one arena where you have the most control. But many will ask you to actively engage your partner.

What you'll need to begin your 30-day "relationship cardio":

- A sense of honesty, adventure and vulnerability - nothing worth it comes easy.
- A partner who is at least somewhat receptive
- A diary to record your thoughts, feelings and perceptions - buy a new and pretty notebook and start fresh on the first page (or, if it feels more appropriate, use a plain, humble notebook... just make sure you are reflecting and recording as you go...)

Day 1 - Catch up on your own housekeeping

Effective communication begins with someone who has something to communicate. This day is all about you. In your notebook, answer the following questions, and jot down any other feelings that emerge. There are no limits - be curious and accepting of what comes out.

- Would you date you? Why or why not?
- If you lived on an alien planet where people didn't even have relationships, what would your life look like?
- Today, are you the person you always hoped you'd be?
- If you had to summarize the essence of your life into just five words, what would those words be?
- Write down your wildest hopes and dreams for the end of the 30 days - what would success look like to you?
- Also write down your biggest fear in beginning this adventure. Be honest. You will have the chance to come back later and examine these fears and hopes.

Resist diagnosing anything or seeing patterns at this point - simply do a check-in on yourself and where you are in your life right now. Do yourself and your partner a favor and take stock today of your sense of self, your goals, your weak spots and what you want for the future.

Day 2 - Turn your antennae on

Today, you need to turn your curious attention outwards and onto the way you and your partner interact. Make notes of your emotions and thoughts, jot down the habits you engage in. In other words, try to make a summary, as if you were an outsider looking in, of what you see when you look at your relationship. Identify, as neutrally as possible, any sources of friction.

At this point, you are still just collecting data. Whatever you notice, put it down in your journal. If you like, you may choose to even start recording your dreams at this time or add something creative and impressionistic to your journal: pictures, drawings or poems.

Day 3: Declare your intention

This may be a difficult day. If you've done your homework on yourself, you'll have a clearer idea of what you need from your partner and why. You cannot "fix" a relationship when only one person is working at improving it, however.

Decide how you'll approach your partner and clarify before you do exactly what has motivated you to embark on improving the communication between you two. Be honest, compassionate and prepared. Record how you feel before and after. Give your partner time to respond.

Depending on the kind of relationship you have, your approach may be very different. You could casually bring it up and ask their opinion, or, if things are more adversarial, ask for some quiet time to address a few points. Notice any feelings of fear or resistance that come up.

Do you feel guilty stating that you are unhappy? How does your partner's reaction make you feel? Note it all down. A good way to start is simply: "Hey, I've been reading a book about improving communication and I'm finding it quite interesting. I'd love to involve you in some of the exercises for the next month or so... what do you think?"

Day 4: Invite your partner to the conversation

Today, you are opening up channels.

Depending on how yesterday went, you might feel more comfortable doing this. You've had the time to note down your feelings, fears and expectations, now extend the offer to your partner. Today, turn your attention to really hearing them, as much as you can. Your goal is to find out, are they happy? What makes them happy? Are they unhappy? Why?

After today, you should have a clarified idea of what both you and your partner believe to be your biggest relationship challenge. Don't try to argue or compare notes. Just open up and listen. Become a reporter, or a scientist.

What are their expectations? Their fears? Try to communicate that you are receptive to whatever it is they have to say. If there is something that upsets you, put it aside for the time being and focus on trying to understand your partner's position fully.

Day 5: Breathing room

Every relationship is different. You may have discovered completely new and possibly upsetting information, or you may have found that speaking to your partner this way is stressful and leaves you feeling quite exposed. Today, just let whatever is, be what it is. Don't think about anything. Give your unconscious mind time to process. If you're depressed and hurt, just engage with it. Jot it all down. Allow your feelings to develop.

Day 6: Goal setting

In your notebook, write down three main goals that you have decided on. These goals can't be something like "I want her to be more X" but have to be goals for *you*. Make sure, also, that the goals can be achieved in 3 weeks or so, and that they are measurable - i.e. you'll know when they've been accomplished. Be realistic. Share these with your partner and encourage them to put down their own goals, if it feels right.

Day 7 to day 27: Your own program

The first week is about setting your intentions, making goals and establishing contact. The next 3 weeks are all about learning new ways to connect and communicate. Because no relationship is the same, it would be silly for everyone to follow the same formula. Instead, take a good look at your goals (and your partner's, if you know them).

Every day from now until day 27, you will pick one of the exercises below for each day. You'll be picking the exercises that relate to the issues your relationship faces as well as both of your goals. The following exercises fall into 4 categories (physical, lifestyle, communication, conflict).

Try not to do the same exercise more than 3 times, but if you find that it's particularly effective, do it again by all means. You might like to do each one once for a good variety.

At the end of each exercise, record in your journal what you have learnt about yourself, your partner and your relationship. Keep focused by returning to previous notes and your ultimate goals. Be gentle - this is a difficult and sometimes scary thing to do. Take a deep breath and keep taking notes.

Physical exercises

For when physical intimacy has faded, when you feel distant or that attraction is gone, or when your expectations and needs around sex do not align with your partner's.

The hug quotient

No matter what is going on in your lives, observe the "hug quotient". From now until the end of the thirty days, throw a dice each morning to determine the amount of non-negotiable hugs to be given to your partner, each of which lasts at least 30 seconds. Even if you're in the middle of a serious fight, do your hugs - no excuses.

No-sex sex

This is a technique prescribed by many sex therapists. Set aside a quiet evening where you can be physical with your partner. But actual sex is off the menu - do everything and anything that pleases your partner, but have no expectations and no direction - simply open up and become curious about how your bodies respond to each other.

The spa

Ask your partner what "spa treatments" they'd like: a massage, a foot rub, breakfast in bed? Devote yourself to them for an evening. Don't rush, just enjoy pampering them. Is it more difficult to give affection and pampering or receive it? What feelings come up when one partner's pleasure becomes the focus? And when things are reversed?

A romantic dinner

Go out somewhere fancy for a dinner. There's a twist though: don't speak about anything besides the restaurant experience. Compare, in detail, the tastes, sights, smells and sounds. Be fully present. Don't talk or think about anything for those few hours. Just let go and revel in the sumptuousness of both of your perceptions in the moment.

"Sexual favors"

For the rest of the month period, allot to both you and your partner 5 "sexual favors", where they can ask for what they would like without shame or rejection, and you can do the same. Make this as fun or as serious as you like. It can even be as simple as using one of your favors to request sex when the other partner isn't particularly interested. Note your reactions.

Love letters

Separately, you and your partner both compile a list of 5 things about the other that you find irresistible. Be flattering, raunchy or tender, you decide. Note the parts of their body you love the best, their smile, when they do X etc. Then, leave the notes somewhere the other partner will find them.

Lifestyle exercises

Sometimes, relationships wilt under the daily onslaught of chores, work, money, child rearing - here are exercises that focus on reorienting your relationship as a daily priority.

The play date

Decide on something fun you can both do together. This doesn't have to be anything serious like taking up a dance class - if you both like board games or rolling down hills in the park, then that's what you do. The trick is: both of you must enjoy it. Work together; have fun.

Role swap

For the day, act out the part of your partner - pretend to be them in every way. Treat them the way you feel treated by them. Speak, think and act like them. Your partner does the same. Are they accurate? What do they think of your rendition? How do you interact when you are, well, them?

Opposite day

Both of you commit you to saying *exactly the opposite* of what you want to say. In an argument? Instead of saying, "Ugh, I've had enough of this", say "I want nothing more than to keep on doing this." Instead of saying, "You're wrong", say "*I'm* wrong". Your partner does the same. What happens?

Make a ritual
Decide on something that you and your partner can do today every day, something ritualistic. It doesn't matter what - just that you keep up the ritual for the remainder of the days. Maybe you read to each other from the newspaper, brush your teeth together before starting the day or call each other every day at lunchtime.

Communication exercises

The following exercises are for strengthening you and your partner's ability to really reach one another and open up healthy channels of communication.

The sound of silence
For the day, communicate with your partner only through body language and facial expression. You can talk to others, but when together, you can only make yourself understood through your body, smile and eyes. How good are you?

Nursing home letters
Imagine you are on your deathbed, about to shuffle off this mortal coil and at the end of a long, full life. Write a letter to your partner. Make it as long or as short as you like. Imagine what you'd say to them after all is said and done, your parting words, your goodbye. What do you say? How does it feel to read your partner's letter to you?

Communicative gifts
Exchange small gifts. Make the gift symbolic and communicative. You don't need to discuss the meaning, just find creative ways to non-verbally put your message out there. You can do whatever you like: a wilted flower, a polished stone, a specific book, a handful of pills, a pile of dog poo wrapped in beautiful paper?

Daily reading
Every day, as you wake, take an emotional "reading" of your partner. Take turns, and tell them how you perceive them that day. Are they exhausted, content, defensive, affectionate? Compare notes and see if you both improve with time.

Conflict exercises

Keeping the ratio right

In all your communications for the day, try to balance every criticism or negative thing with *four* positive ones or compliments. This will slow things down, but do it anyway. Make your compliments sincere. "You have such beautiful hands. I love the way you always cook lasagna so perfectly. You have great taste in movies. I love your jokes. I think it's gross that you leave your towel on the floor like that."

"That's OK"

For one day, accept whatever conflicts arise with you and your partner. They say something stupid or disrespectful? That's OK. You don't agree, even a little? That's OK. Resist trying to solve anything, or trying to change the other one's mind. Look squarely at the conflict and say, in your spirit, *that's OK*. How does it feel to be this accepting?

Practicing acceptance

This exercise can be done alone by you and your partner. Write down everything that you wish you could change about your partner, everything that you think is wrong with them. Now crumple up the paper or burn it to smithereens. Make the vow to accept them for who they are, right now, without any amendments.

Calling time-outs

If your relationship is fraught with bickering, arguments and petty fights, institute a "timeout" strategy. The moment one of you senses a fight coming on, somebody is obliged to call a time-out. After this, both of you take the time to gather your thoughts, take a breather and come back to the issue an hour later.

Day 27: Appraisal

If you've missioned through the full 30 days, engaged the participation of your partner and been thorough and honest with yourself in your diary, you'll have a lot of new experiences to draw on as the 30 days comes to an end.

Go back and look at your original goals, fears and expectations. What has changed? How do you feel now about the issues you had going in? Try to explore what new things you have learnt about your partner in the process.

What habits from the 30 days do you want to keep into the future, and what habits do you want to definitely drop from your repertoire? It may be difficult, but you may have decided to end or dramatically change the course of your relationship.

Where do you want to go from here?

Day 28 and 29: Cool-off

Rest and process. Take a step back and allow your thoughts to develop fully.

Day 30: Projection

Try to summarize the experience of the last month. Write a journal entry and speak to your partner about their experience. If it feels natural, decide on how you'd like to move forward. Do you have new goals? New energy to commit to a different lifestyle?

Here are some questions that may arise that I'd like to address:

- *"My partner thinks all of this is lame and won't play along"*

And, what do you make of the fact that there is this difference between you? It might help in the short term to be the one doing all the work, but will you be happy for the long term to be the only one instigating change? Some of these exercises are awkward and difficult. But do you want to be with someone who isn't even really willing to try?

- *"Actually, I'm the one who is uncomfortable doing some of these things"*

Discomfort is not the end of the world. Can you embark on something new and strange with good humor and resilience? Can you be light and easy about it? At the very least, try. Not every exercise will benefit you, or make sense for your situation. Write down in your diary whether you're resistant just because you are afraid of what you might uncover or whether you genuinely feel uninspired. If you find yourself rejecting one particular exercise strongly, it's a good sign that there's something there worth your attention. Whether you end up doing it or not, what does the exercise show you?

- *"What if we break up?"*

Well, what if you do? Ending a relationship that is not healthy or working is not a failure, it's a step in the right direction. In a sense, your goal is not to make sure you and your partner get on perfectly, it's trying to find that sweet spot where your hopes and goals coincide with your partner's, where your intentions both align. Sometimes, the best thing people can do for each other is to sever their connection. Always ask - are you serving one another's highest good? Any movement in this direction is something to be celebrated, not feared or avoided.

CONCLUSION

When it really comes down to it, the relationships we have with others are just extensions of the relationship we have with ourselves.

In the same way that you wouldn't and shouldn't accept someone who is unclear on their goals, unable to communicate well and unwilling to open up and be vulnerable, so you should work hard at not being that person yourself.

True love, soul mates and love at first sight may or may not be worthwhile topics of discussion, but even the best and strongest love needs the watchful care and maintenance of two healthy, mature people to keep it going. Compassionate communication is part of this.

I hope that in this book, you've been able to unearth some interesting new things about yourself, and discovered a renewed sense of your own values, your own purpose and your own goals when it comes to love.

And if you have, I hope that you've been inspired to communicate that more freely and honestly to those around you.

PIECES OF YOU & ME - HOW LOVERS COMPLETE EACH OTHER: LEARN HOW TO NEGOTIATE INTIMACY, AND THAT FINE LINE BETWEEN "ME" AND "US"

INTRODUCTION

If you live in a modern city, you'll likely pass hundreds, if not thousands, of strangers on the streets every day. You'll look into their faces and they'll look into yours, and then you'll walk right on past one another and forget all about it.

And yet, somehow, people meet, fall in love and build their lives around one another. People bond. In fact, every single person you see is a direct result of a relationship between two people who were originally unknown to one another. Think about it: whoever your partner is, they were once a complete stranger to you, too!

Somewhere along the line, somehow, they went from a person who barely registered on your radar to someone you feel like you'd be miserable without.

So, what happened? How can people so far apart become so close?

That topic is the theme of this book!

You could almost categorize any relationship in your life in terms of *closeness*. Call it intimacy, familiarity, whatever – it's more or less the same thing. How close you are, mentally, physically, even sexually.

Whether someone lives near to you, whether you spend a lot of time together, share a history (or a plan for the future!), it all comes down to one thing: the extent to which they've closed that distance that was once between you, when you were both strangers to one another.

No two people resolve this distance in quite the same way, of course. Relationships are as similar to each other as the people that make them – that, is, not at all! And just as two strangers can eventually become each other's most significant others ...they can also go back to being strangers, with time.

As much as closeness defines relationships, it also defines all the ways they can go *wrong*.

When a woman complains that her boyfriend is moving too fast, she's actually complaining that he's getting *too close*. When a man complains that his wife has emotionally shut him out, he's really upset that she is *too distant*.

This theme of close/distant tension rears its head in more relationship complaints that it would first appear:

- Someone is too "clingy"
- Someone is resistant to committing
- A couple are bored with life and with each other
- Somebody cheats
- The passion fades
- A couple are deciding whether to split
- Someone "loses themselves" in their relationship

In the chapters that follow, we'll be getting to the root that all these problems share: how to negotiate *intimacy* and that fine line between "me" and "us".

But we'll take it a step further: we'll look not only at how to fix these issues in your relationships, but how struggling with intimacy can actually be a blessing in disguise! Because the style that we use to interact with others was learned when we were children, it's possible that fixing those relationship problems fixes a few other things in the process...

As human beings, we are all connected. We all "complete" each other, in one way or another. Wherever your relationship is at the moment, and whatever challenges you're experiencing, this book is about getting to grips with this fact of human connection, and how it's playing out in your own life, right this very moment.

If you'd like to learn to develop more authentic, healthier and joyful connections with others, then read on.

CHAPTER 1: THE ETERNAL DANCE BETWEEN "ME" AND "US"

If you've ever watched one of those old black and white films, you might have laughed at the over-the-top romance parts. You know the kind of thing: manly man clutching his dainty woman, she flops her head back and gushes, "I can't live without you darling! You complete me!" To the modern audience, this is cringe-inducing and beyond old fashioned.

Surely more enlightened people know that it's crazy to expect someone to "complete you"? While our grandparents might have swooned at scenes like these, newer generations are understandably cynical. The movie stars say "we're one soul living in two bodies" and the audience hears "I have a personality disorder and we're going to end up in an unhealthy and possibly abusive relationship".

It's not surprising that attitudes towards what's healthy and unhealthy in relationships have changed so much over the years. Feminism in the western world was all about how women categorically *didn't* need men, and that they needed to learn to be whole, complete individuals by themselves, and not seek someone out to give their lives meaning.

Men have historically experienced this pressure less but the attitudes are still the same: his friends will playfully mock a man who gradually gets wrapped up in a new relationship and forgets about other people, joking that he's "whipped" and no longer a free man.

All of this cultural baggage points to one fundamental tension that exists anytime you put two people together: the tension between "me" and "us".

One one side, you're an individual; unique, complete with your own hopes and dreams, a full set of strengths and weaknesses and a life that's largely your own. In fact, from the time you learnt to walk and from those rocky teenage years where you worked hard to find your own identity, you've been trying to carve out your own sense of self. Something distinct from your parents, your siblings, and everyone else.

This is the "me". It's the person you spend the most time with, the one you're usually thinking of when making plans for the future, and the one you focus on when trying to solve problems. It's the "self" in self-improvement!

On the other side is ...well, everyone else. The world at large. Your teachers, colleagues, parents, friends and family members are all close to you in varying degrees, sure, but they're still separate, off to the side. And how much *you* engage with *them* can vary a whole lot.

Now, while you can have deeply intense relationships with all of these people, it's just a fact that there's one more kind of relationship that's even more intense. It's the kind of relationship that often takes center stage in people's lives. The kind of connection many people spend the most time and money and energy on finding. A kind of relationship so special that people seldom manage more than a handful of them in life, if that.

I'm talking, of course, about *serious romantic relationships.* Married or not, these are the people that come closer to us than anyone else in the world. We may love our mothers and feel that our brothers or sisters are our best friends, but our life partner is something one step further. With them, we are really *intimate.*

And how tempting it is to be intimate! You can be that black and white movie heroine at the end of the film, quivering in your true love's arms, safe in your relationship, able to let go of your boring old "self" for just a few sweet moments and melt into them...

You can see the dynamic emerging: on one side of the spectrum, the bliss of letting go and disappearing into another person, into a relationship, and becoming a "we". On the other side, the confidence of maintaining your own separate individuality, of staying free and untangled and personally responsible for you and only you.

Those old fashioned black and white movies were very much about the first side of the spectrum: an all-or-nothing love that's about *need*, about longing so intense that it's distracting. About the thrill of melting into someone else, finding love at last and melding to them completely.

But are we so different today? Perhaps the only difference is that we've swung to the *other* side of the spectrum. Today's ideal couple is fiercely independent. We raise our eyebrows at the traditional gender roles and insist that each partner have their own friends, their own finances, their own identities. We know we should focus on our careers. Work on our personal development. Love ourselves first, we say, be complete as we are and *then* we can think about bonding with someone else. But not too much!

So, which side is right? Maybe you're now wondering which end *I'm* going to suggest you pick. Well, the fact is that there are pros and cons to both sides. We'll have a closer look at where this dichotomy actually comes from and why it's there in the first place, a little later on. But for now, let's compare these two states of mind. I'll call one side of the spectrum "closeness" and the other side "separateness":

The pros and cons of closeness

Pros:

• A feeling of security, protection from the outside world, "coziness"

• Low anxiety – you know your partner is here, with you, and they're not going anywhere. You feel trusting and safe and stable

• It's kind of beautiful. Deeply romantic, all-encompassing, devoted love. It's the stuff of fairy tales!

• A new identity as a couple, one that affords you lots of privileges in our couple-centric world...

Cons:

• Can be risky – put all your eggs in one love basket and what happens when that basket breaks?
• Can be unhealthy. Could mean forgetting who you are and what you want, outside of the relationship. Can even open the door to exploitation and abuse
• Can be boring. Nothing dulls your interest in getting to know someone like already knowing them. Everything about them. *Everything*
• The weakening of your own identity as an individual

The pros and cons of separateness

Pros:
• A feeling of liveliness and excitement. Higher energy and a relationship that is more dynamic and interesting
• Not overwhelming, it doesn't detract from other areas of your life, feels manageable
• It's sexy! Coming together as two separate people brings all the spark of uncertainty. You're with each other because you *want* to be, not because you need to. And wanting is sexy...
• You're always open and free to discover something new. You're not bound to anyone and have no or few obligations

Cons:
• Not feeling a *really deep* and all-consuming connection with someone, worrying about the solidity of your commitment once in a while
• Having difficulty trusting them (you can trust no one but yourself, right?)
• Knowing that you are not always your partner's priority. You simply have to accept that there are limits to your relationship
• You feel the pressure to settle down, to couple up, to follow the formula of what happy couples *should* look like

You'll probably notice that the pros and cons of both almost complement each other. The closer you get, the less stress and uncertainty you experience. You feel comfy and cozy with that person – but at the same time, that comfort also means the heat and energy fizzles, too.

The further apart you get, the more in control and independent you feel ... but at the expense of intimacy and that same deep feeling of comfort. It's almost as if raw, exciting lust is one end of a rope, and stable, committed love is on the other ...and they're pulling against each other.

Many relationships actually cycle through these two extremes: the initial buzz of two coming together as separate individuals is intense in the first few months of a relationship, but later on gives way to more security and stability ...and boredom. The interplay doesn't stop there, though. A couple has to continually navigate the close/separate tension – when they have children, marry, or when a hot secretary steps into the mix, for instance.

So then, which side is better?

You can probably guess what I'm going to say: neither! Instead, a healthy, strong and loving relationship is one where both of these forces are in *balance*. In fact, a healthy relationship is balanced and moderated by a *third*, separate element altogether. But that's for a later chapter.

In the rest of this book, I want to talk about how so much of what it means to be in a relationship rests on this fundamental tension. Close or apart. Together or different. When the forces are balanced, both people get the benefits of intimacy, but while moderating the risks of throwing away their own identities and forgetting who they are as individuals. The ideal relationship gets the best of both worlds!

I'll also talk about how so many relationship problems stem from difficulties resolving this underlying tension. Whether you're on one side (so embroiled in relationships that you're losing yourself) or the other (too distant and having trouble letting go and being truly intimate) then my hope is that the rest of these chapters will have something that speaks to you.

Near the end of the book, I want to talk about the third element that is necessary if you want to find a meaningful blend between these two. And how this third element can turn your relationship woes into an incredible source of growth and opportunity.

Let's begin by stating what might not be so obvious at first: that there are healthy and unhealthy ways to be both close and separate. There's nothing intrinsically "bad" about either, but there are definitely better ways to express both of these human mindsets.

With conscious awareness and with compassion, nothing that two people do together can ever be "bad".

At the interface where you meet up with the rest of the world, you can choose your degree of engagement. We've already looked at two ends of the spectrum: very close and very separate.

I'm sure you know of some couples who have a loving and stable relationship, but they maintain a degree of separateness between them. Perhaps they go on separate vacations, have separate friends and share very different hobbies. But this separateness isn't a source of trouble for them.

Likewise, I'm sure you can think of people who are with each other 24/7, always fighting, always embroiled in drama and breaking up and getting back together three times a day. There are couples who are bitterly unhappy with the amount of "distance" between them after years, but that same amount of engagement would cause another couple to break out into a cold sweat.

What I'm getting at is that though there are two ends of the spectrum, it very much is a *relative* spectrum. It will differ for different people, in different cultures, in different times of your life. And your partner might be working with a completely different spectrum to you!

The previous section was about the importance of balancing these two forces, but this one is about making sure that wherever you fall on the spectrum, you do so with integrity, self-awareness and kindness.

What's the difference between unhealthy and healthy closeness? What's the difference between healthy and unhealthy separateness? Let's look at a few relationships that show just how complex this simple dynamic can actually be, when two real human beings are playing it out in the real world. See if you can spot not only closeness vs. separateness, but also try to find instances of both in their healthy and less healthy forms.

Can you see yourself in any of the following examples?

Case Study 1: Carl and Sara

In many ways, Carl and Sara share a stereotypical male/female relationship – Carl is the "strong silent type" and Sara is an extroverted homemaker, always encouraging him to open up and get in touch with his emotions. They had a whirlwind romance, married soon after meeting, and have been deeply in love ever since. They communicate well and often, and share a loving bond.

The problem is Carl's "episodes". While he loves being very close and loving with Sara, eventually, he has enough and feels smothered. Instead of mindfully stepping back, though, he shuts her down, completely. He goes off on a mission without telling her and stays away for sometimes days at a time.

Sara grows hysterical, angry at being ignored, panicking he won't come back this time and hating how vulnerable she suddenly feels. Carl eventually does come back, like he always does, but by the time he is ready to be close again, Sara has shut down herself and wants to keep her distance. They take a few weeks or months to grow close again, only for the cycle to continue...

Where do they fall on the spectrum?

Healthy closeness, unhealthy separateness.

Carl and Sara have mastered the art of being close. They weren't afraid to commit early on and are happy and well-adjusted to one another. What they haven't mastered is *how to be separate.* Carl neglects his need for alone time until things become so bad he has to "run away" and Sara responds by shutting down herself. The rifts they create during these episodes last for months afterwards.

What's the way forward?

Carl and Sara don't need to find more ways to share time and affection with each other. They already love one another half to death! What they need to do though, is to find healthier ways to put up boundaries between them. They need to find compassionate ways to take breaks. Instead of letting it get out of hand, Carl could find ways to communicate to Sara that he needs time off the relationship as and when he does, and well before things reach breaking point. Sara needs to figure out ways to be OK with being alone sometimes, too.

Case Study 2: Andrew and Lily

This couple's friends have stopped getting involved in the "drama". Everyone believes they should break up already. They are "on again off again" and caught in extremes. When they are "on", they shut out the rest of the world, throw themselves into one another and forget about their obligations. It's them against the world. They might have a tempestuous relationship, but each believes that they are both the best that they can do.

When they're "off" again, they both get depressed and dysfunctional. Andrew drinks heavily, Lily tries to make him jealous by dating other men she doesn't really care about.

They realize that life sucks without the other one, and that they needed each other all along. Then they're "on" again.

Where do they fall on the spectrum?
Unhealthy closeness, unhealthy separateness.
This is a real "worst of both worlds" scenario. In its mild form this may look like a fiery, passionate setup but at its root it fails at both tasks: finding ways to be both close and separate. Andrew and Lily scorn the rest of the world when they are close, and self-destruct when they are apart. They can't live with each other ...and can't live without each other!

What's the way forward?
If Andrew and Lily's relationship is to survive, it has to find a middle ground: they need to have a less intense connection with healthy space for the rest of the world, as well as learn how to be apart as separate, healthy individuals, outside of the relationship. The all-or-nothing isn't working for them – they need to find mature ways to have a relationship in the grey areas instead.

Case Study 3: Mike and Melanie

They were High School sweethearts and everyone told them that they were getting engaged too young. They were each other's first everything, but after a few years, the boredom and seriousness of a big adult relationship at such a young age started to take its toll. Since they loved each other, they eventually were able to talk about this with each other: they needed other things, outside the relationship. They were both not done "growing up" yet.

So they both agreed to occasionally see other people, to keep up their respective social lives and hobbies, but to stay together. They communicated this well to one another, they shared their fears and desires honestly, and tried to remember to be young and "free", even though they had a very, very long term relationship. The problem is now the question of finally getting married. Both are petrified that tying themselves down will be the kiss of death for their relationship. They're drifting and both want to take "next step", but both are worried that they'll soon get bored of one another once they commit for real.

Where do they fall on the spectrum?
Healthy separateness, unhealthy closeness.
Mike and Melanie have spent considerable time on developing a healthy separateness and distance between them. They did this with respectful and open

communication, and made sure that they didn't lose themselves too early in a serious relationship. The problem is that they're both unsure how to be *close*, as well. They're both fearful of intimacy, inexperienced with what it takes to maintain healthy, adult closeness with each other, and unable to pull the trigger and move to the next stage of commitment.

What's the way forward?

Mike and Melanie's problem is maybe not as common as the others. They nevertheless have to find healthy ways to let go and trust one another in a committed relationship – without jeopardizing the lives they are trying to build for themselves.

Case Study 4: Eric and Celeste

After being married for more than twenty years, Eric and Celeste know each other inside out. Though they started out a little like Sara and Carl, they eventually learned to balance themselves. They both enjoy a close, intimate relationship and share most of their lives together. They've raised children, kept a house and travelled together, and they both have grappled with their own demons and one another's.

Occasionally, Eric gets itchy feet and wants to go on a trip of his own. Celeste knows that he needs it, and wishes him well, letting him disappear for a few days. Because Eric knows how how much this worries Celeste, he doesn't leave her hanging: he explains to her carefully what he needs and lets her know that she is loved and appreciated. He always brings her back something nice from his travels.

Celeste, too, knows that she can depend on him when she needs a breather from their relationship. She gets in bad moods, doesn't much feel like sex and just needs to turn inward and recharge for a few days or weeks. Again, though, she knows to expect these moments and lets Eric know what is happening and why. They both agree to be happy and waiting when the other "returns".

Though their lives are wrapped up in each other, there are spaces that are only Eric's, and spaces that are only Celeste's. She likes to keep the details of her previous marriage private. She has a weekly book club that he's not invited to, family and friends that are her own and a separate savings account. Likewise, he has his own room of the house that Celeste doesn't go into, and he shares hobbies with his brothers that don't have much to do with her. Instead of being threatened by this, both are secure enough in themselves that they don't require constant attention. When they are together, though, they don't hold back. Everyone knows it: Eric and Celeste love one another as much as any two people can.

Where are they on the spectrum?

Healthy separateness, healthy closeness.

Celeste and Eric have found that special balance between being close and together, and being separate and apart.

So …what's the difference?

It's easy to see how important balance is when we imagine hypothetical relationships like these. But it's a tricky question: what makes Eric and Celeste's relationship balanced and joyful and loving, while other's struggle, falling on one or other side too strongly? Why do they succeed? Why do some couples find the balance and others get endlessly tangled up in one another's unhealthy webs?

I'd like to suggest that there is a third vitally important quality that all successful long term relationships share. Before we look at what that quality is, let's take a look at *your* relationship, and where it falls on the spectrum of close vs. separate.

Whether the relationship you're in right now is a long term marriage, a committed partnership or a new-ish connection, there is no other relationship in the world quite like it. You and your partner share a unique place on the spectrum between close and separate, and you'll both have your own unique ways of expressing that.

Read the following check list for both extremes and tick the statements that apply to you and your relationship. But be honest!

Closeness

- My partner and I have no secrets from one another
- We spend the majority of our time together
- My partner is my everything: my best friend, my confidant, my therapist...
- My partner is the single most significant person in my life
- I can't imagine life without them
- Most or all of the activities in my life are shared with my partner
- We share the same opinion on basically everything and never argue
- We live together, shower together, sleep in the same bed, eat together everyday...
- I consider my relationship one of my life's greatest achievements
- My partner is the one I go to with problems or to fill my emotional needs
- I feel safe and secure with my partner
- We are both 100% monogamous and always will be
- There is lots of physical affection in our relationship
- I rely heavily on them for some things – like finances or emotional support
- We are both very comfortable with our sex life
- People think of us as a unit. We're invited out as a couple and it's assumed we share the same position in all things
- We share finances, and one or both of us would suffer financially if we split
- My partner is like my family
- Every long term plan I make for my life includes them
- When they feel bad, I can't help but feel bad too
- If my partner disappeared, my whole world would break apart
- There is a strong sense of obligation to stay with my partner
- I feel that their achievements are a reflection on me
- I'm committed, for the long haul, no matter what
- We are part of the same whole
- We have children and/or pets together
- I get anxious and unhappy when I'm apart from them for too long
- Sex with them is more about love and intimacy than raw lust

Separateness

- I trust my partner, but the day might come when they leave me or I leave them
- My partner can't give me *everything* I need in life
- It's nice to spent time away from them occasionally, and I find it easy to entertain myself when they're gone
- We have many differences between us, but it makes life interesting!
- There are some hobbies and activities we don't share
- I often think how lucky I am to have caught them! I get mildly jealous sometimes
- We often go out on "dates" or plan special trips together
- We don't always have to talk when we're together
- We each have friends or family that we spend time with, without the other one
- We both know that noticing attractive others or a little flirting is normal. It's not like the rest of the world is invisible just because we're together
- There are parts of my life that they don't know about
- They would be just fine without me
- My partner is just one part of my life, not my whole life
- I believe that they are responsible for their own mistakes and I don't always agree with their choices
- We don't have a sex routine; we still flirt and try new things in bed
- We take things day by day
- I can picture a life without them in it
- If they disappeared, I would be hurt, but I could manage and find love again
- We don't have children or pets
- I'm able to separate my own feelings from theirs: if they're in a depressed mood and I'm not, I can be helpful without getting depressed myself
- We sometimes argue or get on each other's nerves
- We have separate politics, separate histories or backgrounds, or separate cultural beliefs
- There's a lot of humor, fun and energy in our relationship – we don't do too much seriousness and lovey-dovey stuff
- We have separate savings accounts, and we'd both be financially stable without one another

Where do you fall on the spectrum?

Just reading through these, you might already be gaining a sense of which aspect is stronger in your relationship.

Do you answer heavily on one or the other?

Do you answer yes to *both* aspects? What do you think this means?

Do you agree with very few statements on either side?

Which statements do you think are healthier and which less healthy? Which ones did you choose?

Are there any particular statements that stand out a lot to you?

Try to figure out the exact areas that your relationship is strong in, as well as those places where it might need some work. You might already know this well: perhaps you struggle with commitment and lack real closeness in your relationship, or perhaps sex is a very particular blind spot that stands out as a problem for you.

If you're still unsure about all of this, there is one question that will cut to the root of whether your degree of relationship closeness is healthy or unhealthy:

Ask yourself, does your relationship actively encourage both of you to be the best and highest versions of one another?

Does your separateness enhance those moments where you are close, and does your closeness enhance you as an individual, when you are separate?

What's the way forward?

Once you've got a better understanding of the strengths and weaknesses of your own position on the spectrum, you can get a better idea of how to move forward through the rest of this book.

I can't tell you what is healthy and unhealthy in your own relationship. What you and your partner consider "too close" or "too separate" is really only up to the both of you! Nevertheless, there are some red flags in any relationship that are warning signs of a bigger problem.

Before we continue, I want to talk about some aspects of relationships that go beyond the spectrum of close vs. separate. While I believe that this spectrum is a good way to think about relationships of all kinds, there are limits to this theory. There are normal variations in how we choose to resolve this fundamental tension. And then there are relationships that are plain and simple *in crisis*.

If you relate to any of the following statements, then this might not be quite the right book for you. Instead, think about ways to address these more pressing problems first:

• You or your partner feel suicidal at the thought of the relationship ending – or it continuing!

• You and your partner are both active and heavy users of narcotics or alcohol

• There is physical violence in your relationship

With that caveat, let's move on!

CHAPTER 4: THE PARADOX OF RELATIONSHIPS

So, we've taken some time to have a look at how your current relationship stands, and how it's balanced between close/separate. And I've talked about the "balance" you can find between both of these. Be close, but not too close. Be separate, but not too separate. Ok, sounds simple enough!

In this chapter, I want to go a bit deeper into what I mean when I say "balance". In fact, what I'd like to suggest is not just a 50/50 split between the two aspects. I'm not saying you should add a little of one or take away a little of the other until the ratio looks right. What I'd like to suggest goes a little deeper.

At this point in the book, I want to replace the term "balanced" with "integrated".

Let me explain. Being separate or close are not really opposites, but rather two sides of the same coin. It's not really that one fights against the other, but that they are both mutually defining. Let's return to the idea of healthy and unhealthy: healthy closeness and separateness are integrated into one another. One feeds off the other, and they both give meaning to each other.

I'll explain what I mean with an example. A man goes out with his friends for the night. He enjoys the "guy time", relaxes, catches up with everyone. He spends no time at all with his fiancé at home. In fact, he barely thinks of her at all, while he's out. But when he gets home, he is reminded all at once about how awesome she is. For a split second, it's though he's meeting her again for the first time. "Oh, I remember you! I remember this awesome relationship! How lucky I am."

When contrasted against his guy friends, he suddenly sees his fiancé clearly again. Even though he was as separate from her that evening as he could have been, the result was that he felt *closer* to her. He felt happy and safe coming home to something familiar, reminded about all the little things he loved about her, able to appreciate her with fresh eyes.

His separateness enhanced his closeness.

So, you can see that in a healthy relationship, separate and together are not opposites, but work together.

It goes the other way round, too. Let's look at his fiancé. He comes home to her after a fun night out with the guys. He is loving, attentive and appreciative of her. They share an intimate, sweet evening together. She feels close to him. They're a team. Together till the end. He loves her, and everything she is, deeply. She soaks all of that up, feeling energized.

In the morning, she wakes up and goes to work. Because she feels so loved and appreciated, so understood and valued as the person she is, she tackles her work with fresh vigor. She feels confident and resilient against the day's setbacks. Knowing that she's loved, she is able to love herself and go out and do her best work. She forgets about her fiancé while she's in the office, but in a way, the closeness they shared that night is with her still, powering her through the work challenges of the day.

She barely thinks of him during that time, but it happens nevertheless: her closeness has enhanced her separateness. She takes the energy from that intimacy and carries it out into the world, developing herself and her individuality. Which she then brings back to the relationship.

So, we can see that separateness and closeness are not really different things, but rather two aspects, or two expressions of these mysterious things called relationships. One fuels the other. They feed each other.

In our private, intimate relationships, we become more and more the individuals we are meant to be. Intimacy and closeness carves out the lines of our individual selves. And when we go out into the world and move as free individuals, we are all the better equipped to appreciate and really understand what it means to be close, later on.

So, intimacy and distance are *not* two different things. They don't "balance" so much as mutually exist, in a joyful dance of push and pull, give and take.

You can only be truly intimate with someone when your own sense of individuality is strong and well developed. And you can only be a healthy individual able to stand on their own and be independent when you have the energy and power gained from intimacy with others.

What it really means to be close

So real, healthy intimacy is not about loss of self, but rather enhancing the self. And being separate can sometimes be the single biggest thing that enhances closeness.

It's now that I want to introduce the *third* aspect that I mentioned earlier on, that extra ingredient that moderates both closeness and separateness in a relationship so that they remain in this beautiful, eternal "dance", both feeding on and encouraging the other.

The third aspect is compassionate awareness.

This comes in two parts. The "awareness" part is being alert and taking notice of what is real, in the present moment. The "compassion" part is about being kind and accepting, to both yourself and your partner. It's about loving and acknowledging what your awareness allows you to see.

Compassionate awareness is what encourages you to stop, look honestly at your life and take conscious, beneficial action. It's what allows you to take responsibility, to be honest with yourself and others, and to be kind. With the light of compassionate awareness behind your choices, things become healthy and deliberate. You take control and feel deeper joy and self-love.

What does this have to do with the close/separate tension?

Well, wherever you fall on the continuum, it pays to do so with kindness and compassion. I asked you this question in the previous chapter:

Does your relationship actively encourage both of you to be the best and highest versions of one another?

This question concerns something in a higher realm, an idea that goes beyond the push and pull of too close or too far. With self-awareness and kindness, it's *all* good. When both you and your partner are committed to living according to your highest selves, the close/separate tension resolves itself. You are both committed to helping each other be the best you can be.

So when you choose to be *close*, you do so mindfully and with compassion. You are aware of who you are and can moderate yourself. You can be kind to yourself and your partner, loving both of you for who you really are. You don't mind wading out into the deep waters of very strong intimacy. After all, we *are* all connected. So long as you maintain awareness, though, this interconnectedness is only a source of joy.

And when you choose to be *apart*, you also do so mindfully and with compassion. You are aware of yourself and your partner as separate people. You accept this with joy. You don't mind zooming in and focusing in on your own life for a while, because after all, we are all 100% unique individuals. So long as you maintain awareness, the separateness is only a source of joy.

We are both separate and apart, both one and many. Two sides of the same coin.

People who find a "balance" between these two have really found a seamless way to *integrate* both of them. And the integration can only happen with an open, aware mind and a heart full of compassion. With this mindset, it becomes a question of finding a smooth, joyful flow between close and separate.

Well, I hope you'll forgive the temporary detour into the new-age stuff!

But I also hope I've convinced you that any blend of together and apart is healthy if done with conscious, mindful compassion – for yourself and your partner. The anchoring question is always, *does this serve not only your higher self, but theirs, too?*

A quick disclaimer: this book is not about "self-help"

It's easy to find information out there on how to be a better "self". If you want to fix your career, work on your personality blind spots or rid yourself of bad behaviors, that's easy enough to do, with some effort.

But this is a book about relationships. And when it comes to other people, it's just no use to use the same framework you use for your "self". We live in a deeply narcissistic world, and we carry these attitudes over to our connections with others. We talk about others as though they were products, and we love them according to how well they fit *our* lives, *our* hopes and dreams, and what *we* want.

We may even see relationships as just another one of life's achievements, something to put in our personal cabinet of trophies. Even when it's a question of how we relate to others, how we love them and put their needs above ours, we may be tempted to do so through the framework of our own selfish needs!

While you're thinking about the ultimate state of your connections with others, try not to think of relationships as something you *have*. They're not something you own, but something you *share*, with someone else. Relationships are not about the self at all!

Try to see both sides: are you ultimately serving others? Are you actively helping them become the best they can be? Not your personal vision of what they should be, but *theirs*? Being a better person and enhancing yourself is only one half of the equation. Actively working for others, with others – this is the root of what it means to be *in relationship*.

Before we move onto the rest of the book, I want to suggest that you don't read the information as one individual next to another individual, but as someone who is truly *together* with someone else.

It's not a book about people, but about the good things they can do, together.

CHAPTER 5: YOUR RELATIONSHIP IS A WONDERFUL LABORATORY

Earlier on we looked at different ways that this close/distant dynamic can play out with real live couples. But why are some couples one way and others completely different? In this chapter, we'll look more deeply into where these patterns and behaviors actually come from.

Before you were even born, you were basically indistinguishable from another person: your mother. This was the "closest" you've ever been to another human – and will ever be again! Even long after the umbilical cord is cut and you learn to use your own lungs to breathe, your own legs to walk ...well, you still depend on your mother. Being close to the people that took care of you wasn't really an option back then. Love was basically the same thing as survival ...which was basically the same thing as dependence.

But as you grew up, you learnt about something else: independence. The more separate you grew from your mother (and those that cared for you) the more you became more fully *yourself.* You learnt you could have your own opinion, make choices, even think and feel things that were hidden from the rest of the world. You developed your own goals and dreams. You started to think of yourself as an "I" and everyone else as a "them".

The reason I'm mentioning all this is that these early experiences are what shape our attitudes throughout the rest of our lives. Not to get too psychoanalytic about it, but these early relationships become very real *models* for every relationship that follows.

That means that if your mother taught you early on that you couldn't really rely on her for affection when you needed it, you may have developed the idea that *all* people in relationships are unreliable, or a little cold. If you were penalized heavily every time you stepped out and tried to think for yourself, you may have developed the idea that being an individual is risky, and will *always* cost you the acceptance you crave.

Of course, what's happened in the past is over. Or is it?

If you've ever met a girl with "daddy issues" or known a "mommy's boy", you'll instinctively understand just how important these early relationships can be. But so what? What can you do with this information now that you're big and grown?

In this chapter, I don't want to get bogged down in blaming your mom for your commitment issues or trying to play detective for things that happened decades ago. But I do want to suggest something exciting: *the relationships we have as adults can offer us key opportunities to understand and resolve these past issues.*

Let me give you an example. Imagine a woman who had a distant mother and a father who barely acknowledged her existence. As a little girl, all she can remember when she thinks about him was how desperately she wanted his attention, for him to care about her. She remembers wishing he'd praise her for her school work or be proud of her achievements. She wanted to please him so badly that she completely shrugged off all the times he was mean, critical and downright abusive to her. In her mind, if she could put up with enough hostility and cruelty, she'd eventually "win" his love.

Sounds heavy, but you'd be surprised how many women have the same experience! In any case, this woman now finds herself in a new dilemma as an adult. Relationship after relationship, she fails to find security and commitment with a man. She instead finds a string of disinterested, mildly abusive men who don't have much respect for her. Her friends can see that she keeps choosing men like this, but to her, the world is just full of this kind of man and nobody else.

In essence, this woman is repeating the same relationship dynamic over and over again. It's always the same story: for her, "love" means begging for and "winning" affection from people who don't really care about her. Just like with her father! It makes her unhappy doing this, but she doesn't know how to do anything else. After all, she learnt this model when she was too young to think critically about it. For her, the abuse she suffers isn't getting in the way of love – for her, it *is* love.

Instead of writing off all men as abusive and non-committal, though, and instead of giving up, this woman can look carefully at what her relationships are really showing her about herself. Instead of running away from the horrible feelings of being invisible and unloved, she goes *deeper* into them. Where did they come from? Why does she have them?

She begins to think of the people that come into her life as people who are there to teach her something. In a way, her relationships become a kind of *laboratory* – a place where she gets to the difficult work of really understanding herself and how she works in the world.

One day she shares this insight with her partner. He loves her, but he has his own baggage from the past. Early on, *his* mother taught him that "love" was the same as smothering, or a loss of freedom. His mother was overbearing, nosy and demanding, and taught him that all women are just as pushy, forcing their love and needs on others. He understood that love was something you had to resist – and he's been resisting it ever since!

As he talks to the woman about why he finds it hard to commit, and why he's unable to treat her with kindness and consideration, he has his own insight: he's working with faulty models, too.

And now, a different situation emerges. No longer do we have two badly matched people who seem to be set up to hurt one another. The advice that they should split or just go see a counselor doesn't go deep enough here. Instead, we can look and see that these two people *attracted each other* into the other one's life. Not only can they both learn from one another, but they are each perfectly suited to target the other one's baggage, head on.

When you meet someone who "pushes your buttons", you're encountering someone special: a person with opposite but complementary weak spots. The places where you fit can be the places of most tension and destruction ...or the greatest opportunity to build on those weaknesses.

Through awareness and compassion, our couple can look at their differences not as something that needs to be avoided and gotten rid of, but something interesting to understand. Something that, when engaged fully, will open up new paths of understanding ...and healing.

So, the woman can work on her self-esteem, learning to ask for what she wants and teaching herself that she is worthy of being loved and respected. And the man can learn that getting close and vulnerable with someone isn't threatening, and that it can actually be wonderful. These two people are not working *against* one another; their blind spots can actually work together.

They each teach the other the lesson they most need to learn.

In fact, some people believe that this is the root of attraction in the first place. When you feel yourself inexplicably drawn to someone, it's not hormones or the stars aligning. Rather, it's the *mutual recognition of some shared "work"*. It's the heart's way of trying to resolve old hurts, to learn, to put things right again ...and being drawn to precisely those people who will most challenge you and force you to do that work.

When I talk of relationships being a laboratory, I mean that every time you engage with another human being, you have the opportunity to *learn*. Relationship trouble can be the single biggest stress in your life. It can be devastating. But if you engage it with compassion and self-awareness, it can also be a signpost pointing the way to much, much better things.

What led you to your current relationships? A technique for learning the lesson, once and for all

• Think of your earliest significant relationships. This can be mom or dad, or anyone you relied on for care as a child. What was that relationship like? What was the "lesson" here? In our example above, the woman was taught that love was something she had to earn. What lessons were you taught early on?

• Can you see any ways that those same lessons are repeating now in your adult life? Our example woman found herself trying to "convince" every man in her life to care for her. Do you see any patterns in your own relationship history?

• Can you identify any ways that you have actively been choosing to put yourself in the same type of relationship, over and over? Do you have a "type"? Do all your relationships end the same way?

• Now ask yourself *what could have been*. Think back to those early relationships: what did you need and want, back then? What did you wish for but didn't get? If there was some kind of trauma or disruption, what did you wish was the outcome?

• Now you've identified your way forward. The woman in our example wanted very badly to be cared for, acknowledged and cherished. But her belief that she wasn't worthy led her to men who confirmed that belief. The woman in the example can find ways to cherish and love herself, first. This breaks the cycle of trying to "win" affection. It puts her on a different path where she can stop reliving poor relationships from the past and start living the relationships she really wants.

• Can you think of a way to start giving yourself what you missed in those early relationships?

• If you have a partner already, can you think of how your "baggage" fits into theirs? Can you see how you're both "hooking" one another? Can you think of a way to stop feeding their vicious cycle and start giving them what they really need and want?

When people talk about their relationship problems, there's always a hidden current of blame. Who's right and wrong? Who's not playing by the rules and who should be punished for it? We try to point fingers at the other person and find what's wrong with them. They're not committing fast enough. They're not being honest. They're too clingy. They don't have the right opinions or the right interests.

But why are they in your life in the first place?

What is it in YOU that called such a person into your world?

We ALL have issues. We have all had imperfect childhoods, we've all suffered losses and disappointments. And deep down, we all want the same thing: to be loved and accepted for the human beings we are. That's it.

Try to be compassionate – your partner's weaknesses could have important lessons for you. Their flaws could shine an important light on your own, and what's more, you could both offer to one another the chance to overcome those flaws, and to move beyond. In adult relationships, you get a second chance to work through the pain of the past. In your "relationship laboratory" you get to experiment and be someone else. Learn new lessons.

This can only happen, though, when that special third factor is included. It's only compassionate awareness that allows you to see deeper into your relationships ...and do something about it.

You could spend a lifetime going round the same old cycles, getting trapped in the same unresolved dynamics with people who are all playing the same role for you. Or, you could stop, become aware, and choose to have compassion for what's really going on, beneath the surface.

You could see relationships as *processes*. Opportunities for both people to grow and become the best versions of themselves that they can. We can all help one another to heal!

CHAPTER 6: MASCULINE, FEMININE AND THE NOTORIOUS S-E-X

Maybe it's so tempting to talk about couples completing one another because there's a primal, fundamental way in which their *bodies* fit together. For most (heterosexual) people, the mechanics of sex point to something very deeply understood: that men and women complete one another. They fit, literally.

As we saw in the previous chapter, we may all have little dents in our psyches where our partners have bulges, and they may have dents where we have bulges. And so we fit. But when it comes to men and women, the potential for truly complementary relationships is even greater.

You won't find many "traditional" values in this book, but very old fashioned models of human sexuality actually do have something right: they understand the value of this "completing" process, i.e. they know that for a relationship to work, there needs to be balance and for each person to complement each other. Strength paired with weakness. Good paired with bad. The whole being so much more than the sum of its parts.

It's unfortunate that most of this traditional thinking centers around how men and women ought to play their respective roles: men do this, women do that. They live happily ever after. Or so it goes.

While most of the world is moving away from these old fashioned conceptions of masculinity and femininity, they're discovering a curious side effect: relationships that are not polarized this way have their own disadvantages, too. Couples who are too much their own individuals, too independent, too separate from one another ...soon become nothing more than roommates.

I'd like to suggest a middle ground: that healthy relationships *do* have a tension between masculine and feminine, and that a happy sex life *is* due to the successful pairing of one with the other. However, this doesn't mean that to have a good sex life you should put on a 50s apron and make a cake while you wait for your husband to come home from work!

Rather, it means becoming aware of your own complementariness, whatever that looks like for you and your relationship.

Think of "masculine" and "feminine" as labels only. Just descriptives for characteristics that *both* men and women can share, and which form opposite ends of human experience, like the ends of a magnet. Any one woman can be more "masculine" than any one man, and that man may be more "masculine" in the morning but more "feminine" that same evening. What I'm getting at is that we can understand the tension between man vs. woman as a deeper tension between different styles of living, of interacting. Just shorthand for understanding the different flavors of the same human experience.

Masculine is supposed to be active, logical and stubborn. Feminine is supposed to be passive, emotional and yielding. Whether these are accurate descriptions of real human beings (hint: they're probably not) they do give us some clues about the ways that these characteristics can *complement* one another. Whoever the people involved are, the fact is that active *does* pair well with passive, and logical and emotional *do* balance one another out.

A relationship can be a space to balance all the traits you and your partner share. The hills and valleys fit together, like a puzzle piece. The extrovert helps the introvert come out their shell, the introvert teaches the extrovert to enjoy their own company. Masculine traits are moderated by feminine traits – whether those traits are possessed by men or women.

If your relationship problem has a gendered flavor to it, I'd like to suggest that you abandon the traditional ideas for a moment, and just look at you and your partner honestly. Ask, again, if you are both supporting one another to be the best you can be, not despite your differences, but because you are different.

Opposites can enhance one another. Are your differences, whatever they are, enhancing one another? Do the idiosyncrasies of your personality stabilize your partners, creating a stable, happy whole?

Take your pick: safe or sexy

Unfortunately, though the trend for relationships is to move towards these stable, happy wholes, the old rules of close vs. distant come into play. Without any distance between you, the sexual tension fizzles. It's safe, but it sure isn't sexy.

Sex is a stage where all the dramas of close vs. separate play out. It's a cruel irony: two flirting strangers can be nearly insane with desire for one another, and would give anything to share a bed together. But fast forward a few years and they're in that very bed, night after night, and the they'd give anything to not have to go through the chore of sex, again. Have you ever known a couple who fight and then have raucous "make-up sex", seemingly fueled by the threat of losing each other? Or what about the guy who's hyper-focused on a conquest but loses all interest the very second she says "yes"?

Loss of sexual interest over time is probably the biggest issue long term couples face. What's the solution? Make a problem.

I'll explain what I mean. If you're having difficulty finding that same lust and excitement for your partner as you did in the early days, the problem may be that ...there isn't one. You're *too* comfortable. Too close already. To get back some of the old sexual tension, you need to add distance again – and with distance comes a little more risk, a little more doubt. It's OK in a long term relationship to trade that white hot passion for a little stability and security. But if your intimacy levels are really suffering, you might need to throw a spanner in the works and stop taking one another for granted.

Get in shape and take pride in your appearance and your life achievements. Don't carry yourself as though you feel you're entitled to your partner's complacency forever just because you're married. Likewise, behave as if you also need to be cared for and seduced each and every day. Go on dates. Flirt a little, be a little unexpected. Put that distance between you ...so you can have the thrill of closing it up again.

CHAPTER 7: THE PICTURE ON THE PUZZLE BOX IS ALWAYS CHANGING

In the last chapter, I hinted a little at the fact that for many couples, stability and squashing out any tension or distance in their relationship actually has the effect of draining the life out of it. This really is most true in the bedroom, where familiarity can soon start to breed contempt.

Nothing saps the spontaneous thrill of enjoying your partner for who they are, in the moment, than the sinking knowledge that you're on a schedule. That you're following a script and need to perform in this or other way.

Why am I mentioning this again? Well, this strict adherence to should and musts *outside* of the bedroom can be just as deadly. The 'opposite" of close is distant. And the opposite of joyful, loving connection with another human being is a connection that is forced and full of obligation.

Whether we know it or not, most of us are walking around with ideas about how relationships should be, and the narratives they have to follow. We may not even realize that we're holding up our own lived experience against these abstract ideas of what we think our experience should be. And curiously, we may be tempted to adjust ourselves to fit the story, rather than consider whether the story really makes sense for us!

As children, we were told stories where two protagonists meet, experience some problem, solve the problem, and then live happily ever after. That's it. The story doesn't go on after that – the couple reaches some ideal equilibrium and then nothing ever changes again. It may take a few decades and failed relationships to see that real life doesn't often match this story!

People are always changing, and so too will the relationships that they're in. We've looked at length about the dynamic dance between male and female, between close and distant, between mindlessness and consciously making the choice to be alert and compassionate.

But all of this changes with time, too. A couple may cycle through many variations of close vs. distant in the course of their relationship. Their connection may stretch and tighten between them over the years, like an elastic. It may even snap. It may stay the same for years, then change completely over the course of a week.

This chapter is about all the principles we've discussed, but with an extra ingredient thrown into the mix: time. Many of the relationship problems that torment people the most are centered around change: getting closer, getting further apart. Here, I'll treat all of these changes as fundamentally the same, whether it's the decision to move in together or the decision to get divorced.

Changes in relationships are inevitable. They may be "good" or "bad", but you always get to control how much awareness and compassion you bring to them, whatever they are. You could fall back on a relationship narrative about how things "should" be, judge your life accordingly and then try to force the changes you see in front of you into that mold. Or you can accept the reality of the moment, with compassion.

Common relationship narrative number 1: the escalator

When you step onto an escalator, it's for one reason only: to get from where you are to where you want to be. You don't care much about the escalator itself, it's just a tool, something in the middle point to help you get to the more important endpoint. Using this narrative is a bit like thinking of relationships this way. You're at point A, point B is off there in the distance, and you need to *keep on moving*.

So you meet someone you like, and go on a few dates and like them even more. That's great and all, but what next? You start looking at the next step. You have to date more. See each other more. Still good. Then the next step is to meet their friends or parents. Then move in together. Just keep going. If you pause along the way, the relationship is officially stalled – and you treat it with as much irritation as you would an escalator that stopped moving. Next is engagement, then marriage. Then kids. Then a bigger house. Then grandkids. Just keep on going.

When you think of every part of your relationship as merely a stepping stone to the next part, what you do is rob yourself of joy in the present moment. You're on a "track" – perhaps to a serious commitment, because that's your point B and the only reason the relationship exists the first place. When it "stalls" or goes backwards, you worry. The sad thing is, all those steps in between *are* the relationship. There's nothing else. And when you hurry along a relationship, forcing it to be more more more ...then you miss out on all the good things it actually is, right now.

If any of this sounds very familiar to you, there's an easy way to challenge this narrative: just ask yourself, are your needs being met in your relationship? Instead of wondering whether your relationship is living up to some external standard, ask if it's living up to the *internal* ones.

Common relationship narrative number 2: the happily ever after

This has a lot in common with the escalator narrative. It goes like this: couples get to know each other, finding themselves more and more a part of one another's lives. Then, they find equilibrium and ...stay that way. They settle down and commit to one another and their relationship. Where the escalator is all about hurrying towards some imagined end, this narrative *is* the imagined end.

The relationship in this story can never, ever change. People fall in love, they commit, and then that's it. Their relationship stays what it is over decades. There are no ups and downs, just one, smooth line of true love all the way along. The biggest characteristic of such a relationship is that it never ends. It doesn't taper off or morph in time into a different kind of affection. Neither partner's libido changes, there are no outside love interests, nobody in the past or the future to threaten the stability, no aging or illness, nobody changing their mind about anything and never, repeat *never* any split ups or divorce.

It's easy to see how silly this is when laid out like that, but this narrative is really, really common. You'd be surprised how many older couples, after decades of loving one another, quietly shift into a more companionate marriage, more like old friends than lovers. Some people have wonderful relationships that run their course within a mere six months. This is all perfectly fine, so long as you don't try to cram it into a narrative that doesn't really fit. Of course, there's nothing wrong with actually having a relationship that is stable and unchanging, but to *force* the fact won't do anyone any good.

If this narrative is one you're guilty of indulging in, try to remember that, like everything else in life, relationships grow and change. Instead of resisting change wherever you see it, become curious about it. What can you learn here? What new things are always waiting, just outside your comfort zone?

As an antidote to some of these relationship narratives you might be carrying around with you, I'd like to suggest a different, more authentic way to cope with changes in your relationships. Whether you're transitioning into a bigger commitment, for example thinking about marriage, or whether you're considering terminating a relationship altogether, these questions will help you narrow in on the right choice – without having to rely on some fairytales that have nothing to do with the human beings in question.

Questions to as yourself as you encounter relationship changes

• How do these changes line up with my values? How do they line up with my partner's values?
  • Am I happy with the level of closeness right now? What about my partner? What would getting closer or actually mean for us and am I happy with that?
  • Am I happy with the level of distance between us right now? And my partner? How would opening up some distance affect our relationship?
  • Am I trying to force the natural progressing of this connection into a shape that doesn't really suit it?
  • Are these changes ultimately going to help me be the best version of myself?
  • Can I say the same for my partner?
  • Do these changes come from outside – i.e. from friends and family, society at large – or are they expectations my partner and I have of each alone?
  • Do these changes come from a place of kindness and compassion, or are they fueled by anger and hurt and fear?
  • Is what I fear really so scary here?
  • Is what I want here really a good thing?
  • What is my real responsibility with these changes? What part have I played here and am I happy with that?
  • Am I forcing a change simply because I think there should be one?
  • Am I being forced into a change?

• Is this change about repeating the same old patterns or about breaking out of them?

• Are there aspects of the situation in front of me that I could be missing?

• Do these changes make me feel happy, fulfilled and excited about myself and the future?

• If you're still not sure – dig deep and ask your intuition/higher self: what conscious choices do you really want to make here?

So often, a relationship problem is not so much a problem, but a change. In particular, it's a change in how distant or close we are to one another. If you can stop, take the time to understand what those changes are and what they mean for you, you give yourself the opportunity to learn.

And to become better!

It's time to get to work!

By this point, I'm hoping I've managed to convince you of a few important points:

• We can understand many relationship problems by understanding the interplay between close and separate.

• Successful relationships are all about balancing both.

• The third secret ingredient, the one that pulls everything together, is *compassionate awareness.*

• Your relationship, and all the problems you experience in it, can be a "laboratory" for you to get to the root of old wounds ...and heal them once and for all.

• The "work" is never finished – relationships are always changing, and so must the way we deal with them.

Of course, as interesting as I hope some of this has been, simply reading about relationships won't make much of a difference out there in the real world! We have to try some of these ideas out, on ourselves and our relationships.

The following exercises are not meant to be followed in any set order. You can also choose to skip one if it really doesn't seem relevant. But try them anyway – they might seem simple but they really come alive when you try to put them into practice.

Exercise 1: a date spent apart

This exercise is great for when you're not really sure *how* to balance the close and the distant aspects of your relationship. Choose a day to commit to a date, only this time a date with a twist. A date where you spend your time apart rather than together.

For example, you could set out for town on a Saturday morning together. At some point, bid each other adieu and then head in separate directions. You can make a game of this (toss a coin – heads goes right, tails goes left) or just follow your noses. Agree to meet back at the same place after a set time, say an hour.

Now, when you're on your own mission, do ...whatever you like. Go into shops or cafes you like the look of, head to a market you've always wanted to go to or buy something that catches your eye just because. Chat to strangers. Go for a walk in the park. It doesn't matter – just make sure it's something you like and find interesting.

Then, when you meet back up again, share with your partner all the interesting things you've found, and listen to what they did. Enjoy how your separateness and difference can actually be a source of closeness ...and it's fun! It might feel a little awkward at first, but try this a few times. You'll get the hang of it. You might like to make themes for your dates – food, exercise, finding out something new about your city that you both don't know – and then add a fun competitive element. The point is that when you return to one another, you have something fun to share and draw you closer together.

Exercise 2: a closeness diagram

Get two big pieces of paper and set aside a few minutes with your partner. It's easy to talk about closeness and separateness as these floaty, abstract concepts, but it can be really illuminating to actually *see* it.

Start first, and draw yourself as a big circle in the middle of your page. This represents you and all the things that make up your life – your interests, your hobbies, your work etc. Now, draw another circle for your partner, but draw them relative to yourself. Do they overlap with your circle about 50%? Is their circle far away off to the other side of the page? Is their circle *inside* yours, or vice versa?

It can be difficult to talk about these issues sometimes but much easier to *show* them to your partner. Ask them to do the same. Do you notice any differences? Anything that surprises you?

Finally, take another color pen if you have one and draw over your current diagram – this time outlining what you wish the situation looked like. Perhaps the overlap is fine but both of your circles feel too small. Perhaps you'd like them to touch but not overlap. Maybe the overlap can be big, but you'd like to draw dashed, open lines rather than solid ones. Have your partner do the same.

Discuss what you find out about one another and your relationship. Why have you drawn your diagram in the way you have? What kind of compromises can you both make? Have there been any miscommunications in what you both understand as "close"?

Exercise 3: switcheroo

When we're in healthy, interdependent relationships, there is always some give and take, some push and pull. We seek out those who are complementary to us, who bring out our best but also make up for our weaknesses!

This is all healthy. What's less healthy, though, is when we expect others to pick up our slack for us, or when we shirk responsibility for things or take on responsibility that isn't ours. This can lead to dependent relationships, where we rely on our partners for things that we should really be supplying for ourselves.

In "traditional" marriages, women were encouraged to forfeit their careers and aspirations and let their husbands take care of it, and husbands were encouraged to let everything that feel outside the realm of work to stagnate, delegating his emotional and social life to his wife to figure out.

While this might work temporarily, the fact is it only works when the relationship is intact. When the relationship hits a crisis, both may suddenly become aware of just how lopsided they have become as people.

If you've ever suspected that you've left some parts of yourself under-developed simply because your partner "took care of it", then this exercise is for you. While it's true that you can feel whole and fulfilled as part of a couple, it's nothing compared to the wholeness and fulfilment you can experience when you can provide *yourself* all the things you seek in a partner. This way, you can engage with them because you choose to and want to, and not because you need to and have no other choice.

To do this exercise, set aside some time (perhaps one day) where you switch roles with your partner. Role-playing is a favorite technique of marriage counsellors, but this is very focused role playing. As you pretend to be your partner, try to manifest all those things that you feel are "their job". They do the same.

For example, in our traditional marriage example above, the woman can try doing what she usually lets her husband do: worry about money. And he can do what he perceives is "her job" – worrying about whether everyone's happy and getting on well, that morale is high, that resources are managed properly, that harmony in the home is maintained.

This is a very obvious example. Be careful though, it's not about the physical and practical differences in your partner's life and your own. Everyone has division of labor and we can't all do one another's jobs. It's more about temporarily taking on the work that you ask your partner to do on your behalf.

In traditional setups like I've described, the woman is often responsible for the "emotional work". Remembering birthdays. Encouraging communication. Instigating therapy or making sure there's a date night every week. When she stops doing this for a second and lets him do it instead, she gives him the chance to develop that side of himself. Likewise, if she's put her career on the back burner because she allowed his career to dominate, she may get some insight into this under-developed side of herself when she tries to be her partner for a day or so.

The goal of the exercise is to try to give yourself whatever it is you rely on your partner for. It's perfectly OK to delegate, to divide up household roles and to settle into an equilibrium. But you might be surprised by what you learn when you walk in your partner's shoes for a while.

Exercise 4: holiday

Take a vacation, *without* your partner.

When you're a couple, you may gradually start to move as *one*, rather than two individuals, together. You may fall into the same tired old routines, nothing new coming in or out of your lives, and things fizzling out and becoming predictable. So with this exercise, give yourself time to feel desire again, to remember what drew you to your partner in the first place.

When you are always with your partner, your desire to be with them is logically at its lowest – after all, you already *are* with them! Inject some distance and you'll also inject some desire. While you're apart, for however long, try to really tune into why you miss them. Really notice how it feels to reunite again, and how you relate to one another.

If this exercise works out well, can you inject mini breaks like this into your life at more regular intervals?

Exercise 5: timeline

As we saw in the last chapter, change is the only constant. This exercise is simple, but it can make you much more aware of this fact, bringing clarity to whatever ails you in your relationship right now. Also, this exercise is better for those couples who have been together for a considerable amount of time – it won't work as well for those who are still quite new to one another.

With your partner, sit down and construct a "timeline" for your relationship. You might like to make a literal graph showing how close and separate you were over the time you knew one another. Take turns tracing your own line – you'll probably notice some dips and peaks, some relatively calm, sections, and some places where you both disagree a little.

Are there any patterns emerging? You might be surprised to find, when laying it all out visually, that change over time is not some worrying exception – but more like the normal state of affairs! If you're currently in a rough patch, can you look back and see past times when things were as difficult but which you nevertheless managed to overcome?

Exercise 6: bring in a third!

Many people choose to freshen up a stale relationship by bending the boundaries of their monogamy and bringing in some extra sexual element from the outside. Many couples know that far from being a threat, this kind of new energy can be like a jolt of excitement and new life into a long term relationship. Old fires are stoked, and both get to feel like they're living a little.

Now, I'm not suggesting you do this. But at the same time, it's a sound principle: your relationship is not a little world made of only two people. You both have families. You both have a place inside your communities, your work structures, your neighborhoods. Can you find a way to bring other people's energy into your relationship?

Volunteer somewhere together with your partner. While you meet new people, you are simultaneously meeting a new and different version of yourselves. Socialize and make friends with other people who share hobbies and interests – and not just other couples! Find room in your relationship for older people, for children, even for animals. It's a little paradoxical: the more you turn outward towards others, as a couple, the stronger your bond can grow – but without all the claustrophobia of shutting everyone else out.

If you're the kind of couple that has cut most of your friends and family out now that you have a significant other, this exercise will be particularly difficult and may prove to be an ongoing challenge.

But there's a reason that wedding rituals all over the world contain an element of community participation. Other people are called on to witness, to bless the couple and accept them as a unit. This is because the supportive structure of a healthy relationship can sometimes be *outside* of that relationship.

We are all connected. No person survives on their own – we all live inside complex webs, mutually defining each other; the same, yet different. Our world can be quite a narcissistic place – but by mindfully and compassionately reaching out to others, *all* your relationships will benefit, not just the one you share with your partner.

CONCLUSION

If you've read this far and had the courage and curiosity to put some of the exercises into practice, my bet is that you think a little differently about your relationship now than you did before. Whatever your challenges at the moment, they can always benefit from calm, compassionate awareness and a willingness to learn.

With this book, I wanted to show that a deeper understanding of what it actually means to be *close* to someone can benefit not only your romantic relationships, but your relationships with everyone, yourself included.

As human beings, we all complete one another, sometimes just a little, sometimes in more obvious ways. But at the root of every connection we share with another, is the fundamental interplay between them and us, close and far, separate and together.

Master a mindful balance between these two and you allow yourself to appreciate the gifts of being in a relationship of any kind. You can look at all your quirks and idiosyncrasies (and your partners!) with fresh, compassionate eyes. You can give more fully and more authentically in each moment, and even when it's time to part ways and move you, you can do this with peace and self-awareness, too.

I encourage you to go out into the world and be grateful for all the people you meet and all the wonderful things they can teach you. Have gratitude for your partner, no matter what your relationship with them is like now, because in knowing and being together with them, you are blessed with the gift of *connection*.

Be curious about these connections, about what really serves you and the people around you, and suddenly there are no "relationship problems" any more.

If you've picked up a relationship self-help book, chances are you find some things in your relationship challenging – I nevertheless encourage you to take on those challenges with an open mind and, more importantly, an open heart!

WHEN LOVE HURTS AND EVERYTHING TURNS TO SH#T - HOW TO REBUILD A BROKEN HEART WHEN YOU CAN'T EVEN FIND THE PIECES

INTRODUCTION

If you've found yourself thinking "could this really be happening to me?" a lot recently, then this book was written for you!

Infidelity is a strange thing: it seems like it's all around us all the time, but when it happens *to us*, we're horrified and can't believe it. Could this really be happening?

When you watch a movie and see the stereotypical angry husband burst in through the door and catch his cheating wife in the act, you feel bad for him. But unless you've actually had this experience yourself, you might not understand just how truly upsetting it can be. If you're reading this book, there's a strong chance that the reality of being cheated on is hitting you ...and it's harder than it looks! After all, the one person who you might have chosen to confide in after such a painful experience is the very person who caused the pain.

The angry guy in the movie doesn't quite show the whole picture. When your partner is unfaithful, you may feel angry, humiliated, sad, numb, brimming with murderous rage, confusion or any awful blend of all of those. And all in the few minutes it takes for the realization to dawn on you. And then you have to keep going to work, doing your chores and getting on with life ...or what you *thought* was your life!

When I think of this kind of thing, I imagine a happy, contented person at a big table, building an enormous jigsaw puzzle. Not just any jigsaw, but a really massive, complex one, the kind that takes weeks to build. You've got the end result in your mind's eye, you've built the corners and edges, and best of all, you have your closest friend and fellow puzzle builder with you: your partner. You're both plugging away at building this beautiful puzzle, together. Then one day, they get up, turn the table over and send every last piece spilling across the floor. Days and days of work, gone. Those four precious corners, lost in the mess. The picture that you were building, together, now lay broken on the floor.

Why would anybody do such a thing? Weren't they working on the puzzle *with* you? For a moment, you stand and look at the mess on the floor and ask yourself (you guessed it) "is this really happening right now?" And before you've made sense of the whole incident, your partner is standing in front of you, crying and pleading for forgiveness. "Please try to understand!" they say, "please don't be angry. Think about how hard it's been for me, let me explain..."

When someone cheats in a relationship, your whole world can turn upside down overnight. The "picture" you were building together, as a team, is thrown out the window. Now what?

I should mention now that this book is not about how to *leave* someone after they've been unfaithful to you. Some people have a zero tolerance policy for it, or they're not invested enough to take on the work required to trust again, or the cheating is really just the end of a relationship that has run its course anyway.

Nobody is entitled to forgiveness after a deception. For some relationships, the deception is so deep, so lasting and so pervasive that there really isn't much to do except separate as gracefully as possible.

But cheating doesn't *have to* be the end of the world. This book is for those people who want to know how to keep going anyway. If you've recently experienced the soul-crushing realization that your partner hasn't been faithful, it might seem strange to hear that in a way, cheating can be a *good* thing. Even though you might feel your heart and mind pulled in a million different directions right now, my hope is that by the end of this book, you have found a new clarity, a fresh calm, and a clear sense of how to move forward.

With compassion, self-awareness and concrete commitment, a relationship can survive any disaster. Even cheating. Of course, the hard part is finding out how to be compassionate, self-aware and committed!

So, your partner cheated. They lied to you, broke a promise and reached out to someone else for attention or sex or love. And you're devastated. But if the cat's out of the bag and your partner is in front of you, begging for forgiveness and another chance, then this book will show you what that actually means.

Your puzzle is broken now. But it IS possible to sit down again, together, and rebuild. It IS possible for your partner to change, for your relationship to change and more importantly, for things to get *better*.

Your new puzzle probably won't be of the same picture anymore, and you'll probably have to go more slowly and carefully when you build it.

But it can be done.

The new picture can be just as beautiful as the old one …or even more so.

CHAPTER 1: GROUND ZERO: THE DAY YOUR WORLD CHANGES

I call the moment when you discover the infidelity "ground zero" because it can feel like your heart has just been blasted with a nuclear bomb.

Whether you've had your suspicions or it came completely from nowhere, staring at hard evidence can be a real blow. Some people discover incriminating photos or texts, others hear a confession and others, like our movie man above, discover the act itself.

Cheating hurts so much for two key reasons, and it's these reasons that makes it different from other kinds of trauma you could experience.

It hurts because it comes from the person you love

We expect murderers to murder, and we know that politicians lie. We are of course affected when people we don't like do something to harm us ...but we expect it. What we don't expect is that our partners – the people we associate with love and security and intimacy and safety – can be a source of pain. The anguish of seeing someone who used to give you so much happiness flip and turn into someone who gives you pain can be disorienting to say the least. When someone hurts you, you've gained a problem. But when *someone you love* hurts you, that's two problems: the hurt they've given you, plus the fact that now you have one less loving, supportive person in your life.

It hurts because of the sexual element

One of the most fundamental parts of sexual intimacy is that it's (usually! Although I'm not judging!) just two people, alone, shutting out the rest of the world and enjoying one another in private. We mark the beginning of a more serious relationship by expecting and committing to sexual exclusivity.

For many people, exclusivity is the defining feature of a relationship. So when that exclusivity is yanked away, it can feel like the whole relationship "is a lie". It's not rational, but the sexual element makes this kind of betrayal so much worse. You feel exposed, cheapened and deeply threatened. It goes a little deeper than jealousy though. It can be a massive shock to realize that you're not The One but One of Many.

It might sound strange, but realizing that you are not the only person that your partner finds attractive can unlock strong emotions that go right back to childhood. When we come into this world, we are perfectly fused with our mothers. In our still-developing minds, love = survival. Literally. Because we're completely helpless, her love and care literally translates to us being able to survive and thrive.

If you've seen how jealous a toddler can get when a second baby enters the family picture, you'll understand how painful it can be to learn that you're not The One, but One of Many. As we grow up, we learn to take turns, and to share. But there's still a little part of us that remembers how amazing it felt to be the center of the universe, to have someone's full love and attention, all for ourselves. For many people, romantic relationships are a place to recreate that warm feeling, if only temporarily. We close the door on the world. It's "just the two of us". "Love chemicals" like oxytocin are released when a mother bonds with her baby ...and when two lovers stare into each other's eyes and forget about everyone else. You love them and they love you and it feels warm and safe and wonderful.

And then they cheat.

If we've learnt in childhood that love = survival, then losing that love can literally feel as though our survival is threatened. It can feel like the end of the world. Rejection and deception of this kind isn't like getting fired or failing at a project. It cuts to the very core of who we are, of the fundamental hope that keeps all of us going: that we are lovable and deserve to be cared for, and to live. Getting cheated on can feel like getting kicked out of the nest and left to die in the cold. I know I'm being dramatic, but feeling like this is not melodrama – it's rooted in the realities of the way our brains work.

The hours and days after you discover an infidelity are going to be chaotic.

Before we continue with the rest of this book, it's important to understand exactly what things are happening inside you, and why. How would you react if you were kissing your partner and they suddenly turned into a ferocious tiger in your arms? Well, that's essentially what *did* happen, according to your brain!

What to expect when your heart's been ripped out and stomped on

Forgive the dramatic title, but as you'll see, hyperbole is also part of a normal response! After an infidelity, all of the following are perfectly normal:

- You're totally numb and don't feel anything.
- You're having trouble thinking clearly or sticking to one train of thought.
- You're mad as hell and feel yourself losing your temper all the time.
- You want cold, hard revenge and you've fantasized about getting even.
- You're sadder than you've ever felt. You feel hopeless, and wonder what the point is.
- You feel paranoid – if people can lie about this, what else is a lie?
- You feel humiliated and like you've been made a fool of. You wonder if people are laughing at your expense.
- You're confused. You just can't reconcile how happy everything seemed with this ugly new piece of information. You really don't get it: *why*?
- You're disappointed, and feel a tired, old cynicism creeping in. How could you be so stupid to trust someone?
- You feel like you just want to run away and never deal with any of it.
- You feel kind of relieved.

All of these emotions (even the last one!) are perfectly normal reactions to being cheated on. You might feel completely awful and unable to function some days, and others you can almost forget about your feelings for a while and get on with life like nothing happened. It's also normal to swing wildly from one emotion to another.

What do you do with this hurricane going on in your head?

Well, nothing. That's right, you just let it be. The most important thing to keep reminding yourself of in the early days is that you don't *have to* feel like anything.

Give yourself permission to feel ...whatever it is you feel.

Your partner may be pressuring you to talk immediately, or to forgive, or to explain and tell them what you think, and what you'll do and why. As kindly as possible, ask them to give you time. If you're like most people, you won't be in a state of mind to deal with any of that. Your first task is to take care of yourself and make sure you're processing all your emotions responsibly.

So, what does that look like?

Take care of the physical stuff

Anchor yourself in the routine of your life. You still need to eat, to run errands and to work. You don't need to force yourself to do things you can't, but don't abandon important routines like good eating and getting adequate sleep.

In fact, you might find it very soothing to just "unplug" for a second and immerse in some quiet task, alone. Have a bath, go for a long walk, read a book you like or get your hair done. Communicate to your body and mind: "you are cared for!" Take your vitamins, keep up your exercise routine and try not to do any serious overeating or drinking, no matter how appealing it might seem!

Avoid making any big decisions

Let's go back to our movie guy. After he discovers his cheating wife, he might jump into his car, drive off in a huff and file for divorce the next day. While this is certainly an option, it's usually better to give yourself time to cool off before going nuclear. You may still make the same decision you would have in the heat of the moment, but you'll feel better about things and more in control if you slow down and give yourself time to process.

It's kind of irritating, when you think of it. Here you are, minding your own business, and your partner drops this huge, awkward, ugly thing in your lap. It's like they're saying, "Here, you figure it out!".

They broke things, it seems, and now you get the privilege of fixing them!

The ball is, as they say, in your court. And you might not like that it is. The assumption is always that the cheater is remorseful, and that the person who was deceived is now in a possession to decide whether they'll forgive or not. Even if it's never laid out this way, the fact is that there will be lines drawn separating out "good guy" and "bad guy" in your situation, and as the good guy, you'll be expected to have an opinion, and to act on it first.

If you've followed the advice of the previous chapter, you've given yourself the gift of letting your emotions cool down a bit so that you can handle the situation with more clarity. Whether this takes you a day or a week or even longer, you're stuck with this question: now what?

I'm a firm believer in being positive and expecting the best when it comes to relationships. Really. But with cheating, you need to moderate that positivity with a healthy dose of reality. Cheating is a problem. A big one. In this book, I want to show you that it can transform from being a problem into being an *opportunity*, and a chance for growth and insight and yes, deeper love.

But that transformation doesn't happen by itself!

Infidelity can be the start of something new and genuine and real – but only under the right conditions.

Before you pour yourself into the project of healing after the betrayal and rebuilding that beautiful jigsaw again, you need to be realistic. Below, I'm outlining three key conditions that need to exist in order for a relationship to survive and thrive after an infidelity.

Condition one: the deception is not ongoing

The first condition for healing a relationship is, obviously, that the deceit that caused the trouble has to actually *end*. Healing can only happen once the pain totally and completely stops. Before you climb the mountain of building trust again, you need to actively start at zero again, where there might not be trust, but there are also no fresh infringements, no new lies.

There are many ways that infidelity can be discovered and wrangled with, all the while not *technically* being dealt with properly. For example, your partner could be "drip feeding" you the truth. Let me explain: you discover a damning text to a work colleague and ask them about it. They deny it for a week, then admit that yes, something was going on, but isn't anymore. You're hurt, so you ask if there's anything else. Was it ever physical? How often did it happen? They say, yes it was physical, but just once. And it happened weeks ago. You push for more details. How often were you in contact? They say only once in a while, but they don't mention emails, only face-to-face contact. They don't tell you about the emails because you didn't ask. But you ask them later, and they deny it at first, but finally admit it. You ask, how many emails, and they say, just one, but later you find out...

As you can see, this kind of thing can make you tear your hair out. To their credit, your partner might be so horrified about what will happen when you know the full extent of the betrayal that they believe they're protecting themselves and you by "softening" the truth. So they feed you the information, bit by bit. Actually, from your side, this looks even worse: are they going to lie about every little thing? Do you have to *drag* it out of them?

Everyone's situation is different, but in order to move forward and heal, you'll have to be deadly honest and real with each other. And the first step to this is knowing what actually happened. You don't need to know every sickening detail, but what is important is this: is your partner forthcoming with information?

Really think about it. The person who comes running to you after a single mistake and tells you everything without prompting is different from the person who was "caught" and forced to confess.

The way that your partner talks to you about the infidelity is very telling, so listen:

Is their attitude one of "coming clean", of telling without prompting and of wanting to level with you as soon as possible? This person has deceived you, but the deception is not ongoing. On the other hand, are they "drip feeding" the truth to you, lying by omission, minimizing their actions or giving information only when pushed for it? This person has deceived you, and they are actively in a mindset that is *not* truthful and open, right now. Pay attention.

Condition two: your partner is remorseful

Almost always, the cheater is going to be "sorry". But again, listen carefully to the nature of this apology and what it really means. Where this sorry comes from could spell the difference between moving on in love and pursuing a relationship that is not worth your time and trust.

Remorse means that the person deeply, truly understands that their actions were wrong. They see the consequences of these actions and regret them, feeling bad that they hurt someone they care about. Their actions make them feel ashamed, because deep down, they don't align with their core values. They have a conscience and know that they've behaved in ways they're not proud of. And worst of all, they feel themselves falling in esteem in your eyes, and are sad by this.

Of course, you can be sad and upset and "sorry" without feeling any of the above. You can be sorry, to put it bluntly, that you were caught out. You can see the consequences and hate that they're happening, but you would have been happy to continue making those choices if you could be guaranteed that you'd avoid the consequences. It's the old, "sorry that you got caught, not sorry that you did it" difference ...and it's a big difference! Such a person regrets their actions not because they feel that they're intrinsically wrong, but because they're inconvenienced by the results and wish they could take them back. The discomfort is not in knowing themselves that they've violated some principles, but in that *someone else* is judging them for doing so. If they were never discovered, they'd feel very little remorse, or none at all.

I don't have to tell you which attitude is more likely to have a better outcome in the long run. But how do you know if your partner is truly remorseful?

Step one: follow your gut. You know your partner. It might feel like they're changing before your eyes, but listen to that voice inside anyway.

Step two: pay attention to the object of their remorse. What I mean is, when they speak about feeling bad about their actions, listen to *who* and *what* they're upset about. If the focus is on you, and how they can't stand to have hurt you, that's a better sign than if they focus on how terrible *they* feel for everything that's happened.

Do they speak about all the things they want you to do now, i.e. to forgive you and to let them explain etc. or do they beg you to tell them what they can do to make it better for *you*? To put it simply, is their focus on you and the relationship itself, or are they concerned with their own wants and needs first?

Condition three: your partner is committed to the practical work of earning your trust again

A partner who has cheated and feels no remorse will get impatient and want you to forgive as soon as possible, but only because *they* don't want to have to deal with their negative feelings. To relieve themselves of guilt, they might push you to understand their perspective and to get over it. In fact, you might be shocked to discover that the work seems to be all yours: they have all the fun of destroying your relationship and you have to be the bigger person and graciously forgive!

The three conditions I'm discussing here are not about revenge or taking the moral high ground. They're not about smugly looking down on our partners and enjoying the fact that they are wrong and we are right. But it is about determining your chances of saving your relationship. This is tricky to do since you are probably not feeling trustworthy of them in the least! So the solution is to not rely on what they say alone. Instead, look at what they *do*.

Has your partner *taken active, real, concrete* steps to put your relationship back in focus and start gaining back your trust?

Be careful here; a promise of what they'll do in future is just not the same thing as actually doing something. You won't fully trust them, they might break that promise anyway, and you'll be stuck in a vicious cycle where their word disintegrates in value to nothing.

Hard as it may be, and tempting as it may feel to believe the promises and hold onto *something*, ignore the words. Look at your partner's behavior instead.

If the infidelity has happened at work, for example, have they taken steps to move to another department, or deliberately talk to the other person and tell them in no uncertain terms that there will be no more contact between them? If you've discovered a secret online dating profile, was the profile destroyed instantly, with no further questions? If there's an actual full blow relationship with someone else, has this relationship been 100% terminated?

It seems crazy to think of it, but I know a woman whose husband calmly explained to her that he didn't want to tell his mistress he was married just yet, for fear of upsetting her. This is a clear indication that the person is not seriously committed to making any changes. A cheater should not only feel remorseful and be committed to telling the truth, they should be funneling their energies into their relationship – it's an emergency, after all!

Chat to your partner about whether they'll be getting STI tests, what they plan to do to cut contact with the other people involved, and how exactly they will start making your relationship a priority. If they seem resistant or surprised by these questions, again, pay attention.

A truly remorseful person dedicated to making your relationship work will jump at a concrete suggestion to make things right.

Now even I'll admit that that previous chapter is something of a downer. It's a little grim to begin such a positive book with what looks like an ultimatum, isn't it? But the reason I list those three conditions is not so that you can gloat or feel superior. It's not so that you can put your partner through the ringer.

It's so that you can *save time*.

Because the "ball is in your court", and your partner will be anxious for some kind of resolution (as will you!) you may be pressured into forgiving and moving on. But the truth is that re-building trust takes work from *both* of you. You may want with all your heart to move past this disaster. You may feel angry and hurt but still have a seed deep down that wants to try make things work and move on. That's great!

But in your faint hope and optimism, don't lose sight of the fact that you cannot save your relationship *on your own*. If it heals, it will be because of both of you. This means that if you're bravely committing to learning to trust again, and your partner has no intention of doing the same, you're needlessly exposing yourself to more hurt and disappointment.

You need to determine, right in the beginning, what the cheating really meant, and why it happened.

Some people cheat because they're sad and lonely and stressed. They make a single poor choice and regret it deeply. They see immediately how it's not what they wanted, and the experience leads them deeper into their relationships, making them more aware of what's important. They learn new things about themselves and the people they love, and embrace the challenge of making things better.

But let's be honest, some people cheat because they can. Some people acknowledge the damage it causes, and still choose to deceive those they love, for a quick thrill in the moment.

Your hard work and effort at building up trust will not be wasted with the first kind of person. But it certainly will with the second. So figure out what's what before you decide to commit to the process of healing. As with anything in relationships, commitment from both partners is necessary. Commitment from just one is not a relationship, it's a delusion.

The great thing about infidelity is that it can be the most genuine thing a relationship experiences! I mean that. For some people, it takes the disaster of an affair to finally force them to have the conversation they should have had years ago. Cheating is nasty and unpleasant and destructive ...but it can also have a way of clearing away the crap and bringing the hard truths to light.

Together with your partner, or alone, consider the following questions very, very carefully.

Of course, asking your partner to have a look at these questions and having them resist is an answer in itself. But be curious. Listen without judgment. Your goal is to understand WHY this has happened. Not to punish and judge, but to understand. This understanding will not only give you a better idea of how to move forward, but whether or not you should be moving forward at all.

Just a warning: going through these questions can be grueling. You may dredge up information and feelings that are raw and painful and scary. Take a break if things become too intense. There's only one rule when going through these questions: be *honest*. The only antidote for deception is honesty, and the journey towards healing after infidelity starts with painfully removing the lies, no matter how many there are and how much it hurts to do so.

1. Ask them directly: why do they think they cheated?
2. What did the cheating provide that they couldn't find somewhere else in their lives?
3. Have they cheated before? For the same or different reasons?
4. Were they caught or did they confess?
5. How extensive is the deception, i.e. did this infidelity takes years of daily lies or was it a single event?
6. Was the cheating pre-meditated, or a spur of the moment mistake involving alcohol, for instance?
7. Did your partner lie to you before, even when you asked, "are you cheating?"
8. If you hadn't found out, would they have continued? Did they plan to tell you ever?
9. What is the size of the infidelity? Is it a passing flirtation or is it a full on, long term loving relationship? Is it an inappropriate friendship, just sexual or are there strong feelings involved?
10. Fundamentally, is your partner happy in your relationship?
11. Before you found out, what were the effects of the affair? Was your partner increasingly distant or did they maintain the same old affection for you, not changing towards you at all?
12. What does your partner actually think about the chances of them remaining faithful in future?
13. Does your partner want your relationship to stay the same as it always was?
14. Have they taken steps to remove all the conditions that caused them to cheat in the first place?
15. What have you done to push your partner away? Have you been doing everything you can to maintain intimacy? Have they?
16. Do you *want* to find trust for them again?

Just answering these questions may bring up extra trauma to deal with. Try to have compassion for yourself if you find it difficult, though. Once you've pushed through, you may discover an incredible calm settling in over you. With dishonesty, the world looks black and scary and unknown. But if you can be brave and take a good hard look at what you're dealing with, you can start to make out some shapes in the darkness, and soon, you can clearly see the full dimensions of the problem in front of you.

This can be a huge relief, I promise! And it's the first step to psychologically coming to terms with your new reality. Think of it as picking up all the puzzle pieces and laying them back on the table. You're surveying the damage. You may have lost a few pieces, forever. There may be some new, unwelcome pieces in the mix. But the first step is to look at all of it, with honesty.

Having trouble staying honest? Well, if your partner is unable to share openly and directly, consider this and what it means. Being brutally honest after years of deception may take time, and may hurt like hell at first. But your partner should be *willing to try*. If the willingness is not there, won't your own willingness be wasted?

Give yourself, and your partner, some time to process what you've discussed. Best case scenario, you're both on the same page and you both want to do what it takes to make things work. Worst case is you discover that the cheating was a symptom of a bigger problem, and one that's beginning to look insurmountable. The most likely outcome is that you'll find you're somewhere between these two extremes.

A possible outcome

After you've gone through each of these questions, and had a few honest conversations, it's time to decide what to do about it!

But before we go onto the next chapter and see what this actually looks like, I want to make a point about boundaries. Your partner has violated yours, and you're processing the fallout. This is a delicate, vulnerable time. What you and your partner do now will have ramifications that may last for years to come.

This book is written for those people who are hurt and sad and confused ...*but who want to move past the infidelity.* They want to forgive, they want to be better, and they love their partners enough to try again. This doesn't mean the violation wasn't serious ...it only means that they take their relationship seriously, too, and want to give it a serious try before calling it quits.

But there's nothing wrong with calling it quits. If you've read the first few pages and thought to yourself, "you know what, this sounds like a lot of work and I'm just not interested", then that's your prerogative. You're not less compassionate or progressive or mature if you check out and decide that the boundary violation was one step too far. In fact, there are situations where stepping away early on is the smartest, most compassionate move.

Likewise, people who push through and do the work of bettering their relationships are not in denial, they aren't doormats and they aren't desperate. They've just decided that the potential to make things right outweighs the original violation.

While you're hashing things out with your partner (or deciding whether they're worth hashing out!) try to ignore the advice and judgment of others. People have their own agendas for wanting you to stay or leave a cheating partner. But it's not about them, it's about *you.*

This book is about helping you reach the best possible outcome given the challenge of infidelity. For some people, that best outcome may be dissolving the relationship sooner rather than later. We'll speak later about mindful breakups and how to make sure that you're moving ahead with crystal clear boundaries in future. But the rest of this guide is written with the assumption that you'd like to try and heal your relationship. I'll be assuming a certain optimism on your end. But honestly? Don't be afraid to check out halfway through. Now, and later, you have the option to stop, graceful disentangle and move on. You don't need anyone's permission for that!

CHAPTER 4: WHAT'S YOURS AND WHAT'S THEIRS

In a divorce, you have to start think about what belongs to who. You separate out the things in your house, the debt, the kids, your own emotional baggage. As you pull apart, you both have to remember what it's like to be individual people again. What's "yours" and what's "theirs"?

Moving on after infidelity is kind of the same. Why? Because the relationship you used to have is gone. It's over. In fact, the agreements and understandings you shared with your partner have changed completely – sure, you weren't consulted on this fact, but all the same the state of your relationship is now forever different. Essentially, you've gotten divorced. The only difference is that you're staying together after the divorce.

It may seem weird to think of your "fresh start" this way, but it does capture nicely just how profound the changes you've experienced are.

In your "divorce", you're going to be dividing up the emotional work.

The reasons for doing this will become clear the longer you try to move on after your Ground Zero moment. Let's say your partner cheats, they're broken up with remorse, promises are made, and long awkward chats are had late into the night. You feel cautiously optimistic. You've reached out a little, tentatively. Things are raw, but you're hopeful. You love each other, after all.

Then one day your partner does something mildly irritating and all of a sudden you lash out at them. A few minutes into the fight you're already dredging up the "incident". Your partner feels this isn't fair – how many times do they have to apologize for the same thing? And does their past affair have anything to do with the fact that they keep breaking the dishwasher? You, on the other hand, are incensed that you're getting told off for being angry. You *are* angry. Very angry. Are they really suggesting that you get over things just like that? How convenient for them!

You can see where this kind of thing goes. Who's "right" in this situation? No matter how heartfelt the late-night discussions and no matter how sincere the promises, eventually, a couple in this situation will encounter the hard question: whose stuff is whose?

Getting stuck in blame and resentment is the single surest way to dissolve what little trust you're able to build back up. It's important to decide *who is responsible for what* early on, so that you are not getting pulled into reliving the transgression over and over, never giving your partner the chance to move on.

On your path to healing, life will be made up of all the little things it used to be made of, except now there will be a pall of doubt and tension hanging over it. You get rid of this by deliberately choosing happiness, trust and compassion, instead of dwelling in the past. This is hard, and the subject of our next chapter, but for now, stay mindful enough to ask yourself regularly, "is this mine?"

Your "stuff"

If your first thought is, "I don't have any stuff, all of this is the other guy's fault" then know that you're deliberately engaging with that pall of doubt and tension. When someone hurts you, it's natural to place the blame at the hands of the transgressor. And yes, it is your partner's "fault" that they hurt you. But it is *your responsibility* to heal from that.

This can be a difficult concept to grasp, especially when your idiot partner breaks the dishwasher for the second time that month. They are responsible for hurting you. But you are responsible for how you manage the resulting emotions. Is this fair? No. Not at all. But the brutal fact is that human beings do hurt each other, and your reactions are your own business. Own them.

You'll soon see that demanding that your partner be responsible for soothing you is not only unhealthy – it doesn't even work! You may get suspicious one day about a text or a look or an evening they spend late at the office. Those suspicions are a natural result of the infidelity. Of course you feel that way! But what you choose to do with that is actually nobody's business but yours. If you pester your partner, don't believe their answers and demand they keep providing you "proof", you soon see that they don't have the ability to assuage your doubts anyway. Only *you* do.

At some point, you reach a wall: it's not possible to see into your partner's very soul. It's not possible to trace their every move, to know anything with 100% certainty. At some point, you have to *trust*. Not for them. Not as a reward they earn for repenting, but for YOU, because it feels better to trust and honestly, it's more practical. Living in paranoia is profoundly disempowering and crazy-making.

You're going to be sensitized and doubtful after an infidelity. Your partner has eroded your sense of trust. The world was one way, and then they yanked the carpet out from under you, and now you're wary of taking anything at face value again. And that's normal! But if you want to heal and move on ...eventually, you do have to move on. Eventually you have to disengage your own feelings from their actions.

I know someone whose girlfriend cheated on him. Their relationship went through the grinder, but they stayed together. However, things were never the same. He demanded every password and access to every social media account she owned. He read her mail, kept tabs on her throughout the day and secretly enlisted the help of others to keep an eye on her. He felt that this was a kind of "solution". His girlfriend went along with it, wracked by grief and the feeling that she deserved to be surveyed, and even punished a little. But the result was that more than a year later, they were still in the same doubtful limbo. They eventually did break up. She never cheated again, but it didn't matter – the real damage to the relationship came in the months *after* she cheated.

What went wrong? Well, I think the problem was that they were both unclear of what belonged to whom. He was torn up (of course he was!) but instead of dealing with his own emotions, he made her responsible for them. He conditioned his well-being on her "behaving". Instead of controlling himself, he controlled her. And she, instead of processing her own emotions (guilt, self-hate) she allowed *him* to process them for her by continually punishing her for a crime that was done and dusted. They both never took responsibility for their part in the dynamic, and so blame and resentment abounded. The trust was gone. The infidelity was the catalyst. But what really killed their relationship, I think, was their inability to take responsibility for their own baggage …and refuse to carry the baggage of anyone else!

Sounds great, but how do you determine what's yours and what's theirs anyway?

Start by remembering this: *your emotions, good and bad, are your own.*

Sure, other people's actions affect us. That's kind of the point of this book. But you are an adult, and how you behave in adversity is your responsibility. Nobody can "make" you feel anything. If you feel mistrustful, recognize that you are actively choosing to feed and maintain that feeling in yourself. And that you can just as actively choose to starve out that emotion and nurture a different one.

I know what you're thinking: "but I can't do that! Do you have any idea what he did to me? It's not so easy to forgive, you know!"

I know. It isn't easy. But it is necessary. This is the "work".

Think of this. If you are hurt, and you close your heart, the person who hurt you has taken *two* things from you: they have taken your trust in them, but they've also taken all the trust you would have given in the future. You've also allowed them to rob you of the ability to enjoy and trust others again, forever. Are you happy to take that damage and dwell on it so that it takes over your whole life?

If the hurt has taken its toll, wouldn't you rather minimize that damage? Wouldn't you rather shake it off and get back to being healthy and trusting and open as soon as possible? We sometimes imagine that allowing bitterness and doubt and resentment into our hearts will somehow punish the one who hurt us. It's a spiteful mindset, one in which we unconsciously say, 'fine, I will take my delicate self and hide it away forever, so it can't be hurt again."

But doing this doesn't punish anyone *except us*. They have hurt you. But don't allow them to also take away your natural trust and faith in other people, your curiosity, your willingness to believe that people can be good. *That* is the real damage. And it is a damage that you are complicit in creating.

What is your "stuff"? It's the sum total of your thoughts, feelings, actions and beliefs that together form your mindset. Life is unfair, but this domain is 100% under your control, always.

- Keep events in their rightful place. If you're upset with your partner about something, stick to that *specific* thing. Don't use minor arguments as an arena to fight about big, unsettled resentments.

- Don't make it your partner's problem to soothe you. They can certainly try, but deciding "I'm going to relax and trust now" is only ever up to you. Don't force your partner to produce never-ending "evidence". Don't grill them. They will behave how they behave, and you will feel how you feel. The two are actually not as connected as you think! If you feel awful, ask, "what thoughts am I holding that are perpetuating this awful feeling?" You'll likely find that the source of your discomfort is inside you, and not in something your partner is currently doing wrong.

- Own your needs and voice them assertively. You'll feel raw that your needs weren't met *in the past*. But the past is over. Have respect for your partner and express your needs, in the moment. Are you feeling sad and lonely and just want some affection?

Don't get angry at your partner for not reading your mind and pre-empting your needs. Just ask!

- Forget about "closure". You may be tempted to ask for gruesome details of the infidelity or ask your partner awkward questions that you won't like the answer to. You'll convince yourself that doing this is cathartic somehow. What's probably happening, though, is that you're traumatized. A common symptom of PTSD is "re-experiencing", which means the brain wants to keep returning to the traumatic moment in a desperate bid to "make sense" of what happened. You feel that if you can just understand, just know all the nasty details, then you'll have control somehow. But let it go. Your healing lies in front of you, not behind.

Their "stuff"

Well, all of that's great and all, but what about them? Aren't they responsible for *anything*?

Here's something to hold onto when you feel yourself slipping into anger and resentment over your partner's bad behavior: it's not your stuff, it's theirs. You don't have control over what they think, how they act, or what they say. None whatsoever. You can love and trust them, you can express your needs and limits, but at the end of the day, what they choose to do is 100% their stuff ...just like yours is yours!

What stuff are they responsible for? Exactly how much are they to blame?

Well, does it matter?

Revenge and judgment can feel good. For a while. But they never lead to true healing. You might be thinking that what I'm explaining here is foolish. That if you completely stop trying to control your partner, if you give them your trust and forgive them, that you've somehow made it more likely that they'll hurt you again.

But here's the truth (and this truth may be liberating or horrifying, depending on your mindset!): *nothing that you do has any effect on whether they hurt you or not.* Really. You were not in control of them before, and you are not in control now. You may have *felt* like you were in control, before they cheated, but that was not because of something they were doing, it was because of something *you* were doing. They are no more or less trustworthy now, only your mindset towards them has changed. If someone wants to cheat on you, they will. Being extra vigilant or being caring and trusting will make no difference to whether they ultimately do it. Why? Because it's their decision, not yours.

But, being trusting will *feel* much better for you. So if it doesn't matter what you do, why not choose to do the thing that makes you happy?

If you're thinking, "because then they'll cheat on me and then I'll be the idiot who let themselves get hurt", well, here's where your boundaries come in. You don't need to be angry and spiteful to have a boundary. You can be open, trusting and light in your spirit right up until someone violates that boundary. And then, since you are in charge, you can terminate your connection. Not in anger to the violator, but in love to yourself.

You are warranted in "checking up" on your partner here and there, especially if trust has been broken. But don't torture yourself. Determine if your boundaries are being respected. Express your needs. Be kind, in the moment. *That* is your business. They can cheat on you again, sure. They can throw away your trust and act against their principles and yours. But that is *their* business.

CHAPTER 5: COMMITTING AFTER YOUR TRUST IS GONE

Healing after infidelity is a bit of a Catch-22: The only way you can heal after cheating is to *commit* to forgiving, to give everyone the chance to tell a different story and do something else. But this is precisely what you don't feel like doing!

You can't trust your partner again because they broke your trust the last time they had it.

Now what?

Trust is something that builds on itself. You give a little, it works out well, you give a little more. You open up a little, your partner respects and cares for you, you open up a little more. You give, they give, you give again. Soon, you have a history and a relationship that is predictable and secure.

When your partner cheated, they smashed all your saved progress to bits. Now, to build back up again, you need that first, crucial bit of trust. The bit of trust that will allow you trust a little bit more next time, and then a little more. But someone has to "go first". Who's it going to be?

Maybe you can guess, but I'm going to say that the answer is *you*. You have to go first. More than likely, your partner still trusts you. You didn't damage their trust, and so it's still there. But now it's asymmetrical. Your trust in them is at a big fat zero. And it's "your stuff" to place that first piece down so that trust can be built up slowly again.

You may start looking for a reason to pay them that trust. We talk of trust as something people "earn". And that's true. Trust is not handed out willy-nilly, free for anyone. That's what makes it valuable. So maybe you think, has my partner apologized enough yet? Has my anger and hurt diminished enough? Have they earned me taking that first step yet?

I would like to suggest that this first piece of the trust mountain is different from the others. This first piece is not earned. It's just given. It's just an act of faith, something you give and hold thumbs that you made a good choice and that the person you gave it to will return the favor.

If you are waiting for your partner to prove themselves to you, it might work, it might not. You might wait a very long time! Whether it works or not, asking your partner to take the first step is putting yourself in a reactive frame of mind, rather than a proactive one. It might not feel like it's fair for you to take a risk and trust again since they're the bad guys, and they broke everything in the first place. But this is life. This is the grace of healing. And it can be an incredible gift – not to the cheater, but to *yourself*!

Now, I'm not a fool and I'm not asking you to be romantically and stupidly trusting right after your trust has been broken. But what I am suggesting is that you are *selectively* compassionate. Your attitude to someone who has hurt you will be different – and it should be! So here is my suggested compromise. Think of this as a way to protect your heart without shutting it down:

Give 100% of yourself, and trust completely. But do so *intermittently*.

If you don't feel 100% trusting of your partner in the moment, then don't trust. Easy. Don't close your heart, just don't open it to them, for now. Don't linger in that space, though. You don't achieve anything by being partly forgiving, partly compassionate, half in and half out. Commit to trusting when you feel strong and able. Be with your partner, in the present moment. Choose to love and trust and be vulnerable and all that other good stuff.

And when you don't, don't. Your trust "tank" is not as full as it was before. You're on emergency stores. But instead of running the tap on a low trickle, eking out what little goodwill you can for your partner, open it fully and completely. Let it flow. Immerse yourself completely and utterly in the moment and *trust*. If you can only do that for short periods, great. You gain nothing by half measures.

The reason for doing this is that it saves you from growing a new relationship built on impartial trust. You take the leap of faith and "go first". Instead of feeding your doubts, you give yourself the chance to learn what it's like to live without them. And something special happens: during those authentic, trusting and open moments with your partner, they get to put down fresh trust pieces, building up that mountain again. When you're begrudgingly giving trust little by little, your partner can only build little by little too. Stinginess of spirit begets more stinginess of spirit.

So, set the pace. Invite your partner to be kind and open with you again, and trust that they can rise to the challenge. You are not signing away your life or asking to be a doormat. You're just making that first move. It's not forgiveness yet, but it's opening a space where you can forgive. There is no need to martyr yourself. Make your move and then step back and wait for your partner to meet you there.

CHAPTER 6: CAN YOU PREVENT INFIDELITY FROM HAPPENING AGAIN?

I think I can imagine what went through your mind as you read the previous chapter.

Maybe it *seems* so sweet and nice, just to trust again. But maybe you read something like that and all you can think about was being hurt again, or the sinking paranoia that your partner no longer loves you, that there can never be those same feelings of comfort between you ever again.

I get that.

When you try to put back those little jigsaw pieces, you may be wincing, wondering if your partner is about to jump in and ruin it all again. Try to remember, though, that you give trust for yourself, and because it feels good to give it. You can't force yourself. You can only let go. Picture it not as something unpleasant you have to endure, but a deliberate reorienting: you loved your partner once before, and you trusted once before. It's just a matter of finding that again.

It's risky, though. And it's risky for a very good reason: you may be deceived, *again*.

Your partner may well feel like they got off easy, that they can take your trust and forgiveness for granted. They may simply cheat again.

But even here, acting in compassion and self-awareness will never lead you astray. Here's why: if your partner does cheat again, then you are in the supremely easy position of knowing with 100% certainty that you can leave. Ending a relationship can be nerve-wracking because you're not sure if it's worth saving, how much is your own fault, what can be forgiven and blah blah blah. But if this happens? It's kind of a blessing. Your partner has told you clear and plain as day that there is nothing left for you to pursue with them, and you can leave with an open heart and a clear conscience. *That* is why you give them a "second chance".

Remember, you can only control your business. If people don't respect your boundaries, it's your business to reinforce those boundaries by following through with consequences. Love freely and openly, but if your boundaries are violated – repeatedly! – then relax and know that there's nothing more you can do but remove yourself from that situation. In a way, it's the cleanest, easiest outcome. There's nothing to really think about. It might hurt like hell, yes, but letting go of someone's disrespect for you can be a surprising relief.

When you're in the process of healing and building up trust again, make some boundaries for yourself. And make sure that both you and your partner know exactly what it means when those boundaries are broken. Not everyone deserves your trust. Some people cheat over and over because they have an unconscious belief that commitment = loss of freedom. Some cheat because their self-esteem is low and they crave validation and attention. Some cheat because they are addicted to sex or thrill-seeking. Some cheat because they lack the maturity to pursue the things they want, and would rather relationships blow up than decisively end them themselves.

In any case, it's not your business *why* someone would choose to keep on deceiving you. You only need to acknowledge that they have, and that you won't let it happen again. If you start building the puzzle again with your partner, and they break it, again, then leave. Break all contact and move far, far away from that person. You will only damage yourself (and them!) by staying.

So, onto the question of this chapter: can you prevent infidelity from happening again?

This question is actually fear in disguise. It's asking, if I close my heart up in the right ways, will I be able to prevent someone from hurting me again?"

It's the wrong question. The answer to this question is easy: no. You can never change how people choose to live *their* lives. There is no trick or magic talisman that will protect you from that, ever.

But you can live your life the best way you know how. You can make healthy choices for yourself. You can set up boundaries, defend them and gravitate towards people who respect and cherish you. And then, so what if anyone cheats on you? Feel sorry for them – it's a whole separate hell to live life as a deceitful person. And they lose the trust of someone great: you!

Many of us feel that if we're slow to trust again, we can inoculate ourselves from getting hurt in the future. But this approach has its drawbacks. Getting really close to someone means allowing a degree of vulnerability. Close yourself up and you'll protect yourself from pain ...but you'll also numb yourself to all the good things, too.

You don't have to do anything special to make sure people don't hurt you. You don't need to build walls or try desperately to be better so that people will not be tempted to abandon you. The best way to mitigate the pain of relying on other people is not to pretend you don't need to rely on them, it's to say "to hell with it", and to love deeply, even though it might hurt.

Don't allow your partner's (or ex-partner's) bad decisions to warp your life. I'm talking about developing a nasty dislike for the opposite sex, or becoming cynical or shutting yourself off from any romantic engagement. As long as there are people, they will hurt one another. But so what? The cost is worth it.

If you're prone to landing up in abusive or manipulative situations, or you keep being drawn to people who (for whatever reason) don't want to commit fully to you, now's the time to do your homework and make sure you're going out into the world in "good working order", single or not:

- Take an honest look at your relationship history and the patterns there. Have you pursued people who have directly or indirectly told you that they will not prioritize your feelings or their relationship with you? Many women who are repeatedly cheated on unconsciously choose men they know will reject them, simply because this fits in with their view of themselves. If you feel like you've been begging to be someone's "number one" since you were a little girl, look closely at the ways you may be seeking out that same dynamic now. You may just need practice in what it feels like to be respected and cherished!

- Nobody deserves to be lied to. But many people cheat because their partners have shut them down, taken them for granted or denied them sex and affection for years. Ask yourself honestly if you have been nurturing your partner and making them feel cared for and wanted. Do you actively maintain the relationship or just assume it'll run on its own?

- People who cheat do not, in most cases, see their partners as *primary*. Ask yourself why this is. Try to understand your own needs and wants when it comes to commitment. Have you asked for what you need? Have you carried yourself in a way that communicates the respect you have for yourself? Many of us go into relationships just assuming that both people are on the same page when it comes to what counts as cheating, but is there a *spirit of commitment* running through your relationship? Or are you in a limbo, waiting for something? Infidelity can sometimes have the surprising result of revealing how differently people actually think of "commitment". The next relationship you're in (including version 2.0 of your old relationship!) be clear about what you expect and why.

So ...what about non-monogamy?

No book about infidelity would be complete without a consideration of monogamy, right? Well, maybe. I want to say, though, that commitment has nothing to do with the number of people in a relationship. Polyamorous people or those in open or non-monogamous relationships will emphatically say that their relationship model is *not* about infidelity. That what they do isn't "commitment-lite" or glorified cheating. In fact, commitment, honesty and responsibility are just as important in these kinds of arrangements as ever. Maybe even more so.

If you've had the thought that maybe you should "downgrade" your cheating relationship to an open one, since its already technically open, think again! Those with experience will tell you that polyamorous setups almost always fail when they begin with deception. And why wouldn't they? If you couldn't trust your partner with one set of rules and expectations, why would it work with a different set?

Of course, it's a legitimate wonder. Your partner may have cheated because deep down, they crave the affection and love of more than one person, and this has nothing to do with how much they love *you*. This is more common than you think. People are perfectly capable of forming deep, meaningful attachments to more than one person at a time.

But there is a mature and compassionate way to deal with these feelings. Many people are open and honest with their partners. They share their desires thoughtfully, and discuss them in a trusting context. And there is nothing to say that two loving, thoughtful people can't transition from a monogamous to a non-monogamous relationship. It happens all the time!

The problem is the *deception*. Whether a person identifies with the philosophy of non-monogamy or not is almost beside the point: if they've been lying to their partners, that's the most salient feature of their relationship. And cheating and lying are no easier or more natural in a non-monogamous setup.

So, will switching to an open relationship redeem your cheating partner? It's highly unlikely. If this is the way that your conversations are going, well, great. But the fact remains: the hard work of healing your connection isn't going anywhere.

You have to do that work.

Bringing other people into your relationship is a privilege for those who have already earned deep trust and security with one another. If you've just cheated, your relationship is nowhere near ready for that, and so it's kind of pointless to wonder whether that relationship model is right for you.

Heal the trust you have with your partner first. Build it up again. *Then* you can decide on the varsity-level relationship stuff.

A man goes out with friends to a bachelor's party. They're all at the groom's house, people are drinking, things are slowly getting raucous.

Then the strippers arrive.

This is a surprise to some of the guests, who were promised a "tame" evening. Uncomfortable, they leave soon after. Our man, however, stays. His girlfriend texts him a message to say she hopes he's having fun. He sees the message, and thinks about responding.

But he doesn't.

Naturally, things get more and more out of hand. Our man sees that 1am rolls around, and remembers that he told his girlfriend to expect him home at midnight. He's quite drunk, though, and thinks, what the hell. He's already there, he's not *technically* doing anything wrong.

When one of the strippers turns her focus to him and starts touching him, he feels a little guilty. But, this *is* a bachelor's party, after all. He never asked for her to do that. More guests leave, going back home to wives, girlfriends or families.

Our man does not.

Eventually, the stripper goes even further.

The next morning, his girlfriend is understandably livid. Someone's put a very embarrassing picture on Facebook of our man and the stripper, and she is beyond hurt. Our man feels awful. He is sorry. "It was a mistake" he tells her. He had too much to drink, he was just there supporting his buddy, it was a bachelor's party, after all, that's just the kind of thing that happens, it meant nothing. It was an *accident*.

Now consider another man. He dates a woman for three years, and they break up because they both move to different cities. They lose touch but eventually, by some twist of fate, they end up working at the same company. Both of them are married now, but they strike up a friendship again.

One day it's a Christmas year-end party at the office and the woman is emotional, confessing to the man that she missed him terribly all these years, that she wished they had never broken up, that she might even still love him. In the heat of the moment, they kiss.

Both are wracked with guilt and cut contact immediately. Our second man goes home, confesses to his wife and tries to explain what happened. It wasn't what he intended. He loves her a lot and they were just caught up in the moment, nostalgic, a little carried away with things. It was a mistake. It was an accident.

Now, which of these cheating stories is "worse"?

Is man 1 or man 2 the more deceptive? On the surface, maybe you're tempted to say the first guy is just a bit of a moron. He got drunk, he didn't mean it to happen ...and it was a bachelor's party, after all. Looks like an innocent mistake, even if he was kind of an ass about it. Maybe you think that the second scenario sounds scarier. Here, the two in question loved each other. It just seems more serious. They're both married!

The best way to understand all the millions of ways that people can bend and test the "technical" rules of what counts as cheating and what doesn't, is to look at the intention behind the behavior. Though Man 1 claims he made an accident, in truth, he made several perfectly conscious decisions to harm his relationship with his girlfriend well before there was a stripper grinding in his lap.

He chose to ignore her texts. He chose to stay when he saw things getting heated. He chose to drink, chose to stay out later than he said he would, and chose not to mention the incident when he got home. None of this was an accident. These were actions taken that reveal an attitude of disrespect. It's the behavior of someone who hasn't prioritized his partner. To say "it's a stag party, that's just what happens" is to shirk responsibility.

If your partner has repeatedly chosen to put themselves in a situation where cheating is likely, well, don't let those choices go unnoticed. People who follow the letter of the law in their relationships have already been unfaithful in spirit. They are already looking for ways to act without consequences. The "accident" may just be the natural fulfilment of what they really want, deep down. Who knows what tempting little situations that person might repeatedly find themselves in later on?

Beware of "accidents" that happen over and over again. We are all human and having some compassion for your partner is always a good idea. We all can succumb to the attention of someone else, to the lure of a different life, of something forbidden and new and even a little dangerous. But once you make a decision in that direction, *and then keep going*, then you are no longer making a mistake. You are making poor decisions.

Cheating can be a moment of carelessness and weakness. Or it can be a manifestation of a deeper problem.

Man number 2 shouldn't have kissed his ex. But he has more right to call it an accident. Once both of them realized the line they had crossed, the situation was shut down and the other spouses were informed. It's not natural to expect that people magically stop having feelings for others the second they say "I do". "Slip ups" like this are not only likely, they're actually pretty common. But if handled correctly, they can strengthen a commitment. Both partners can see evidence of one another choosing, in each passing moment, to devote their energies to the relationship that matters, to prioritize it, and to defend it.

If your cheating story has an "accident" flavor to it, look closely and see what this actually means. Look at the *intention* behind the choices, as poor as they may be. Look at what leads up to accidents. Sometimes, negligence is worse than malice. If your partner's defense was that they "weren't thinking", ask yourself if you're happy to have your feelings so unvalued that they don't even register when you're not there to speak up.

I like to think that people, on the whole, are good. When people hurt others, most do so out of their own weakness, and when you can be kind to them, they can learn to be better. I'm a big believer in compassion. It's human to lust after others, to wonder what life would be like if you chose boy B rather boy A, to wish for a little thrill once in a while or feel the rush of being noticed by someone new.

But it's also human to want to push through those momentary distractions and remember to act according to what's *really* important at the end of the day. It's also human to want to be better than passing temptations and to commit to something bigger.

Hurting one another is par for the course. But if you are going to be compassionate with someone, look for evidence that there is a matching compassion in them, too.

If it seems like we've spent ages on the previous sections, it's only because *laying the groundwork* is so important in healing from infidelity.

When your partner cheats, you're not having a problem with your relationship, rather, your entire relationship is the problem! It might seem overly-dramatic, but infidelity eats away at the most fundamental layers of a partnership. To undo the damage, you need to get right in at the root of things.

The following exercises should only be attempted once you've determined that you are both willing to do the work it takes to start building again. If you are brimming over with resentment and lauding your "second chance" over them as a form of punishment, you won't heal. If your partner is squirming away from taking responsibility and unwilling to make changes going forward, then they won't heal, either.

But if you're both courageous enough to start with a commitment to something new, these exercises can bring some order to the chaos.

Exercise one: dates with the present moment

There are going to be a few tearful and awkward conversations along the way. But that doesn't mean your whole life must become one big tearful and awkward conversation! Give yourself and your partner the chance to actually enjoy one another again, to build up a relationship that isn't defined by this awful, ground zero moment. You'll be upset, possibly for a long time, but for this exercise, put that aside just for one evening, and go on a "date with the present moment".

Do something fun with your partner. But the trick is to *not bring up the past in any way, shape or form.* Not even to reminisce or remember something good. Just be in the moment, forget about the infidelity for a second and enjoy the moment. Flirt a little, enjoy the activity at hand and try to see your partner, as they are, in front of you. Of course, you don't have to pretend that your anger and hurt and doubt don't exist anymore. But "shelve" those feelings and come back to them later. For now, just relax and enjoy.

Exercise two: create "checkpoints"

As the partner who's been deceived, you might feel the burning need to check that your partner is not still deceiving you. You might demand to see their text histories or follow them to make sure they're going where they say they go. I can promise you, these feelings are normal, but acting on them will *not* make you feel better.

You'll make your partner feel like a scolded child and you'll only reinforce your mistrust of them. And worse, if you discover that everything's fine, deep down you'll only start to wonder if they're behaving themselves simply because they know they're being watched! If you don't want a Cold War style atmosphere in your home, don't do this, to yourself or your partner.

Instead of spying on your partner or looking for "evidence", set up your lifestyle with "checkpoints" that will help soothe your doubts but won't establish a parent/child dynamic with your partner. This could be daily rituals like texts when they leave or arrive at a place, or a commitment to meeting at the same place and time every afternoon for coffee. Pick checkpoints together. They don't have to be big things, just little spots in both of your schedules where you can reach out, touch base and confirm, "yes, I'm here, everything's fine."

This gives your partner many small opportunities to be on time, to show that they're present and paying attention. These little "mini commitments" accumulate. You may even decide to keep things more open ended and tell your partner that while things heal, you need them to reach out and arrange a special meeting each and every week with you. Don't nag, don't bully, just let them know that doing so will soothe you and help you build up trust. Then wait. Give your partner the chance to show you, over and over again, that they "choose" you, that they're present and focused on you.

Whatever your checkpoints are, though, make them voluntary. You don't build up any trust by forcing your partner to confess, badgering them for details about their day, spying on them etc. You build up trust when you create opportunities for them to take care of you, and see that they choose to do that, of their own will.

Exercise three: have "give and take" jars

As we've seen, moving on after infidelity can be hard because the past and all the doubts it stirs up can taint the present, no matter how good it is. No matter how many sincere promises are made, no matter how many new leaves have been turned over, the ghost of the past lingers. This exercise is all about making sure those fears and resentments don't get the chance to get out hand.

It's normal for you to feel a range of emotions. Eventually, you *will* hurt less, and you *will* move on. But what to do in the meantime, when your partner is trying to make amends but all you want to do is tear their head off?

Here's a little way to process those horrible emotions as they bubble up, and deal with them before they have a chance to build up and undo all the hard work you've made to reconnect with your partner. Have two jars. One for you and one for your partner. Use beans, coins or other small pieces to represent trust, comfort and feelings of safety. When you begin this exercise, have your jar empty, and theirs full. This is a visual reminder: your trust will have to be earned, piece by piece, and it has to come *from them*.

Now, as the week goes on, you can move beans from your partner's jar into your own. Every time you feel that they've acted in a way that makes you feel loved, secure and happy, move a bean (or many beans) from their jar over to your jar. When they behave in ways that undermine your trust and have you feeling doubtful, move those beans back into their jar.

This is a great exercise because it captures very simply the process of give and take that you'll both have to commit to. Your partner will see that they have to do more than one or two grand gestures to win back your trust. And they will see that that trust gained is not permanent either, and can be lost at any time. The jars show us that trust is not usually a black and white thing. It comes in degrees. If you have a big store of trust earned, a few slip ups are not going to be so bad. But if you have no more beans left in the jar, a slip up suddenly becomes a very big deal indeed.

This is also a good exercise because it spares you from having endless conversations about how everyone is doing. It communicates directly what can be hard to put in words. It gives the cheating partner concrete feedback about how to win back your trust, and it gives you a sense of control and the feeling that you're expressing yourself and being heard. Keep the jars up for as long as you need.

Exercise four: sharing needs

If your partner is like most people, they probably cheated for (what they think is) a very good reason. If you've done the work of discussing this and taking responsibility where you need to, you already know the reason why. It might not be something you're happy to think about, but this exercise takes the spotlight off of you and asks: how is your partner? Are they getting their needs met?

Try this exercise last, after you've built up at least a small store of goodwill towards them again. Sit down with your partner. Both of you will write down, on a piece of paper, ten of your relationship needs. These are the things that you both require to feel happy, safe and fulfilled in a relationship. Choose a mix of non-negotiable, serious ones plus some that are nice to have, but not absolutely necessary all the time.

Now, exchange lists. You each can choose three things off the list that you will commit to making a reality for your partner. If they've written, "I need sex at least 3 times a week" and you choose that one, you will commit to having sex with them 3 times a week. If it feels difficult to do something new, remember that they are doing the same for you, and they are working hard to learn to do what *you* need and want to be happy.

You'll probably start with the easy ones, but don't stop there. Once you're comfortable with any changes you've made, come right back to the list. Can you commit to bringing any more to life? Some you may already be doing, but not quite enough. Ask your partner for specific details (for example, "do more around the house" might translate to doing the laundry once a week) and then get to work. While it's not a transaction, the idea is that you *both* commit to making the other one happy.

When one partner cheats, it's easy to get stuck in a "forgiveness loop" where one partner is eternally repentant and the other is sitting on a throne, pondering whether to forgive or not. But this ignores the other partner's needs. Worryingly, it ignores those needs that might have propelled them to cheat in the first place.

Just because your partner has cheated, doesn't mean they don't get to have demands on you anymore. Just because you are trying to forgive a hurt, doesn't mean that they don't have their own hurts. You will need extra care and attention as they build up your trust again, but you are never exempt from taking care of them and their needs.

Exercise five: a forgiveness meditation

"Forgiveness" is overrated. You don't forgive a mosquito when it bites you, because it means to bite you, and it wants to, and if it can it will bite you again. You simply accept that mosquitos bite and take the right measures to make sure you're protected. We live in a world that doesn't do much to distinguish between "justice" and "revenge". We think of forgiveness as a gift we give to perpetrators, something that makes us a gracious "bigger person".

This kind of forgiveness is really just about ego and power play. I think it's far better to *accept and be compassionate* than it is to forgive. You don't need to "forgive' a mosquito because it's just being what it is! Here, when I say "acceptance" I mean the ability to really see people, for what they are and not what you wish they were. It's the ability to acknowledge imperfection and the fact that as humans, we are all on our own paths, all struggling, all learning. It's not wiping the slate clean or writing off a debt. It's just seeing people, all the bad included. Mosquitos bite. Humans hurt one another.

Here's an exercise that you can do alone, any time you feel your compassion for your partner running low. Simply sit or lie somewhere quiet where you won't be disturbed. Close your eyes and focus on your breathing; take a moment to pay attention to your body, the environment, your thoughts and feelings.

Now, picture your partner in front of you. Spend plenty of time really imagining every aspect of them. Remember their faces, their voices, their mannerisms. Try to see their *whole* person. Picture them as children, and all their little passions and disappointments. Picture their fears and hopes and dreams. See them achieving things, and failing at things. See them at their best and worst. See all of it. Can you feel a deep sense of appreciation for this person in front of you, and everything that they are? Can you feel love and compassion and understanding for this person? They are just like you! Mostly good, learning all the time, imperfect, human.

Now also picture yourself in their life. See them falling in love with you. See them together with you, two imperfect people who nevertheless love one another. See them enjoying life with you. See them cheating on you. It will hurt to think of this last part. But can you extend your love and compassion still, even to contain the fact that your partner has hurt you? Can you see that even though they have hurt you, that they are still people who deserve compassion and understanding?

Imagine that your partner's choices and behaviors are sitting off to the side, connected to them but not part of them. Can you look at their actions for all they are, while still loving your partner? Can you commit to and love *them*, if not their actions?

Imagine seeing potential futures unfolding for this person in front of you. See how they can grow and become better. See yourself in that picture, and how good it feels to be kind to another person. Forgive yourself and how you're not perfect either. Feel that compassion is endless, and that transgressions are only temporary.

In your heart and mind, try to *accept*.

CONCLUSION

For many relationships, infidelity is the kiss of death.

Depending on the details, willfully deceiving the person you claim to love is a crossed line that is difficult to uncross again. There is no point sugar-coating it: a relationship where one person cheats is one that is in serious crisis, and to heal it again is no easy feat.

But it *can* be done.

My hope with this book is that after the chaos and disruption of infidelity, you're able to stop, gather yourself and move forward with clarity and compassion.

With effort and a true commitment to do what it takes to rebuild a damaged relationship, it is more than possible to turn a relationship built on deceit into one built on trust. In fact, it's possible for the lowest point in your relationship to spur on changes that make it stronger and more authentic than ever before.

No two people are the same, and neither are any two relationships. Cheating is complex and upsetting. There are no shortcuts to finding your own unique way out of the pain and mistrust that comes with infidelity. But one thing is for sure: if it can be done, it will only happen with compassion and self-awareness.

And more importantly, it will happen *with* your partner.

RETHINKING BUDGETING - HOW TO ESCAPE THE
POVERTY MINDSET AND CREATE A LIFESTYLE THAT
WORKS FOR YOU

"We cannot solve our problems with the same thinking we used when we created them."
~ Albert Einstein

This is *not* a book about money. It's a book about *thinking* about money.

In it, you won't find a few quick ways to save a hundred bucks this month or how to cheat the system here and there to save on your utility bills. But what you might find is a new way to think about yourself, the money you make and how it all fits into your broader worldview.

This book in particular was written for those of us who might not have grown up with the right financial role models, or who have ingrained habits that are holding us back. This book is for those of us who grew up poor.

There is a famous Broadway musical currently running that has a lead actress who comes from a severely impoverished Ugandan village. In one scene, she belts out an emotional ballad about how she hopes and dreams about moving to America one day. In her song, she dreams big: imagining that this glorious new city she could live in would have all the vitamin injections you could ever want, warlords who were kind to you and an endless supply of flour at the corner shop.

The song is really funny because the audience knows what she doesn't: that she isn't even able to *think* about something outside her realm of experience. She can't see outside of her mindset. Even her wildest dreams are just a slight variation of her current reality!

Why am I mentioning this? Because so much budget and personal finance advice out there is about solving problems *using the same thinking that created them*. In essence, it's just about being more efficient at keeping yourself stuck in the same old mindset and repeating the same old mistakes. Not about how to actually break away from those mindsets, or learning why exactly you make the mistakes you do.

This is why I won't be making suggestions about how to dilute your fabric softener to save money or how to shop around for interest rates. For the curious, that information is easily available, usually for free.

Instead, this book tries to go a little deeper.

It starts with a fact that many personal finance guides out there avoid like the plague: that we are *not* all created equal, we *aren't* all coming from the same place and we're *not* all blessed with a basic, neutral understanding of what money is and how to use it. In fact, most people stay poor not because they don't know to dilute their fabric softener or get the best interest rates. It's because they're *thinking* poor. And they don't know how to think in any other way.

Of course, I'm not suggesting that generations of institutionalized poverty comes down to nothing more than attitude. Certainly, people who've never had the opportunity to develop a different mindset are at a disadvantage. But what I *am* saying is that if you identify as having grown up poor, the only way "out" is to change your mindset. It's beyond this book to explain why you have that mindset to start with, and in most cases, it's nobody's "fault".

Nevertheless, we are all equal in one fundamental way: at every point, no matter who we are or what we've endured in the past, we can make conscious, beneficial decisions for ourselves. No matter what, we can act now in ways that will make tomorrow better than it was today. No matter how broke we are now or how much we've struggled, there's nothing to stop us from stopping, taking control, and *thinking* our way into a different lifestyle, one choice at a time.

That's what I hope to show you in the chapters that follow.

CHAPTER 1: WHY MOST BUDGETING ADVICE IS JUNK

I'll never forget the first time I set out to take charge of my own financial life.

I had gotten the idea that drawing up a budget was a good thing that I needed to do. I purchased a book that was popular the time and which promised to teach me all the useful personal finance skills I had never been taught by my parents …who were frankly horrible with money.

Here's the part where I tell you how poor I grew up. And I did. I'm better off now, but I grew up, like so many other people, barely scraping by. My family lived hand to mouth, we frequently had to do without and money was a constant source of stress and irritation in our home. My parents didn't sort out their retirement properly, we were often in awful debt, and although everyone worked their butts off, we never really seemed to get anywhere. Tale as old as time, right?

But I had just landed my first job, and I decided I wanted to be better than that, and I was going to start with a budget. Very soon, though, it dawned on me: what I was reading wasn't written *for me*. I nearly laughed out loud at the "examples" in this book, the authors giving estimates for stringent household spending that would have felt like Christmas to my family. The authors spoke of financial terms and concepts I had no idea about. I soon felt like a massive loser. Too poor even to budget properly! It hurt.

I read other books subsequently and found the same thing: sanitized, euphemistic talk about money that just didn't seem to belong in my world at all. I realized what was missing from all these books: they all seemed to pretend that social class didn't really exist. That in the modern world, we were all starting from the same point, all comfortably middle class and all sharing the same financial problems.

As I grew up I accumulated the knowledge of all the standard budgeting advice. But it never seemed to sink in. Why? Because *my mindset was still poor*. Because I had learnt behaviors and attitudes during my childhood that I hadn't actually shaken yet. The advice books I read conveniently skipped over any of this awkward talk, and so I never got the opportunity to ask myself seriously: how did growing up poor affect my personal finance skills? How was my mindset different from those around me, and those who grew up more comfortably?

Once I asked this question, stuff started to make more sense for me. I soon realized that what was keeping me from making sound financial choices wasn't that I didn't know all the tricks and tips on saving, or how to do my tax or invest wisely. What was keeping me from living the lifestyle I wanted was my *thoughts*. I realized that I differed in the way I thought about things when compared to wealthier people.

I needed to change my habits, and to do that, I needed to change the mindset I held when it came to money. That is what this book is all about. Most budgeting advice is junk because it doesn't take into account that we *aren't* all starting from the same point. In fact, many of us enter into our adult lives with mindsets that almost guarantee we'll stay where we are, making the same mistakes over and over again. The same mistakes our parents made.

In the chapters that follow, I'd like to suggest a way to get to the root of the mindset that may be holding you back, no matter how much well-intentioned advice you follow.

CHAPTER 2: THE CYCLE YOU NEVER KNEW YOU WERE TRAPPED IN

Growing up poor can change the way you think about life.

Your parents teach you many things, but you were too young at the time to actively notice it. So, you adopted their version of reality as reality itself and even if you did start to question it, it was well after these associations and beliefs were cemented in your mind.

You may have the belief that you need to lie and be greedy and unethical to succeed in life (did you see your parents denigrate and mock people wealthier than them?). You may believe that people "like you" simply don't ever succeed – or that you do but within very defined limits. You learnt from those around you what to expect from the world, how to behave, what to do in the face of failure, how large your dreams were allowed to be and what it meant to be "rich" or "poor".

The thing is, everything that you learnt is *not* reality – just one version of it.

You know who didn't receive that same version? People who don't share your socioeconomic bracket. People think that the only difference between rich and poor is that wealthier people can afford more things, but this isn't all they can afford. They can afford different *ideas*. They teach their children to expect a lot, to work hard, to automatically assume that something can be done rather than the opposite. We'll get into this idea a little later in the book.

"Poor": An Expanded Definition

But what does it actually mean to be poor, anyway?

I've just been throwing the word around and assuming you know exactly what I'm talking about. But what makes someone "poor" and someone else "rich"?

Every once in a while a politician or public finger finds themselves in the media when people discover just how much their house is worth, how much money they take home every year, or what disgusting amount their wives have spent on designer handbags. The politician jumps in and defends himself: he's *middle class*, you guys. He might even say he grew up poor. He's not rich at all, in fact, after he pays all his staff and employees, he actually has very little left over...

Every once in a while you also read about lifestyles or quality of life in other countries, and are shocked to find out just how little others have, even though they might protest and explain that they are, in fact, quite wealthy. They're *middles class*, they tell you, they have everything they need...

Looking at all of this it's easy to conclude two things: first, that "middle class" is a limbo land and can mean whatever you want it to mean, and second, that poverty is more of a *mindset* than an objective fact.

Poverty is, in fact, a feeling.

Cold hard cash and how much you have of it – this is an objective fact. Whether you have food to put in your mouth and a way to protect yourself from the elements – also an objective fact.

But deciding how successful you are, deciding whether you have "enough" and what that even means, comparing yourself to your peers and your own internal standards, feeling how well your lifestyle supports all your dreams and desires... these things couldn't be any further from objective fact.

The definition of poverty I'm going to be using in this book is the same one *you're* using. Whatever that is.

What "counts" as poor depends on where you live, how you were raised and your own principles. How you define yourself is entirely up to you. My hope is that by the end of this book, you'll be thinking of yourself a little differently. But for now, I want to point out that there's a reason so many people disagree on the definitions of "rich" and "poor": the reason is because there *aren't* any definitions!

One more thing: I'll talk about poverty here in a very broad way. I want to convince you that being "impoverished" is something that extends far, far beyond how much you have in your bank account. Lack of money can be just that, a lack of money. But in the real world, consistently being deprived of the things you need to live your best life can have far-reaching consequences.

You can be impoverished in thought. In the same way that lacking money limits your options for the food or clothing you can buy or the places you can live, it also limits the kind of thoughts you can have. It clips your dreams and your self identity into smaller shapes. In the same way that you might buy lower quality clothes or settle for no-name groceries, you might only be able to "afford" a certain attitude, a certain life philosophy and worldview.

This is what this book is about: being impoverished. Of course, you can add money and hope that everything sorts itself out. But look at "poor" people who win the lottery. They don't suddenly develop a taste for steak and caviar and have the urge to develop their investment portfolio. Their attitude to life remains impoverished.

So, you can be "poor" with a lot of money, or "rich" with much less. Being impoverished, however, goes a little deeper. It's this attitude that's hard to pin down, but once you start looking for it, you'll notice it everywhere. Let me show you what I mean in the next chapter...

CHAPTER 3: THREE BELIEFS THAT IMPOVERISH YOU

As we've already seen, almost everything we know about money originally came from our parents. They outlined for us all the things that were possible in the world we inhabit. They told us what money was and what it was for, and by watching them, we learnt (or didn't learn!) how to manage it.

If you read the title of this chapter and thought, "nah, I don't have any impoverishing beliefs, after all, I'm just middle class anyway..." then I want to challenge you to keep reading. You might be surprised by what you learn about yourself!

Active or Reactive?

Psychologists call the characteristic that I'm about to talk about "locus of control". Fundamentally, it's all about *where* you see power and control coming from, in your life. It's the way that you answer the question, "who's running the show here?"

So, for example, someone with an internal locus of control might get promoted at work and conclude that *they* are the reason why. They caused the promotion to happen, they are responsible for it and now they'll take the kudos for it.

A person with an external locus of control, on the other hand, might also get promoted but explain that event in a completely different way. They may believe that they were favored by the higher ups, that they just got lucky this time, or that they've been handed an opportunity by someone other than themselves. It's not their doing, the promotion came from outside somehow.

That seems simple enough, but zoom out a little and think of the biggest possible picture. How does the universe itself work? Where do you fit into it and what causes things to happen to you? In other words, who's running the show?

Even people who are proactive and responsible in their work and life can fall back on worldviews that are very, very different. They may believe that ultimately, they don't really get a say in what happens to them. Whether it's God, or karma, or evil corporations that control the world, the sentiment is the same: their lives are run by things outside of their control.

An impoverished person believes:

• That "old money" dynasties and special secret networks are really controlling all the wealth in the world and you can't do anything about it if you're not a part of that.

• That money has to be *given* to you. That money is a reward you earn from someone who has more than you, in exchange for playing by their rules.

• That there are specific degrees and qualifications that will open doors and whisk you from one income bracket to the next.

• That proper money management is all about passively saving as much money as possible.
• That the way to advance in life is to get more and more prestigious job titles, and own assets and property.

An un-impoverished person thinks:
• That there are rules and hierarchies in the world, but that you don't always have to play by the rules, and if there are any secret inner circles, there's no reason why they can't be part of them.
• That the super wealthy are not some alien species, but just regular people that you could emulate.
• That money has to be *made*. That money is a reward you earn from creating something of value, in exchange for taking risks.
• That education is important, but there are no secret handshakes or degrees that fast track you into success. That learning practical, real-world skills is just as important, and you don't need any institute to validate that learning for you.
• That proper management of money is all about actively enhancing your ability to earn as much as possible. Saving is secondary.
• That the way to advance in life is to gain skills and a mindset that are intrinsically valuable, no matter what.

Ultimately, it's the difference between active and passive. The passive, external locus of control asks, "what are all my limitations here? What rules do I have to follow? What is expected of me and how I can win at the game that others have set up for me?"

The active, internal locus of control asks, "what do I want and how can I get it?"

One is focused on the outside, with all its constraints, and the other on the inside, and everything that you have under your control. One sees wealth as coming from the outside, the other, from the inside. It's the difference between hoping for a good salary and becoming an entrepreneur so you can decide on your income *yourself*.

Logical or Emotional?
As I mentioned before, poverty is a feeling. Wealth, abundance and security are states of mind.

Because of the way less fortunate people are raised (and sadly, this is the case for *most* people!), money becomes a symbol for a whole host of tangled emotions, thoughts, beliefs, expectations and automatic habits. Money becomes a stand in for lots of complicated states of mind: success in life, how you measure up to your peers, your feeling of safety and wellness in the world – it all comes together in this hot button called "money".

Money can be shameful, a source of deep unhappiness and stress, something embarrassing and hard to figure out, something you always want to avoid even thinking about, something that wears you out and saps your joy in life. "Money is the root of all evil".

Because of this, many people have attitudes towards money and those who have it that don't make a lot of sense. Disdain for "snobs" can hide deep insecurity and jealousy. Some people convince themselves that those better off are actually faulty somehow, that they must have gotten their wealth illegitimately or they must lack something special in life, like faith or a happy family. But all these stories and feelings and thoughts are just that: stories.

Having an overly emotional attachment to money makes you all the worse at managing it!

How do wealthier people think about money? Well, they think of it as what it actually is: a tool. A resource. Something to use to allow them to manage the rest of their lives. A thing to manage and moderate, to build, to develop.

It may be unfair, but such people, for whatever reason, lack the strong emotional attachment to money that poorer people have. They may enjoy their wealth or stress about it occasionally, but nowhere near on the same scale.

Let me make an analogy. A person who has terrible hang ups about their teeth, a fear of needles and no understanding of how the body works will find going to the dentist a really horrific experience. You could probably guess that such a person won't make the best health decisions when it comes to their dental care.

But a person without such hang ups or fears just ...goes to the dentist. It's a normal, everyday thing for them. They might not find it totally pleasant, but they just calmly get on with it: what do they need to do? What's the story and how do they fix any problems and move on with the rest of their lives?

This is the way that people without money hang ups behave. Richer people have an ease and familiarity with money that makes them better at managing it. They think about it logically. They don't avoid discussing it, and don't have those burning, unpleasant associations with their self-worth and identity. It's just money. It's a paradox actually: the rich can afford to just chill out and *stop thinking about money* quite as often. It's the poor, paradoxically, that are obsessed with it.

This ties in a little to the previous point – that of control. For wealthier people, money doesn't control them. They control it. For poorer people, money is a big, scary, frightening, exhausting thing that controls them.

Audacious or Doubtful?

I have a friend who is an incredibly talented artist. After much encouragement by others, she decided to try and sell some of her work. But her attitude was always, "nobody likes this kind of thing anyway, nobody will buy it, and I hate the sales and marketing side of things so much that I would probably just mess it all up anyway."

Do you notice the external locus of control? The emotional attitude? My friend also had a third "impoverished belief", namely doubt. What she ended up doing was pricing her work way, way too low. She had internalized the idea that it wasn't worth much, and acted accordingly. She was so doubtful about the possibility of even being a little successful that she acted as though she had already failed. After many people bought her work at the (extremely) low price, it began to make sense to her: why had she settled on this low, arbitrary number for her prices? Why had she immediately put a ceiling on herself?

She thought she'd lose customers if she priced higher. She didn't. So she priced even higher still, always riddled with doubt, as though she couldn't even imagine something other than just getting by or failing outright. But she kept selling. She had an impoverished mindset, and it had been seriously holding her back.

Rich people have a certain audacity about life. They don't even bother with doing what my friend did, they would have dived right in with the *highest* price they could get away with first and watched to see what would happen.

An impoverished person thinks:
- Life is something to survive.
- That the ultimate goal is to be comfortable and not take too many risks.
- That they can only succeed by the kindness of others, by luck, by being "fortunate" or by convincing others that they're worth it.
- That they need to ask permission, and are just waiting for conditions to improve or for someone else to show them how to succeed.
- That it's arrogant and greedy to always push for more, and you shouldn't go "above your station" and act like someone you're not.

An un-impoverished person thinks:
- That life is something to optimize – and there's always something more to improve on.
- That risk is just part of life!
- That they can succeed if they work at it.
- That they are in charge and don't need anyone's permission to take risks, or make a plan and follow it.
- That if they don't push for more, they won't get it. That they have to be a little uncomfortable and try new things to make money and get what they want.

The "audacity" that wealthier people have is really like an unshakeable confidence. They believe, more thoroughly than poorer people, that they deserve things and that the only thing standing in their way of getting those things are challenges that are easily surmounted. A rich person doesn't secretly believe that they're unworthy. In fact, it's the opposite; they know that in life they'll get precisely what they fight and work for!

A poor person, on the other hand, is unconfident. They're unsure about life in general, doubtful about their abilities to master it. They assume the world is holding them back and so they behave in ways that *hold themselves back*.

It's a self-fulfilling prophesy that goes like this:

I am not good enough, not like those rich and successful people, so all I can hope for is to survive and make do (and be "middle class"!) as best I can. Life is hard and difficult to figure out, and it's stupid to take risks when just getting by is so difficult already. So I don't take risks and don't step out of line. It's tiring so I'll spend money on entertaining myself and giving myself treats now and then. I'll stay in the hierarchy, take orders and wait for a promotion. Make myself useful to others and the dreams they have for themselves – I can get to your own dream later, when my life doesn't suck as much as it does now...

Such a person makes poor financial decisions, sees the results as proof that their worldview was right all along, and gets themselves stuck in a nice cycle of more and more impoverishment.

A person with less emotional attachment to money, more audacity and an internal locus of control is going to have a totally different thought process going on:

I'd really like to make more money and live a particular kind of lifestyle that I know will support all the dreams and goals I have for myself. That's going to take a lot of work and planning, so I'd better just get used to taking risks and being out of my comfort zone. I'll spend my money on learning as much useful stuff as I can. How can I be better? What needs to be improved on here? I'll keep asking that question and appraise my plan of attack as I go along. My dreams are not going to happen by themselves, and I'll need money to make it all work! I'd better stop wasting time on distractions and focus my energies...

Which person is going to be prepared and ready to strike when opportunity knocks? Which person is going to price their artwork really low and be satisfied with it? Which person will keep on their toes and learn all the skills they need to adapt and thrive and which person is going to believe they deserve a "treat" for surviving a long work day?

"Entertainment" – a trap

Why do people who have less money to spend sometimes buy very expensive sneakers or spend a fortune on things that even wealthier people think is wasteful? If you asked them (or if you do this yourself!) the answer won't be that they're just bad at finances and don't truly understand what they're doing. More likely, the answer will be, "I work so hard all week long. My life is difficult and stressful, just let me have this *one thing*..."

Before we move on to the next chapter, I want to quickly talk about what's so cyclical about the "cycle of poverty" and what exactly you need to be breaking out of. What poorer people "should" spend their money on is understandably a touchy topic. Who are we to tell someone who's scraping by that the few luxuries they have in life are all wrong somehow? If you work a long, hard day and want to come home and veg out with junk food and alcohol, who's to say you don't deserve it?

But this could be the start of a cycle that's difficult to break out of. When life is stressful and uncertain, it's tempting to grab what little scraps of pleasure and relief you can when you can. But these bad habits could eat away at what could otherwise be savings. They could rob you of time you could spend not just recovering from the stress in your life, but actually finding ways to address the root causes of that stress.

Don't be tempted to blow huge amounts of money to soothe yourself from how stressful it was to earn that money! It's like busting your ass at the gym to burn an extra 300 calories, then rewarding yourself later on by scoffing down 600. It's obvious how this can keep you trapped, going round and round and never really getting anywhere. You'll feel like you work yourself to death but never make any progress.

Do you identify with any of this? Perhaps you spend too much money on numbing/distracting yourself from a lifestyle you hate (i.e. "entertainment") instead of stopping, deciding what you actually want and spending your energy and money on making it a reality.

Of course, if you're the kind of person who would be utterly miserable without your little vice (clothes or shoes you can't afford, expensive games or consoles, alcohol, cigarettes or substances, junk food, gambling, beauty treatments and makeup you don't really need...) then you're probably wondering what the hell you're supposed to do without it.

First, divide every task you encounter in life into two categories:

1. maintenance, and

2. growth

Everything you do either keeps things ticking over, just as they are (maintenance) or it actually moves you *forward* somehow, bringing something new and better into your life (growth). When something in your house breaks, and you fix it, it's maintenance. You're just actively working to keep things from getting worse. But if you take an afternoon off and lay in some new tiles on your bathroom floor, that's making a renovation. Things are better now. This is growth.

The reason I make the distinction is because when you're in a cycle of poverty, all your actions are maintenance actions. That's why you get nowhere – there's never any time or money to do growth activities. So you just run and run to stay in the same place. "But I *have to* go to work" you say, and it's true. For most people, sadly, their work is going to be 90 – 100% maintenance, never truly moving them anywhere. And they're so tired after work that they don't have the energy to do any other tasks, like learning something new, bettering themselves, spending time with hobbies or passions or family. A horrible situation to be in!

To break the cycle, make sure you're doing at least one growth activity, every single day. Don't have the time? Have a look at your "entertainment" and you'll find some, I promise. Take the money you spend on junk food, the time you waste in front of the TV, the cash you fritter away on the weekends ...all of it adds up and can be put to far better use in a million other ways.

It may be difficult at first because you'll feel like you're losing your "reward", but try to remind yourself that it may take a little effort to break out of the cycle. It's staying in the cycle that's easy!

Trim down your weekend beer habit and spend that money on a weekend programming course instead. Instead of blowing away every windfall you get, put it away in a savings account for something you know will move your life forward – an eventual deposit on a house, education, or tools or equipment that you could start a small business with. Resist the urge to make a mediocre, unfulfilling life more comfortable and instead invest in things you won't get to enjoy for a while, but will pay off eventually.

When you're exhausted after a long day and all you can think about is zoning out in front of TV, eating something nice and falling asleep, try to remember that although it looks like it, this actually *isn't* a reward, or a treat, or a way to spoil yourself. It's just maintenance – and what you are maintaining is a lifestyle that you don't actually enjoy. Spend some time every day on moving things forward.

Though I've mentioned three beliefs here, ultimately, these "impoverished beliefs" come down to one fundamental idea that is much more than just your bank balance. They're the physical manifestation of your worldview, your attitudes made real, out there in the world.

One is rooted in fear and scarcity, the belief that life is just meant to suck a little, and that you can never have it all, never really succeed, never really get what you want. The other is rooted in something far more hopeful: if you are focused, self-aware and work hard, there's no reason why you can't make money work for you, and use it to achieve the things that are important to you.

Some of what you've read in the previous chapter may not have seemed relevant …although I'm sure at least some of it hit close to home!

In this chapter, take a good, honest look at where you stand in your attitude towards money right now. From there, you can start to get a clearer idea of the cycles you're trapped in – and how to get out of them!

For this quick quiz, tick all the statements that apply to you. Don't think too hard about it – just answer naturally (and honestly!).

A relationship with money is like any other relationship – 100% unique. So take a few moments to also jot down any thoughts and feelings you have but which aren't listed above. Understanding your strengths and weaknesses when it comes to your finances will make it so much easier to start making changes that count.

Money Personality One: The Dreamer

1. I feel like if I just had $100 000 tomorrow morning, all my life problems would go away
2. My spouse/parents/someone else handles all my financial decisions
3. I often fantasize about a rich lifestyle with all the trimmings, but not so much about the work it would take to make it a reality
4. Deep down, I think that all wealthy and successful people must be awful, although I am very jealous…
5. I'd rather wait for a promotion in my current job than look for a better one
6. Success with money comes down to luck and privilege
7. Marrying well or inheriting a lot of money are core parts of my financial plan for the future
8. I like playing the lottery or gambling
9. I have "expensive tastes" and like the finer things in life
10. If my parents were richer, or if I had been born in a different time or culture, life would have been much, much better than it is now

Can you recognize the external locus of control in The Dreamer's beliefs? For this personality type, money is a wonderful, desirable thing, but it always comes from *outside*. It's always something they have little control over, some magical, faraway thing that they can dream of but can't imagine actually living.

If you've ticked a lot of these beliefs, maybe you flip wistfully through magazines and daydream about all the symbols of a wealthy lifestyle, but never with any firm intention of what it actually means to achieve those dreams. You might shrug and believe that financial security is something for other people, but not you. The Dreamer is walking around with their own internal ceiling: they can visualize all the good things in life they want, but they position themselves well outside of it, looking in, and dreaming. That is, not *doing* anything about it!

Money Personality Two: The Emotional Ostrich
1. I never open my bank statements
2. I'm just not good with money – I've never been good with numbers
3. I pay a lot of money on late fees or overdraft fees...
4. I've always had debt, or I have a lot now
5. I could never be a cut-throat entrepreneur – not in this dog-eat-dog world!
6. I'd rather live a good life than chase money!
7. I just avoid talking about these kinds of things, to be honest
8. I haven't thought too much about retirement – I can solve that problem when I get there
9. Talking about money is kind of shameful
10. I was never taught anything about money, I've just muddled my way through till now

The Ostrich thinks that money is scary and painful they so if I pretend it doesn't exist, maybe it won't! Behind this personality type's denial is a lot of unbearable emotion – money is somewhere along the line interpreted as threatening, boring, embarrassing or depressing. So they avoid it!

If you've ticked a lot of these, don't worry – I would bet that Ostriches are the most common of these types. Many of us are never taught sound personal finance skills, and had parents and even communities who taught us to fear and avoid taking responsibility for our money. Because the Ostrich avoids engaging with these painful feelings, they also avoid wealthy, successful people, even believing deep down that financial success is bad somehow, and that they never really wanted it anyway...

Money Personality Three: The Big Spender
1. I'd die of embarrassment to let some people know my true spending habits
2. No matter how much money I have, I always seem to run out too soon
3. If I get a windfall, I spend it immediately
4. I love spoiling my friends and family and enjoying the good life
5. It's important for me to be perceived as completely in control financially ...even better if people believe I'm quite successful
6. I sometimes try to appear as though I'm wealthier than I actually am
7. I'm an impulse buyer
8. I feel like I'm way, way behind my peers when it comes to finances
9. Fake it till you make it!

10. I have a lush lifestyle and spend heavily, but have few assets and no savings

The Big Spender has a lot in common with the previous types: namely, the external locus of control and the emotional rather than logical attachment to money. But they go a little further, committing only to the *image* of wealth and success, rather than the work and planning that realistically goes into it. The Big Spender values financial success not for its own sake, but because it forms part of their identity. They may "keep up with the Joneses" a lot or live beyond their means.

Money Personality Four: The Money Martyr
1. I often buy something and feel really guilty afterwards
2. My job isn't really going anywhere
3. Even though it makes me feel stingy, I'd do anything to get the best deals or buy the cheapest possible item
4. I often blow a lot of money to de-stress and then regret it later
5. People like me never really get rich, we just get by, and I'm fine with that. After all, what's so special about me that I deserve a fancy life?
6. I find that a lot of my life revolves around stressing about money
7. I never feel secure when it comes to money
8. I don't play the game to win, I play it just to *not* lose!
9. I resent those who seem more successful and happier than I am
10. Life is just one financial obstacle after another, and I almost always lose

Just reading The Money Martyrs list is depressing, don't you think? This personality type sees money as nothing but a massive tormentor. They're slaves in their own lives, hopeless and unable to improve, only ever keeping their heads above water and hating those who seem to find a way out.

This is a pessimistic, limited way of thinking. People with this mindset will never take risks, and will constantly feel like their jobs and finances are something to survive, rather than to thrive within. Money is a source of stress and misery, rather than a practical way to reach your goals. Goals? The martyr doesn't even dare to have goals – they can't afford them!

Money Personality Five: The Confident Realist
1. I have a five-year plan
2. I understand everything that's deducted from my salary and know exactly what I take home each month
3. I can tell you what I spent on entertainment last month
4. I'll be OK financially – I'm not afraid of a few bumps in the road, I always land on my feet, because I'm willing to do what it takes!

5. I think of money as a tool

6. I use the money I earn to pay for a life that makes me happy and fulfilled

7. I always look for opportunities and try to find the bright side in my situation, whatever it is

8. I admire and look up to those who have done better than I have, and I'm really curious about how they did it

9. There are plenty of problems in my life – but I'm bigger than those problems, and I don't let them control me

10. I think of my life in terms of time and value, and not so much in terms of hours worked or what my salary is.

And finally, we get to the ***Money Realist.***

These people are quietly optimistic, a little forceful and cocky sometimes, but convinced of their own innate ability to control and determine their own destiny. Such a person doesn't "hope" for anything, take gambles or wish that something would fall in their lap – they simply become curious about opportunities around them and do their damndest to make the best of those, through determined hard work.

This personality may have some emotional associations with money, and they may have hiccups and setbacks like everyone else, but their mindset is fundamentally different. They don't ever question whether they deserve success or security, and they certainly don't ask anyone's permission to do it. They just do it. And they keep on doing it.

How many on this list did you tick?

CHAPTER 5: ATTITUDES LEAD TO BEHAVIORS, WHICH LEAD TO ATTITUDES

The point of shining a light on the inner workings of your money-mind is not to feel bad about yourself or shrug and conclude that nothing can be done.

Attitudes lead to behavior. And when you behave, you actively change and shape the world around you ...which in turn confirms and maintains those same attitudes.

Our attitudes have a way of bringing themselves into being – we can only choose from the options our attitudes have allowed us to notice. When we have a setback, it's our attitude that helps us explain what happened and decide what to do next.

Once you know exactly what thoughts are steering your behavior, you can start getting to the exciting stuff: *changing*. Simply plonking down some new behaviors on top of your old life will never really change much. But if you can dig deep and root out those underlying beliefs that are powering those behaviors, you start making meaningful progress.

Let's say you identified with the Big Spender money personality above. For you, money is like food or love – something you just don't want to put limits on! Your belief may be that we should "eat, drink and be merry, for tomorrow we'll die!" and so whenever you have money, you spend it. All of it. You have the belief that money is for enjoying, but of course, this means that you have no savings, no safety net of any kind, and no strategy for the future.

So when you're faced with that kind of financial insecurity, your belief is confirmed: money can disappear at any time! You had better enjoy it while it lasts! So the next time you get money, you blow it again, celebrating its return into your life. The cycle continues.

Maybe your relationship to money is more like The Emotional Ostrich. Dealing with money is so unpleasant you just ignore it and hope it'll all go away somehow. So, your belief is, "if I close my eyes and shut my ears and don't look at all this scary stuff, it won't exist anymore." Of course, it's a faulty belief. While you're in denial, your finances are doing whatever they're doing, and likely getting worse. Your behavior might lead you to miss important deadlines, fail to notice weird charges or fees that you really should query, file late on your taxes or do it incorrectly, get ripped off when buying things or lose important documents.

The result of this attitude, though, is the opposite of what you hoped: not only do your problems not go away, you're just inviting more and more of them into your life! The cycle continues.

Of course, these are just examples, and your real life will be far more complex, probably with a few elements from more than one type. But that's fine. Though the details may differ here and there, everyone still follows the same principle: your beliefs inform your behavior.

Change the beliefs, and the behaviors will change as well. You can try to force an attitude change by forcing yourself to behave differently (like most personal finance books would suggest) but this is likely to be much less successful!

I'd like to ask you to do an exercise now to try and zoom in on your own beliefs and the behaviors they're keeping in your life. Return to the beliefs you identified for yourself from the last chapter, and choose around three or four of the strongest ones. For example, you could go with:

• I resent those who seem more successful and happier than I am
• I find that a lot of my life revolves around stressing about money
• Even though it makes me feel stingy, I'd do anything to get the best deals or buy the cheapest possible item

Now, you might identify with the The Money Martyr stereotype. Always scrimping and scrooging, letting money (or the lack of it!) completely sap the joy from your life. Now, what are the specific *behaviors* that stem from these attitudes? You could note down:

• Because I resent others who are wealthier and more successful than I am, I avoid them and associate with those like me, or those who are even less successful than I am. I don't seek out those who could teach me something new or offer me new opportunities.
• Because I always stress about money, I try to get relief by not thinking about it, but then problems get out of hand, which cause me more stress anyway, and then I get stuck in a vicious cycle...
• Because I always go for the cheapest option or the best budget deal, I often drastically reduce my quality of life for very small savings. This depresses me and confirms my belief that I'm not worth nicer things, which makes me less likely to work to bring them into my life.

When you sit down and have a good honest look at your beliefs, you'll probably find that many of them are self-sustaining – in other words, believing them traps you in a vicious cycle that's hard to break free of, so you keep believing them.

In the example above, you can see how stingy, fear-driven beliefs lead to a life that is focused on lack and on reducing. You're always about making things less, about minimizing, about saving and retaining. How could you ever dream big or take risks or be joyfully expressive if all your beliefs are focused on *lack*? When so much doubt controls your life, you don't even entertain the notion that with some effort and risk, things could improve. And so you prove to yourself that the world is harsh and that scarcity and misery are just the norm.

Take some time to really look at the beliefs you hold and how exactly they manifest in your life. If you've held your beliefs for a long time, this may seem difficult. You may be tempted to say, well, this *is* the way things are, this isn't a belief. Fair enough. For now, just become curious about the links between what you believe and what you *do* in the real world because of that belief.

A good way to zoom in on this is to ask, where would you be *without* this belief?

Ask yourself, is your current mindset actually working for you? What would happen if you abandoned it? If you do nothing at all and carry on going as you are, will you be happy with the result a few years down the line?

CHAPTER 6: THIS IS NOT A MOTIVATIONAL BOOK

Perhaps you've read this far, and you've identified your blind spots when it comes to thinking about money. Maybe you've been honest and had a good look at the beliefs and feelings that are holding you back from taking financial responsibility in your life. Great. Now what?

There is a dangerous "law of attraction" vibe around personal finance improvement. You're probably already familiar with it: have the right mindset, and the universe will deliver. Just think the right things, truly believe and then wealth and abundance will just rain down onto your lap with no effort.

Do you recognize The Dreamer personality type in this? This is the ultimate in external locus of control. In place of "my boss" or "my father" or "God himself" you have "the universe" and whatever mysterious processes it runs on. You believe that if you just hold thumbs and have the right attitude, you'll be *rewarded* with everything you want and need.

While I want to emphasize just how fundamental mindset truly is, I also want to emphasize that this attitude is actually quite disempowering. Why? Because attitude alone is not enough. Because nobody gives you the reward but you.

Here are some harsh truths – if you were raised poor, you're starting at a disadvantage. You've been lied to and told that hard work will get you out of the hole, but that might not be true. Or maybe you've been told that you'll never be more than what you are now.

Simply changing your mindset will likely not help. Money and resources are real, and they don't care about your politics, or whatever mystical self-help book you've read, or what you "deserve" or how much you pray.

To be rich, you have to think rich, not because *thinking* means anything, but because it maps onto specific behaviors. In the end, it's all about ACTION.

Money is a deeply emotional topic. It always will be. As you read this book, your head may be swirling with ideas of what you do and don't "deserve" in life, about the morality of greed, of what it really means to add value in life, of give and take, of whether capitalism is evil and whether money corrupts people, of your social status, you gender, your race...

But none of that matters. We could dwell right now on how young women often make poorer financial choices because they unconsciously expect the men in their lives to take care of them. We could consider whether belonging to a disadvantaged class and being poor is really your "fault" and how institutionalized discrimination may have ensured that you were poor before you were even born. We could talk about the death of the middle class or how evil corporations are or how really smart people should unplug form the system and become gypsy entrepreneurs...

But we won't, because none of that matters. None of that is under your control, so while it may be interesting to think about, in the end it doesn't mean much. What matters is the action you take, right now, whatever your circumstances.

And to make sure you're making the best possible choices for yourself and the life you want, you need to look closely and unravel all the beliefs you hold – especially all those that are actively keeping you in a lifestyle you don't want to have.

So, from this point in the book, we'll switch from thinking about thoughts and beliefs, to engaging with the real-life *behaviors* that come with those beliefs. Zoom in and you'll see: being "rich", managing your resources and living a life that fulfils you is nothing more than a habit. People who are financially secure and in control are not any different from you – except in the way they think about things.

Once you've got a thorough understanding of your ideas and beliefs, it's time to dismantle them. In the following chapter, we'll move onto how to start picking out those beliefs and substituting them with ones that will lead to the kind of life you actually want. But a caveat before we start: none of what follows means anything unless you take the time to really ACT.

Even though you might understand an exercise intellectually, or even though it seems simple on the surface, you won't get the true benefit unless you take the leap and bring it to life in the real world. The biggest characteristic missing in the personality types we've discussed, and the biggest antidote to the three beliefs that keep you trapped in unhelpful cycles, is ACTION.

Mindsets are important. But they're important because of what they lead to: beneficial action. If you're committed to making real changes, then let's move on to the next chapter...

The way that you tackle your limiting beliefs and behaviors will be specific to you and your unique situation, right now.

The advice that follows is general, but try to keep an eye to tailoring everything here to fit your personal situation. Don't get disheartened if something seems not to apply to you, and don't write off advice that seems very obvious or low-level to you.

Each of the following exercises is tailored to fit each of the money personalities, but I suggest looking at all of them anyway, as most people can find something useful from each group.

Breaking the cycle if you're The Dreamer

If you're a dreamer, you may share the very common beliefs that financial success is something lucky that happens to you, or it doesn't, and you don't get much say in the matter. When it comes to explaining financial success, you may point to:

• Genes
• Family wealth
• Luck
• Genius
• Entrepreneurial skills
• Fate
• Something mystical, like God answering your prayers

But the truth is that none of these things has anything to do with how successful you are. How do I know this?

In studies and surveys done on the attitudes held by people in different socio-economic brackets, the above beliefs are shared by poorer people ...and NOT by wealthier people.

Think about it.

Holding the above beliefs are strong predictors that you'll stay poor. And of course they are! If you believe that something's out of your control, why bother trying to change it?

The corresponding "rich" beliefs are different. Richer people are more likely to explain financial success by pointing to:

• Hard work
• Creativity
• Being proactive
• Realistic optimism

What's the difference between these two sets of beliefs? One favors ACTION.

If you identified with this personality type and set of beliefs, your challenge will be to find ways to turn your locus of control inward, and remember all the power you have in determining your own fate. There is no master plan, no finance gods or strokes of luck – there is only you and the actions you take for your own life.

That's all.

Exercise One: What can I do?

The question "what can I do?" has two parts:

The "I" part and the "do" part. When you ask yourself this question, you're focusing your attention on the only thing you have realistic control over: yourself. You don't waste time dwelling on how your parents screwed you over or whether the government taxes you too much – this is disempowering. Instead, you take control and become curious about *your* scope of influence. No matter how small that may be, *you* own that possibility, and *you* are responsible for taking it – or forfeiting it.

The second part is about doing, about action. To take responsibility for your own role in your future is to become aware of the actions open to you. As we've seen, mindset is nothing without action to bring it to life.

What can you do?

For one day this week, commit to changing your channel from external to internal. Keep asking yourself this question, whenever you're faced with any money decision. Let's say you do some online banking and freak out at some hidden charge you never knew about. You could say, "damn the banks, I hate them, always exploiting the little guys..." and so on. But what good does that do? Nothing. Instead ask, "what can I do?"

This immediately cuts the emotion out, and focuses your attention on what matters: what actions you can take, as the supreme agent of your own life. If there's something you can change to avoid those charges in future, do it. If not, accept it. Keep your mind open for opportunities in the future. Maybe the banks are evil and exploitative. Maybe not. It doesn't matter though ...what can you do?

Try this for a day, and then push it to a week and then longer. See how long you can maintain this frame of mind. And follow through! Once you've identified a course of action, take it and see how different life looks after some proactive choices. When you switch from passive to active, external to internal, suddenly your financial future is completely in your control. Do this with both small and big things and you'll be surprised by how many new ideas and avenues open up to you.

Breaking the cycle if you're an Emotional Ostrich

At the root of the Ostrich's need to live in denial is one very strong emotion: fear.

Many of us are instilled with this fear in childhood. Fear that we'll have to do without. Fear of failure or letting our families down. Fear that money is this big, scary, unmanageable thing that can ruin lives and crush you. If we grew up poor, we may have seen our parents struggle financially. We may have experienced shame in being poor, panic and insecurity over never having enough, neglect or having to watch others experience good fortune while we made do with less.

The irony is that fear keeps the Ostrich in the very cycle they want to escape so badly. By continually engaging with money in fear (and resentment and doubt and all those other nasty emotions) the Ostrich never gets to develop a more neutral, relaxed attitude to money. How do you break out of this cycle?

Exercise Two: Find Your Rock Bottom

Breaking out of this cycle of fear is easy: challenge the underlying fear, and engage with it. For this exercise, you'll need one thing the Ostrich doesn't have: bravery. This exercise will be horrible to do, but that's the point here; you'll dive deep down into the thing you believe is unbearable ...and then bear it!

Wealthier people, especially those who work their way up from poverty, often have a fearlessness to them. They simply *stop caring* about the risks quite as much. They have a "nothing to lose" vibe about them and don't care if they have to suffer a little on the way. If you read any biographies about supremely successful individuals, they often talk about the early days before they succeeded: bad jobs, scrimping, sacrificing, doing without.

The difference is that they didn't try to *avoid* this state at any cost. Instead of running away from those unpleasant sensations, they dug deep and engaged with them. They didn't enjoy it any more than anyone else, but they looked the hardship square in the face and acknowledged it for what it was. Then they overcame it.

If you identify strongly with the fearful Ostrich, it's time to get over your fear and see that actually, it's not so bad.

In a journal somewhere, take a moment to jot down *the worst thing that could happen*. Enjoy it. Let your imagination run wild. Whatever financial outcome you fear, put it down: bankruptcy, a life of mediocrity, disappointing your family, having no retirement... Dwell on whatever it is that freaks you out and makes you turn your head away whenever you look at it.

Now, ask yourself, is it really so bad?

Is the situation you're imagining really unfixable? Even if the literal worst thing happened, would it be so bad that you couldn't improve on it some way? Often, when you look at your fears up close, you see that they're not really the end of the world. Bad, sure, but nothing you can't survive and deal with. Have you ever heard the saying, "the thing you fear the most has already happened to you"? What's more, your avoidance of that fear could actually have more consequence on your life than that fear ever will.

For this exercise, try to engage instead of avoid. Let's say you receive your bank statement in the mail. You get a sinking feeling and put it aside – you don't want to open it. You don't want to know how bad your debt is getting, how much your overdraft fees are or how much you've overspent this month. Instead of putting your head in the sand, though, deliberately *enjoy* the fear. Go deeper into it. Open your bank statement and revel in whatever is in front of you. Let's say it's bad. Really bad. Let's say your financial life is a total wreck. But again, if even *the worst thing that could happen* is manageable, isn't your current problem even more bearable? Stand there and really feel it: you're still alive, present, aware. You still can make decisions. At any point, you can choose and act. However bad things are, they will end eventually.

Look at the things that scare you. Look at how much you actually earn; look at the exact figure of the debt you owe. Look at how much you're putting away for retirement and how it won't be enough. Take it all in. It's bad? Ok. Fine. It's not the worst thing that could happen, and even if it was, you know that even the worst thing that could happen is manageable. Find that bottom. Be comfortable with it. Know that you can fail even more and you'll still be OK. Fearlessness is not about having no fear – it's more about learning to tolerate that fear, and even thrive with it.

Take a little grit and fearlessness from your wealthier peers: say, to hell with it. When you understand a problem and look at it honestly, you start to dissolve the fear, and dissolve the hold it has on you. And then you can start taking meaningful action. So, do the opposite of what you want to. Go into the fear. See how bad it gets. See that ...it's not so bad!

• Print out all your bank statements and take a good look at where your money goes each month, even the embarrassing details you'd rather not admit

• Look at your credit card statements and see how much you owe and how much you're paying on your debt. Don't try to hide it or minimize it

• Look at your salary and what proportion of it goes to different areas of your life

• When you get that panicky feeling that tells you to turn away, *that's* the place you need to look even closer. Let your avoidance be a signpost for the things you most need to focus on

Breaking the cycle if you're a Big Spender

Big Spenders are somewhere in the middle – they *know* how important it is to take charge of their financial situations and desperately want to. The trouble is the way they approach it. Many cultures emphasize the outward symbols of financial success: expensive assets, a particular lifestyle. It's tempting to imagine that you could access wealth if you could just access the symbols that are *associated* with it. You may be heavily pressured by others and what you "should" be doing in all spheres of life, but perhaps you haven't spent as much time thinking about what money actually means to *you*.

Exercise Three: Find Real Value

A nasty surprise waits in store for the Big Spender: even if they reach a measure of success and financial stability, they realize too late that it all feels kind of empty. Their achievements and possessions might have a sort of "so what?" feel about them. This is because the main driver of the Big Spender's behavior is, you guessed it, *external*.

Instead of deciding on *why* he wants money in his life and *for what* exactly, he's momentarily focused on just getting it. Money is viewed as an end in itself. But then even if you get money, then what? Then you're faced with the question you might have asked yourself in the first place: what is money's true role in your life? What do you VALUE?

For this exercise, you'll take money out of the equation completely. You'll focus instead on a more concrete, more personal question: what actually matters to you? You'll never be wealthy if you can't figure out how to spend your money in ways that benefit your life. What's the point of wealth and security if it never translates into fulfilment and happiness?

You need to stop thinking of money as a goal in itself and start thinking of the overarching goals in your life – those that may or may not need money to be realized.

In a journal somewhere, try to answer the following questions as honestly as possible.

Step one: Identify your values

• What do you care about more than anything else in the world? Family? Behaving ethically? Finding and giving love? Creating? Having fun? Building useful things?

• Think about the times in life you felt happiest, most content and most fulfilled with yourself. What were you doing? Where and with whom? This gives you an idea of what will ultimately satisfy you in life.

• When you're old and on your death bed, and remembering your life, what actions and achievements will allow you to say, "I'm at peace, I did a good job"? Are you doing those things now?

Step two: Are you investing in those values?

Sure, you might spend reasonable amounts during the month and have an exemplary budget. But you're failing hard if there's nothing in your spending habits that supports those things you care most about.

If you value building a loving family and home life, and you spend almost no money on that, your budget and financial habits are not serving you. If you value creativity and expression the most, then why spend most of your resources on things that don't feed that value in any way?

Look closely and you'll realize that nobody has the ultimate value of "I want to appear wealthy to my peers" or "I want to make sure I live in the way that everyone else is living".

• Look at a typical month and what you spend. Visualize the information in many different ways to get a sense of where most of your money (i.e. energy!) is really going. Much of it will be towards keeping you housed and fed, but after that? You may find that mindless entertainment and distraction are not your truest, deepest values, and yet your budget says otherwise! Does your budget support what you ultimately value? If not, it's probably working *against* it.

• How much of what you spend each month is because you should, and how much is because you want to? We all need to pay tax and rent/mortgage. But are you spending money on a big, beautiful home when deep down, you couldn't care less about that kind of thing?

• What percentage of your income is going to actually improving your life? Not just maintaining it, but improving it. Is your lifestyle working to maintain you or are you working to maintain your lifestyle?

Step three: Re-allocate

The best budgeting doesn't require you to cut your spending at all. You only need to *re-allocate* resources you already have. Imagine a person who hates coming home each evening and blowing hours watching Netflix, feeling guilty they do nothing with their lives. They look at their budget, and add up everything they spend on binge eating in front of the couch, watching TV series.

They take that money and pay instead for sewing classes in the evenings. Their net expenditure is the same, but they've added value to their lives: they've put their money where their passion is and made a step towards a lifestyle that fulfils them rather than just keeps them ticking over.

• Take the low hanging fruit first: find those places in your budget that actively undermine your quality of life. Now's the time to quit a wasteful habit, stop smoking or cut down on low-return behaviors like gambling or drinking too much.

• Find places in your budget where you spend money on things you don't actually care about and won't miss if they're gone, or will miss very little.

• Ask yourself, can this money be put to better use somewhere else? What dreams and goals and ideas have gone neglected because you didn't have the time or money? Can you find a way to pout those resources there, instead of into wasting time or buying things you don't want?

If you're a Big Spender, be thankful: you're guided by a real sense that life should be enjoyable, and that you want to enjoy it. Your only challenge is to identify more efficient ways of using the resources you have.

Better yet, find ways to add value to your life that don't include money at all! Big Spenders often build their identities around generosity, but can you show love and celebrate and enjoy life without spending money? Think of places to volunteer, or choose memorable activities to do with loved ones rather than lavishing them with gifts.

The deeper question for someone with this money personality is: *what is truly valuable*? Not what culture tells you to want or what your family and friends pressure you into wanting. But what do *you* want, deep down? And how can you arrange your life in a way that gets you closer to that?

Breaking the cycle if you're a Money Martyr

We've seen that Money Martyrs are all about focusing on *scarcity*. If you grew up poor and watched those around you be tormented by the "root of all evil", you may have developed some pretty dire attitudes towards finances in general. You may have internalized the fact that life is just crappy and you don't dare hope for otherwise. You want to keep your head down, make rent and not get an ulcer from all the stress.

If you try following traditional money advice, you may be tempted to go for the kind that really just tells you how to live on even less. Clip coupons, make extra cheap meals and scrape by with even less money than you do right now. This kind of advice will just bum you out even more, and keep your cycle going.

Exercise Four: Think Big

Martyrs think small. Very small. They ask others what the rules are and then try to do the bare minimum to satisfy those rules so they can carry on with their lives and not think about it again. They don't ever think they can win at life, so they don't try. The world looks like a series of hoops to jump through, bosses to satisfy and bills to pay. What's missing from the Martyrs life? Their *own* dreams.

You may feel browbeaten and exhausted for very good reasons. But at the end of the day, thinking small will never help you. People don't make money or enhance their lifestyles without taking risks, or without having the audacity to ask for more. And really, there's no "asking" at all – rather, there's just taking!

For this exercise, try to invert your natural scarcity mindset. Try to open your mind to another idea: that the world can actually be a wonderfully abundant place, filled with possibility and all the resources you need to build a life you don't just tolerate, but *love*. But nobody will hand it to you. If you decide that you're not worthy of making the effort, then nobody will come along and convince you otherwise.

Go back to the list of beliefs you jotted down for yourself earlier in the book. You can expand on those now or just choose two or three that speak most closely to your experience. Now, have some fun: turn that idea completely on its head.

Let's say you wrote, "People like me never really get rich, we just get by, and I'm fine with that. After all, what's so special about me that I deserve a fancy life?"

Now, invert that belief. Write instead: "People like me can and do get rich, and I'm not happy settling when I know I can do better. I don't need to be special – and I don't need to 'deserve' anything!"

Now, how does that feel, just to say it?

Do this for all the beliefs and thoughts you've jotted down. Where there's apathy, switch it out for audacity and confidence. Where there's a hate and suspicion of wealth and all those who have it, replace it with an attitude of appreciation, curiosity or playful competition. Congratulations – you're on your way to thinking like many "rich" people do!

When you catch yourself in negative self-talk of this kind, switch over to your inverted belief. Now, most importantly, what does that belief lead you to *do*? As we've seen, beliefs on their own mean nothing without the behaviors that manifest them in the real world. As with exercise 1, ask yourself, what can I do?

You may be overwhelmed by this, since it may be the first time you've ever even entertained the idea that you could *do* anything about your situation, but keep asking the question anyway.

When you see "evidence" that your old ways of thinking are true, reject them. Invert your natural tendency to be pessimistic and have the audacity to think something else: you deserve it. You can achieve what you want to. You don't need to wait for permission.

Try replacing your thoughts like this for a few days, but keep coming back to concrete actions, too, for example:

• Look at your job and assess it objectively. Can you do better? Is this really the best job for you right now, and will it grow with you and fulfil you in the long term?

• Instead of saving every last scrap, do you need to focus your attention on earning more? Do you need a raise or a promotion?

• It might be time to upskill and make yourself more valuable in the world (i.e. stop trying to take up less space, but take up more!). Can you take the time to enhance your abilities and gain experience?

• Think about where you'll be in one, two and five years' time. Look at your current lifestyle setup and ask whether it scales up and appreciates over time – or whether it plateaus. What steps can you take now to put yourself in a better position this time next year?

• Raise your prices, ask for a salary increase or invest in buying things that are better quality and not the cheapest. This takes a leap of faith

• When you find yourself stressing about money, stop and become aware of your thoughts for a second. Look and see if your inner dialogue is actually helping you in any way. Are you encouraged to take any beneficial actions? If not, drop the worry and move on with life. Stressing helps nobody and is a waste of your time. Stress only if it propels you into useful action – otherwise, you might as well just relax!

• Ask for help. All those people who you quietly resent for being more successful or financially stable than you? Ask their advice. Or just spend time with them and try to learn what they're doing that you aren't. Compliment those who work hard and take risks. Find a mentor and emulate them

• When you encounter an obstacle, rejoice! Look closely and you'll see that it's just an opportunity in disguise. Every moment in time is an opportunity to learn something, to make money, to hone in on your values or to let go of things that just aren't working. Expect and value negative feedback – and commit to putting it to use

• When you're feeling miserly, double check what's really causing the scarcity. If you're honest, you may discover that it's only YOU who's limiting and constraining yourself.

CHAPTER 8: BUDGET LIKE A RICH PERSON

When you budget like a poor person (and by now I hope you know exactly what I mean when I talk about a "poor person" – not someone who simply doesn't have that much money, but someone who is stuck in an impoverished mindset, whether they have money or not), you start with your income, minus the expenses, and hope the balance is positive.

You might forget that money is a tool, that it's something there for you to use to enhance your life, your dreams and your goals. You might get trapped in the minutiae like how to shave a few dollars here and there by buying cheaper produce or getting things on sale.

You may focus on lack instead of abundance, on retaining rather than expanding and taking risks. You look at the money you have and ask, "how can I make this go as far as possible?" instead of, "what is the ultimate best use of this money, right now?"

Get cheap – REALLY cheap – with the things that don't matter to you

Common sense tells us to trim away the luxuries first. Get rid of unnecessary spending on fancy coffees or junk food, or little trinkets you fritter your money away on. Right? Actually, this is the wrong way to go about things. What counts as a "luxury" is really only up to you, and even then, the things that give you most pleasure in life are the things you should try hard to *keep* in your budget. Think about it: you get more utility and pleasure from every dollar you spend here than on other things you don't care too much about.

When you're trying to shave down expenses – and there's no shame in needing to do that – start with things that lack a real, subjective value to you. If having the quiet time of a daily coffee ritual is the last thing keeping you sane these days, cutting that spending is a bad move. Instead, look at those things that don't speak to your higher values. If you're going to scrimp, do it on things that don't matter at all. This may not match up with everyone else's idea of what counts as a luxury and what doesn't, but whatever, your budget's not for them.

I know of a guy who couldn't care less about fashion, looking good or fancy clothing. He worked like a dog all through his degree and did it on almost no money because more than anything, he wanted that degree and what it meant for his future. And so he wore, throughout the entire 3 years I knew him, the same two pairs of trousers and the same two shirts. They were identical. While one was getting washed, he wore the other. They had tiny holes in the corners and were pretty ugly, but he didn't care. It was a sacrifice to not buy clothing for years – but a sacrifice he could make easily. He blew his money on gadgets and software and evening classes and conferences. And he went to those conferences in shirts with tiny holes in them.

If you're struggling with money, it'll be so much easier to deal with temporary hardship when you remember that you can *choose where to allocate that hardship.* Keep feeding your passions, and the hardship won't sting that much anyway.

Dream first, then think about the money later

Many people only dream as big as they think they're allowed to. They have an inbuilt "I can't" that they don't even realized they're walking around with. Any financial growth is going to start with a dream that's slightly (or a lot!) larger than the reality you're living in right now. But have the audacity to have that dream anyway, and be curious about how to bring it to life.

Most budgets follow the Money Martyr style of thinking: trim and cut and reduce, at any cost. Of course, the other end of the equation is to think of bringing more *in.* Wealthier people don't stress too much about what they don't have at the moment. They know that resources come and go. They're more concerned with the next opportunity, with finding out which exact path is going to lead them to what they want. Do the same.

Permanently be on a job hunt, and keep feelers out for opportunities at every moment. Are you being compensated properly for your work? Or, are you really adding value to the lives of others? Are you actually *asking* for what you want? So many people just assume they can never negotiate for more money, but why not?

Start with what you want first, and go from there. Don't look around to see all the ways your current situation is lacking and then assume that's proof that you've dreamt too big. Do you remember when you were a little kid and you had grand plans for how you'd live when your parents weren't the boss of you and you could do whatever you wanted? Well, here you are. Time to dream big!

If your dream is large and far away, that's fine. Just identify one thing you *can* do, right now, and get going. You'd be amazed how much time you have when you cut out junk entertainment from your life. And you'd be amazed at how many opportunities you notice when you give yourself permission to accept that they're there at all.

Go back to university. Start your own business. Retire and go backpacking. Ask for a raise. Buy that little thing you want but think you shouldn't get. Or, make any small step in the right direction.

At the end of your life, there's no prize for how well you followed the rules. Nobody is keeping score. The only thing that will matter is whether you can sit with yourself in your last hours and know deep down that you lived well. It won't matter then whether you played it safe. Even reaching for your dreams and failing will seem more valuable to you than never having tried at all.

Stay focused

Think of a budget as a lens that focuses your energy and effort in just the right place. When a laser can concentrate diffuse beams of light into just one point, it becomes really powerful. Do the same. Decide on the goals you value and then tune out everything that distracts you from that. You can waste your whole life "getting ready" or "taking a break" or putting off things till tomorrow.

Your time, your energy and your money are finite resources. So use them wisely. When you budget, keep other things in mind, not just money. Are you using your time carefully? Are you spending your energy in the right place? Are your actions and movements geared towards what really counts?

If so, it doesn't much matter how much money you have. Money becomes a tool. The question is not, "do I have enough money?" but "do I have enough money to live my values?" When you expand your budget to include your own personal, deeper sense of value, you change on a cognitive and emotional level. You give yourself the chance to step out of self-limiting vicious cycles, and to create a lifestyle that fulfills you. You stop thinking poor.

CONCLUSION

"We cannot solve our problems with the same thinking we used when we created them."
~ Albert Einstein

I want to end this short book with the same quote I began it with.

Einstein was a brilliant man in part because he was able to think the unthinkable, to push his imagination to places where nobody else's had gone before. He could have been an exemplary scientist by working within the same realm that physicists of his day occupied, and he would have done very well for himself. But he was interested in going a little deeper.

When you become curious about why and how you are all the things you are, you give yourself a great opportunity to truly change. Not just on the surface, but in a more profound way.

Those who grow up impoverished are taught certain attitudes and beliefs that keep them trapped in cycles of behavior that are largely their own doing. If you've always struggled with money, you may have seen something of yourself in the personalities described here. And my hope is that at the very least, I've convinced you that thinking this way is completely, 100% optional.

There are forces that are beyond our control, and political and economic factors that no one person can ever claim to have overcome. We are all part of bigger systems that we don't have perfect knowledge or control over. With money, this is just a fact.

Nevertheless, we always have the power to stop, turn inwards, and become aware of the thoughts and behaviors that we choose to have and which maintain our lives in ways we don't actually want. No matter how much hardship you go through, no matter whether you become very successful or just putter along for the rest of your life, taking responsibility for your mindset will automatically make you "richer" than you were before.

With a clear understanding of what you value, your dreams and your own blind spots, you are prepared, empowered and able to improve your personal finances, no matter what they are.

My hope is that this book has encouraged you to think of yourself, and the money you have, a little differently.

Be proactive, be a little audacious, and remember that your dreams are just as valuable as anyone else's.

DOLLARS & NO SENSE - WHY ARE YOU SPENDING
MONEY LIKE AN IDIOT?

INTRODUCTION

Let's kick off this book with a simple question: what is money?

No, this is not a rhetorical question.

Find a pen and paper and jot down a few sentences explaining what *you* think money is. Imagine aliens landed on your lawn and demanded a quick explanation for this strange phenomenon called money. What would you tell them?

Seems simple, but try it and you'll soon realize that it's tricky to answer. Money is many different things to people.

What is it to you?

In this book, we'll be tackling the familiar challenges of personal finance management ... but in an unfamiliar way. In the chapters that follow, we'll consider that money is whatever you make of it; it's pure potential and possibility, something you can yourself define and use to your own ends.

If your main money problem is simply "I don't have enough of it!" you may be surprised at the approach we take below. Here, you won't find the same old tips and tricks on how to save money by re-using teabags or buying rice in bulk. Instead, we'll get to the very heart of what money actually *means*, how we spend it and why, and what you can do to start using what you have right now to create a lifestyle that has meaning for you.

We'll consider the root causes of careless spending, as well as the three biggest but largely invisible money myths we all believe in to some extent. We'll then consider ways to start creating a budget that works *for* you and your goals, rather than against it.

Ready?

CHAPTER 1: SPENDING LIKE CRAZY – SIGNS THAT YOUR MONEY HABITS NEED THERAPY

Have you ever opened your wallet and thought, hey where did all my money go?

Have you ever seen someone who ostensibly earns less money than you yet somehow they seem to have a much nicer lifestyle?

Do you ever get the creeping sensation that you're just a rat in a wheel, and that you're never really *getting anywhere* when it comes to money?

Are you often obsessed with buying something and then immediately lose interest in it the second you own it?

Do you feel like you have so much "stuff" but that you don't really need or even like most of it?

Do you ever sit at work and think, "what's the point of all this?"

Does it seem like you spend a lot of your day stressing about money instead of just living?

Do you feel like you're moving from one minor money crisis to the next?

Are you in massive debt and feel sick to the stomach just thinking about how much you owe?

Are you often in relationships, jobs or living situations that you hate simply because you can't afford to try anything else?

If any of the above hit a little too close to home, then this book was written for you. Our culture has a strange blind spot when it comes to money – we'll watch ads for erectile dysfunction medicine on TV without flinching, overshare about our bowel movements and mother issues on social media, but when it comes to a frank discussion about money, many of us are more than a little shy. Money is a leading cause of relationship dissatisfaction, of stress and burnout, and yet we're all super reluctant about bringing it up. You're not supposed to talk about how much you earn. Or how much you *owe*, for that matter.

The result? Many of us have pretty dysfunctional relationships when it comes to money. Even the most put-together person can have an attitude to money that's a little bonkers. Read the following descriptions and see if any of them (or all of them!) sound like you.

The manic depressive spender:
The few days just before payday feel like Christmas Eve to you. You wait and anticipate, and the second you see your new bank balance, you're spending like there's no tomorrow, "treating" yourself to every little thing you know you deserve, spoiling your friends and enjoying the finer things in life. But by the time mid-month comes rolling by, you've overspent and have a horrible money hangover – and have to endure a

miserable few weeks where you scrape by, borrow or live on beans and humiliation. But it's ok because your next payday is coming!

The money addict:

You're probably wealthier now than you've ever been, yet somehow life's expenses have just racked up at the same pace, and your sense of always slightly struggling seems to be the only constant. If money was a drug, well, you developed a tolerance for it a long time ago. What a younger version of yourself would have thought of as success and luxury barely registers at all for you anymore. You're pretty sure there's only one thing that would puncture your thickening skin of boredom and entitlement: more money...

The denial case:

Money is the root of all evil. And it also makes the world go round? Or something. You don't pay too much attention to your credit card statements and you plan on dying young anyway so you never have to stress too much about a pension. You've never been "good with money," you tell yourself, and the only thing you know for sure is that there's always somehow never enough of it. Financial planning and saving sound like things other people do. Things always work out, right? Until they don't. The more irresponsible you are with your finances, the deeper you stick your head into the sand...

Of course, these descriptions are just tongue-in-cheek – poor spending habits and unhealthy attitudes to money can seriously undermine your happiness and wellbeing and are no laughing matter. Money is a resource. It's a symbol. A tool. The way you think about yourself, your life and your worth is keenly reflected in the way you think about money. But in the next chapter, we'll see that most of us don't take money nearly as seriously as we should...

CHAPTER 2: WHY NORMAL BUDGETING ADVICE SELDOM WORKS

So, knowing all of the above, you might decide that you need some expert advice. After all, the next biggest section at the bookstore after self help ...is personal finance.

People grinning like politicians grace the covers of these books, promising that if only you'd just sit down and organize yourself properly, you can get your life together, like them.

So you force yourself to read through these pep-talks, feeling sheepish to discover that you don't really understand compound interest after all, and that at the rate you're going, you can probably only think about retiring at about 95. Depressing!

Let's say you push through and do actually learn a few new tips and tricks to hack yourself into financial shape. Even though you keep it up for a while, your real life is never quite reflected in those pages. People on online personal finance forums tell you to register a business in the Cayman Islands so you can avoid tax, or to keep a piggy bank by your front door so you can save a bit here and there. It's not like these are *bad* ideas, but it's just that somehow... it doesn't seem to fit your life. Why?

Most budgeting advice likes to pretend that poverty is never really an issue

There are lots of reasons your standard personal finance advice never quite "sticks." Let's get the most awkward and uncomfortable one out in the open first, the big elephant in the room that many of the above finance books will just conveniently pretend doesn't exist.

Call it poverty, "struggling", hardship or just plain old not having quite as much money as you need or want, it all amounts to the same thing. And in the same way that a book about dieting macros isn't much help to someone struggling to feed themselves at all, lofty personal finance philosophies that teach you what kind of property you'd best invest in first are ...a bit of a slap in the face.

An acquaintance once told me at a party, "Honestly at our age, if you're not saving at least X each month, you're crazy." The X he was alluding to was astronomically high to me; more, in fact, than many people in my area even made in a month – myself included. The shame and panic I felt then is characteristic of so much financial advice out there. Instead of helping people solve the real lifestyle issues they actually face in life, it makes hurtful assumptions. Pair this with the fact that most people are socialized to never talk about money, to never admit it if they're not doing too well, and you get a nasty cocktail of secrecy and shame around money, instead of realistic ways to tackle problems.

Most budgeting advice fails to take YOU into account

This is really an extension of the above. Most budgeting advice out there assumes you're living a Standard American Life with all the trimmings, are in relatively stable employment, have a spouse and live with the unspoken assumption that you'll want a pension plan and an Xbox and a house for your 2.4 children.

The funny thing about this weird dream is how few people *actually* live it. We've all somehow agreed that this is the way it should be, or the way we want it to be, all the while living lives that are completely different. People are marrying less and cohabiting more, switching careers more, working many part time jobs instead of a single full time one, working from home, or doing strange blends of all of the above. People are leaving home ...then moving back in with their parents. Property has never cost so much for most of the developed world. People spend more on electronics and holidays now, less on cars, furniture, or raising children.

If you're a single parent, a mature student with two part-time jobs, struggling after a divorce or sharing a mortgage with your three sisters, most budgeting advice out there is going to look like a 1950s fairytale to you – nice, but not exactly realistic.

Most budgeting advice is value-neutral

This is not exactly true. Most advice you'll stumble on *is* actually built on a series of beliefs the author will assume you share with them. It's just that these assumptions are so entrenched it's hard to even notice they're there. We all instinctively know that money is a Big Deal, but perhaps because it's such an emotional and touchy subject for so many of us, we like to keep our distance and treat money literacy the same we treat household maintenance or yearly dental checkups.

But money is right at the heart of the way we live our lives. It's part of our identities, part of how we se ourselves and our achievements, part of how we construct meaning for ourselves and others. It's as personal as religion or sexual orientation. It's not value neutral.

It's possible to learn to deal with money on a surface level – but unless you look a little deeper and explore what money actually means to you, you'll be missing what makes money such a big deal in the first place.

Money is a proxy for *value*. It's human shorthand for all the things we've decided are worth something. And because of this, no discussion about money is complete without a discussion about value – specifically *our values*.

CHAPTER 3: TAPPING INTO YOUR MONEY PSYCHOLOGY

All well and good, but so what? What does that mean for you, someone who wants to learn healthier spending habits and take charge of their financial life?

Well, the advice in this book will try buck the trend and offer money advice from a completely different perspective. If you want to learn more about your 401k or what schemes are available for first time home owners, that information is easily available to you. If you need to understand how to pay down your credit card more effectively or what to do with your student loans, then rest assured you'll find answers at your local bank, or online, or by asking your accountant (if you have one!).

This book will simply not cover these issues – or at least, not directly.

Instead, we'll take a step back and ask ourselves *why*. Why do some people rack up huge amounts of debt and others don't? Why do some people make so much but seem to spend it all, while others earn half what they do and seem twice as happy? Why do people buy things the way they do? Why are some people petrified to open their credit card statements while some trade forex "for fun"?

These are not just idle questions though: once you truly understand *why* and *how* you think about money, then you can actually start to make lasting, realistic changes to the way you make, spend and save it.

If you read through the first chapter of this book and found yourself nodding in agreement, chances are you're guilty of a few "money misconceptions." These are myths about money that we've all either been taught or have learnt from our life experiences – but which are nevertheless keeping us back. These unquestioned beliefs about money can keep us from taking an honest, realistic look at where were we really are in our financial lives ...and were we really want to be.

By the end of this book, my hope is that you have a clarified idea of what money *really* means to you, and its role in helping you live a life that aligns with your own principles. But before we can do that, let's have a look at some ideas that may be limiting you in your life right now. You'll get the opportunity to ask yourself, is this really what *I* believe? Is this idea helping my ultimate goals – or hindering them?

CHAPTER 4: THREE BIG MONEY MYTHS – AND WHY THEY DON'T MAKE SENSE

Money Can Buy You Love:

If you've ever casually studied advertising, you'll know that this is one of the fundamental underlying principles. Somewhere along the line, companies realized that merely telling their prospective customers about the characteristics of their product was no good – what they needed to do was sell a lifestyle. In other words, promote the idea that money can buy you love.

And it can buy you every other wonderful emotion, too. When you see the toilet cleaner ad on TV, it's not advertising toilet cleaner, it's selling you the opportunity to be a good wife, to create a safe and hygienic environment for your children. People don't sell cars, they sell freedom. They don't advertise perfume by telling you that it smells like neroli and jasmine, but that it smells like *scantily clad Charlize Theron ascending a luxurious silk rope, pearls and jewels smashing to the floor beneath her.*

Though most of us pay lip service to the idea that money can't buy you love, our spending habits betray the fact that actually ...that's exactly what we're hoping for. In a capitalist society, everything is for sale. You don't only buy a product to do a particular job, you buy yourself, an image of you in the future, using that product, living the kind of life of someone who uses that product.

This is why so many advertisements show people and not the product they're selling. This is why Apple had such extraordinary success marketing themselves against the boring "PC guy" – their marketers understood keenly that their customers weren't only shopping for good laptops and phones, they were primarily *shopping for their own identities.*

Now all of this makes good sense if you're in the business of selling things to impressionable people. Marketing departments spend huge amounts of money to make sure they're digging deep into people's psyches and tweaking just the right strings to get them to buy. They make unspoken promises that spending money will make you more attractive, more sophisticated, more intelligent, more successful.

If you think you're immune to this kind of thing, think again. Advertising evolves as people become more aware – if you've ever paid a little extra for "artisanal" anything or happily bought a product because it promised it was fair trade, you've been had in just the same way. Marketers understand that modern man doesn't want to be manipulated and sold to – so they are careful to make products that people can buy and which show how alternative/progressive they are, how savvy and countercultural. How *un*manipulable they are! It's dirty business.

If you've bought into any of this, one obvious consequence is that you develop the habit of solving problems by *buying* things. Bored? Buy something entertaining. Feeling like life is meaningless? Buy something that makes you feel like you're important. Lonely? Buy some drinks. Get your nails done. Save for a car.

Trying to buy positive emotions doesn't make sense because, for the most part, it just doesn't work. If you buy some expensive high heels because they make you feel like you're finally an adult with a sophisticated grown-up, legitimate job – well, what happens when those shoes break or get dirty or go out of fashion? You never learn to develop your *own* inner sense of worth and confidence. You defer the lesson, you put the psychological work outside of yourself, and into a thing that is inevitably short lived and fleeting. In a few weeks your new shoes start to look just as boring as all your other shoes.

So you're flipping through a magazine one day and see a beautiful, young girl with dazzling ruby lips. Your brain thinks it's finally found a solution. You never needed those old shoes anyway, no, what you really need now is to buy this gorgeous lipstick. And the cycle continues. What never changes is who you are, inside. You never ask yourself, who am I? What does it mean to be an "adult"? What am I looking for? What am I proud of? What do I want to do in this world, today, right now? These nagging questions are soothed temporarily by the rush of something new and shiny – but they never go away. The people who invented the term "retail therapy" knew what they were talking about…

How to stop BUYING solutions to life's problems:

If you identify with this myth, well, you have your work cut out for you. Taking a moment to stop and truly think about your behavior takes a lot of effort. Spending carelessly, being drawn to endless new things but never satisfied, well, that's the default. That's the easy setting. Breaking out of this can be difficult. But it can be done!

To begin, get into the habit of asking yourself *why* before every purchase. No need to send yourself into a weird existential spiral about it, though. Just ask yourself, as honestly as possible, if you're trying to buy an emotion.

Are you trying to redeem your bad lifestyle choices and feel morally superior by buying some overpriced "health food"? Are you buying one brand of smartphone instead of the other because of its price and features, or because you're hoping unconsciously to be one of the "cool kids' by having that particular phone?

Of course, there's no law to say you can't do any of this …only try to be aware. Once you're in the habit of seeing why you're *really* buying something (peer pressure, advertising) you'll loosen its grip on you. You'll also give yourself the opportunity to address your issues *directly*. If you're bored or sad or frustrated, pause before you jump in to buy a solution.

Is there another way to give yourself that feeling? A way that doesn't involve spending money?

Challenge: Sometime within the next week, challenge yourself to not buy something you were thinking of buying. Now, instead of consuming, see if you can turn things around and *produce* instead. Instead of going out for a fancy dinner, why not stay home, challenge yourself to make your own gourmet meal and invite your favorite person to enjoy it with you in a pillow fort in your living room? Instead of blowing money on a premium handcrafted children's bunk bed you saw on Pinterest, enjoy your children by taking them on an impromptu road trip or picnic where you paint watercolors for the afternoon, or take the opportunity to teach your children about woodwork and painting and build a bed yourself. Don't binge on chocolate when you're feeling down, call your mom. You get the idea!

Your Bank Balance = Your Life Report Card:

When you were in school, the custom was to give you a periodic report card to let your parents know that you were keeping up (officially) and how you rated compared to the other kids (unofficially). Though many parents and schools have abandoned the idea of ranking and scoring children in a learning environment this way, the fact is that this attitude is just as prevalent as ever. Most of us still cling to a vague sense of being measured and ranked according to our peers.

We approach our 30th or 40th birthdays, wondering whether our peers are ahead of us in just the same way our mothers stressed when we were the last ones to learn to spell, or when we didn't score high enough in our exams. From early on in life, we are told that human life, learning and progress can be quantified, and once it is, the name of the game is competition.

So, although most people who disagree that they think this way, we all secretly understand that the engineer who earns $200 000 a year is "worth" more than the teacher who earns $20 000. We encourage people to ask for raises by telling them, "you're *worth* it!"

But is this really true?

Far be it for me to downplay the achievements of the world's businessmen and entrepreneurs, and all those who have earned money from their ideas, talents and hard work. It would be strange to suggest that those who are skilled and work hard should not be rewarded.

But.

Thinking of your bank balance as your "life report card" is what is truly diminishing. It reduces a person's entire life achievements to a figure (or several figures), focusing only on those things that can be priced, quantified and put into a spread sheet. In other words, what can be bought or sold.

What you get when you look at the world this way is one-dimensional people. You get the super-successful CEO who sits alone in his expensive condo at night, feeling that for all his money, he's still strangely unfulfilled. You get stay at home parents who experience deep and profound feelings about the work they do, confident about their life's meaning right up to the point were someone dismisses them as "unemployed" and therefore worth exactly nothing.

When you view yourself as a being whose purpose is to make money, and the balance in your bank account as your "score," you rob yourself of a fuller experience of your life. You tick all the financial boxes and feel empty. You wonder what it's all for.

How to stop being defined by your salary:

Challenge: Make a "Life Resume." You don't have to literally write out a CV as you would when looking for a job, but give it some thought: what are your life's achievements? Not as a cog in a machine or as an employee in someone else's company, but as a human being.

What skills do you have? We often write off everything we are and know if it can't be sold on the job market. We forget that we are also husbands and wives, parents, friends, community members. Who we are is so much more than what we can sell ourselves for in the marketplace. Thinking of yourself as earning a score just leads you to ugly feelings of competition where you downplay all the things that make you unique – not to mention all the ways *other* people are unique too! Competition shuts you off from creative solutions. Ironically, it's the real visionaries and free-thinking entrepreneurs, the ones that follows their hearts, that end up making the most money and being more successful anyway!

I Did It All for the Money:

Go to any big-box homeware store in the suburbs and you will see a familiar sight: a busy woman dragging around her bored-to-death partner who can't fake any more enthusiasm for flower shaped candleholders or ceramic birds or beaded lampshades. "But what's this all *for*?" he whines to his girlfriend, who thinks of him as some kind of uncultured idiot.

He has a good point. What is it all for?

For our final "money misconception," lets look at all the ways that you might be tempted to treat money as a goal in and of itself, rather than a tool that helps you achieve your life goals. This is the difference between working for money, rather than money working for you, as cheesy as it sounds. It's a subtle difference, but it lies in the fact that money isn't actually a thing, it's a thing that allows you access to *other things*. What those other things are is entirely up to you. But surprisingly, many of us forfeit this question entirely.

We make enough money to get buy. We save because it's what we're told we should do. We pay the bills and get on with it. But unless you have a *plan* for the things you spend money on, then they're all just as useless as those homeware knick knacks the girl in our story wastes money on. Think about it.

If an item or service adds literally nothing to your life, it's basically the same as you taking that money and throwing it away. You may feel as though you've achieved something in merely earning it, but unless that money was actually put to use in helping you achieve your life's goals – what was it for? You have a lump of savings, which feels nice, but again, what's it for?

Most of us are told to just earn money – and the more the better. Keep getting promotions. Keep earning more. There's a dim understanding of what you'll eventually do with it (buy a house? Retire eventually?) but very few people actually sit down, look at what they earn and ask themselves, how am I going to *use* this?

It can be sobering to look at someone who earns less than what we do, living our dreams and carving out a lifestyle for themselves that we ourselves want. But if you never ask yourself the question (what do I want?) your money will come and it will go again …and your dreams will languish, never actualized. You'll die and maybe leave a chunk of your life's earnings to the next generation, and your only legacy will be a material one – if that. Bleak, isn't it?

This misconception ties into the others, and is built on the idea that money by itself is enough, that money isn't a shorthand for value, but *is* value, not just a symbol for success, but all of what success is. That merely earning it and squirrelling it away is more or less the same thing as living life successfully. It's a rather elaborate way that we tell ourselves we can buy an emotion – in this case, the emotion is one of success, of completeness and accomplishments. When a rapper rolls around in a bath of cash in a music video, the implication is clear – the money *itself* is the achievement.

The trouble is, again, that this line of thinking just doesn't make any sense. Your unfulfilled goals and dreams are still there, nagging at you, your misconceptions remain unchallenged, and your values and principles remain untested. The sheer number of wealthy and yet personally undeveloped people in this world is proof enough that money is just a tool. And like any other tool, it can be used well, or it can sit there and do nothing useful.

How to remember that money is just a tool:

Maybe you can remember being a kid and thinking how when you grew up, you'd be in charge and could do and buy whatever you wanted. What happened to those dreams?

In the previous challenge, you tried to re-imagine a Life Resume that focused on all of your life's accomplishments and skills, not just those that can be labeled with a price tag. While you'll obviously need some marketable skills out there, the idea of this challenge was to remind you of your other dimensions, and that you are so much more than an employee or a tax payer.

In this challenge, we'll do something a little similar. Instead of looking at your budget and seeing only the cold, hard figures, draw up an alternative "Values Budget." In this budget, you won't merely be tallying up the actual money you have coming in and going out – you'll instead be tracking *how well you use that money*, however much it is.

If you're routinely squandering money on things you just don't care about, and which add nothing to your own sense of fulfillment, then you have a bad budget, and it doesn't matter how much you earn.

Sit down with a pen and paper and start brainstorming two or three of your ultimate life values.

These are the things that are important to you, the non negotiables of your life, the things, maybe, that you'd be prepared to die for. This is what gives you a sense of satisfaction and purpose at the end the day, or what guides each of your actions. Don't worry if you haven't worked out a crystal clear set of values for yourself, but ask yourself the question anyway.

Now, let's say you've narrowed it down to two very special life values that you believe are more important to you than anything else: the happiness of your family and the belief that you should always, no matter what, try to grow and expand your mind, and learn new things. Other possible values could include independence, artistic expression, romantic love, building something useful, fame or spiritual connection. It doesn't really matter.

Now, if you're like the average human being, you'll probably be using around a third of your total time sleeping or doing general "life admin" like eating, showering, getting dressed, walking from one place to another. That's around 8 hours. For argument's sake, let's say you're in full time employment and expected to work 8 hours a day. The remaining 8 hours are yours, let's say for recreation.

Though there's not much wiggle room when it comes to sleeping or "life admin," the rest of your day is up to you. Look at the relative proportions of time you spend on different activities and ask yourself if they match your principles and values. If you value your family's happiness and the ability to learn new things more than anything else – does your schedule actually reflect that?

Don't only look at how much time you're "spending" on certain activities, but also how much actual money. You may well re-consider your identity as a lifelong learner and family man if you only total $45 and 2.5 hours per month on both of these values. Look at what you *are* spending time and money on. Are these the things that deeply move you and give your life meaning?

You may discover a pretty obvious root cause of unhappiness: that your daily habits (including your money habits) don't truly align with your higher values. You may be wasting precious time working at a job you don't really care about only to spend all that money on things and activities you don't really care about either.

The great thing about an expanded budget such as this one is that it's *not* value neutral. Money has value in your life to the extent that you can use it for the things that make you happy and fulfilled. What does it matter to be frugal and pinch pennies if you have no real sense of what a saved penny can do for you anyway? What good is a raise or end-of-year bonus if it can only buy you *more* of the same things that don't really fulfill you?

Decide on your values (pick two or three). Look at what you actually spend your time and money on – are your habits and values well-aligned? Can you take the time and money you spend on things that don't enrich you and funnel them towards things that do?

You could find novel ways to use coupons to buy budget cereal or buy a second hand appliance instead of a new one. But you reap greater rewards when you take a *full, comprehensive* look at your life and ask how money is and isn't serving you. With that in mind, let's move onto some real, practical ways to start improving your relationship with money, from the ground up.

CHAPTER 5: SMART WAYS TO THINK ABOUT YOUR MONEY

The only way to make meaningful changes in your life is to do something you haven't done before.

Begin with the attitude, "what if this wasn't the way it is, but some other way?"

Be willing to drop all the assumptions you make each and every day, and be open to new possibilities. Like any lifestyle change, revamping your attitude to money takes patience and the willingness to form new and healthier habits. As you complete the exercises listed here, as well as those that will follow, try to maintain a curious, open frame of mind:

Be aware, be in control:

You can't change what you're not aware of. Decide today that you'll take charge of money, rather than feeling like it is in charge of you. For people who've grown up in homes where money was scarce, the feeling that resources will always be scarce is hard to shake. But you are in control. You decide what thoughts you have, and the thoughts you have determine your behaviors and habits.

It may seem like a small thing at first, but often, the biggest transformations in life happen when we look honestly at our thoughts, feelings and behaviors and see them for what they are. You might have an out of control spending habit, one where you blow huge amounts of money every weekend on overpriced drinks. But one day you stop for a second, look at the drink in your hand and think, *is this really worth it*? And then you look closely at just how much money you waste every month this way, and you add it up over each year, over a lifetime. You think about how you've stupidly told your friends, "I'd love to study part time, I just can't afford it." You decide to change your lifestyle, to start spending money on the things you really value. It's hard work, but none of it would have started without that first thought, that first moment of awareness.

Have the courage to keep asking yourself, what am I doing now? Why am I doing this? Is this what I want? Am I happy? What if this wasn't the way it is now, but some other way?

Make the choice:

It's an old truism that if you don't choose, someone else will be happy to choose for you, and this is also true of all things money-related. If you don't negotiate for a higher salary, you'll get the default one. If you don't make an effort to make and stick to a budget, there will be millions of people out there who will happily take your money from you. If you don't actively choose where to spend your money, you may find that it somehow gets eaten up by the end of the month anyway.

Be proactive when it comes to your finances. Realize that money is nothing but *potential*. It can be whatever you want it to be: savings for a rainy day, a smaller investment into something big and important, a momentary bit of pleasure, security, a way to survive, something fun and ego-boosting ...anything. So use it wisely.

Don't focus on lack – be grateful instead:

It's easy to fall into the frame of mind where you're punishing yourself, where you're on a kind of diet where you're not allowed to spend or enjoy yourself. This may be the case for those "manic depressive spenders" we spoke about above. The problem with this kind of attitude is that you work against yourself, and set yourself up for failure. And you make overspending seem extra attractive!

If you feel miserable when moderating your spending, take some time to remind yourself that you're making active choices, and that you don't *have to*, rather you want to. Remind yourself of your values. Try not to focus on all the things you don't have, but be grateful for the things you do.

Many people recommend a "gratitude journal" and as cheesy as it sounds, it's a remarkably easy way to remind yourself of how fortunate you already are. Instead of becoming numb to all the wonderful things that are already in your life, take the time to remember how lucky you are to eat well, to have the luxuries you do, to have friends and family, or even for the blessing of sitting outside in a park with the warm sun on your face.

Try jotting down 10 things that you're grateful for every single day. This will not only unlock old wells of pleasure and life satisfaction you might have forgotten about, but it will keep you aligned with your higher values and principles.

Adapt and learn:

Things change ...and so should you. What works in your early twenties won't work in your retirement years. As your life circumstances change and develop, your attitude to money should be flexible enough to change along with it.

Have a five-year plan, but make it a flexible one, one that can grow and adapt as needed. As you make changes to your spending habits and money lifestyle, you may of course stumble on something that doesn't work. That's OK. Trial and error (emphasis on the error) is just part of learning.

Keep in mind that just because you did something once before, doesn't mean you have to keep doing it. You're allowed to change your mind. And you're allowed to be wrong. Think of it this way: you either succeed, or you learn. You only fail when you look at the outcomes of a lifestyle change and fail to take any lessons from it. So, feel free to read something in these pages, try it out for yourself and then decide that nope, it won't work for you.

We've looked at three of the most common underlying money misconceptions that are probably getting in the way of a money lifestyle that truly serves you. We've looked at some of the hidden beliefs that may be quietly limiting your ability to use money for what it is: a tool that can help you achieve your goals and create a life that fits with your values and principles.

Let's take a more practical look at your actual budget now, but try to keep in mind this bigger picture. Below we're going to look at ways to bring your actual spending habits closer in line with what's important to you. We'll look at ways to take the insanity out of spending and get a greater sense of control and awareness over how you use your money. You can follow the outline suggested below as often as you like. And since money advice is only good advice if it actually works for your life, feel free to adapt and adjust it as necessary.

Step One - Take a good hard look:

If you haven't already, it's time to look at what you spend in a typical month. You'd be surprised how few people know exactly what they spend and where. In fact, if you're hesitant to even look properly, ask yourself if there's something you're trying to avoid looking at too closely.

You can appraise your monthly spending in a few ways: looking at bank statements and going through each item carefully, highlighting every expense according to the type (eating, entertainment, clothing, schooling, debt etc.) is an easy and obvious way to start. You might like to download a money management app that will allow you to look at your expenses in a variety of ways – sometimes graphs and pie graphs really drive the point home.

Look at what percentage of your total income you're spending on each area (i.e. 30% on rent, 10% on food), look at savings and if you can, try to identify any long term trends (i.e. your rent keeps going up but your salary is staying the same, or you keep going into debt every January after Christmas).

It's just data at this point so try to stay curious and pretend it's someone else's spending you're looking at. If something feels too scary or depressing to look at, that's your cue to look even closer at it...

Step Two - Rate how well this budget is suiting your needs:

As we've seen, most money management advice out there has a very simplistic take on budgets: more money is good, less is bad. But I hope you've been convinced now to look at your budget with higher expectations.

Look at your spending habits in all their glory. Look at that awkward lump of debt you'd rather not think about. Look at your salary, what you (really!) spend on gym, on internet, on coffee and snacks, on medical expenses. Now, recall to mind your "life resume" and "values budget" from earlier chapters. Whether you did this exercise in full or merely thought about it, try to remember now what your ultimate values are as a human being, and what your achievements in life thus far have been.

Now, ask yourself, are your spending habits helping or hindering you in these values and achievements? Are you spending in alignment with these ideas – or in direct opposition to them?

Look for areas where you bleed a lot of money into things you don't actually care about. If you only buy a coffee and a snack every day at work because you're bored and unfulfilled, you're spending inefficiently. If you can identify where you are trying to "buy your emotions," then you can cut that spending and think of real ways to address that emotional need – you'll help yourself and save that cash all at the same time.

You may notice that wasting a hundred dollars each month on expensive coffee and treats during lunch hour is just a small thread – but pull on it and you may discover it leads to bigger lifestyle changes you might be ready for. You may discover that overspending in this area only happens because you're bored with your job and need to ask for more challenging projects. This may be just the impetus to admit that it's time to ask for a promotion or look for another job. Had you merely tried the standard budgeting advice (buy a coffee machine for home instead and take it work in a thermos! Have tea instead, it's cheaper!) you've gone a step further and made meaningful changes to your lifestyle.

Take a moment to look and see whether your spending habits and attitude to money is doing its job of helping you achieve your goals.

Step Three - Re-prioritize:

If you're reading this book, the answer to the previous question may be "hell no." That's fine. Without changing your total income or your total expenditure, attempt now to reshuffle and put your resources to their *best* possible use. Is your lifelong goal of learning to play the violin more important than wasting hours every evening binge watching series? Then stop paying for TV each month and funnel that money instead into a fund for violin lessons. If you value the idea of making meaningful change in the world, or of doing the right thing, cut that useless gym membership you keep paying for and offer to volunteer at a dog shelter instead. You still get some exercise, you save money *and* you do something that's ultimately worth so much more to you.

Think creatively here. Don't assume you "need" something. Ask yourself honestly if you just *want* it. Some choices can be difficult of course, and most of us are working with very limited incomes. But make this easier for yourself by contextualizing: going to the movies every weekend feels indispensable ...but is it *more* valuable to you than paying down that depressing debt?

When you use your deepest values as your yardstick, these choices become easier. It may feel miserable to trim down your food or eating budget, but it may energize you to make those same cuts if you know that the money you're saving is going to wards buying a gift for someone you love, or for the holiday of a lifetime, or your child's education. The great thing about editing your budget according to *your own values* is that you're not making or saving more money, but using the money you already have to its best purpose. You're optimizing. And so you don't have to feel miserable forcing yourself to be frugal, because your actions are naturally geared towards a lifestyle that means something to you. You're not trimming your budget, you're enriching your life. You're not taking away, but *adding*.

Step Four - Develop active habits:

All the money epiphanies in the world mean nothing until they're put into action. The whole point of looking closely at your spending habits, your money psychology and the misconceptions fuelling your spending habits is simple: *do* something about it.

Thankfully, the smallest changes are sometimes the best. Don't worry about making grand one-time gestures to fix up your money troubles once and for all. Rather, focus on small, realistic habits that you can do each and every day. It's these changes, after all, that will accumulate and go to making up the bulk of the life you want to create.

Let's say you commit to dropping expensive dinners with your partner. Many of us just default to eating as entertainment – but there's so much more to life than eating! Instead spend that money on things that you both actually enjoy: buy board games, save up for a hobby you can both do together or go to interesting talks or workshops. Instead of taking public transport, take your bike and you save money and get some fitness into your schedule at the same time.

Here's a more extreme example. Let's say you look at your budget and realize that although you deeply value travelling and learning about new and exciting places, you haven't actually been able to afford a real holiday for years. But you fritter away money every year on travelling to visit distant family members, people who you don't like much and who don't seem to like you either. Not only do these family members add nothing to your life, they actively make you less happy by adding stress and keeping you from putting that money towards a trip that would actually make you happy.

Just by looking realistically at your budget, you've discovered that you have also been spending too much time on unfulfilling relationships that are more about obligation than anything else. Without spending an extra cent, you make it a habit to treat yourself each year to a weekly vacation somewhere *you* want to go.

Step Five - Rinse and repeat:

As we've seen, happy spending habits are more or less always a work in progress. Make daily changes to your life and try on new habits for size. Then have another look and ask how those changes are working for you. Can you change something else? Is there something new you've learnt? Have you learnt how *not* to do it?

Tips on Surviving a Money Crazy World:

Avoid, wherever you can, the temptation to spend on impulse. If you always give yourself a "cooling off period," you'll minimize emotional spending or buying something just because of sneaky advertising. For smaller purchases, wait 24 hours, and for bigger purchases, sleep on it for a few days before committing.

When you're spending money on something, don't focus only on the price you see in front of you. Ask yourself what this item *really costs you*. How long did you have to work to afford it? By working that long and exchanging that time for money for this item, did you really get a "good deal"? Could you use that time or that money on something else, that's worth more to you? Is that money actually worth more *unspent*, i.e. do you really have to buy anything at all?

Fast forward purchases a few years. Many of us throw away huge amounts of junk from our homes every year, and also keep buying things obsessively, never making the connection between the two. Are you going to get bored of this item within a few months? Will it really last? How will it fit into your life? Are you actually just buying next year's junk?

Don't go to shopping malls unless you're feeling calm, rational and in control. This means avoiding the shops when you're hungry, sad, bored, angry... You'll only be extra susceptible to advertising and pressure to "buy solutions." You'll have to work extra hard to resist temptation and may fall into the trap of feeling that you're depriving yourself.

Be prepared. It's so much easier to act wisely when you're acting according to a plan you've spent time on beforehand. Know how much you can afford to spend on a night out before you leave. Go shopping with a list and don't buy anything not on that list. Pack a work lunch the night before so you're not tempted to buy something expensive on the spur of the moment when you get hungry.

Try to see if you can spend your money on lived experiences rather than things. Things get old. They break. People get bored of them. But happy memories can last a lifetime, and if your experience teaches you a new skill or gives you a fresh insight on life, even better. Think of travelling somewhere novel, seeing a show, going to a class to learn something new, challenging yourself to a marathon or climb, donating to a charity that means something to you, experiencing beautiful music or performances, going into nature ...all of these things have so much more value compared to something like a phone upgrade or a new piece of furniture for your home.

Carry only small amounts of cash on you, for emergencies. This will deter you from spending mindlessly. It's easy to think of a few coins in your wallet as nothing much, but they add up. Spending on bank cards has the added advantage of letting you track exactly how much and on what you spend your money.

If you're trying to develop your professional career, you might like to consider negotiating for and working towards a higher hourly rate with less total time worked rather than endlessly angling for more work. In the long term, you'll value your *time* more and more. As you upskill and become more experienced, look for more job flexibility, more benefits and more free time rather than just a higher salary. Employers are usually a bit happier to negotiate on these anyway, and they'll actually have a greater impact on your quality of life.

When making big spending decisions, consider how a choice will mature with time. It may be that it's better to spend on X rather than Y in the present moment, but wait ten years and X just gets worse and worse as a choice. When considering big purchases, spending on education or paying off debt, ask yourself what will give you the greatest flexibility and control in the future. Ask which choice gives you more choices later on. Give less weight to choices that can't be undone or modified and more weight to those that can.

Don't be afraid to talk about money. Let go of hang ups and ask for help and advice when you need it. There's no shame in having money difficulties or being stuck with debt – but it's a real shame if you let hang ups about money prevent you from tackling a serious problem head on.

Some of our most nonsensical spending habits are closely tied with our worst life habits in general. Do you have an unhealthy drinking or smoking habit? This is the kind of thing you pay for over and over again – you pay for the substance itself, you pay with diminished health and you may even have to pay later on for medicine or treatment for health problems you bring on yourself. When it comes to any kind of addiction, it's never worth it. If this is you, the best thing you can do for yourself is clean up this bad habit. Drop your nasty sugar addiction. Quit smoking. Cut back on drinking. Vow to stay away from junk food.

Speaking of habits, there's one that you can get rid of instantly: gambling. If you're throwing away money on casinos or lottery tickets (or, as my grandmother called it, "idiot tax") then just stop. That money will do far more for you as savings.

Avoid comparing yourself to others. There's a lot of ego bound up in money, and it's hard to break the automatic connection that money = success. If you're suffering from trying to keep up with your peers, try to remember that people willfully display the life they want you to see, and there are invariably problems that you never know about. Keep going towards your own goals. If someone's success feels intimidating, try turn that feeling into inspiration – how can you do the same? What can you learn from them?

Avoid, wherever you can, the temptation to spend on impulse. If you always give yourself a "cooling off period," you'll minimize emotional spending or buying something just because of sneaky advertising. For smaller purchases, wait 24 hours, and for bigger purchases, sleep on it for a few days before committing.

When you're spending money on something, don't focus only on the price you see in front of you. Ask yourself what this item *really costs you*. How long did you have to work to afford it? By working that long and exchanging that time for money for this item, did you really get a "good deal"? Could you use that time or that money on something else, that's worth more to you? Is that money actually worth more *unspent*, i.e. do you really have to buy anything at all?

Fast forward purchases a few years. Many of us throw away huge amounts of junk from our homes every year, and also keep buying things obsessively, never making the connection between the two. Are you going to get bored of this item within a few months? Will it really last? How will it fit into your life? Are you actually just buying next year's junk?

Don't go to shopping malls unless you're feeling calm, rational and in control. This means avoiding the shops when you're hungry, sad, bored, angry... You'll only be extra susceptible to advertising and pressure to "buy solutions." You'll have to work extra hard to resist temptation and may fall into the trap of feeling that you're depriving yourself.

Be prepared. It's so much easier to act wisely when you're acting according to a plan you've spent time on beforehand. Know how much you can afford to spend on a night out before you leave. Go shopping with a list and don't buy anything not on that list. Pack a work lunch the night before so you're not tempted to buy something expensive on the spur of the moment when you get hungry.

Try to see if you can spend your money on lived experiences rather than things. Things get old. They break. People get bored of them. But happy memories can last a lifetime, and if your experience teaches you a new skill or gives you a fresh insight on life, even better. Think of travelling somewhere novel, seeing a show, going to a class to learn something new, challenging yourself to a marathon or climb, donating to a charity that means something to you, experiencing beautiful music or performances, going into nature ...all of these things have so much more value compared to something like a phone upgrade or a new piece of furniture for your home.

Carry only small amounts of cash on you, for emergencies. This will deter you from spending mindlessly. It's easy to think of a few coins in your wallet as nothing much, but they add up. Spending on bank cards has the added advantage of letting you track exactly how much and on what you spend your money.

If you're trying to develop your professional career, you might like to consider negotiating for and working towards a higher hourly rate with less total time worked rather than endlessly angling for more work. In the long term, you'll value your *time* more and more. As you upskill and become more experienced, look for more job flexibility, more benefits and more free time rather than just a higher salary. Employers are usually a bit happier to negotiate on these anyway, and they'll actually have a greater impact on your quality of life.

When making big spending decisions, consider how a choice will mature with time. It may be that it's better to spend on X rather than Y in the present moment, but wait ten years and X just gets worse and worse as a choice. When considering big purchases, spending on education or paying off debt, ask yourself what will give you the greatest flexibility and control in the future. Ask which choice gives you more choices later on. Give less weight to choices that can't be undone or modified and more weight to those that can.

Don't be afraid to talk about money. Let go of hang ups and ask for help and advice when you need it. There's no shame in having money difficulties or being stuck with debt – but it's a real shame if you let hang ups about money prevent you from tackling a serious problem head on.

Some of our most nonsensical spending habits are closely tied with our worst life habits in general. Do you have an unhealthy drinking or smoking habit? This is the kind of thing you pay for over and over again – you pay for the substance itself, you pay with diminished health and you may even have to pay later on for medicine or treatment for health problems you bring on yourself. When it comes to any kind of addiction, it's never worth it. If this is you, the best thing you can do for yourself is clean up this bad habit. Drop your nasty sugar addiction. Quit smoking. Cut back on drinking. Vow to stay away from junk food.

Speaking of habits, there's one that you can get rid of instantly: gambling. If you're throwing away money on casinos or lottery tickets (or, as my grandmother called it, "idiot tax") then just stop. That money will do far more for you as savings.

Avoid comparing yourself to others. There's a lot of ego bound up in money, and it's hard to break the automatic connection that money = success. If you're suffering from trying to keep up with your peers, try to remember that people willfully display the life they want you to see, and there are invariably problems that you never know about. Keep going towards your own goals. If someone's success feels intimidating, try turn that feeling into inspiration – how can you do the same?

What can you learn from them?

CONCLUSION

At the beginning of this book, I asked you to answer the question, "what is money?"

Well, let's look again at this question as we come to the end of the book. Do you still have the same definition of money? Or have you altered it slightly, or made it a little larger?

The way you think about money is highly personal – your attitude to money is a reflection of your upbringing, your culture, your personality with all its virtues and shortcomings. Money can be a literal prison, tying you down to work and habits that drain you of motivation and purpose. It can also be a bridge that carries you to your life goals, a tool and a resource that allows you to access the things you truly value in life.

The role that money ultimately plays in your life is entirely up to you. It rests in having the self awareness to be honest about the choices we make every day, in the bravery to know what we value and hold dear, and the dedication to make rational strategies to reach those goals.

My hope is that this book has given you a starting point to begin to reconsider your relationship to money and, by extension, your relationship to yourself and the world you live in. My hope is that you've found something here that inspires you to think differently and make different choices, ones that will leave you feeling more in control and more fulfilled than before.

We each only have one life – here's to spending it wisely!

THE MINIMALIST BUDGET - A PRACTICAL GUIDE ON HOW TO SAVE MONEY, SPEND LESS AND LIVE MORE WITH A MINIMALIST LIFESTYLE

INTRODUCTION

What's the first thing you think of when you hear the word "budget"? It's a meager little word, one that all too often comes after *"tight"*.

Maybe you think of this word as an adjective, something to describe a cheap and substandard car or hotel. "Budget" brings to mind rationing, a kind of money diet.

If you're like many people, budgeting is something you do with a kind of deflated spirit: budgeting means bargain bin quality and the sad sense that what you want is going to be just out of reach.

This book will try a different approach to budgeting all together. It's a pity that the idea of living within one's means should be experienced as such a deficit – this book will try to show that when you apply the principles of minimalism to budgeting, you are neither in a state of self-denial or trying to survive a financial scrape. In fact, a minimalist budget is a particular approach to abundance and fulfillment that may seem counterintuitive to most.

Undoubtedly, what came into your mind when you heard the word "budget" was simple: money. Money is a thing to be feared, to be saved, to be celebrated when it's there and mourned when it isn't. Budgeting, we are told, is necessary. When you live in a world where there is always one more thing to buy, being cognizant of the fact that you don't have endless resources is just the practical thing to do.

However, budgeting can be much more than this. To put it simply, money is only *one* of the resources that we should be managing in our lives, and possibly not even the most important one.

As humans, it is our lot to deal with being finite beings: we have only so much time to spend on this earth, only so much time that we are allotted each day, only so much energy that we can give away before we run into a deficit.

In a sense, the principles of minimalism rest on a more fundamental interpretation of "budget". Just as you need to match your financial expenditure with your income, minimalism encourages us to match our needs with our actions. It doesn't make sense to buy food for 12 when you have a family of 4 in the same way it doesn't make sense to clutter up your home with things you don't want, like or need. Trimming away at unessential elements in your day-to-day life is an exercise in budgeting and minimalism both, whether you are trimming away excess expenses, destructive thoughts or junk in your spare room.

This book will offer an expanded notion of what it means to budget. We'll look at how money is not the only resource that needs to be managed, and a "life budget" that acknowledges your emotional, behavioral, social and even spiritual capital is more likely to lead to smarter decisions.

Minimalism is not, of course, about starvation or punishment. It's not about doing with less than you need. Rather, minimalism is about finding what you need and fulfilling that need exactly, without excess. It's a subtle point and one that the average person who has grown up in an industrialized capitalist society can miss: *to have exactly enough is not suffering*. Budgeting is therefore about understanding what you need to have enough, and how best you can allocate your resources to that end.

Most of the budgeting advice out there will come firmly out of the scarcity paradigm – you're usually offered a few ways to shave off money here and there. You are asked to look at all the instances where you are not spending or living on the bare minimum, and usually anything extra is framed as unnecessary, indulgent or, depending on who you talk to, bordering on immoral. These tips will tell you that after enough cheap toothpaste, homemade laundry soap and clothes bought out of season, you'll save enough money and make it all work. You're asked to look over your life and find places where you could manage, without too much discomfort, to do with less or even without.

While thriftiness and being money-conscious are excellent skills to have (and for some, absolutely necessary), minimalist budgeting is more about conscious decision making and less about stinginess and trying to endure a lack.

To show the difference, consider a purchase someone might make: a new dishwasher. On paper, the initial cost of a dishwasher might make it look like a kind of luxury. After all, you can simply wash the dishes *for free* yourself, right? In traditional budgetland, a dishwasher may fall well into the category of "unnecessary". Can you do without it? Of course. Then, it doesn't belong in your pared down budget. On the face of it, this logic seems sound. In fact, while you're laboring away washing dishes by hand, you may even get the impression that doing it all yourself is kind of noble.

The "minimalist budgeting" in this book will ask you to take a more expanded view of the dishwasher. Not buying one will certainly result in less of your money spent. But, as mentioned, since money is not your only resource, by focusing on only this aspect you're not getting the full picture. Is the cost of doing dishes by hand *really* free? In your budget, have you factored in the fact that washing dishes saps hours of your life each week and makes you grumpy? If you're so wiped out at the prospect of another 45 minutes of housework at the end of the day that you give up and splash out on expensive restaurant food, you haven't even saved money, anyway.

When you lay alone in bed at night and ponder your existence, which will mean more to you: the extra cash you saved by not buying a dishwasher, or the lifestyle you gave up as the person who never has to worry about dishes again? You can't take your possessions with you when you die, they say, but which will be more soothing to you on your deathbed - the fact that your life was thrifty or that it was enjoyable and meaningful?

Simple budgeting doesn't take these kinds of things into account. The primary purpose of your life, at least in some sense, is to be happy. Money usually facilitates this. But if you're maximizing your money to the point that it makes you less happy, your budget is no longer serving its purpose. Minimalist budgeting is like regular budgeting, only with an eye to what is truly important. While this book will certainly show you nifty ways to save a buck here and there, it will also regularly ask you to examine what that buck means to you at the end of the day.

We'll explore shopping and spending habits, identify problem areas, think about debt and make achievable goals for home, work and more. We'll look at concrete ways to put some of these principles into action, and look at resources that will keep you focused and motivated. But at the same time, this book is also about the philosophy of minimalism, not thriftiness.

If you can pair your budget plan with a more nuanced understanding of your relationship with money and how it ties into how you want to live, the changes you make will be more authentic and longer lasting.

CHAPTER 1: THE PURCHASE

Let's start at the very beginning – the moment when we buy something, when money changes hands and we go home with a new item that suddenly is part of our lives.

The fact that so many people buy things when they barely even thought of buying them before they actually stepped into a shop speaks to the power of advertising. The typical shopping experience is an exercise in mindlessness. In fact, one of its primary characteristics is that you can't think about it for too long – otherwise you'd probably come to your senses and leave with the same amount of money you came in with. If you've ever arrived at home and looked at a purchase, almost as if for the first time, and regretted it deeply, you've fallen victim to the forces that can trap the mindless customer.

Mindful consuming means having principles set firmly in place before going into this fray. When you know what you want and why, you're somewhat immune to advertising. If you waltz into a shop without a firm sense of why you're there and what you need and want, you're basically inviting the forces of marketing to come and take your money and time from you. Here are some ways to become a more savvy consumer:

Avoid going to shops and malls when you feel tired, sad or bored

Advertising doesn't appeal to your highest self; it speaks to your weakness – your emotions of greed or fear. For advertising of most items to work, the customer needs to feel that they are lacking somehow: your children's clothes are filthy, your phone is old and outdated, you look and feel terrible and only a new X can fix the problem. If you enter into a retail space already in a compromised mood, you'll be even more primed to receive these messages. For much of the Western world, people are encouraged to solve problems by buying things. Be mindful of negative emotions and be careful of making decisions when you are trying to escape them.

Get a real sense of your options

As modern day hunter-gatherers, we have a long history of ferreting out a good bargain, or finding exactly the item that we need. It's no exaggeration that the quality of our choices can never be better than the quality of the options we have at hand. If you are simply not aware of something better, you can't possibly choose it. Don't be a person who makes poor purchasing choices simply because you didn't know any better. There may be a close and convenient store that you always go to, but ask yourself, are there any other options worth considering? Could you buy your item online? A common advertising trick is to provide the customer with plenty of options – but don't forget: you can always *not* choose and go somewhere else where the choices are different.

Have a plan

Spur-of-the-moment style decisions can work out OK sometimes, but more often than not, choices made spontaneously only serve to increase confusion and dim focus in your life. Before you head out to shop, visualize what you need and why. Imagine a filter going down over your eyes that allows you to only perceive what is relevant. Write a list if it helps, and plan to go when you have adequate time and the shops will not be too busy.

Be realistic

People build entire careers out of making merchandise look more appealing to you in the store. Lighting, special displays and music make everything look better. You may unconsciously buy into the hype that a mannequin and special marketing help to create around a particular item of clothing, for instance. You then get home and realize: you simply bought a very ordinary sweater. Try, as much as you can, to take each item and imagine it in your actual life. How will this fit you? Will your family *actually* eat this? Where in your day do you plan to use this new gadget?

Learn to look for quality

Get into the habit of examining the workmanship of new items. Check seams of clothing, look at how tools or toys are constructed, examine the warranties of appliances and think of how much maintenance each item will require once purchased. Never buy an item with the intention of it only lasting a short time. Just the same as you imagine a new item and how it will fit with your life, try to imagine what it will look in a year or two.

Keep it simple

Food, for example, is an area where there is a lot of "added value" thrown into the mix. You wrote "potatoes" on your list but now you see that there are at least five different options for potatoes – different prices, different degrees of being pre-processed, organic or nonorganic etc.

If you only wrote "potatoes", there's a strong chance this item in your life is simply not that important to stress about. Don't waste another 5 minutes of your existence trying to maximize on a decision that, truthfully, means very little to you. Buy any old potatoes and get on with it. This frees up time to track down and optimize the more specific needs you have, for example the other possible item on your list, "Two bottles of fresh orange juice – the one with the green label."

Keep your other resources in mind

You've probably heard the advice that buying fresh vegetables is cheaper than ones that are pre-cut or processed somehow. This is true. But with an eye to minimalism and not just thriftiness (or worse, being cheap), we need to consider the bigger picture. A bag of bulk, unwashed and unpeeled potatoes may save you a little money. But before you reach for them, add into the price your time and effort it will take to cut and peel them yourself. If you can earn more money in your job during the time it would take you to cut and peel than the money you save by buying the cheaper version, then you haven't really saved anything. In fact, you've lost money and purposefully chosen to fill your time – your other precious resource – with potato peeling. Sometimes time really is money – strike a balance.

Think in relative terms

Get into the habit of looking at the price of things in terms of the price of other things. $100 may not seem like much for such a fabulous new gadget, but when you think of it in terms of costing the same as 20 cups of coffee, two shirts or food for your dog for a month, you get a little more perspective. Better yet, frame it in terms of hours you'd need to work. Is the item worth, say, four hours of your life? Let's be dramatic here, it's not four hours of work you're paying, it's four hours of time, also known as... your life.

Commit to not comparing yourself to others

Thank goodness for advertisers that human beings are such insecure social creatures. How much has been bought in the history of the world simply to keep up with someone else who bought something too? How much of the value of an item is merely the value of everyone else's approval? Don't pressure yourself into buying something just because you feel like it's the thing people should do. We like to think we grow out of this peer pressure with age, but many an adult has taken on ungodly amounts of debt to buy their homes simply because that's what the world expects of people their particular age.

If all else fails, don't give money to people who tell you that you suck

90% of advertising is based on telling you how awful and stupid your life is without their product. Do you want to reward this kind of thing by giving these people your money?

CHAPTER 2: MAKING YOUR BUDGET, PART ONE: FINDING THE CORE

Because this book is not just about financial budgeting, but takes into account other important factors, too, our budgets are going to be a little different. Our main goal for this expanded type of budget is to find that sweet spot in between what we want and need, and the resources we have to give towards this end – not just money.

Perhaps you're familiar with Oscar Wilde's advice: when you only have two pennies left in the world, spend one on bread and the other on a lily.

Oscar may have been a bit flamboyant, but he understood something about budgeting and value. He valued his own inspiration, his own sense of well being and believing that the world was a beautiful place *as much as* he valued the need to eat. For Oscar, being filled up with twice as much bread was simply not worth it if you had neglected to nourish your soul. That we want to be mindful and smart with our money is a given. But there are two other resources that people routinely forget to factor into their budgets: time and value.

Time

Your salary could always change, and even if you lose your job, you'll likely have some savings or a severance package to tide you over for a while. It's always possible to borrow or lend money, or, in that case, steal it even. Time is not so forgiving. All we know is that we are alive right now – how much time we still have is anyone's guess, and we could suddenly run out in an instant. Money can be made and spent, but time is more fixed. We will all die. None of us, no matter our station in life, wakes up to the luxury of more than 24 hours each day. In this, we are all equal.

Trading in time for money is the basis of all work – you sell a piece of your work and effort (i.e. your time) in exchange for money. This works out fine if you intend to use that money to enrich the remaining time you have, but sadly, people can forget this part of the dynamic. The balance between time and money is forgotten about – we make choices as if time was infinite and money was the most important.

Rather than begin with money, a solid minimalist budget begins with time, the most absolute and precious of your resources. You may feel it's counterproductive to dawdle with your time management when your credit card debt needs attention, but the two are inextricably linked. A budget that takes into account money will only ever solve half of your problems.

Begin with the capital you have: 24 hours each day, seven days in each week. Decide on your needs and work backwards. Sleep is a good place to start – you may block out seven or eight hours of each day to sleep. Next block out time taken for meals, exercise and grooming. Try not to be idealistic – you may think you only spend an hour each morning getting ready, but be honest and look at what you really spend. No time is "dead". If you feel like you need at least an hour to unwind and do nothing at the end of each day, factor that in.

When you begin to break down your life in this way, you may notice how much of your time is frittered away on things that you don't ultimately care about. People lament the lack of quality relaxation time they have in their lives and yet waste hours on TV or trashy websites that add nothing to their experience. This points to a problem in time budgeting: sometimes, our spending habits are not in tune with our values and goals.

Just as you don't want to pay extra for an insurance service you have no need for, you don't want to use up your time in a way that doesn't fit your main goals. At the end of the day, no matter what you have done, the 24 hours is up, and your decisions are made. End of story. The fact that our lives are finite is scary enough – to know that you squandered what you had on looking at gossip on the Internet or flipping past infomercials on the couch will make this fact even harder to swallow.

The thing about time is that it's not possible to go into debt – if you spend more time on a task than you really want to, that time is taken away from something else. Zoning out in front of a game seems pretty innocuous, until you think that that activity is actively *displacing* another one. In other words, it's an opportunity cost, and you're usually losing out on other, better opportunities.

When you choose to play computer games for 4 hours straight you are making a choice, even if you don't think you are: you are saying that this activity is more important than anything else you could be doing at the moment. Better than spending time with those you love, better than learning to play that instrument you've been meaning to, better than exercise or a good meal or sex. So, is it? Budgeting your time is asking yourself this deliberately: is this the best way to spend your time?

Here's a clue that you have been squandering your time: you're always busy but feel like you never have any time. You go to bed at night with the creeping suspicion that, on the grand "to do" list of life, you've forgotten to tick something off. You get depressed on Sunday evenings thinking about going back to work. You feel old. You say to people around you, "Hey, where did September go?"

Value

The second valuable resource is a little more subtle. For the most part, money is a stand-in for "value". It is a symbol of worth that we attach to things, and entire economies are built on the patterns that emerge when we all agree on how much an item is worth. Usually, money is a pretty accurate indicator of something's value. But the important thing is that an item's monetary value is not fixed, and certainly not absolute. An item's value shifts with something more fundamental: our *perception* of its value.

An example: someone may sell you a gadget that is worth exactly $10. In a real and indisputable way, this item is "worth" $10. Yet, whether this item translates to $10 of *value* in your life, in your actual lived experience, is something completely different. Your quality of life, your well-being and your sense of achieving your own *personal* goals may or may not coincide with the market value of $10 given to this item. On the ground, such an item may provide you the equivalent of $20 in peace of mind and happiness, or drain you of $10 in the form of extra stress and fuss.

The only one that can decide an item's real-life value is you – the person living the life. Money is a stand in only – we need to learn to consistently ask ourselves what value things bring to our lives, regardless of what the market tells us they are worth.

Budgeting with an eye to more fundamental value means asking what things add to the experience of your being alive. The tone of your living, the texture of how you move about, interact with people, how you feel about yourself, your well-being and sense of purpose, these are all hidden yet extremely important parts of your decision-making process. You may end up going with the unwashed and unpeeled potatoes in the end because you realize that the experience of spending time in your kitchen is quality time and something you cherish.

You cannot add more time to your day or your life, but you *can* enhance the quality of the time that you do have. Time passed well is the experience of value. Passing time in a way that feels satisfactory is something to seriously consider when you make choices. Importantly, nobody can tell you what you value. If you read a book encouraging you to spend more special time with your children, you may never realize the simple fact that you are quite happy with how much time you spend with them already. Then you may wonder why spending more quality time with them only seems to aggravate everyone involved. The choice you made that was intended to make you happier is actually doing precisely the opposite.

The simple way to find out how to factor value into your budget is to become aware of what really matters to you. What is the point of your life? When do you feel most energized, happiest and most fulfilled? If you don't build into your life moments where you actively pursue these principles, then you cannot be surprised when you get to the end of it and feel as though it's all been a waste. It's sad that many people feel like their true passions and values are more of an afterthought, something to indulge in only after they fulfill all their obligations. The problem with this approach is that once you fulfill those obligations, you'll probably be left with a sense of emptiness: what was it all for anyway?

A budget will be more effective and more meaningful if it takes into account the fact that you are a human being who has a real need to be emotionally and spiritually fulfilled. If practically that means you are unwilling to devote anything less than three hours a week to choir practice, then blocking that in becomes as fixed and permanent as the need for sleep.

Now that you've identified the parts of your life that are non-negotiable, you can turn your attention to the parts that are less so.

By drawing a line around the things that are unchangeable (the amount of time you have) and the things that you don't *want* to change (your passions and values) you are left with the parts of your life that can be practically moderated. Vow to not touch these important aspects.

If you have allotted yourself an hour each day to pursuing something that is deeply important to you, don't shortchange yourself by sacrificing that hour to admin or errands when in a pinch. It may not feel like it matters much now, but believe that the loss of well being and sense of purpose in the present becomes important, sooner or later.

This section will most strongly resemble the traditional budgeting advice you may have encountered so far.

The principle is simple: if it's not that important, it won't be a big deal to reduce the amount of resources you allocate to it.

A dysfunctional budget doesn't reflect your true values. For example, if what you crave more than anything is alone time and the bliss of zoning out with a mindless book, your budget is dysfunctional if there is no time that acknowledges that. More obviously, if you don't care much about what coffee you drink in the morning and simply care about getting caffeine in your system in the quickest way possible, it doesn't make sense to splash out on expensive cappuccinos every day. If your mother drilled it into you since you were little that superhero figurines were a sad and embarrassing way to spend your time and money, a good budget for you may be realizing that, actually, to hell with it, those figurines make you really, really happy.

Again, the difference between regular budgeting and minimalist budgeting: we are not attempting to remove everything, but to remove that which doesn't serve us or is unnecessary to our deep sense of value. The paradox is that trimming away the clutter often allows us to enjoy our true passions *more*, not less. Freed of distraction and the need to maintain pointless rubbish in our day-to-day life, we can turn our full attention to the things we are happy to dedicate hours and money to.

Using the tips provided later in this book as inspiration, make a thorough inventory of every single point of expenditure during a month period. It may help you to convert these figures into percentages (percentage of total expenditure), which give a better *relative* value of how they compare to other expenses. For example, you may find that you spend $70 on average every month on your superhero figurine habit.

But when you look at the rest of the list, other than spending time with your baby nephew, this ranks as the most enjoyable activity in your life. In the next column, allocate a *value* percentage – this is the beginning stage of setting budget goals for yourself. How much does this item add to your life? How much, percentage wise, are you willing to devote of your total income to this hobby? If it were the one thing that makes you really happy, then it'd be fair to say you can allocate a full 10% of your income to this. Why not? People struggle their whole lives to find happiness - if you've found it, then nourish it. So if your salary is $2000, and you only spend $70 of it on figurines when in your heart you are willing to spend up to $200, your budget is not right. If anything, your budget has taken into consideration your mother's goals and ideals and not yours.

This ideal percentage also relates back to the concept of time outlined earlier. If you are spending 2% of your total expenditure on magazines, is that an accurate reflection of how much value magazines add to your life? Also, if magazines, on further examination, actually add very little to your life, your ideal percentage will be much, much lower. Perhaps you will realize that they add nothing to your life at all. Think of the time that this magazine adds and takes to your life, and put this in the "time" column. Magazines are the sort of thing that might take an extra half hour a week to flip through, and they need to be bought and then thrown away. Tally this up and put it in the time column. How many hours do you lose to this activity you feel so-so about? A dishwasher, for example, would have a positive value, since it allows you to save the time you would have spent washing dishes by hand.

Go through each group of items. You needn't be too exact, only keep to the spirit of tallying up each item's true impact and cost on your life. It may emerge that your budget is spent on things that you don't care about or which actively make your life worse. Do you notice how little time and money you spend on your own values? It may turn out that you only *think* you are spending a certain amount of time, money and energy on something but are spending much more or less. This exercise can show you the discrepancies that may exist between your ideal lifestyle and the one you actually live.

"Cutting" a budget sounds bad, doesn't it? But as you turn your attention to what needs to be sliced away, think of it as spring cleaning. A minimalist budget isn't just about reduction and frugality, it's about *efficiency*. As you chop away at your monthly expenditure, think of it as making way for the things that really matter to you. First look at money that is spent on things you don't value. Cut it away. Look at things that take more time than is strictly justified. A certain item may be fine when looked at in financial terms, but when you consider the time drain, would be better eliminated or reduced.

Cut it away.

If you've spent any time at all living the way you live, you may be rather entrenched in the habit and need some time to "cut" away at certain items. Certain items, people or rituals take time to phase out. This may be as big a deal as moving house or something as trivial as cutting out morning coffee or finding a different route to work.

A "smart" goal is a goal that has the best chance of being achieved. Don't sabotage a good idea by making vague or unreachable goals, like "I'm going to eat better" or "I'm going to stop wasting money on magazines".

A SMART goal is:

Specific

Don't be vague. What does "eat better" mean? More vegetables? How much more? A specific goal is "I'm going to eat vegetables every night with dinner".

Measurable

Simply, how will you know you've achieved your goal? "Buy fewer magazines each month" is not measurable, but "Buy only one magazine each month" is one you can measure.

Attainable

Naturally, only a goal that you can actually achieve is going to be, well, achieved. Be realistic. Making a goal to slash your monthly medication bill when you're managing several chronic illnesses is asking for failure.

Realistic

Related to attainability. We make goals because we aspire to be better, but don't set the bar *too* high. Making the goal to cut your monthly expenditure by half is basically building failure into it.

Time Based

A good goal has an expiration date. "Someday" is giving your unconscious mind permission to slack. Set a date in the future where you expect to reach your goal.

Examples:

Not so smart goal: "I'm going to be more efficient when I do the grocery shopping."

Smart goal: "By this time next month, I'm going to be spending 10% less on groceries."

Not so smart goal: "I'm going to wash my clothes less to save on detergent."

Smart goal: "Tomorrow, I'm going to buy detergent in bulk to save on laundry costs."

Not so smart goal: "I'm going to spend quality time with my children."

Smart goal: "Every Tuesday, I'm going to spend at least one hour with the children playing football."

Hopefully, by becoming more aware of what's truly important to you, as well as acknowledging your hard limits (time, money), you're closer to creating a budget that not only saves you money, but offers you the best path to wellness and fulfillment in your life in general, given the fact that our time on this earth is limited.

Once you have identified your values, the time you have available and the money you have coming in, you are better able to cut away at what is unessential to reveal what truly is.

This next section will focus more concretely on practical ways you can reduce the time, money and energy you lose to things that ultimately don't serve your highest goals. Since everyone has different sets of resources at their disposal, their solutions are going to be different, too. Some of these solutions won't apply to you, and that's OK. If spending money or time in one area is vital to feeling fulfilled and happy, then you don't need to save money in those areas.

Food

One of the easiest ways to lose track of spending and consequently, one of the easiest places to save money without even trying. Decide on your main motivation and move from there:

When you don't have time to spend on food

If you prioritize convenience over health (naughty!) then it makes sense to splash out on convenience foods. There is no shame in this. Perhaps at this point in your life, you are focused on building your business or are sorting out some other area. Convert your time fussing over food preparation into money which you spend on food delivery services or pre-made meals. The advice to prepare more of your own meals at home is only going to make you more miserable, so chalk up restaurant bills to time saving.

When you don't have money to spend on food

If you prioritize healthy eating, there are plenty of ways to eat healthily without spending too much. If time spent in the kitchen is not an issue, save money by preparing fresh and unprocessed foods yourself. Buy in bulk, cook and freeze. Opt for cheap foods like potatoes, eggs, leafy greens, carrots, pulses and legumes of all kinds and cheap vegetables like cabbage. The money saving tips below are for you.

When you don't have time OR money to spend on food

However, if you want to reduce both time spent on food as well as money, your only choice is to eat foods that are cheap but also require very little preparation. Buy a cookbook that shows you how to prepare food quickly and with only a few ingredients, use a crock-pot and learn to eat mostly salads and simple dishes. Smoothies, three-ingredient meals and sandwiches are your best bet.

Action Steps for shaving money off your food expenditure:

- Make a grocery list and stick to it.
- Don't be embarrassed about buying own-brand food at the supermarket. For things like rice and flour, there's just not that much room for difference in quality.
- Go to Sunday or farmers' markets. The outing can double as a fun family activity and the produce is usually cheaper and fresher. Pick up something for brunch and you've killed a few birds with one stone.
- Here's a trick to remember in supermarkets: the most expensive items will always be placed at eye height. Look up or down and you'll find, sometimes almost hidden away, a cheaper brand.
- Only eat at restaurants when the food is something you can't easily prepare yourself – e.g. sushi or complicated exotic dishes.
- Make eating out really worth it by choosing places with all you can eat specials. This way you can have breakfast, skip lunch and pig out for dinner. Also keep an eye out for places that have discounts for meals for your children.
- Buy fruit and vegetables in season.
- If you have the space, grow your own spinach, tomatoes and herbs – they cost next to nothing and are a fun way to add nutrients to your meals without spending much.
- Make stock/broth at home. By using bones, vegetable scraps and herbs, you can make an extremely nutritious and tasty base for almost every meal, using things you would have thrown away anyway.
- In the same vein, start a compost heap. Recycling is one of the truest forms of thrift, and your garden will thank you.
- Buy food that doesn't spoil in bulk.
- Buy a healthy snack while you're shopping so that you're not tempted by the rows of chocolates at the checkout line.
- Buy whole fruit and vegetables in minimal packaging.
- Make stews and soups from cheaper cuts of meat.
- Skip organic foods unless it's a really high priority for you. Some vegetables and fruits, like pineapples, are immune to most pests and so don't suffer from exposure to pesticides. Others, especially those that have thin skins or stay on the plant for a long time, benefit more from being organic. Apples, strawberries and bell peppers are notorious for having high pesticide residue, so buy these organic if you can or otherwise scrub them well and eat only occasionally.

- Eat out less frequently but make it more of an event when you do – sometimes a big three course meal in a beautiful restaurant is worth way more than three or four visits to a noisy coffee shop for a quick bite.
- Cook in big batches and put the rest away for later. Otherwise, try roping in friends or family to pool bulk purchases and divide out big quantities of food.
- Try making your own bread. The ingredients are cheap and you might enjoy the process. Plus, fresh, hot homemade bread is pretty hard to beat.
- Eat mindfully and become aware of what triggers you to eat more than you really should. Consider intermittent fasting - seriously. Skipping a meal here and there does wonders for body and mind and saves you the money and energy it takes to prepare food all the time.
- When friends come over, stick to simple meals and ask everyone to pitch in for a potluck style gathering.
- If you see a "2 for 1" deal, check whether you can get the discounted price even if you only buy one.
- At restaurants, avoid padding your bill with overpriced drinks and desserts, most of which are fairly underwhelming. Ask for a glass of water instead and get a filling main dish.
- Pay close attention to food that gets thrown away. Up the quality of your storage to make sure fruits and vegetables aren't spoiling, or buy fresh food in smaller quantities.
- Consider signing up for an online grocery shopping service. You can get your weekly or monthly staples delivered to your door and save both time and effort.
- Take leftover dinner to work or get into the habit of packing a sandwich and a fruit. You'll save hundreds of dollars over the course of a year.
- Think about having a meatless night during the week if you eat meat. A light meal based around eggs or legumes and vegetables is cheap and gives your system a rest.

Clothes

Following food, people can often sacrifice enormous quantities of money on buying clothing.

When you're up against a clothing industry that wants to convince you to ditch your entire wardrobe every season and stock it again, this is no mean feat. Clothes can be a touchy area because for so many people, clothes have come to represent self esteem, success, comfort, and a certain image they want to project. Their very identity is bound up with the clothing they wear – a far cry from thinking of clothes as merely protection from the elements.

From a minimalist perspective, if someone truly derives immense pleasure from the creativity and spirit in dressing elaborately and paying for it, the goal is not to suggest that they stop. The minimalist philosophy, as we know by now, is about making sure that only those things that truly serve our highest good are focused on; everything else can be downplayed.

Signs your clothes spending habits are hindering rather than helping: you feel like you are always thinking about what to wear, and never feel satisfied in what you choose;

you have tons of clothing and hate all of it; people get frustrated with you because they end up having to take care of buying clothes *for* you; you throw things away before they get worn out; you make impulse purchases; you buy clothing to feel better about yourself – and it doesn't really work... you get the picture.

When you don't have time to spend on clothing

Many men have this attitude to clothing, but deal with their unwillingness to engage with it by fobbing off the responsibility onto wives or mothers. If this works for you, consider yourself spoiled, but otherwise, those who want to look presentable but couldn't be bothered to spend hours in shopping malls have a few other options. If you can, consider hiring a personal shopper to go out and find exactly what you need. Base your new purchases on what has worked in the past, and defer to a stylish friend or work colleagues to give you ideas on what you should go for. Buy quality with the understanding that the better the craftsmanship, the longer you can go without thinking about this problem again.

When you don't have money to spend on clothing

Some of the most painfully chic and creative people have come from backgrounds of poverty. Today, the Internet is teeming with blogs showing you how to turn old or second hand clothing into beautiful pieces that tick all the fashion boxes. If you have the time, learn to sew a little, and nurture the crafter in you to renovate and rework what you already have. When buying new, get wardrobe staples to go with everything in all weather, and make sure the quality of the garment will carry you through a few years.

When you don't have time OR money to spend on clothing

If you don't care at all about clothing and also have no money to spend on it, then, enjoy it! Maybe you're an eccentric college professor, mom of eight or chronic scruffy person. Turn your attention to other areas of your life that do matter.

Action Steps for saving money on clothing expenditure:

- Build a "capsule wardrobe" - high quality pieces in neutral colors that can be combined with almost anything. A multipurpose dress, good trousers, a simple cardigan and a few tops that can all be worn with each other is an excellent wardrobe backbone.
- Avoid sales. If you wouldn't have bought it otherwise, don't buy it now just because it's cheaper.
- Throw out, sell or give away clothing that you plan to wear when you are thinner, more daring etc. A good rule: if it hasn't been worn in a year, it's just taking up space and needs to go.
- Watch out for "dry clean only" garments – dry cleaning costs can really add up.

- Invest in a quality sewing kit to repair torn or damaged clothing. Don't throw broken shoes away: you can often get them fixed or re-soled at dry cleaners for a reasonable fee. Similarly, don't throw away clothing that has become stained. Cover up the stain with dark blue or black dye and the item is as good as new.

- Store clothing properly. When in use, let clothes hang in a well-aired cupboard on padded hangers. If put away for the season, seal in vacuum packed bags or fold away with moth balls to prevent damage.

- Forget about the tumble dryer. Unless it's an emergency and it's rainy, hang your clothes to dry. This saves money and lengthens the life of the material.

- Wash clothing only when it's actually dirty. Especially for top clothing layers that don't touch the skin, a simple airing in a closet will be enough to keep it going for two or three wears. You save on detergent and wear and tear on your clothes.

- Consider switching to natural detergents that are gentler on your clothes, or else try "soap nuts." These are a fun and dirt-cheap alternative - they literally grow on trees and produce natural soap that cleans your clothes when put into the washing machine. You can use them many times over and compost them when you're done (look at wellnessmama.com, an online stockist).

- Iron on the coolest setting to avoid wearing away the fibers.

- Wash lingerie and hosiery by hand using a little hair shampoo, and dry flat.

- For big events like weddings or graduations, buy something simple and elegant enough to be formal, but that can be dressed down and worn again later. A simple black cotton dress in the right cut can become very formal if paired with the right accessories. Think a big statement necklace or luxurious silk scarf. For things like tuxedos or wedding dresses, it's almost always better to rent.

- If you're crafty, use old clothes to make quilts or recycle into other items. At the very least, you can often turn an old garment into cleaning rags or stuffing for a throw pillow.

- Choose clothing in natural fibers. Pure cotton or wool wears well and often won't stretch or fade over time. Leather items can last a lifetime.

Health

Sadly, it usually takes an iffy test result from the doctor or a few days in bed with a serious health issue to remind us how important good health is.

Like oxygen, you only notice how much you need it when all of a sudden you don't have it anymore. From a consumerist perspective, good health is often packaged and sold as something purely aspirational. Tapping into our very real fears of death, unattractiveness or both, many people think health is merely another thing to put on the "to do" list. Get the number on the scale right, end of story. How often have you decided to start a new health regime and discovered that your very next step was to *buy* something – a gym membership, running shoes or new vitamins? As with the other areas covered so far, a minimalist approach to budgeting for our health should focus on the core and trim away the time and money-draining extras.

When you don't have time to spend on good health

You *want* to exercise more, sure, but just look at your schedule! This is a little paradoxical, when you think about it. Being in better health means you live longer, in a general sense. You buy yourself more time. Are you sure you want to struggle away at a life that is so demanding it doesn't even allow you to care for your own body? Nevertheless, if time is an issue, decide beforehand, realistically, how much time you can "sacrifice" each week to maintaining your health. Your goal in this case would be to identify the least amount of effort you can put in for the most health benefit. We don't all have to be gym bunnies who eat right. If a run once a week or the occasional dance class is keeping illness at bay, then do that and return your attention to whatever else you find more worthy at that moment.

When you don't have money to spend on good health

A more common but easier to fix problem. Once you stop buying into the idea that you need gadgets and goodies to be healthful, you're halfway there. Don't try bolstering a weak will or lack of interest with dieting apps, special equipment, classes, juicers, books, supplements or outfits. Companies selling these items will advertise hard that they are a key to, even a replacement for, simply doing the work. But don't believe it. The tips that follow will give you some ideas of how to love your body a little without spending much.

When you don't have time OR money to spend on good health

This book has tried to show that once you identify your true passions and values, the work of a budget is to make sure your behavior is aligning with them. The case of not being willing or able to invest anything towards your health is perhaps an exception. You can go a long way abusing your body before it gives out, but health is pretty close to being a non negotiable. If you have no time, money or energy to devote to staying alive and happy, it may be time to start reassessing your priorities.

Action Steps for saving money on health:

- Make friends with Youtube. There you can find workout videos of every kind, from yoga to weight lifting to cardio. They're free, you have a lot of variety and you can do them at home in your pajamas.

- Healthy eating, with the exception of good quality meat, is usually also cheap. Fill up half your plate with vegetables and you kill two birds with one stone. Leafy greens, eggs, cabbage and tomatoes are healthful and cost very little for the nutrients they provide.

- Really research your vitamins thoroughly and make sure you aren't throwing away money on useless supplements. Homeopathic remedies and special "superfoods" like goji berries have all been shown to have little effect. Save your money. An Omega 3 oil and a general multivitamin are usually more than enough.

- If you go to gym less than 3 or 4 times a week, it's time to get over the fact that it may not be worth it. You'll spend less on drop-in classes that you actually go to.

- Floss!

- If you choose to keep going to gym, make full use of all the amenities there. Shower, use the pool and sauna and take the opportunity to learn about gym equipment you may have avoided. You might even find a handy childcare solution as many gyms have a crèche or children's swimming classes, for instance.

- Don't buy Vitamin C to "boost your immune system". Vitamin C has been shown time and time again to offer no protection against colds and flus.

- Take up walking or running. If you're a beginner you needn't splash out on expensive trainers. A cheaper pair of light trail running shoes will see you through most situations, if you feel you must kit yourself out. Running or walking can double up as a social or meditative activity.

- If you live in a country where you need to buy health insurance, comb over your policy and see if you might downgrade to a smaller plan. Healthy bodies under forty seldom need a full, comprehensive medical plan, as unpopular as that opinion may be .

- Consider getting glasses instead of contact lenses. They may be more convenient, but the cost over years and years will add up. Not to mention that contact lenses pose risks to the health of your eye that glasses don't.

- Depending heavily on where you live, things like hormonal contraception or condoms are often available for free from planned parenthood or community clinics. This saves a nice sum over the course of a year, and you can often get enough for a few months at a time.

- This may sounds silly, but: wash your hands. This is a really simple way to reduce your exposure to viruses and bacteria and consequently, colds and flu.

- It's the unglamorous truth, but sometimes the best health decisions you make are not active decisions at all. Merely refrain from damaging your health deliberately and the battle is half won. Unless it adds immeasurable happiness to your life, quit drinking, smoking or recreational drug use.

- If you insist on smoking, consider rolling your own. It's cheaper and has a certain charm to it.

- Always, always ask if there's a generic medication available.

- Sleep properly and give your body the best defense against stress and disease. Decide on your personal bare minimum and stick to it.

- Drinking water is likewise cheap or free and can only add to your quality of life.

- Vegetable juices are a good way to get your vitamins and can even be cheaper and more convenient than preparing vegetables from scratch.

- Buy cheap disposable razors and sharpen them when they get dull.

- Don't bother with foods labeled as "diet". Speciality cereals, drinks and the like almost always have more affordable alternatives. Ordinary oats are dirt cheap and better for you than cereal, for example.

- Switch to tea instead of coffee and bring your own thermos to work. Tea is a fraction of the cost of coffee, it's healthier and it comes in more fun varieties.

- Build in daily activities that encourage more exercise indirectly. Walk the dog, play with children, dance, build something, etc. Exercise at the gym doesn't hold a candle to exercise that is fun and actually enriches your life.

Home and Cleaning

Is your home a peaceful sanctuary that you return to at the end of a busy day to recharge? Or is it a "gilded cage" that constantly demands your attention to maintain it? The best budget solutions for your household are those that save you time and money, and add to your quality of life, either by removing an annoyance or directly making life more pleasant.

Save time:

- Invest in appliances for chores you need to do everyday, for example a washing machine, dishwasher or pressure cooker. Give away or sell appliances that you use less than once a week. You could likely put their cash value to better use.
- If you can afford to, consider housekeeping help. This may take the form of dropping clothes off at a laundry service or getting a monthly garden service.
- Arrange for debit orders for recurrent payments.
- Shop online and get your regular groceries delivered to you home.

Save money:

- Split costs by carpooling.
- Buy food in bulk from wholesalers and divide between friends and family.
- Unbranded detergent is usually pretty effective but cheaper. Better still are natural cleaners like white vinegar, bleach and bicarbonate of soda.
- Make sure your home is weather proof and seal door and window cracks to save on heating.
- Commit to only having indigenous and low water plants in your garden.
- Unless you are a true collector, don't buy magazines or newspapers. Everything in them is readily available online.
- When you're trying to decide whether to buy something new, give yourself a mandatory "cooling off" period. For smaller purchases, this could be a week, and for larger, up to a month. If you still want it after this time, then go ahead.
- Buy books on a Kindle or get them from the library.
- Try to combine separate car trips to ensure you don't drive around unnecessarily.
- Turn off the TV. You'd be surprised how much junk you're convinced to buy by watching ads, and you'll save electricity and, more importantly, time.
- Only buy prepackaged foods if the time you gain from not chopping and peeling is worth more than their cost.
- It might be worth it to turn your water heater on and off as needed.
- Replace old showerheads with low flow or more efficient shower heads.

- Put a brick in your toilet cistern to displace some water. You'll waste less with each flush.
- Turn lights off when nobody is in the room. Use candles for a cozy atmosphere.
- Buy energy saving bulbs.
- Buy furniture from second hand shops or online. An hour or so of good hunting could save you half the cost of an item in the end.
- The world is becoming more and more digital. Carefully evaluate if you need your full satellite TV package, or get movies and series online instead.
- Have a clothes swap evening with friends to trade clothing you've fallen out of love with.
- A yard sale can be a fun way to connect with neighbors, get rid of junk and make a little profit in the process.
- If you're a crafty type, you might like the sense of satisfaction you feel from learning a new DIY skill. You can save a lot of money by repairing things or making small items yourself.
- Ask a butcher for off cuts or scraps that your dog or cat could enjoy. Quality pet food without fillers generally satisfies your cat or dog in much smaller helpings, too.
- Reuse items you already have. This takes some imagination but is more environmentally sound, cheaper and simpler. Wash and keep jars and bottles to hold spices, or take the time to repair broken items rather than buying new ones.
- Think about what loyalty programs you might benefit from being a part of. Points for shopping at particular stores, discounts on air travel or medical insurance or reduced banking fees all add up and don't require you to scrimp since they are things you already buy.

Children

There's no easy way to say it, but for some, their children can be a real blind spot when it comes to their finances. The sentiment of "nothing but the best" and being able to provide that for their children is strong. And it wouldn't be overstating the case to say that making their children happy and successful is basically the point of many people's lives. Unfortunately, advertising has burrowed its way into many well meaning parents' brains (and pockets!) and convinced them that unless they shower their offspring with material things, they simply aren't being raised right.

As with other things, it can be sobering to settle on what it truly is you want to leave your children with in this life. Material possessions are one thing, but what often mean the most to children are the lessons they learn from their parents. Were their parents fulfilled, dignified people? Did they show them by example how to navigate life? Did they give them skills or a strong sense of self worth or a lifetime of memories that they'll cherish forever?

Budgeting as a parent often feels awful because of the guilt associated with not providing enough for your children. An easy way around this is to consistently train yourself to reorient to basic principles. The really fundamental ones seldom involve material possessions. Ask yourself what each item represents to your children. For example, you may want to send your child to an expensive art camp that tries to encourage children to make friends and be more creative over the summer holidays. Before feeling bad about not being able to afford it, ask yourself what the value of it truly is. If you hope to teach your child the value in creativity and out of the box thinking, what better way can you show them this lesson than by being creative yourself? Embark on an art project together, build or grow something as a family. You save money and in the process deepen your connection to your child.

Action Steps for saving money on parenting:
- For younger children, practice "toy cycling". Let your child play with one or two main toys and put the rest away. Children can't focus on too many things at once anyway, and when they tire of their current toys, switch them out and it'll be as if they were new. Have a few cycles of toys and you'll encourage more focus and appreciation for each one.
- Choose toys that encourage creative thinking, building or imagination. Cards, balls and simple art supplies give you endless possibilities.
- Give parenting books a skip. At best you'll get a few obvious tips on how not to kill your children accidentally, and at worst they'll turn you into a paranoid parent who needs to buy more parenting books.
- Similarly, Baby Einstein style products are largely a scam. You don't need to spend money on making sure that your child is mentally stimulated. Have you ever really seen a two year old? The world is their playground. Everything is new and wild to them. Have faith that their brains are not going to wither unless you buy them a fancy new baby development program when they're only two months old.
- Give children aged from five up household responsibilities and chores. This builds their sense of competence, keeps them occupied and takes a little off your plate. For instance, delegate feeding the pets to your 6 year old, and they'll learn responsibility as well as give you one less thing to worry about.
- Focus children's birthday parties around fun activities and avoid spending it on table decorations or expensive cake. Children love being the center of attention on their birthdays, and this can be achieved with games and rituals, rather than splashing out on expensive party trinkets.
- Children's hair can usually be cut at home.
- Up to a certain age, children don't care about the kind of clothing they wear or what their room looks like. A 2 year old cannot appreciate the adorable baby booties you spent a fortune on and will be outgrown in a few months, but they certainly will benefit from a college fund that their parents had the foresight to begin early on.
- Leave children at home when you go shopping if possible. You'll need an iron will to turn down a nagging child pushing you to buy that toy or treat.
- Instead of just giving children an allowance and leaving it at that, try to teach them age-appropriate saving and investing skills early on. Have them open a savings account so they can learn how interest works. Help them make goals for big purchases they want

and encourage them to be enterprising and spin up money through mowing lawns, selling baked goods or starting a paper route.

- Don't give children too many options. Child psychologists have shown that too much variety can be stressful for younger minds. Tone it down and you'll likely be surprised by how children naturally gravitate towards simplicity when given the chance.

Debt and Finances

Psychologically, debt is a horrible place to be in.

The smart use of credit is a skill every financially savvy adult needs to master, but at the same time, less debt is almost always better. There are the obvious golden rules when it comes to credit, namely only incur credit for very large purchases or those that appreciate over time, and always pay down the most expensive debt first, which is usually your credit card.

Consider yourself lucky if you are budgeting to save more or merely downsize your lifestyle - paying down credit is another ball game and requires even more dedication. Fortunately there are resources out there to help people get on top of their debt. If you find your debt is spinning out of control, it's urgent that you get professional help as soon as possible. Remedying a full-blown debt crisis is beyond the scope of this book, although the tips and ideas outlined here will still be of use.

A financial advisor or coach can give you sound advice for a plan to tackle debt and manage finances better. Here are some tips to take control:

- Try to save each month, no matter what. Even if you can only manage a small amount, save it. Saving puts you in a special frame of mind. You are telling yourself that no matter how small your goals are, they are worth pursuing diligently.

- Push yourself to overpay on your mortgage or credit card repayments. A few extra hundred now could mean years saved down the line.

- Consider selling your car. You can save on the cost of a car by buying from auctions, second hand dealers or even rental companies who sell second hand rental models. New cars should be bought with their cost-to-maintain as the primary focus.

- Re-evaluate your insurance payments each month. There are almost always hidden fees and extras that you didn't notice before.

- Service your car regularly. You won't notice a car that is running less than efficiently, but you will notice the money you save on fuel when you keep your car well maintained.

- If you're flying, book flights as early as humanly possible. Try Skyscanner online to compare rates across airlines, and you could save a lot without even trying.

- Look in to the world of housesitting for when you are away on vacation, or else as an alternative to paying for hotel accommodation. Housesitting is where you agree to watch and take care of someone's home while they're away in exchange for rent. There are millions of resources and profile sites online to hook up with people who are looking for house sitters. Alternatively try "couchsurfing" which is more informal.

- Look at taking a small course in personal finance management. Local colleges might offer short programs or else find an online course.

- Switch to a bank with lower fees. You may even convince your current bank to cut you a deal.
- Consider installing a water or electricity meter into your home. Depending on where you live, this should be quite easy to do and will save you a ton. Getting constant feedback about how much you are spending on things you take for granted means you'll invariably use them more wisely.
- See if you can change your phone contract to a pay as you go option, then give yourself a monthly limit to stick to. Otherwise, try to shift most of your communication to free or cheap platforms like Skype, email or Whatsapp.
- Whatever you do, stop buying lottery tickets. The lottery has rightly been called "idiot tax" and there is just no logical reason for you to literally throw money away on it. Likewise, curb most or all of your gambling, if you do.
- Arrange for an accountant to look over your tax return and give you some advice on what can be written off as tax exempt. More efficiently filed reports could save you hundreds of dollars with zero change to your lifestyle.
- Also make sure you are claiming any government benefits you are entitled to. This may not be a lot on the face of it, but certain benefits really add up over time.
- This may seem obvious, but make a serious effort to stop speeding. Your efforts scrimping and saving in one area could be undone in the one minute you decided to speed on the highway. If you do get fines, pay them quickly to avoid incurring any penalties.
- If you have a problem with frittering away cash, make it a habit to only carry a small amount of cash on you and use cards instead. The extra effort to use this or draw at an ATM can deter many impulse buys. Plus, you'll be able to see very clearly where everything went on your monthly statement.
- If you have a problem with abusing your credit card, hide it away somewhere at home instead of keeping it on you. You'll be forced to think through any purchase more clearly.
- Speaking of statements, get them emailed to you and you can use any of the thousands of handy apps out there designed to manage the data.

Miscellaneous tips and tricks
- Sign up for a course on Coursera.com. These are top-notch university level courses on everything from business to programming to linguistics, and can be done for free in the privacy of your own home. A lower key option for self improvement without breaking the bank is watching a daily TED talk or downloading some classic novels on Kindle, many of which are in the public domain and free, too.
- Museums, galleries and even zoos are good choices for money-conscious outings.
- Keep a literal piggy bank. It's good to have a visual reminder of your savings, and you can dedicate the result to pay for something special. Get into the habit of cleaning out your wallet or pockets at the end of the day and feeding your piggy.
- Wherever possible, walk, cycle or take public transport. This doubles up as great exercise.

- When driving, keep your speed and acceleration as constant as possible. Avoiding sudden stops or erratic driving saves wear and tear on car parts as well as fuel.

- Become familiar with your library. Most libraries are about so much more than just the books. See what classes, talks or performances they have, and try checking out magazines, DVDs or music.

- Buy Christmas and birthday gifts early on. To avoid the situation where people are gifted piles of unnecessary and sort of unwanted stuff, give gift vouchers instead. If you're worried about this being too impersonal, give a gift card together with a more thoughtful item like handmade cookies. These are cheap to make and always welcome, plus you can make them in a batch to give to everyone over the holiday period. Alternatively try a "secret Santa" format for Christmas with everyone writing down what they'd like. Making Christmas dinner a potluck affair means less stress and financial burden on just one or two people.

- Go drinking during happy hour only.

- Choose easy to maintain hairstyles that don't require constant upkeep. This means ditching relaxers, heat stylers that sap hours of your life and damage your hair, and hair color that needs professional attention every six weeks.

CHAPTER 6: THE CHALLENGE - PUTTING EVERYTHING INTO PRACTICE

The trick to minimalist budgeting is finding what works for you, and continually working to zoom in on the lifestyle that is optimized to make you the happiest while spending the least amount of time, money and energy.

Too many budgeting gurus will give you ample advice on how to maximize on only one variable, which doesn't succeed because the other variables suffer.

So even though you've sliced through your monthly expenses, your state of mind has become so miserly and anxious that you can't enjoy the money you're supposed to be saving. Or you try so hard to find the sweet spot between your financial resources and your own happiness that you don't notice the hours of your life you throw away to save a crumb here and there. I had this thought when I read a post by a popular homemaker and blogger. Her advice on how to save a few dollars by sewing her own dishcloths was at odds with the time and effort she had clearly squandered in putting together a professional two thousand word tutorial with several photographs taken with a high end camera.

Let's turn our attention to some hypothetical people who decided to approach their budgeting from a minimalist perspective. It doesn't take a genius to understand that to budget well, one must simply find ways to either spend less money or make more. That's it. Any advice over and above that is frankly condescending. The budget guru will ask if you buy gasoline and if so, will tell you to buy less. Wasting a lot of money on fantasy action figures each month? Then stop doing that, the budget guru will tell you.

Minimalist budgeting takes a broader look and asks you to consider what it really means to have "less" or "more", and why you should care. One man's suffering is another man's luxury living, so it pays to get to the bottom of this value judgment first, rather than simply assuming less is always more, and in always the same way. After we look at some hypothetical people's budgets, you may get a more inspired view of how to start constructing your own. Not through tricks and hacks and finding the courage to just say no, but with a conscious, deliberate consideration of what is important.

Case Study 1 – Amanda's uphill battle

Amanda always felt like a tiny hurricane was constantly whirling around her head. Raising three children under ten, she felt deficient in every way possible. She worked herself half to death but found her salary just barely covering costs. She was exhausted to the bone but couldn't take even one day off of her life to get the rest she deserved. Her solution up till then had been to take on more at work to try to pay for a nanny, but there was only so much she could pay. Her husband's job kept them afloat for the most part, but the relationship between them had barely any time to thrive in the flurry of everyday responsibilities. Every day of Amanda's life ended with her in bed at night, quietly wondering to herself whether this was all there was to life.

Amanda sat down with her husband and drew up a comprehensive accounting of where every cent of their money was going, as well as every second of their time. Rather than merely counting up money in versus money out, they also looked at what value they were deriving from their children, their home, their jobs. What emerged was how little pleasure any of it gave Amanda. Everything was a chore. There was no time or money to do what she wanted. Her reward for managing to juggle all the balls she had to was merely to do it all over again the next day.

Things needed to change. Amanda discovered that a lot of stress arose from housework for their frankly large house. They decided that within 6 months, they wanted to move to a house that was smaller and easier to care for. They found new homes for their demanding pets. Amanda took a long hard look at her life and realized how little of it served her. It was a tough decision to make, but she realized that owning a home with the stereotypical white picket fence, husband, kids and two dogs was not really, when she looked closely, what she wanted for herself.

Her next step was to negotiate a part time schedule with her work. She agreed to work remotely at home for a few hours each day for greatly reduced pay. Rather than crash the family financially, Amanda found renewed vigor and decided that she would like to homeschool her children. What emerged is that when she had a close, loving and involved relationship with them, the pressing need to escape on vacation lessened. Becoming more involved with her children gave her a renewed sense of purpose, and the family saved money on schooling, after school care and babysitters.

As they transitioned, there were moments when Amanda had to get used to their new, downsized lifestyle, but when she considered the time and happiness she gained in exchange it seemed worth it. After a few months she realized how little the trappings of middle class life actually meant to her anyway. With free time to spend watching her children grow, the opportunity to connect again with her husband and the relief from not having to run like a rat in a wheel, the changes she had to make in her expenditure felt pretty manageable.

A few years down the line, Amanda followed her dreams a little further and found that "homesteading" was immensely fulfilling. She took courses on how to build her own house and how to farm her own food at home. She raised goats and chickens and even started to coach other people on how to live a more natural, self-sufficient lifestyle.

None of this would have happened if Amanda had merely learnt to deal with her crummy life a little bit better, i.e. made a budget to cut her expenses. Amanda's problem was not that she needed tips and tricks to squeeze in more work hours or stretch a dollar even more to care for her family, it was that she had lost her center of value. In finding her principles, the need to budget became redundant over time.

Case Study 2 – Kim's 3 in 1 solution

Kim had never been a spendthrift. As a matter of fact, she was raised to be frugal and money conscious, and had always kept track of her money habits well enough. When she evaluated her lifestyle in detail, though, one thing was clear: she had a problem with buying clothing. Whereas every other area of her life was under control, including food, entertainment and how much she spent on her home, she had a nasty habit of buying clothes she didn't need and seldom wore anyway. She hated her job and felt it was a way to ease stress, pass the time and inject a little beauty and excitement into her life. But when she looked at how much more she spent on clothes than she did on buying books or exercising making friends or hobbies or trying new things, she had to admit that the ratio was very off.

Kim had tried unsuccessfully to just stop before. After thinking it over very carefully, she realized that shopping clothes *was* her hobby. In a job that stifled her creativity, she found that buying beautiful clothes was the only outlet for her to indulge in creative expression. No wonder she was unwilling to give it up! Kim decided not to cut down, but to re-channel her resources to where it really mattered.

After tallying up the cost she usually spent on clothing each month, she vowed to take that money and buy a sewing machine instead. She made a new hobby of going to thrift stores and finding cheap items that she then revamped into amazing creations that she got immense joy and pride out of. She also joined a knitting group and made friends there with other similarly minded people. They encouraged her to get more joy out of her creative urges.

At the end of the day, the total money spent is more or less the same for Kim. But what she gained in quality of life means she was using her resources smartly. By rerouting the money she spent on a pointless shopping habit, she cut down on unnecessary spending, made new friends and found a hobby that not only saved her money, it enriched her life. It may even be that in five years' time, Kim has discovered that her passion for creative clothing is lucrative. She might open her own boutique or write a How To book sharing her knowledge. What started as a way to save money could well turn into a way to *make* money.

Case Study 3 – Jeff's Dilemma

Like a lot of people his age, Jeff had been trying to break away from under his parents' wings and get his life started. He had a few problems. While looking for work, he couldn't realistically afford the rent to get his own apartment, but he was slowly going crazy staying with his folks. While he was constantly short on cash, he had lots of free time. His self esteem took a beating the longer he stayed home and had his parents pay for him. What's worse, he was getting depressed and out of shape.

Jeff's challenge was to transform the excess time he had into money and quality of life. He sat down and organized his priorities. He needed to keep his spirits up, find a job and get out of the house as quickly as possible. He decided he would volunteer for a few days a week at a community center and offer to help coach a children's football team. The position paid nothing, but Jeff made connections, kept motivated and spent large amounts of time away from his parents. He also connected with someone who offered to help him put together a CV. He conveniently had access to regular, free exercise which got him feeling better about life in general, and discovered that the satisfaction he got from bonding with the children gave him the motivation to find work.

People can be strange about money. Something about our culture ties self worth so strongly into the number value of how much we earn and own, that your social class becomes as much a part of you as your hair color or occupation.

A lot of budget/thrift resources out there will skim around this topic or pretend it's not even there. Wanting to cut down on expenses because you care about the environment? Great. All power to you. Want to get rid of some of your stuff because you crave "simplicity" in your life? Excellent, how very enlightened of you. Scratching around for coupons because, well, you're poor? Hm, not so good.

The principles of minimalism followed here in this book don't assume any level of wealth in particular. Minimalism is about getting down to essentials, and the essentials are different for each person. What's important is the *spirit* behind the material things and the money. It's possible for a very wealthy person to live a minimalist lifestyle, and it's possible for someone living on the poverty line to be living a materialistic one. What is "enough" or "simple" for one is extravagant for another.

That being said, many people come to minimalism at least in part out of necessity. For some, being laid off at work or trying to absorb the cost of a new child or other blow to their finances forces them to reconsider their lifestyle. What begins as a failure to keep up within the capitalist system as we understand it turns out to be an opportunity to step outside of that system and look at it for what it is.

It's not nice to say, but very often the feeling is that voluntary frugality is somehow nobler than the involuntary kind. Living off of government handouts and scraping by on cheap food and rent just doesn't have the same shine to it as a pretty stay at home mom who sews her children's clothing in her free time because her husband's salary gives her the luxury to.

It's important to recognize that the choice to live minimally, the ability to identify your priorities and work with them, is a privilege, and it's own kind of wealth. Those stuck in cyclic, long-term poverty are often so tired and cynical that it's almost a luxury to take the time to meditate on their values, hopes and dreams. So, yes, poverty is not the same as minimalism. But wherever your hard limits come from, minimalism can help with the *spirit* behind finding a way to work with them.

The approach in this book is designed to appeal to everyone, but of course, you may have read something and thought, "Wow, that is totally not how my life works." and felt a little alienated. I know it's happened a few times that I've heard someone talk about "cutting down" on this or that expense – and their new value is so much higher than my upper limit that it's almost embarrassing. But don't let things like this deter you. The principles remain the same, whether you think $10 is a lot of money or whether you wouldn't even notice if it fell out of your wallet.

Minimalism is about being real. The case studies so far have been short and necessarily a little simplistic. Sometimes, there isn't enough money, enough time *or* enough energy. No matter which way you spin it or what you reshuffle, there just isn't enough to go around. This ties in with how we think about budgeting in general, and that sickening feeling you may feel when you hear that word. Sometimes in life, you have to go without.

What does minimalism have to say about, well, being poor?

The time element, as we've discovered, is nonnegotiable. Money can be earned, but there are also, to varying degrees, limits to what we can earn and how little we can spend. The only area that can be controlled the most by us is the subjective value we assign to money, to things. We can control how we look at our achievements, how we think about money and our own happiness. Learning that we can still be happy and fulfilled and have a life that is as rich as anybody else's, no matter how in debt we may be, is a hard but sweet lesson to learn.

If you find these issues frequently touch a nerve, your path to minimalism may include an exploration of your own attitudes towards and relationship with money. The psychology of money is complicated. If you are in the mindset of an ascetic, or are unconsciously punishing yourself by doing with less, you are no less entwined and obsessed with material possessions as the ostentatious show off you are trying not to be like. There is a reason people give away their possessions after deciding they want to commit suicide. Minimalism is about being mindful of material things and how they interact with your world and your happiness.

Though we all come to minimalism with a different background, set of values and goals, the principles are the same for us all.

CHAPTER 8: A NOTE ON MARRIAGE AND MONEY

Stress around money constitutes the most common reason that marriages fail.

Who pays for what and why can be so stressful a concept to negotiate that some couples end up separating before they figure it out. In a marriage partnership, there are two income sources (usually) and more complicated expenditures. Add children and the complexity increases even more still.

But the basic principles of money management hold true. In partnerships, each person's contributions and rights to shared wealth need to be very thoroughly understood. As a couple or a family, you need to regularly do check ups on what everyone is bringing to the table (and, um, taking off of the table...)

Many men unwittingly put themselves into damaging financial binds with their wives, and wives can unwittingly fall into the homemaker role and shoot themselves in the financial foot when it comes to their own personal savings and retirement. As you sit down with your spouse or partner, tally up income that stems from all areas, including the more abstract ones of time and value. Stay at home mothers may contribute nothing in the way of money but single handedly enhance the value of the household through raising children, as well as saving time and energy by taking on the management of the household. A good accounting will recognize all of this in the decision making process. A better accounting will see how well this picture aligns with both of your values and principles.

CHAPTER 9: THE FIRST STEPS TO YOUR OWN MINIMALIST BUDGET

So, are you ready to begin your own minimalist budget story?

Week One

Hopefully, by now, you have a stronger sense of how the principles outlined here will apply to your specific lifestyle. In this first week, your goal will seem like the simplest but will in fact be the most important step. Here, you will find your "core" around which you will structure the rest of your budget. Without this core, your budget goals are meaningless and you're unlikely to stick to them for long.

For the time being, just plan. Keep the three elements – time, money and value – in mind. Look with honest and realistic eyes at the time that is available to you. It may help to draw up a schedule that shows, in hours, where all your time goes. If you're a visual person, block these out in different colors – the effect can really hit home when it's staring you in the face in neon pink and yellow. You may tally up how many hours you spend on various activities, i.e. sleep, work, chores, eating, relaxing etc.

Next, have a very rough idea of your overall income and your overall expenditure for a month period. This doesn't have to be 100% accurate for now, but be in the general ballpark. Don't guess – go on what records you have.

Lastly, and this is the most important part, meditate a little on your goals, values and passions. What adds to your life? What makes you happy and fulfilled? What gives you purpose? When are the moments in your schedule that bring you the most joy? Make a note of them.

Now, be curious about emerging patterns. As mentioned earlier on, you may find it helpful to have a column that ranks each category according to how valuable it is in your life. Do this with percentages or rank them in order. This will let you see if the actual time, money and energy you spend in any one area actually makes sense when you consider how much meaning it brings you.

Start to hone in on some goals for yourself. Choose what looks like the stickiest area – there will always be one! The one with the biggest discrepancy between your subjective appraisal and how much money you spend on it, the item that shocks you, *that's* the one to start with.

Week Two

With a little bit of direction, make a goal to work on for the rest of the month. One goal may not seem like much, but in many cases the biggest problem is usually one specific area that, if addressed, would help everything else fall into place. Remember to make your goals SMART. Specific, measurable, attainable, realistic and time based goals are the only ones you'll be able to achieve, so take some time making a good, solid goal.

Sit down with a calendar and map out the time frame/s for your goals/s. It's a good idea to break down bigger goals into smaller ones and then have them spaced out over a realistic time frame. So, start with the goal of spending 10% less on groceries, and then move onto 20% and more gradually over the course of six months.

Your goals could be money based or have to do with how you allocate the resources you already have. Your goal could also be to simply get more enjoyment out of the money you spend. Once you have some realistic goals laid out, you need to commit to them. If you've chosen them wisely, your goals shouldn't be some Herculean task that takes mountains of will power. In fact, you should feel energized and keen to reach these goals because they are all about getting you closer to the lifestyle you actually value.

The Next Month

Over the course of the month, keep a close eye on your goal. Notice if the goal needs adjusting and don't be afraid to tweak it if it's not quite right. Mindful budgeting means making smart decisions, it isn't about punishing yourself or forcing yourself to do with less when you can't or don't want to. With a firmer idea of what your core principles are, the less important details can be shuffled around without too much stress.

Try to avoid pushing yourself to make too many changes at once as this actually increases the chance you'll revert back to old habits. Go slowly and step by step. Importantly, don't let anyone tell you what you should and shouldn't value. If you really feel like a particular item will add something to your life, get it. If after a while of budgeting and assessing your goals you discover you could completely do away with the things you're supposed to need, just do it.

Six Months and Beyond

As you start ticking off your goals, you may be inspired to make more or to turn to maintaining your lifestyle. Your journey will be your own, but if you regularly take the time to check in with your core values and beliefs, your choices will never be too far removed from those that will ultimately make your life more meaningful.

In the end, budgeting is just a natural extension from a way of looking at life in general. It is pointless to ask yourself to cut down your spending so that you are only buying the "essentials" when you haven't actually defined what is essential for your life. A budget is only as good as the purpose it's meant to fulfill, and only you can decide what that purpose is.

Saving money is easy. Earn more, spend less. That's about it, really. The reason why so many people fail to make something so simple work for them is because money is not, as we've been taught, an objective, static thing. It's bound up in our histories, our psychology and our own personal values. A budget that has any chance of being actually implemented must take into account these values. In fact, these values have to be the main inspiration.

Moving forward:

Life is short. Money and material things can make our time on this earth better, and they can help us inch closer to what we find meaningful and worthwhile. *But, they are not meaningful and worthwhile in themselves.* This short book has been about examining this relationship between money and happiness. The goal of a revamped and better budget is never to just save money, rather, to make your spending and earning habits match more closely with what your life really is and what you really want it to be. Saving money when you feel directionless and living a life without purpose counts for very little.

CONCLUSION

Money is a resource, and a very important one, but it is not the only metric of success or efficiency.

You can change your life entirely without saving a cent by learning to think of what you have differently. Conventional budgeting offers a narrow view, a purely mechanistic perspective on money. Want more of it? Spend less of it. Invest. Save.

But money is a tool and how we spend it is an expression of our values and what we think is important. How much would you pay for peace of mind and the calm you get from knowing you are living well? How much of your life do you give away when you work? How much of that do you recoup in the form of your salary? Of all your expenses, have you remembered to include the time you waste stressing about money?

These may seem like vague or overly philosophical questions, but they get to the root of how we earn, spend and think of money. Once we understand these roots, our efforts to save here and there not only become easier, they become more meaningful.